FreeBSD

An Open-Source Operating System For Your Personal Computer

John — Thanks! Annelise

Annelise Anderson

The Bit Tree Press

Portola Valley, California

FreeBSD: An Open-Source Operating System for Your Personal Computer

by Annelise Anderson

Published by The Bit Tree Press, 108 Portola Road, Suite 115, Portola Valley, CA 94028-7899

bittree@andrsn.stanford.edu

Printed in the United States of America

10 9 8 7 6 5 4 3 2 1

ISBN 0-9712045-0-0

Contents

Introduction

This book is an introduction to FreeBSD, a powerful, stable, fast UNIX-style operating system that runs on a personal computer, for people who have never used FreeBSD or any flavor of UNIX before.

FreeBSD is one of the operating systems that powers our new technology—industrial strength, multi-user, Internet capable. Yet it's free, open source, and runs on the same increasingly inexpensive hardware on which we run Microsoft Windows.

The purpose of this book is to make it easier for people who are not (or not yet) full-time computer professions or UNIX experts to install, configure, and run FreeBSD.

You, the Reader

You're the reader and, I hope, the installer! I assume you don't know anything about FreeBSD or any other variety of UNIX, but can't resist the temptation to try out something new on your computer—a whole new operating system.

Why do you want to do this? To tell you the truth, I don't know. Maybe you're just curious about what your computer can do *besides* running Windows. Maybe you secretly yearn to write computer programs or be an Internet service provider, connect all your computers at home or in your dorm together, run a web server, or get a jump start on your friends and classmates on a career in computers.

You're getting frustrated with Windows and with the way the graphics hide what's going on underneath? You're in a box that Microsoft built. It's time to get out. And yes, you can play Quake on FreeBSD.

So I assume:

- You have a computer.
- You run some variety of Microsoft Windows (or maybe Linux) on that computer.
- The computer has a CD-ROM drive.
- You know about the parts of the computer you can kick or drop.

How to Use This Book

You can use this book and the CD-ROM it includes to install FreeBSD and experiment with using it. The book tries to tell you enough about what you need to know when you need to know it, and to give you some pointers about getting more information when you want it.

This is an introduction rather than a comprehensive guide or a final reference. It doesn't tell you how to manage a machine with 1,000 users, run a web server that gets a million hits a day, program in C, or hack the kernel. But it does tell you how to get the system up and running, connect to the rest of the world, and use FreeBSD as part of a local network.

How This Book is Organized

This book has six main parts and a couple of appendixes. The first two parts deal with installation and getting acquainted with FreeBSD. Part II covers basic skills you will need later. After that, the chapters get more specific, and you may want to jump to a chapter on installing software, getting sound to work, or connecting to the Internet. When you need to know something covered elsewhere, cross-references tell you where to look.

I: FreeBSD—What It Is and How to Install It

Part I explains what FreeBSD is, how it fits into the family of UNIX operating systems, and what you can do with it. It also tells you how you can install

FreeBSD alongside whatever version of Windows you happen to be using and how much space its various components take.

II: Getting FreeBSD Running

Part II covers the nuts and bolts of running the system—logging on, shutting it down, moving around, looking around, and using the floppy and the CD-ROM drive. This part also explains how you can set up FreeBSD to make your life easier, how to find out what the system is doing, and how to edit files so you can change what the system does.

III: FreeBSD and Software

In addition to FreeBSD itself, more than 5,000 software applications, most of them free, are available and ready to install on FreeBSD. New ones are added almost every day. Each application usually comes in two forms—as a package and as a port. Part III explains how you install FreeBSD-ready software and find out enough about it so you can run it. It also provides an overview of the software available and what it does so you can decide what you might like to install.

IV: Connections, Sound, Graphics, and Printing

Part IV explains how to get your connection to the Internet up and running, how to make sound work, how to get X, the graphical user interface, to work (you need it to run Netscape), and how to print from FreeBSD.

V: Customizing Your Kernel and Updating the System

To get specialized hardware working with FreeBSD (possibly even your sound card) and to get maximum performance from your system, you need to customize your kernel, the "brain" of the operating system. Part V explains three ways to customize your kernel, including building your own kernel. It also tells you how to upgrade the entire system.

VI: Other Challenges, Other Resources

This part includes a chapter on miscellaneous tasks that didn't fit elsewhere, a chapter on crisis management, and a chapter on other sources of information about FreeBSD—the Internet, books, and your own hard drive.

VII: Appendixes

Appendix A lists hardware that works with FreeBSD. Appendix B tells you about the installation CD-ROM—the first CD-ROM of the FreeBSD set—included with this book.

Conventions Used in This Book

Something you type on your keyboard is shown in the book's text in `fixed width` type or in **`bold.`** You might see something like this:

```
xanne@killer ~ $ whoami
xanne
```

`xanne@killer ~ $` is the prompt, like a `C:\>` in DOS, on my computer. The computer's name is `killer` and my username is `xanne.` The bold text, **`whoami,`** is what I typed—my polite request to the computer to tell me my name. The next line—`xanne`—is the answer the computer printed out.

When you have to fill in something of your choice, like a file to edit, the place where you fill in your choice is shown inside angle brackets in *`italic`* type. The following command:

```
xanne@killer ~ $ ee <filename>
```

would use the `ee` editor to load the file you fill in for <*`filename`*> so you can edit it.

Icons Used in This Book

ON CD-1 This icon alerts you to software that's on the CD-ROM. The CD-ROM is virtually identical to the first of the four CD-ROMs that come with the set you can buy from Wind River Systems (http://www.freebsdmall.com). The CD-ROM includes the entire FreeBSD operating system and quite a lot of third-party software. The third-party software varies a little from release to release, so a 4.3 installation CD-ROM may be a little different from a 4.2 or 4.4 installation CD-ROM.

TIP A nifty shortcut or a one-line summary: this may be all you need! Sometimes, a hint for where to go when things don't work or where to get additional information.

WARNING It's easier to stay out of trouble than to fix trouble (although you learn a lot getting out of trouble). This icon will help you avoid sandtraps, quicksand, and similar hazards.

X-REF This icon tells you there's related information somewhere else in the book that might be useful..

REMINDER Just a reminder.

LINUX The penguin alerts you to something in FreeBSD that's different from Linux, or maybe something that's identical in both. Linux is another UNIX-style free operating system. If you've never used it, you can ignore the penguin.

What to Do Next

It's much more fun *doing* than just *reading*, so you'll want to get FreeBSD installed right away. It's one of those tasks, like jumping a ditch, that's nice to do right the first time. After some background about the wonders of FreeBSD in Chapter 1, Chapters 2 and 3 get right to it, and Chapter 4 finishes it up in style.

If you have comments you'd like to communicate, write to me by email at andrsn@andrsn.stanford.edu. I'll also post some files and other updates (I hope they won't have to be corrections) on my web page at http://andrsn.stanford.edu/FreeBSD.

Acknowledgments

I appreciate without bounds the support and encouragement of my husband, Martin Anderson.

Many people, from new users to experts, read part or all of drafts of this book and offered corrections and suggestions. Nik Clayton was especially helpful, and so was Doug Barton. Greg Lehey provided comments on early chapters.

John Murphy read the entire text twice and was especially helpful in finding typos, inconsistencies, and several substantive mistakes. Other people to whom I am grateful for catching typos and providing suggestions include Bruce Harding, Roddie Hasan, Yuri Korobkov, Brian Raynes, Eric Rehnke, Charlie Schloemer, and Christoph Sold.

Several people, including Jordan Hubbard, Terry Lambert, and Josef Grosch, provided encouragement. So did many new users who downloaded an electronic copy of the one or more chapters and declared that it was just what they needed. Various people on EFNet's #freebsdhelp channel helped by both asking and answering questions, and people on other EFNet channels answered questions as well. Susan Schendel did a great job of copy editing a difficult manuscript. Remaining errors are, of course, my own.

The ultimate debt is, however, to those who write the code and the documentation that goes with it. An operating system that is free, open source, and the outcome of voluntary effort owes its existence and its pizzaz to the hard work of many special people. I have tried, where possible, to identify the individuals responsible for some of these contributions. But many major contributors and maintainers of code and documentation are not mentioned either because I don't know who's responsible or the topics don't lend themselves to attribution in a book of this type.

Finally, I want to thank the Hoover Institution at Stanford University, and its director, John Raisian, for continued support.

Chapter 1

FreeBSD and UNIX

FreeBSD is a powerful, free operating system based on the UNIX developed at the University of California at Berkeley in the late 1970s and the 1980s.

- FreeBSD runs on an ordinary personal computer—the same computer on which you run Windows 98 or Windows 2000.
- FreeBSD is a multi-tasking, multi-user system, although it doesn't mind having only one user.
- FreeBSD is used by Yahoo!, MCI WorldCom's UUNet, Mindspring, and many other Internet service providers (ISPs).
- FreeBSD was used to do the graphics for the movie *The Matrix* and is used for animation at a number of companies, including Disney.
- FreeBSD is open source. That means you can look at what the programmers actually wrote. You don't have to do so if you don't want to—but it's nice to know that other people do.

FreeBSD: The Operating System

FreeBSD is an operating system that works both as a personal computer (call it a work station, if you want to get serious, or call it a play station) and as a network operating system simultaneously.

- As your personal computer, it can be used just as you use Microsoft Windows—to read, send, and sort email, display wallpaper, play music, process photos from your digital camera, connect to your Internet service provider, run Netscape, download files, and write term papers. You can even play quite a few games, although on that score Windows 98 still has the edge.

FreeBSD's Genealogy

UNIX was originally developed at AT&T's Bell Labs, which sent some free (but copyrighted) copies around to universities. The Computer Systems Research Group at the University of California at Berkeley, under a contract from the Department of Defense, added a crucial component—the internet protocol, or TCP/IP. Without that—no World Wide Web. They did a lot of other work on the system and made it available to others under the name Berkeley Software Distributions.

In the early 1990s the Berkeley boys reinvented the parts of UNIX that were copyrighted by AT&T until there was nothing left that couldn't be freely distributed, including the most fundamental part of the system: the source code that the programmers themselves wrote. Nevertheless, AT&T sued BSDI, which was selling BSD/OS, a commercial operating system based on the work at Berkeley. The suit was settled out of court. FreeBSD as it exists today was developed from the last Berkeley Software Distribution, 4.4 BSD, and it has always been open source.

UNIX, both AT&T UNIX (known in its most recent commercial incarnations as System V) and BSD UNIX, originally ran on expensive computers bought by governments, corporations, and universities. By the early 1990s, the personal computers with Intel processors that people were buying for desktop use at home and at the office got powerful enough to run UNIX, and Berkeley's UNIX got ported to the PC.

The UNIX family includes several commercial varieties stemming from AT&T UNIX (HP-UX from Hewlett-Packard, IRIX from Silicon Graphics, AIX from IBM, Solaris from Sun Microsystems) and several that owe more to Berkeley UNIX (SunOS, DEC Ultrix, and BSD/OS). Only a few of these run on a PC.

For more information, see the file `/usr/share/misc/bsd-family-tree` after you have installed FreeBSD.

- At the same time, FreeBSD can serve up web pages, connect to other UNIX and Windows computers and share files with them, provide a firewall, offer files for download, function as a USENET news server, run mailing lists, allow users to log in from remote locations—and do everything else you'd expect from a network server .

What Comes With FreeBSD

FreeBSD comes with just about everything.

- The base system has editors, email, software for connecting to your ISP, and all the heavy-duty networking stuff, all on the installation CD-ROM.

- The base FreeBSD system always comes with the X Window System (often called just X). X is the GUI (graphical user interface, or in real life, gooey) that's the UNIX counterpart to Microsoft's Windows. Only one window with X? Of course not. But that's what they chose to call it.

- Besides the base system and X, FreeBSD comes with over 5,000 third-party ready-to-install software packages, including a couple of office suites (word processor, spreadsheet, presentation creator, and database). Most are free and open source.

- FreeBSD runs nearly all the software available specifically for Linux. The software that makes this possible is also on the installation CD-ROM.

- Finally, the payware. Some commercial programs, like the Applixware office suite, are available in versions made specifically for FreeBSD at competitive prices.

Ready to Serve

FreeBSD does its network serving tasks extraordinarily well, which is why it's used by Yahoo!, one of the busiest sites on the Internet, by many Internet service providers, and by major providers of files for download.

What makes FreeBSD so appealing is its stability. It runs and runs and runs. Often a FreeBSD machine gets rebooted only when its operating system gets upgraded or it gets some new hardware, like another disk drive—or when the power fails.

Unlike Windows, FreeBSD doesn't need to be rebooted when new software is installed or settings are changed. Many FreeBSD machines have been running continually—24/7, or 24 hours a day, 7 days a week—for over a year, and FreeBSD dominates Netcraft's top-50 uptime list (how long major servers have been running without rebooting).

See http://uptime.netcraft.com/up/today/top.avg.html to find out how good FreeBSD really is.

Open Source vs. Microsoft Windows

FreeBSD (and NetBSD and OpenBSD) and the various distributions of Linux are all *open source*, which means you can get the source code—what the programmers wrote. That makes them different from any version of Microsoft Windows, where you get only *binaries*—the versions of the programs that only the computer itself understands.

With a Windows operating system and most of the software you buy for it, you can't find out how it's really put together and what it's doing. Neither you nor anyone else (except the people who work for the companies who make it) can look at the source code.

What difference does it make?

First, with open source anyone can look at the code and make improvements and fix bugs. A problem or a feature doesn't have to be on a company's "to do" list to get attention, and contributions can come from many different people, not just people who work for the company. Sources of support are also more diverse, but not necessarily as well organized. The jury is still out on whether open source is a better way to develop software—both operating systems and applications—than the closed-source approach, where access to the code is limited and central direction is greater.

Second, when we run software available only as binaries, you and I can't find out what our computers are really doing. Our computers store a lot of personal information and personal documents—passwords, financial data, email we hope is confidential. A business has trade secrets and business plans to protect. Even encryption and firewall software may be binary only.

It's probably not such a great idea for all of us to run, all the time, software whose mysteries and true behavior are known only to the companies that wrote it. Jörg Wunsch, a FreeBSD developer who grew up in what was then East Germany, signs his email messages with the line "Never trust an operating system you don't have sources for." There's some wisdom in that.

A New System: Fun or Work?

Learning a new operating system isn't easy. The best advice I got when I started out with FreeBSD, though, was that it wasn't so hard—it was just a different way of thinking.

Windows (and Apple's Mac) have almost entirely isolated users from typing anything at a command prompt, like the infamous `C:\>` of DOS. Now it's clicking and double-clicking, pulling down menus, and dragging and dropping. Graphical aids to set up and manage the system are becoming available for FreeBSD and other flavors of UNIX, but most of the work—and most of the fun—is still at the command line.

FreeBSD and Linux

Linux is another free UNIX-style operating system—or rather, a Linux distribution is an operating system. Linux itself is just the kernel—the basic program that runs the computer. All the other parts of the system are put together to create a distribution (a full operating system) like RedHat or Debian or SuSE or Slackware. Each of these distros (which is what they are called for short) comes with a somewhat different set of add-ons and a different way to manage add-on software.

Which is better, FreeBSD or some variety of Linux?

- Many people think the BSDs, and especially FreeBSD, are better at handling Internet communications (technically, TCP/IP) because there's a much longer history of development with the BSDs. Windows NT/2000 and Mac OS X have turned to BSD code for their networking, thus bringing in the strengths BSD has developed over the years.

- FreeBSD enthusiasts also think its file system is safer—you can use some speed-up techniques with less risk that your files will get trashed.

- Users like the way FreeBSD handles third-party software in comparison to most Linux distros; it's easier to find what you want, install it, and get it working—although the Debian distro of Linux is pretty good at this.

- X, the graphical user interface, is identical in Linux distros and FreeBSD. So are Apache (a major web server) and Samba (the software for communicating with PCs running Windows) and many other software packages.

- FreeBSD runs most Linux software—often better than Linux does, according to some people.

- Linux can sometimes handle a particular piece of hardware that FreeBSD can't, but hardware drivers for both systems are continually being written and upgraded.

- The FreeBSD license allows developers to use FreeBSD code in other applications and distribute only binaries. Linux uses the GPL license, which requires (with some exceptions) that the full source code of any application in which any GPL code is used must be made freely available.

FreeBSD and Linux are competitors, but they are competitors with a lot in common. Together they are challenging Microsoft in the server market and increasingly on the desktop and the laptop as well. The third edition of the *UNIX System Administration Handbook* uses FreeBSD and RedHat Linux as two of its four example systems (the other two are recent versions of Solaris and HP-UX).

Computer professionals find themselves working with both Linux variants and BSD-style systems (as well as Microsoft's offerings). Trying to learn Linux and FreeBSD at the same time would be as confusing as learning French and Spanish at the same time. Pick one, and stick with it until you know it. And hey, make it FreeBSD!

Linux and FreeBSD differ in one major respect. Because Linux distributions have only the kernel (with modifications) in common and put the rest of the system (userland) together in many different ways, the Linux development community is many groups: the kernel developers (with Linus Torvalds at the center) and the various groups that work on different distributions.

FreeBSD is more unified, with one development group (the programmers who write the code) that works on the entire system, kernel and userland. The developers elect a core group, one of whose responsibilities is to approve and welcome new developers, known as committers once they are given the privilege of making changes to the system.

Many developers with commit privileges are seasoned professionals; a few are still in high school. People who aren't formally committers also contribute to FreeBSD. Most of the communication is done through mailing lists, where people post their suggested changes to the system.

The BSD Family

BSD varieties of UNIX are all descended from the UNIX developed at the University of California at Berkeley. Of these, FreeBSD is the most popular.

FreeBSD has a couple of close cousins—OpenBSD and NetBSD—that are, like FreeBSD, open source and free. OpenBSD concentrates on security. NetBSD runs on many other kinds of computers as well as PCs. Someone once said that NetBSD will run on a squirrel carcass in a cardboard box. (I don't believe that, but then I haven't tried it.)

FreeBSD also has a sister, BSD/OS, a commercial member of the BSD family.

With Apple's new operating system for the Mac, called Mac OS X, the BSD family acquires another cousin.

Where to Get FreeBSD

You can get FreeBSD on CD-ROMs or over the Internet.

The CD-ROM and This Book

Version 4.3 or later of FreeBSD is on the CD-ROM in this book along with many of the ready-to-install third-party software packages available for FreeBSD. This CD-ROM is identical to the first CD-ROM in the set of four sold by Wind River. The installation CD-ROM is also available as an ISO-image: you download it over the Internet and burn your own CD-ROM.

The Full CD-ROM Set

The full set of four CD-ROMs can be ordered from Wind River Systems (http://www.freebsdmall.com) and is often available in computer stores. The first CD-ROM is the installation CD-ROM. The other three in the set include more third-party software, a live file system (great for when you accidentally erase files), and something called the cvs repository from which it's possible to extract any version of FreeBSD that existed when the CD-ROM was made.

The FreeBSD CD-ROMs were originally marketed by Walnut Creek CDROM, which was bought by BSDI in 2000. The software division of BSDI was in turn bought by Wind River Systems in 2001, but FreeBSD itself is not owned by anyone.

Downloading FreeBSD from the Internet

TIP

The set of four CD-ROMs is great to have, and buying it supports the FreeBSD Project. But many people install FreeBSD over the Internet and get software by downloading files from ftp.freebsd.org or one of the mirror sites around the world that has the files. If you don't have an installation CD-ROM (or it's not bootable on your hardware), you need bootable floppies—at least two—to get started; you get the rest of the system by FTP. It may take a while depending on the speed of your connection.

Chapter 2

Preparing to Install FreeBSD

Installing FreeBSD—and keeping the operating system you already know and love safe—takes some planning. You want to get it right the first time, and you can. This chapter takes you through the preliminary steps:

- checking out your hardware
- making space for FreeBSD
- choosing what to install
- making boot floppies, and
- printing out a few documents

—right up to the point where you put the CD-ROM in the drive and boot up the installer.

The Bare Facts

- FreeBSD needs its own space—not just some unused space on your Windows drive, but a *partition* of its own. That partition has to be a primary partition—not an extended partition or a logical drive in an extended partition. A PC hard drive can have up to four partitions.

- Unless you have either a partition that you can delete entirely (losing all the data there now, perhaps after copying it elsewhere) or unpartitioned space, you must add a new disk to your system or shrink your Windows partitions to create unpartitioned space.

- FreeBSD (and every other operating system on a PC) needs some of its files close enough to the beginning of the disk so the computer can find them when it boots. Unlike Windows, these files can be on a second hard drive instead of the first drive.

- You can install FreeBSD in as little as 110 megabytes (MB). All the networking stuff will work, but there won't be room for the X Window System or graphical applications like Netscape—nothing pretty. If you can squeeze out a gigabyte, it would be nice. The details on how much space you need for the various bells and whistles come later in this chapter.

- A computer with two (or more) operating systems installed needs a way to give you a choice—what do you want to run today? It needs a *boot manager.*

Getting Ready

Like checking the tires and stashing a road map in the glove compartment before driving cross-country, a little advance work helps a lot.

Making Backups

WARNING

If you never make backups, this is the time to bite the bullet. Of course, bullets don't taste very good, and FreeBSD doesn't eat hard drives for lunch. But we all make mistakes.

Windows Backup Software

Windows 95/98/NT/2000 come with built-in backup software, although in Windows 95/98 you may have chosen not to install it.

If Backup is not installed, for Windows 98 do the following:

1. **Click** Start->Settings->Control Panel->Add/Remove Programs

2. **Click the** Windows Setup **tab.**

3. **Click on** System Tools **to highlight that selection, as shown in Figure 2-1.**

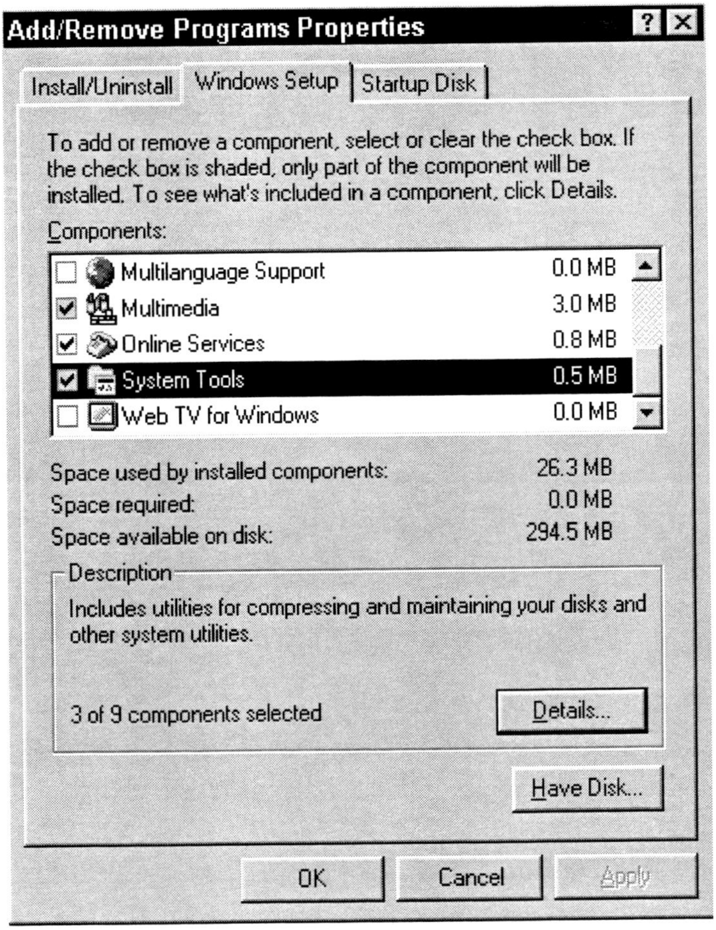

Figure 2-1: Where the Backup Software Comes From

4. **Click on** Details....

5. **Check the box next to** Backup**, as shown in Figure 2-1.**

WARNING

Don't uncheck any checked boxes; doing so tells Windows to delete installed programs.

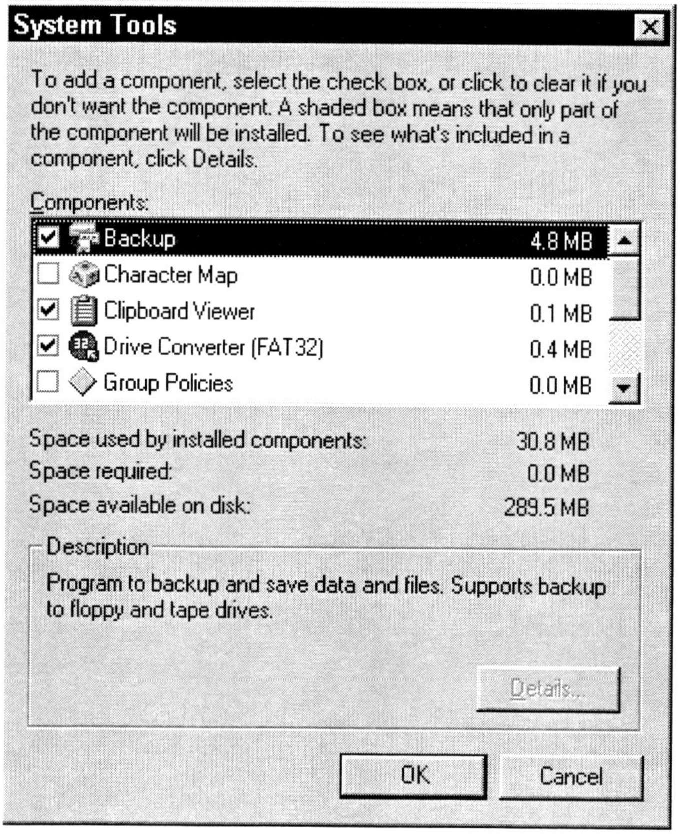

Figure 2-2: Click OK to Install Backup Software on Windows 95/98

6. **Click** OK

7. **Follow the instructions on the screen, which may ask for your Windows installation disk or a floppy.**

The process is the same for Windows 95, except that Backup is located under Disk Tools instead of System Tools.

Once installed, find the Windows 98 Backup with Start->Programs->Accessories->Systems Tools->Backup (again, Disk Tools instead of System Tools for Windows 95) and run the program.

In NT Backup is on Start->Programs->Administrative Tools (Common)>Backup. Check the box that invites you to back up the registry.

The problem, of course, is not in running the program but in finding a place to back up the huge hard drives we're getting used to using.

Living on the Edge

If you live on the edge and don't make backups, at least consider what you really don't want to lose.

To prepare for the worst case—you accidentally delete an entire partition (like C or D) on your hard drive—preserve what you can't reinstall.

The fractal gif you created that looks like a dragon. Your first draft of the next great American sitcom. Your spreadsheet data on road kill and UFOs. Your email demonstrating that you really were charged for two copies of Quake III. The phone numbers and addresses of people you hope you can stay with on your cross-country skateboard trip. The date of your mother's birthday. Software licenses, passwords, encryption keys. Financial and tax data, if you're lucky enough to have some and your accountant doesn't take care of it for you. Your browser bookmarks.

Most of this data will fit on a floppy or two. If you have a Zip or Jaz drive or a writable CD drive, all the better.

Consult your Windows manuals or on-line help for different approaches to backing up the Windows registry and making a Startup Disk or Emergency Repair Disk.

Checking Out Your Hardware

FreeBSD installs on a variety of different PC hardware. Appendix A: Supported Hardware lists supported hardware for the version of FreeBSD on the CD-ROM—a long and rather cryptic list. Here are the basics:

- A computer with a 486 or better (a Pentium is better!) CPU, although an 386SX might work. AMD and Cyrix CPUs are also supported.
- At least 8MB RAM—16 is better.
- An IDE or SCSI hard drive with at least 110MB available. For the total

experience, a gigabyte or even two.

- A CD-ROM drive and, if it's not a bootable CD-ROM drive, a floppy drive.
- A floppy drive and a good Internet connection if you don't have a CD-ROM drive and want to install from the Internet.
- Keyboard, monitor, and video card.
- Optional: mouse (but required for X, the graphical user interface), sound card, modem, ethernet card, and printer.

What Windows Can Tell You

You want nitty-gritty details about your hardware for two reasons—to check in Appendix A: Supported Hardware to see if it's supported by FreeBSD, and to tell the FreeBSD installer about it on the chance that you need to do so. Consult your own Microsoft Windows:

In Windows 95/98:

1. **Click** Start->Settings->Control Panel.
2. **Double-click on** System **when you see a display like that in Figure 2-3.** You see a display that tells you the computer's operating system, its CPU (like 80486), and how much RAM it has.
3. **Click the** Device Manager **tab**. The View Devices by Type radio button will be selected. You see a display like Figure 2.4.
4. **Right-click on a kind (Windows calls them classes) of hardware and click** Print **to print the information to your printer.** The radio button Selected Class or Device will be selected. **Click** OK.
5. **Repeat for each kind, or class, of hardware** except System Devices, which you don't need.

At the end, you have a sheaf of papers called Selected Resource Reports that tells you about your hardware—make and model (except for standard computer parts) and resources used.

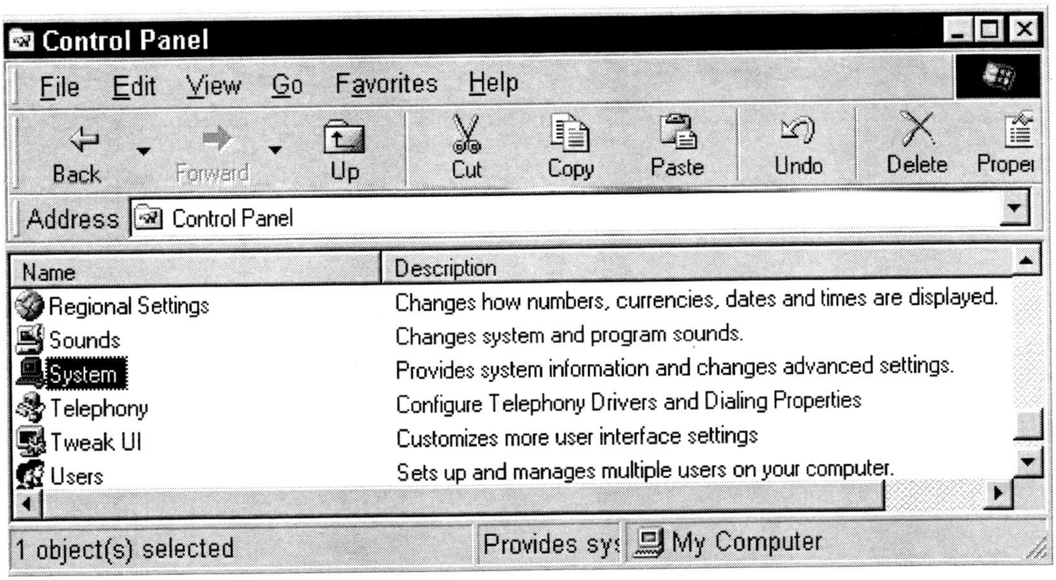

Figure 2-3: Getting Info from Windows about Your Hardware

To print everything at once, click Print and select the All Devices and System Summary radio button. This option kills more trees and it's harder to find what you want in the print-out, but you get everything Windows knows about. Expect 18-20 pages of information, called a System Resource Report.

For Windows NT, follow these steps:

1. **Click** Start->Programs->Administrative Tools(Common)->Windows NT Diagnostics.

2. **Click the** Resources **tab**. You see a display like Figure 2.5.

3. **Click** Print **to print everything.**

   To see the IRQ, DMA, and I/O for each piece of hardware, click on the Devices tab, right-click on an item in the list, and click Properties.

   Unfortunately no printing is available from this dialog box, and the hardware names are more mysterious than clues in *London Times* crossword puzzles. Figure 2.6 shows resources for a Soundblaster 16.

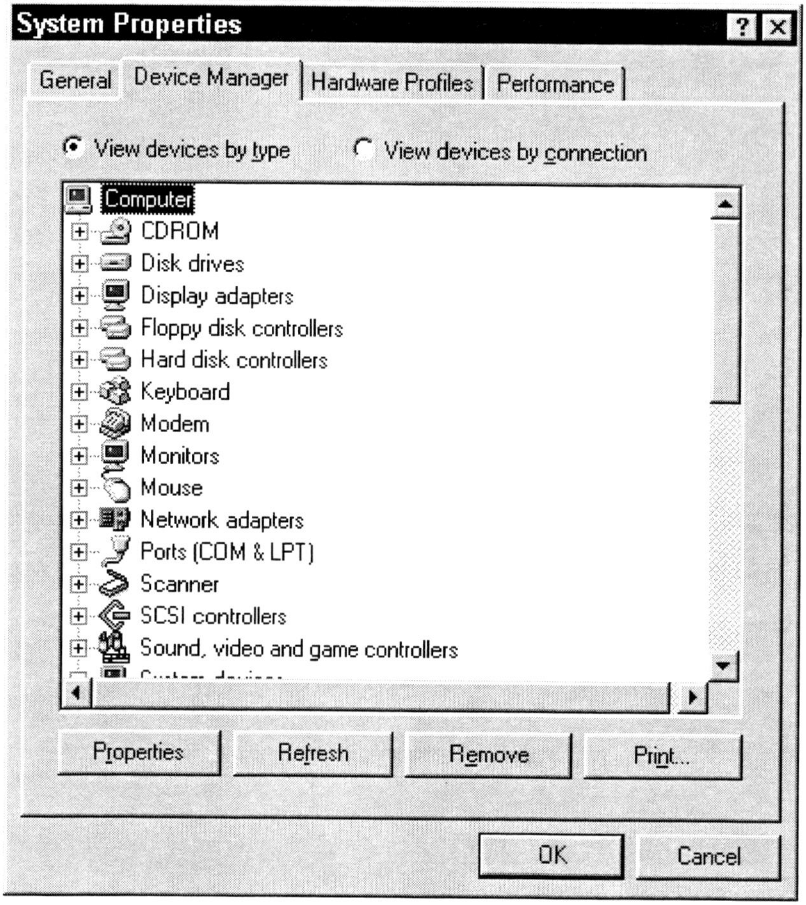

Figure 2-4: Classes of Hardware Devices, in Windows Terms

Your print-outs (I hope you didn't have to write all that down) give you just about all the information you need to install and configure FreeBSD. Use a marking pen to highlight the names of the different hardware items and the IRQs (interrupt requests) and I/O (input/output) addresses they use in Windows.

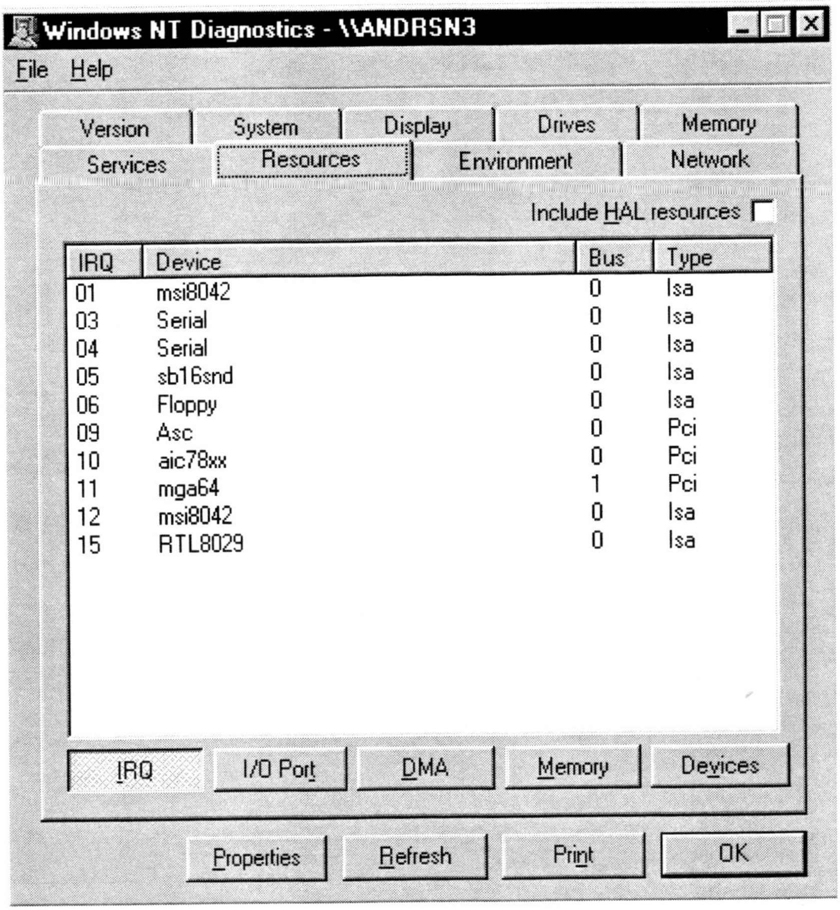

Figure 2-5: Windows NT Hardware Listing

A typical entries for communications (serial) ports looks like this:

```
Class: Ports (COM & LPT)

Device: Communications Port (COM 1)
Resources:
     IRQ: 04
     I/O: 03F8h-03FFh
```

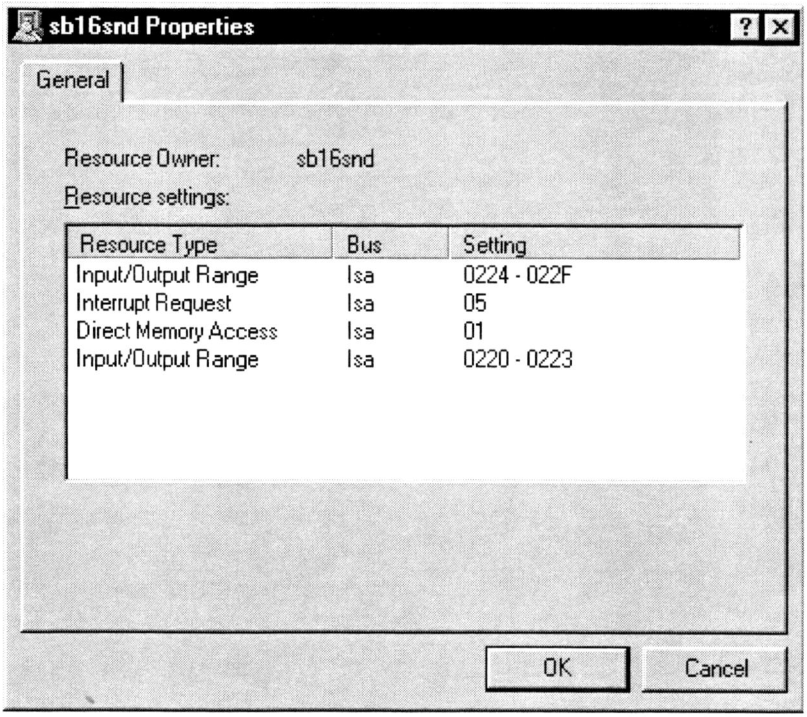

Figure 2-6: Windows NT's Display for One Hardware Item—A Sound Card

```
Class: Ports (COM & LPT)
Device: Communications Port (COM 2)
Resources:
     IRQ: 03
     I/O: 02F8h-02FFh
```

A sound card might show up like this:

```
Class: Sound, video and game controllers
Device: Creative AWE64 16-bit Audio (SB16
     compatible)
Resources:
     IRQ: 05
     I/O: 0220h-022Fh
     I/O: 0330h-0331h
```

```
I/O: 0388h-038Bh
DMA: 01
DMA: 05
```

You use your print-outs to check your hardware and the resources it uses against the list of supported hardware in Appendix A: Supported Hardware. If your hardware uses resources different from those listed in the hardware appendix (like a different IRQ), mark the hardware entry in the appendix and write down there what *your* hardware is using in Windows.

Special Handling: The Modem and the Video Card

It's nice to know you've got serial ports, but which one does your modem really use and how do you connect to your Internet service provider? You need this information to install from the Internet (if you can't use a CD-ROM) and to connect to your ISP once FreeBSD is installed. Now is the time to get Windows to tell you:

1. **In Windows 95/98, double-click** My Computer.
2. **Double-click** Dial-up Networking.
3. **Select the connection you usually use and know works as configured, right-click on it, and select** Properties. **Write down the phone number.**
4. **In the "Connect using" box, click** Configure **and note the port (probably COM1 or COM2) the modem uses. Click** Cancel.
5. **Click** Server Types **and then** TCP/IP settings **(if that's what you use) and write down the configuration information—the IP address you use (probably assigned) and the name server IP addresses.**

Where's your monitor manual? This manual will be a big help getting the X Window System running. What you want to know are a couple of numbers called the horizontal and vertical refresh rates, sometimes known as synchronization ranges. If the monitor manual has wandered away as most of them do, fire up your web browser and try the manufacturer's web page on the Internet, http://www.sony.com, for example. Search the manufacturer's site by the model number on the back of your monitor and find the "specs" that go with your monitor model. Print them to your printer.

How Much Space Is Enough?

FreeBSD can be installed in as little as 110MB—about 90MB of files and 20MB of *swap* space, or space to use as a substitute for memory. This is what you get if you choose *minimal* at installation time.

FreeBSD installs in chunks called *distributions*. Fortunately the install menu lets you pick more intuitive categories, each of which includes a bunch of distributions. The minimal install is just the *bin* distribution, which includes files that get put in several essential directories.

The distributions and the space (the space keeps edging up, of course, just like housing prices) they need are shown in Table 2-1, Space Requirements. The items with an asterisk aren't actually distributions, but are essential space or software you install to use the distros.

- Even a minimal installation needs some swap space. You need more if you run graphics programs that use a lot of memory. Two times your computer's memory (RAM) is the standard (e.g., 64MB swap if you have 32MB RAM), but if you don't have much RAM and you want to run Netscape, you may need more than two times RAM. You can't make a swap partition bigger than its original size, but you can add one if you have unpartitioned space.

- The help stuff—`man`, `doc`, `info`, throw in `dict` and `games`—is good to have on your own computer so you don't have to go to the Internet with every look-up. The "`compats`" are necessary for the X Window System, at least some of them. They don't take much space. Unless you choose a minimal installation and go back later to install more stuff, all these small but tasty potatoes are automatically installed. The installer may ask if you want `crypto`, and you should get it.

- The heavy hitting comes with ports—the framework that makes it easy to install third-party software. The ports collection is one of FreeBSD's nicest features. Try to make space for it.

Table 2-1 **Space Requirements**

Distribution	*What It Is*	*MB*	*Running Total*
bin	essentials	90	90
swap*	RAM substitute	20	110
man	on-line help	7	117
compats	compatibility with older stuff, X	8	125
doc	FAQ, handbook	24	149
dict	spell-checking	2	151
games	includes fortunes	6	157
info	more help files	2	159
crypto	security	10	169
XFree86	GUI (version 3.3.6)	30	199
ports	third-party software framework	65	264
kernel source	to rebuild kernel, get sound working	45	309
other source	to upgrade system	225	534
desktop*	X-Window cool stuff (choices)	36	570
software, files*	for doing updates, locating data	30	600
linux support	for running Linux programs	60	660
space*	to rebuild system	300	960
more swap*	substitute for RAM	108	1068

- Kernel source may be necessary to get a sound card working (see Chapter

13) and for several other purposes.

- The X Window System's biggest space requirement comes from graphics programs rather than X itself. The FreeBSD installer lets you choose only the parts of X you need. GNOME and a featureful *window manager* like `afterstep` (X always needs a window manager) are examples of programs you add to X for desktop convenience (and eye candy). Other choices might take a little less (or more) space.

- The installer will ask if you want support for Linux programs. Quite a few different kinds of software use Linux support (recommended).

- The biggest demand is full source, about 225MB in addition to the kernel source, and especially the space you need to use it after you install it—about 300MB.

Table 2-1 allows 30MB or so for software and files (like email and the database that gets built to help you find files). That's minimal. Software and files seem to expand to fill the space available. And where are you going to put the office suite?

Planning Your Install Strategy

Once you know how much space you want to give FreeBSD, you decide where to put it.

Getting Up Front

FreeBSD can run from a second hard drive, unlike Windows, which won't perform from anywhere but the first hard drive. But FreeBSD needs a few of its files (those in the / or "slash" root file system) close enough to the front of the drive so the computer can find them. And every other operating system needs some files up front too. This is the way personal computers work. The front rows can get a little crowded, with everybody wanting to be close to the stage.

How close to the front is close enough? On IDE hard drives (the most common kind), the boot sector of every operating system needs to be entirely under the 1,024 cylinder mark. Where's that cylinder mark? If only you could pry open the hard drive and find it, even if you had to count up to 1,023. Unfortunately, it's not that easy. It's really a problem the computer itself has working with big hard drives.

In the worst case, the 1,024 cylinder mark occurs at the first 504MB of the drive. Newer computers, built after 1994 or so, come with built-in ways to handle bigger drives, called Logical Block Addressing or LBA. If you have a large IDE drive, LBA is probably already turned on in the BIOS. You usually change the BIOS settings by pressing the Delete key when the computer boots and says "Press DEL to enter setup" or something similar. You follow the directions on the screen.

LBA should be enabled for a new hard drive, and if yours is installed at a store, the service department usually does this for you. Changing the settings for a drive that already has an operating system on it will probably make that system unusable. Software solutions also exist, but may conflict with a boot manager or FreeBSD.

In the best case, you can boot from any partition under the first two gigabytes, and usually the first 8 gigabytes for SCSI systems on newer computers. SCSI drives are more expensive, gigabyte for gigabyte, than IDE drives, plus there's the expense of the SCSI controller card and the SCSI cables. But you can attach up to seven devices on a cable, and some of the cards allow two cables and external devices as well. If you have a SCSI controller, it will show up when you boot the computer, possibly inviting you to press Ctrl-A to enter the SCSI configuration utility. This happens before the operating system loads. SCSI drives are easier to work with than IDE drives.

Checking Space

If your Windows `C:` drive occupies the entire first two gigabytes, either you shrink it (putting some programs and data in a `D:` drive farther out on the disk) or you get another hard drive. In this new millennium when you can get a huge IDE drive for under $100 plus installation (if you're not handy with screwdrivers and cables), that may be the easiest way to go.

To find out how much space your programs and data occupy on each drive:

1. **Double-click** My Computer.

2. **Right-click on the drive you want to check.**

3. **Select** Properties.

You see on the screen how much space is occupied and how much is free (but not unpartitioned) in both numbers and a graphic.

Checking Partitions

On personal computers you're limited to four *partitions* on a each hard disk drive. One of these partitions can be what's called an *extended* partition, which can hold other *logical* partitions (that sounds like cheating, and it is). FreeBSD cannot be installed in an extended partition, but Windows NT and Linux can. An extended partition could hold logical drives for Linux and a logical drive for Windows applications, for example. But FreeBSD, like Windows 95/98, needs a *primary* partition.

Windows 95/98 doesn't tell you how your hard drives are partitioned (that's up to the tech at the store, right?) unless you run a DOS program called `fdisk`. Like the tool kit in your car, a bootable DOS floppy with some tools on it may come in handy. (Windows NT cannot create a bootable DOS floppy.) Make one this way:

1. **Double-click the** MS-DOS icon **on your desk top (or use** Start->Programs->Command Prompt).

2. **Change to the** `C:\Windows\command` **directory by typing:**

```
C:\>C:
C:\>cd Windows
C:\Windows>cd command
```

   If Windows is installed in a different directory, substitute the appropriate directory.

3. **Type:**

```
C:\Windows\command> format a: /s
```

4. **Put a floppy in the drive when it asks. Answer the screen prompts and wait for it to finish.**

5. **Copy files to the floppy by typing at the prompt:**

```
C:\Windows\command>copy fdisk.exe a:
C:\Windows\command>copy format.com a:
C:\Windows\command>copy chkdsk.exe a:
```

Copy `edit.com`, `qbasic.exe`, and `qbasic.hlp` to the floppy if you have them (optional).

All your DOS files on the floppy need to be the same DOS version or they won't run.

You boot the computer (if you need to find out how the hard drive is partitioned) with your new floppy in the `A:` drive and type `fdisk` at the `A:>` prompt.

You see the plainest menu imaginable. Type a number to select a choice. Typing 4 displays partition information. That's all you want to do right now. You press Esc to exit to a previous menu or the DOS prompt. You can then reboot the computer and remove the disk from the drive.

The display `fdisk` produces tells you the disk number. It lists the partitions and their type (EXT for extended, PRI for primary), and also the size, file system, and percentage of the disk the partition is using. If you have a large disk, `fdisk` may not see all of it.

Windows NT is blissful by comparison. Clicking Start->Programs->Administrative Tools(Common)->Disk Administrator gives you a graphical or text portrayal (selected on the View menu) of your disks, how they are partitioned, unpartitioned space on them, and free space within partitions. It also lets you delete partitions.

Here's how a 2-gigabyte hard drive might look with all the sensitive stuff up front, within the 504 megabyte limit:

- 400MB primary partition:

- One GB primary for all of FreeBSD including the / file system
- 600MB extended for Windows applications and data.

LINUX

One way to get Windows 98, FreeBSD, and Linux on the same hard drive would look like this:

- Windows in the first 300MB primary partition
- FreeBSD's / file system of about 70MB in next primary partition
- FreeBSD's other files systems (usually `/var` and `/usr`, and swap) out in the hinterlands at the end of the disk in a primary. They won't mind.
- Linux in an extended partition with its / file system, which in some incarnations of Linux needs to be 150MB, up front, the rest in various logical partitions, and other Windows files also occupying a logical partition in the same extended partition Linux uses.

Shaping Up Your Hard Drive

To make space for FreeBSD on an existing hard drive, you check the drive for errors, save what's precious and throw out the garbage, consolidate what's left, and finally resize the partition. Here's the list of things to do:

1. **Error-checking:** Click My Computer. Right-click on the drive you want to check, click Properties, click the Tools tab, and click on Check Now to check for errors.

2. **Cleaning up**: Move or delete files until the used space on the drive is small enough to allow it to be resized (you'll do that later).

3. **Defragmenting**: Click My Computer. Right-click on the drive you want to defragment, click Properties, click the `Tools` tab, and click on Defragment Now.

   Defragmenting puts pieces of files back together and places them at the beginning of the drive, consolidating free space at the end of the drive—essential to shrinking it and making unpartitioned space available.

Windows 95/98 comes with a disk defragmenter. For Windows NT you need third-party software (perhaps Norton Utilities for NT). Defragmenting takes a long time—plan on a couple of TV programs.

4. **Resizing**: Resize the drive's partition to make it smaller, so you get unpartitioned space, with special software.

Resizing

Moving files and resizing partitions takes less muscle than moving furniture, but it's just as sweaty. Both freeware and payware are available to help you.

ON CD-1

Two utilities in the `tools` directory on the CD-ROM resize or move partitions, `presizer` and `fips`. `Presizer.exe` comes with a how-to in `presizer.doc`. The documentation for `fips.exe` is in `fips.faq` and `fips.doc`. Both authors want you to read their rather extensive descriptions of how things work and the process before you risk ruin with their software. Get ready to use them with these steps:

1. **Copy the binaries** (`fips.exe` or `presizer.exe`) **to a boot floppy (like the one you already made). Also copy** `restorbb.exe`, **which can be used with** `fips`.

2. **Print the documentation files from the CD-ROM, where E: is your CD-ROM drive, from a DOS window by doing the following:**

   Type `write E:\TOOLS\fips.doc`. The WordPad accessory will start and open `fips.doc`.

   Click on the `File` menu and choose `Print` to print the document.

   Repeat for other documents, including `fips.faq` and `presizer.doc`.

3. **Read the documentation to see if the program will work in your situation and how to use it.**

Commercial software, including Partition Magic from PowerQuest (http://www.powerquest.com) and System Commander from VCOM (http://www.v-com.com), also can do this kind of work. PowerQuest's

DriveImage can move an entire partition to a new drive.

The commercial programs get updated more often than the freeware versions and have more features and more elegant manuals. They change the cluster size when they resize partitions, which is good.

You do not partition or format the space you create by resizing. FreeBSD will do that for you when you install. If you have a partition you plan to delete, FreeBSD will do that for you too.

Keeping Windows

You might be tempted to just wipe Windows off your hard drive. FreeBSD is great, but Windows—whatever variety you use—is useful too, and not just for those old applications you want to run.

- An installed DOS or Windows 95/98 partition makes it easier for FreeBSD to know how to handle the disk drive—to get its geometry right.

- Hardware—like ethernet cards—often comes with software for setting up the hardware. This software is usually exclusively for DOS/Windows.

- A DOS/Windows partition provides a place for a full-fledged boot manager—the software that gives you the choice of which operating system you want to run.

  A boot manager can live in the small space on the hard drive that comes before the partitions where the operating systems are located, and FreeBSD offers two such boot managers. But given the space limits, you can't do much with these boot managers, like telling them what text to display on the screen or which operating system to boot by default.

- A DOS/Windows partition provides some space to save a few files if you decide to reinstall FreeBSD—more space than you get on a floppy.

And Windows gives you another option for installing FreeBSD if you have space within a partition. You can use a payware program (about $99 for individual users) called `vmware` (http://www.vmware.com) to create a *virtual machine* on your Windows hard drive.

The virtual machine behaves as if it were a PC running another operating system. If you have a gigabyte or two of space, lots of memory, and don't want to shrink partitions or repartition, this may be for you. Not all the capabilities of FreeBSD (or any operating system running in a virtual machine) are available this way, but overall it works. The advantage is that you have FreeBSD running at the same time as Windows, in a window like any other program. The disadvantages are that your memory is split between the two systems, neither one runs as fast as it would otherwise, and the CD-ROM, floppy, and printer are available to only one system at a time.

Picking a Boot Manager

If two operating systems exist on the same computer, you need a way to choose which one to run when the computer boots. This is called a boot manager (or, informally, a boot mangler). A boot manager puts a menu on the screen of the operating systems on the computer. Some or all of a boot manager's files live in cramped quarters called the Master Boot Record, a part of the hard drive that comes before any partitions.

The FreeBSD installer offers to install its default boot manager, `booteasy`. If you do not already have a boot manager on the system, you install it. It can be reinstalled if it gets trashed, or you can install a different boot manager. One option is the free `osbsbeta.exe` in the `tools` directory on the CD-ROM. From the `tools` directory in the CD-ROM, copy the files for the boot managers to one of your DOS boot floppies. These files are:

- `bootinst.exe` and `boot.bin` for FreeBSD's `booteasy`
- `osbsbeta.exe` for the alternative boot manager

System Commander and some versions of Partition Magic, two commercial programs for repartitioning, also come with boot managers. These boot managers need a DOS or Windows FAT (or FAT32) partition in which to keep files too large for the Master Boot Record. Using space on a regular partition allows them to offer more features—you can customize the menu, set the time-out, choose a default system to boot, and more. Older versions of Partition Magic come with the IBM OS/2 boot manager, which needs its own primary partition (one of your precious four).

You can install the System Commander or Partition Magic boot manager before you install FreeBSD.

Windows NT/2000 comes with a boot loader that can also be used as a boot manager. Linux has `lilo` or `GRUB`.

WARNING

Installing Windows 95/98 wipes out any boot manager installed in the Master Boot Record. Hey, this is for your own good! It's virus protection. If you install Windows after you install FreeBSD, the boot manager (not your installed system) needs to be reinstalled, either from a DOS boot floppy or from Windows 95/98's MS-DOS mode.

X-REF

If you don't want to install a boot manager at all, you can use a specially set-up floppy to boot FreeBSD from the hard drive. See Chapter 18.

Making Floppies and Printing Docs

Only two more tasks before you reinvent your computer.

Your computer may be able to start the FreeBSD installer directly from the CD-ROM if you reboot the computer with the CD in the drive. Otherwise you need FreeBSD boot floppies called `kern.flp` and `mfsroot.flp`. The floppies are also good for emergencies, along with the third floppy, `fixit.flp`.

WARNING

FreeBSD boot floppies are images and won't work if they're just copied in the ordinary way. You must use the special program, `fdimage.exe`, to make boot floppies.

Flopping Around

The easiest way to make boot floppies from Windows is to use the `makeflp.bat` utility on the CD-ROM:

1. **Put the CD in the CD-ROM drive (don't reboot).**
2. **Click on** My Computer.
3. **Click on the icon for your CD-ROM.**
4. **Click on the** `tools` **directory.**

5. **Click on** `makeflp.bat` **and follow the instructions.**

The third floppy you want is `fixit.flp`. To make this floppy:

1. **Put a freshly formatted floppy (not a boot floppy) in the a: drive.**

   Can you trust factory-formatted floppies? Some people don't; others do. If you try them and they don't work, format them yourself, just with `format a:` (no system files).

2. **Double-click on the MS-DOS icon to open a DOS window.**

3. **Type** `C:` **to get to the** C:\> **prompt.**

4. **Type** `mkdir bsd` **to create a** `bsd` **directory (call it whatever you like).**

5. **Type** `cd bsd`.

6. **Type** `copy E:\tools\fdimage.exe`**, where E is the drive letter of your CD-ROM.**

7. **Type** `fdimage E:\floppies\fixit.flp a:`

   You can make the `kern.flp` and the `mfsroot.flp` the same way if you didn't use `makeflp.bat` to make them. If you download floppy images by FTP instead of using the CD-ROM and put them in the same directory where you keep `fdimage.exe`, you can make a floppy by typing `fdimage kern.flp a:`, for example.

DANGER

Don't be taken in by `boot.flp`. A lawyer would call it an attractive nuisance. It sounds like just the right thing, but it's for 2.88MB floppy drives. Most floppy drives are 1.44MB.

Printing Docs

ON CD-1

You get context-sensitive help while installing by pressing F1 at any time.

Several help files are also available on the CD-ROM as files with the `.txt` extension. You can look at them ahead of time and even print them out. Clicking on the file names doesn't work because they get loaded with the Windows Notepad utility, and they're not formatted properly for Notepad.

You look at these files ahead of time by clicking My Computer, clicking the icon for your CD-ROM drive, and then clicking `View.exe`. You see a menu of files and commands at the bottom of the screen for navigating. Nice, but you can't print from it. To print a file:

1. **Put the CD-ROM in the drive.**

2. **Open an MS-DOS window by double-clicking on the MS-DOS icon on your desk top or using** Start->Programs->Command Prompt.

3. **At the** C:\> **prompt in the Command Prompt window type** `E: Enter` **where E is the drive letter of your CD-ROM drive.**

4. **Type** `dir *.txt` **to get a directory listing of the text files in the root directory of the CD-ROM.**

5. **Type** `write trouble.txt` **to use the** `write` **accessory to view the** `TROUBLE.TXT` **file.**

6. **Print** `TROUBLE.TXT` **by using the Print command on the File menu.**

TIP

`TROUBLE.TXT` is a good document to print because it tells you what to do about boot problems after installing. Look at the others just to find out what kind of help will be close at hand while installing.

Common trouble on installation or hardware detection after installation is the BIOS setting that tells your computer whether the operating system is Plug and Play. FreeBSD is not a Plug and Play operating system, and things may work better if you set this to No.

And now to do it.

Chapter 3

Installing FreeBSD

Installing FreeBSD is fun. It has one of the best installers around.

This chapter tells you how to:

- start the installer
- create a FreeBSD partition in unpartitioned space and chop it up into usable parts
- choose what you want to install
- tell the installer where to get what you want to install (the media), and
- make a commitment to go ahead.

You make the choices and the FreeBSD installer goes to work. In half an hour or so it will ask if you want to do anything more, and you can make more choices for setting up FreeBSD. (That's in the next chapter.)

The best part is that you can return to the installation program—it will be on your hard drive—any time to add software and do set-ups you bypassed on the first round.

Starting the Installer

To start the installer, use the floppies you made (see Chapter 2):

1. **Put `kern.flp` in the A: drive and reboot the computer.**

   You see boot messages (with some differences since your computer and mine aren't identical):

```
BTX loader 1.0 BTX version is 1.01
Console: internal video/keyboard
BIOS drive A: is disk0
BIOS drive C: is disk1
BIOS 635kB/65535kB available memory
FreeBSD/i386 bootstrap loader, Revision 0.7
(jkh@narf.osd.bsdi.com, Tue Apr 10 18:40:45 GMT
     2001)
/kernel text = 0x24f1fb data = 0x307a4+0x20594 |
Please insert MFS root floppy and press enter:
```

2. **Put** `mfsroot.flp` **in the A: drive and press** Enter.

   You see the twirling baton and this message:

```
Hit [Enter] to boot immediately or any other key
     for the command prompt.
Booting kernel in 9 seconds ...
```

3. **Press** Enter**—or do nothing. The installer will proceed on its own.**

   TIP

   If your computer is capable of booting directly from a CD-ROM, you don't have to use the boot floppies (although it's good to have them).

   You see this, with additional text about configuring the kernel:

```
Kernel Configuration Menu
Skip kernel configuration and continue with
     installation
Start kernel configuration in full screen visual
     mode
Start kernel configuration in CLI mode
```

4. **Press** Enter **and continue with the installation.**

Moving Around the Menus

You move around the menus this way:

Pressing the **up arrow** or **down arrow** moves up or down the options list.

Pressing **Enter** when a menu option is highlighted takes you to the highlighted submenu. When a checkbox like **[ ]** appears next to items in the list, you select an item by pressing the spacebar, and you get **[X]** next to the item. Pressing **Enter** doesn't select an item.

Sometimes pressing the spacebar takes you directly to a submenu. This is scary, but nothing is wrong.

The **Tab** key moves right through fields in a dialog box; so does the **right arrow** key. The **Shift+Tab** and **left arrow** keys move left or backward.

Pressing **Enter** leaves a menu. It accepts your choices if **[OK]** or **[Yes]** or **[Select]** at the bottom of the screen is highlighted. But it cancels or rejects an option if **[Cancel]** or **[No]** is highlighted.

Pressing **F1** at any time (well, just about any time) will bring up help. The lower-left portion of the screen often has helpful hints and explanations.

You can get out of the installation program by selecting **[Cancel]** on each menu until you get to **[X Exit Install],** or just reboot the computer, take the disk out of the drive, and start over—any time before the installer starts writing to your hard drive (you'll get a warning). A dry run or two is OK!

You probably do not need to configure the kernel unless your hardware review (see Chapter 2) turned up some unconventional resources. For now, assume everything is OK.

If the computer hangs and fails to continue with the installation, start the installation over, press the down arrow to select `Start kernel configuration in full screen visual mode`, and use the F1 key for help. The HARDWARE.TXT document on the CD-ROM tells about kernel configuration and can be printed from the CD-ROM while you're in DOS/Windows. Chapter 2 tells you how to do this.

You see the boot messages from the kernel (the main program that runs the computer) and this message:

```
Probing for devices, please wait (this can take
    a while)....
```

After 90 seconds (or sooner) the installer will display its first menu.

The First Menu

The installer's basic menu isn't quite as jazzy as a Windows InstallShield, but it's OK. It looks like Figure 3-1.

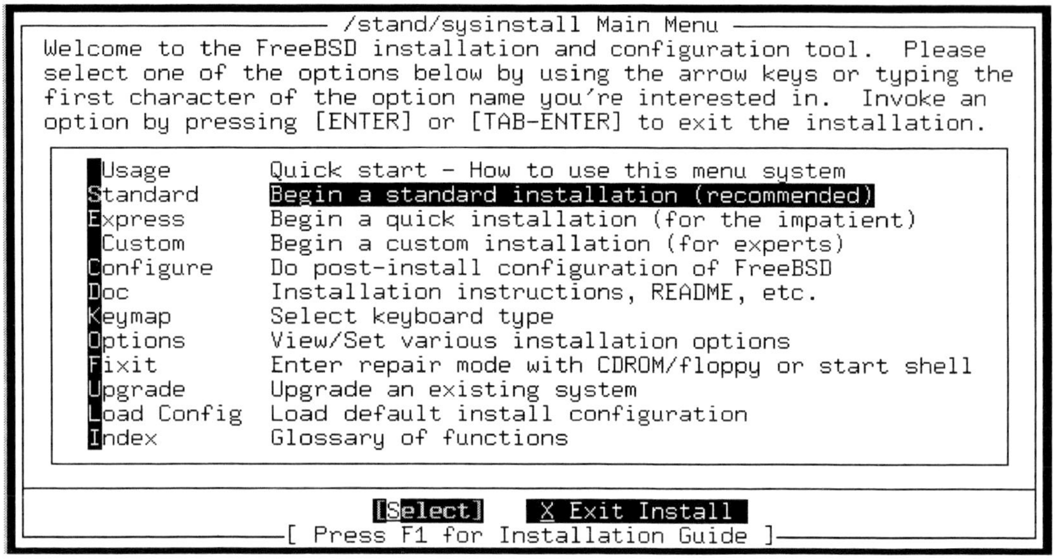

Figure 3-1: The Main Menu

If you use a keyboard other than the standard U.S. one, the first step is to select `Keymap  Select keyboard type` on the main menu, highlight your choice, press the spacebar to get a * next to your choice, press Enter with the highlight on [OK], and proceed:

1. **Press the arrow keys until you highlight:**

```
Standard     Begin a standard installation
     (recommended)
```

2. **Press** Enter.

   You see a message about setting up a DOS-style fdisk partition on your disk. Is this dangerous? You betcha. This is jumping out of the airplane. Your parachute (the backup I encouraged you to make in Chapter 2) is in a safe place, right? FreeBSD will warn you before anything is written to your disk and you have quite a few things to do before that happens, but you can also press a wrong key here and destroy a partition.

3. **Press** Enter.

   If you have more than one hard drive, you see a screen for selecting the drive you want to use with the spacebar. The `ad0` drive (or `da0` for SCSI drives) is the first hard drive in your computer. The second is `da1` (for SCSI) or `ad1`, `ad2`, or even `ad3` for IDE drives, depending on what else (like your CD-ROM) is attached to an IDE controller. Highlight the drive name by pressing the down (or up) arrow key and press the spacebar.

   You see a screen like Figure 3-2. Not shown in the figure is the Z option, which lets you toggle the units in which Size is shown (ST for standard, or 512K blocks; MB for megabytes; and KB for kilobytes).

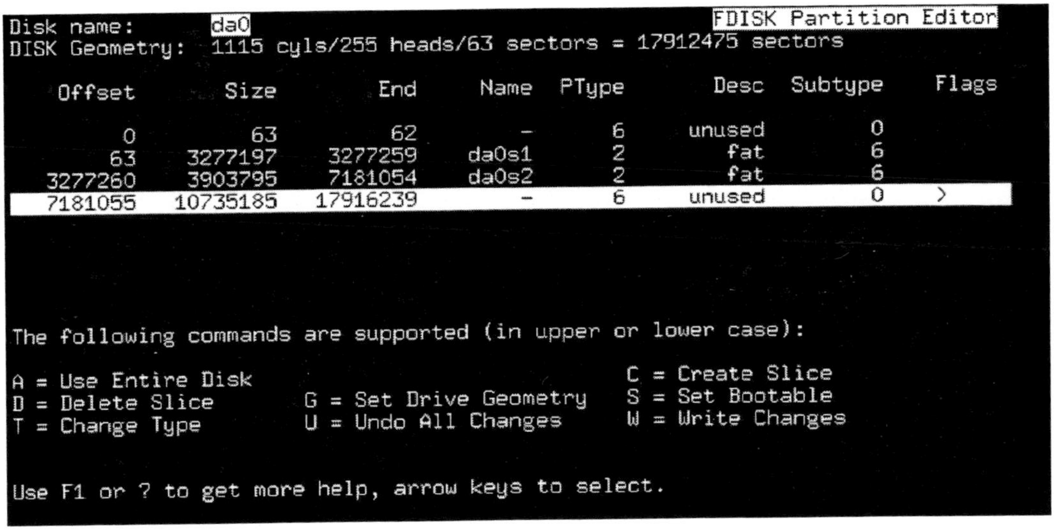

Figure 3-2: FDISK Partition Editor

At the upper left is the `Disk name: da0`. If you have an IDE hard drive, it will say `Disk name: ad0`. If you have two disks and want FreeBSD on the second, the number will be higher.

WARNING

Be sure you select the disk you really want to use.

I assume you don't want to use the entire disk for FreeBSD. So don't press `A`. Even if you want to use the entire drive, you get better results (my judgment here) by not using `A`.

You also don't use `W` when installing—in fact, in version 4.3 of FreeBSD, you won't even see this option on your menu. You should not have to use `T` to change the type of a partition or `G` to enter geometry.

Maybe—just maybe—you moved all of the files you care about out of a partition you want to delete. That's what `D` is for.

Slicing It Up

What's this `D = Delete Slice` in the list of commands, and what does the `da0s1` (or `ad0s1`) mean in the list of Names? Where are the partitions? Isn't this the `FDISK` Partition Editor?

Yes, it's the `FDISK` Partition Editor.

A DOS partition (no matter what kind of file system it has on it) is a FreeBSD slice. No kidding. That's what FreeBSD calls them—slices. That's why the "s" is in the Name. Slices (DOS partitions) are numbered beginning with 1, whereas disks start with 0. Therefore `da0s1` is the first DOS partition (and the first FreeBSD slice) on the first SCSI hard drive (no matter what kind of file system is on it). And you thought Alice had trouble in Wonderland.

Except in the `FDISK` Partition Editor, FreeBSD uses *partition* to mean a part of a slice. This use of the word *partition* is actually standard Unix terminology, in use before any variety of Unix was ported to personal computers. So *partition* meant one thing on a personal computer, another thing on Unix. "When I make a word do a lot of work like that," said Humpty Dumpty to Alice, "I always pay it extra."

WARNING

When you delete a slice, you delete a DOS-style partition. If you really want to delete a slice, move the highlight to the slice and press `D`.

To create a DOS-style partition (FreeBSD slice) for FreeBSD:

1. **Move the highlight to the unused space you want to partition.**

2. **Press** C.

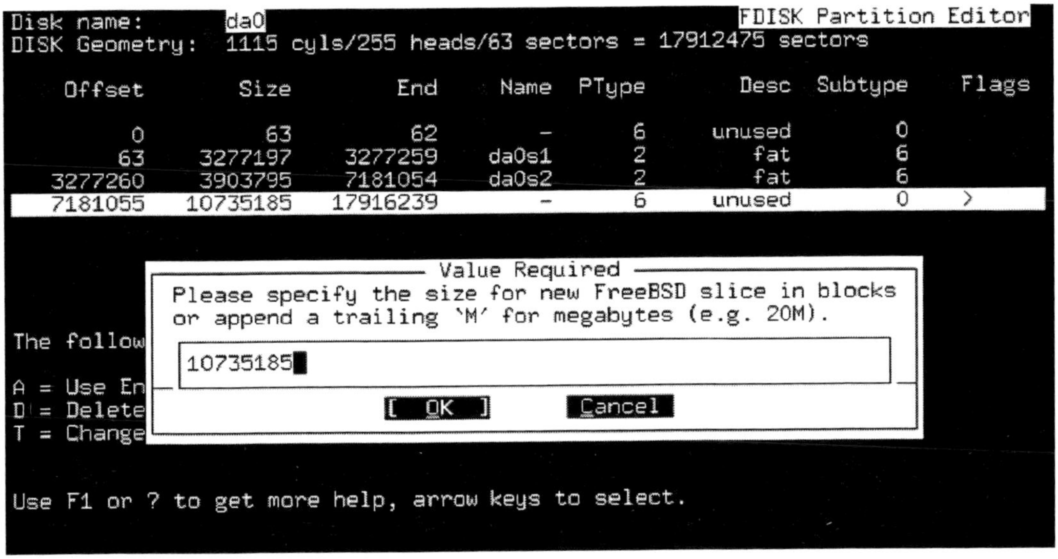

Figure 3-3: Creating a Partition for FreeBSD

You see a screen like that in Figure 3-3. The full size of the unpartitioned space is displayed in the dialog box. This size (in the figure) is in 512 kilobyte blocks. You divide blocks by two to get kilobyte-size blocks, or press `Z` to toggle the units in which the size is displayed. The space shown in the dialog box is about 5.3GB, or 5300M.

3. **Press** Enter **to use all the unused space for FreeBSD.** This is probably what you want, since you prepared this space for FreeBSD.

   If you don't want to use all the unpartitioned space for FreeBSD, press Backspace until the number in the dialog box is deleted, and enter the size of the space you want to use in megabytes with `M` immediately after it. Example: `2300M` for 2.3 gigabytes (GB). Press Enter.

   You see another dialog box asking for the type of partition to create, with 165 (the FreeBSD type) already in the box.

4. **Press** Enter.

   You see the partition you created in the list of partitions. In the right-hand column under `Flags` the new partition will have a `C` (in the right-hand column).

5. **Press the** up arrow **key (or** down arrow**, if necessary) to highlight the partition with the** C **in the Flags column.**

6. **Press** S.

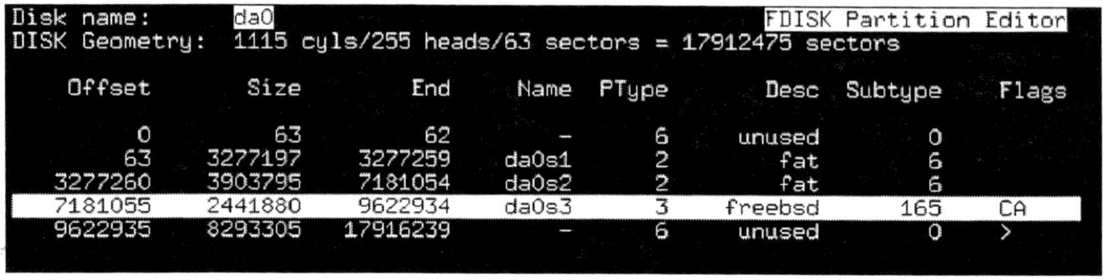

Figure 3-4: A New Partition Set Bootable

You see an A after the C. The A indicates that the partition has been set bootable. Figure 3-4 is an example.

You really do press S to get A next to the C under Flags. Bill Gates would never do that to you, but FreeBSD wasn't made in Redmond. And you're not done until you have a CA in the Flags column.

7. **Press** Q. You're finished with this screen.

The Boot Manager

The next dialog box is for the boot manager. It's shown in Figure 3-5.

You select one of the three choices in this dialog box—install the boot manager, install a standard Master Boot Record (MBR), or leave the MBR untouched.

If you have two hard drives, press F1 and read the help message; it's your only opportunity to do so.

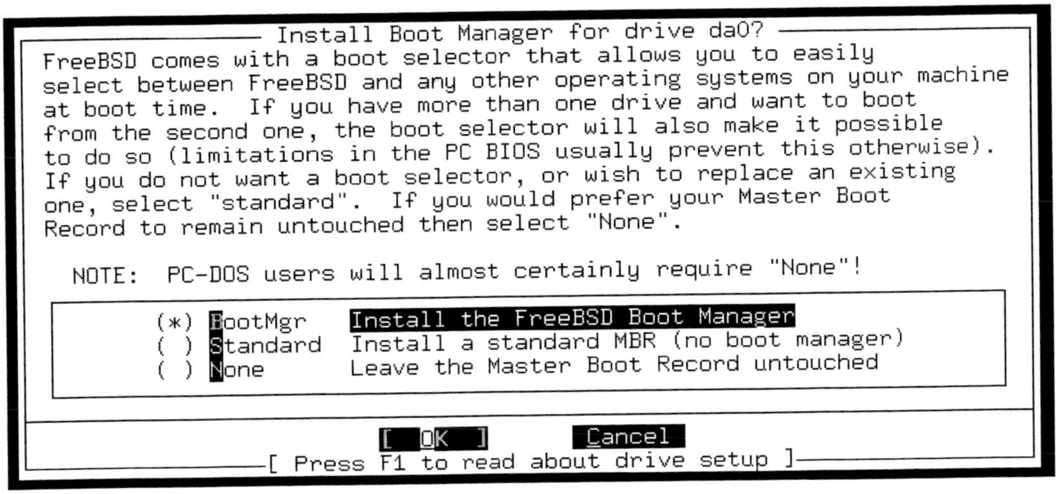

Figure 3-5: The Boot Manager Dialog

You install the boot manager if you have no boot manager on the disk on which you're installing, unless you're installing on a second drive and have a boot manager on the first drive that will take care of things—like System Commander, for example. Then you leave the MBR untouched. You also leave it untouched if you want to boot (always) from a floppy.

TIP

If you are installing on a second hard drive and you don't have a boot manager like System Commander, you need the FreeBSD boot manager on both the second hard drive and on your first hard drive, and you can't do that from this screen. Coming soon, though.

To make your boot manager choice:

1. **Use the arrow keys to highlight your selection.**

2. **Press the spacebar to get a * (an asterisk) next to your choice.**

3. **Press** Enter.

If you have more than one drive, you end up back at the menu where you choose the disk on which you want to install. If you have been working on your second hard drive and you want to install the FreeBSD boot manager on your first hard drive, do the following:

1. **Press the arrow keys to highlight the first hard drive, numbered 0.**

2. **Press the spacebar to get an `[X]` next to the drive.**

3. **Press** Enter.

   You see the `FDISK Partition Editor` for the first hard drive.

4. **Press** `Q`. (Don't do anything else!)

   You see the boot manager dialog again, but at the top it will ask about disk 0 instead of disk 1 (or 2).

5. **Make sure the highlight is on your choice and press the spacebar to get a * next to it if necessary.**

6. **Press** Enter.

The last hurrah of the FDISK Partition Editor (you will see it if the drive on which you plan to install has more than one primary FAT partition) is this:

```
Disk slicing warning:
Max one 'fat' allowed as child of the 'whole'
[ OK ]
```

It's a little unclear here who the parents and kids are, why they're so fat, and what, if anything, should be done. No options are offered. I get this warning whenever I have NT and Windows 98 on the same hard drive on which I'm installing FreeBSD. My boot manager handles this situation. I press Enter. So should you.

Partitioning—UNIX Style

Now you carve your slices into partitions on which you put file systems—BSD partitions inside DOS `fdisk` partitions.

Press Enter to dismiss the introductory screen.

```
                            FreeBSD Disklabel Editor

Disk: da0        Partition name: da0s3    Free: 2441880 blocks (1192MB)

Part        Mount               Size Newfs  Part        Mount          Size Newfs
----        -----               ---- -----  ----        -----          ---- -----
da0s1       <none>            1600MB DOS
da0s2       <none>            1906MB DOS







The following commands are valid here (upper or lower case):
C = Create       D = Delete          M = Mount pt. W = Write
N = Newfs Opts   T = Newfs Toggle    U = Undo       Q = Finish
A = Auto Defaults for all!

Use F1 or ? to get more help, arrow keys to select.
```

Figure 3-6: The FreeBSD Disklabel Editor

A screen like Figure 3-6 appears, and you think you're back in the FDISK Partition Editor, but you're not. You've come a long way, baby, and you're doing fine. This is the FreeBSD Disklabel Editor. You operate entirely on the partition (slice) you created before out of unused space, dividing it into useful pieces. An example is shown in Figure 3-6.

The free space in the partition you created is reported in the banner at the top—1192MB in the example shown in Figure 3-6. As you use up the space in the banner, what you choose will be shown in the lists under the headings.

You want, traditionally, four items: a `/` file system partition (for the kernel and boot stuff), a swap partition to use as a memory substitute, a `/var` file system partition for messages and logs and mail queues, and a `/usr` file system partition for working software and users' home directories. The `/usr` partition (in Unixspeak) gets whatever is left after you give space to the others, but it should be the lion's share of the space.

In a small installation—300MB or less—you can dispense with separate file systems for `/var` and `/usr`. Choose a swap size and give the rest of the space to `/`. That's more efficient use of your limited space.

With a 1GB partition, a carving up might give 80MB to `/`, 128GB to swap (depending on your RAM), 80MB to `/var`, and what's left to `/usr`, although the screen shots use smaller amounts for `/` and `/var`. The `/`, `/var`, and `/usr` labels are called mount points. Here's the process:

1. **Highlight the bar at the top with the free space by moving the cursor with the arrow keys.**

2. **Press** C **to create a partition.**

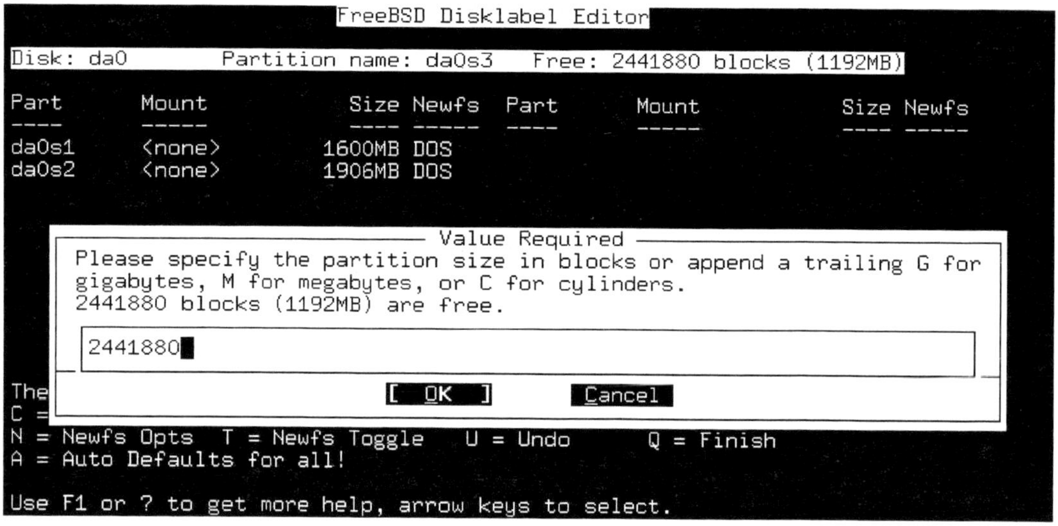

Figure 3-7: Disklabel Editor Dialog on Partition Size

A dialog box appears with a number of blocks in it—always all the free space available. See Figure 3-7 for an example.

3. **Backspace over the amount in the box and put in your own number, say** `60M`. **Figure 3-8 shows how it will look.**

4. **Press** Enter.

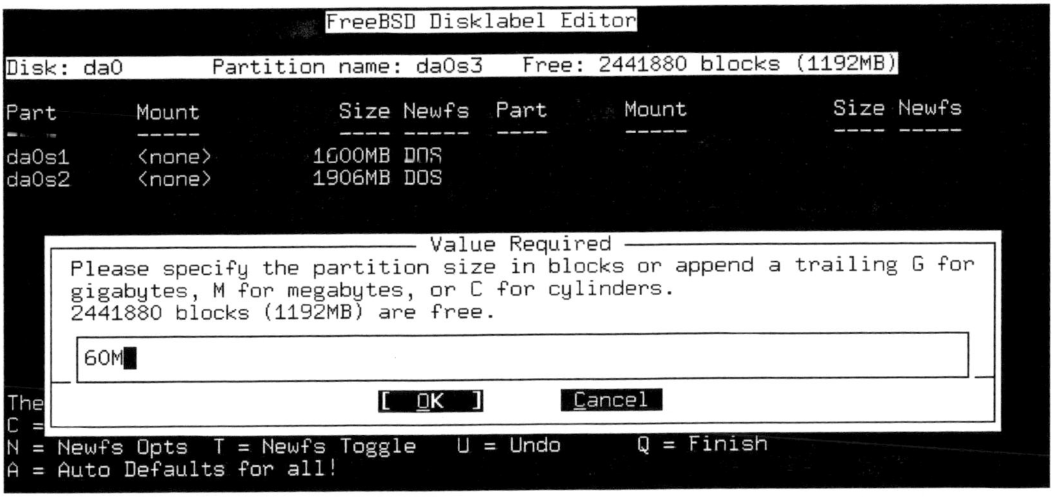

Figure 3-8: Disklabel Editor with a Size Entered in MB

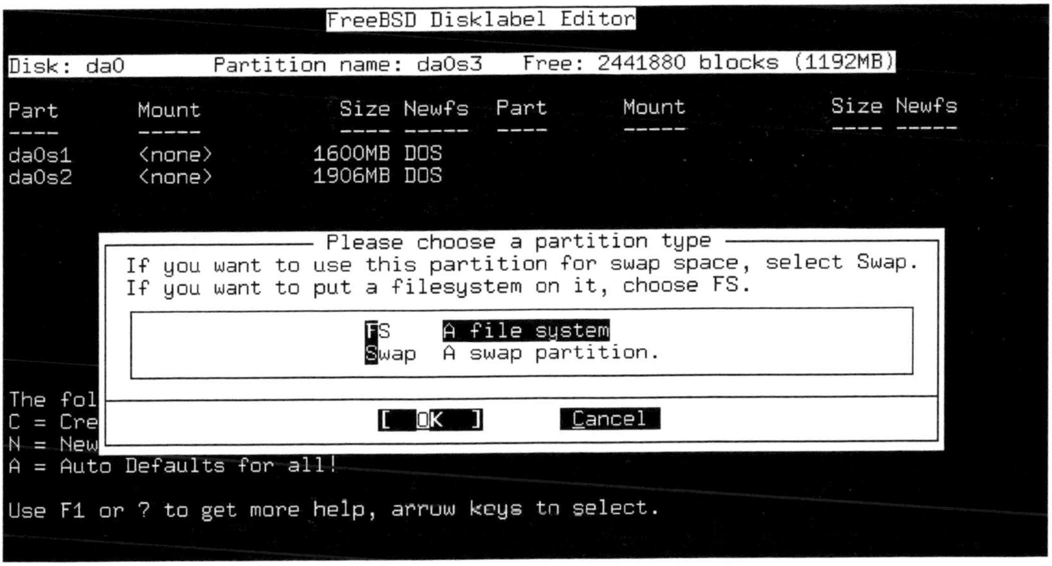

Figure 3-9: Disklabel Editor Dialog on Partition Type

A dialog box asks for a partition type—either a file system or swap. See Figure 3-9.

5. **Highlight FS and press** Enter.

   You see a dialog box asking for a mount point for the partition.

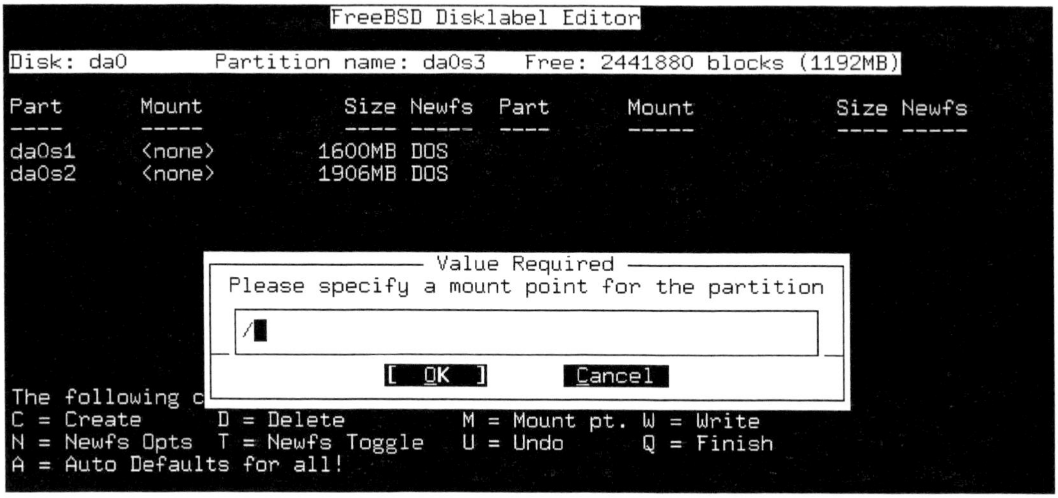

Figure 3-10: Disklabel Editor with a Mount Point Entered

6. **Enter / in the box as shown in Figure 3-10 and press** Enter.

   You see the result in Figure 3-11. The list now includes a new Part(ition), `da0s3a`, the Mount point is /, its size is 60MB, the file system will be UFS (that's what FreeBSD uses), and a new file system will be created. The amount Free in the banner at the top has been reduced to 1132MB.

7. **Press** C.

8. **Backspace over the amount in the dialog box and type in** 128M **(or some other amount of your choice, about twice the amount of RAM you have). Press** Enter.

9. **Move the highlight in the dialog box to Swap and press** Enter.

   No dialog box for a mount point appears, because swap partitions don't need mount points.

10. **Press** C.

11. **Backspace over the amount in the size dialog box and type in**

40M **(or** 60M **or even** 80M **if you have a little more space). Press** Enter.

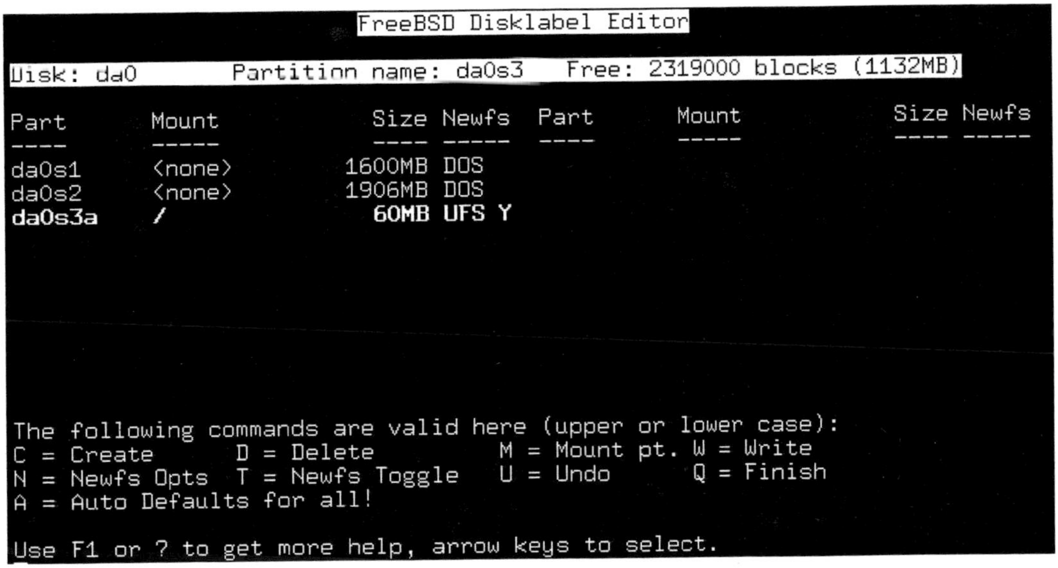

Figure 3-11: Disklabel Editor Showing New File System

12. **Move the highlight in the partition type dialog box to FS for file system. Press** Enter.

13. **In the mount point dialog box type** `/var`. **Press** Enter.

14. **Press** C.

15. **Press** Enter.

    Pressing Enter uses all the remaining space, which is the right thing to do now.

16. **Move the highlight in the partition type dialog box to FS for file system. Press** Enter.

17. **In the mount point dialog box type** `/usr`. **Press** Enter.

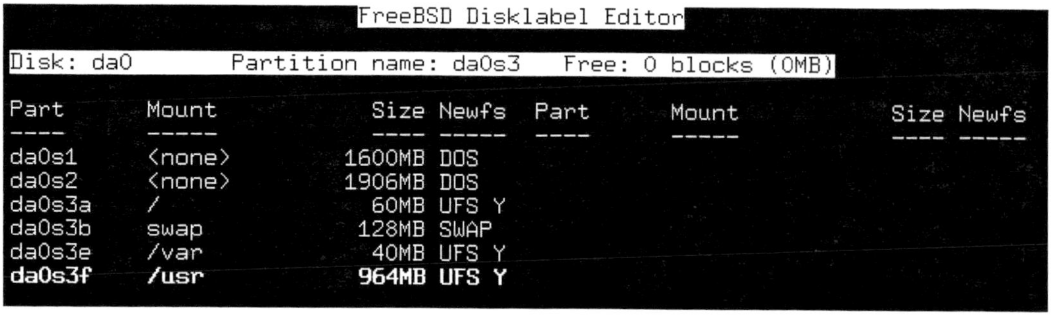

Figure 3-12: Disklabel Editor Done

Figure 3-12 shows how the Disklabel Editor will look after /, swap, `/var`, and `/usr` are created. The banner at the top shows 0 blocks free—everything's been used. Your disk name and the partitions listed under Part, as well as the Size list, will be different. But the letters `a`, `b`, `e`, and `f` are typically attached for `/`, `swap`, `/var`, and `/usr` respectively, and will be if you create them in that order.

Write down on a slip of paper the name of the partition on which / will be mounted—in the example, `da0s1a`. That information will be just what you need if you have trouble booting.

18. **Press** Q **to leave the Disklabel Editor.**

TIP

If you make a mistake typing a mount point, you move the highlight with the arrow keys to the line on the screen with the typo and use M to revise the mount point. Put the highlight back on the banner at the top of the screen to continue.

The Selection Menus

After the FDISK Partition Editor and the FreeBSD Disklabel Editor are done, you get a series of menus where you choose what to install.

The Base System

Figure 3-13 is the basic selection list. Chapter 2 (Table 2-1) tells you how much space different stuff takes (some items come up on later menus, not this one). The purpose in Chapter 2 was to help you decide how much space to make available for FreeBSD. But making the right choice here is not terribly important because you can easily add stuff after FreeBSD is installed.

```
                         Choose Distributions
 As a convenience, we provide several "canned" distribution sets.
 These select what we consider to be the most reasonable defaults for the
 type of system in question.  If you would prefer to pick and choose the
 list of distributions yourself, simply select "Custom".  You can also
 pick a canned distribution set and then fine-tune it with the Custom item.

 Choose an item by pressing [SPACE]. When you are finished, choose the Exit
 item or press [ENTER].

 <<<  Exit             Exit this menu (returning to previous)
      All              All system sources, binaries and X Window System)
      Reset            Reset selected distribution list to nothing
 [ ] 4 Developer       Full sources, binaries and doc but no games
 [ ] 5 X-Developer     Same as above + X Window System
 [ ] 6 Kern-Developer  Full binaries and doc, kernel sources only
 [ ] 7 X-Kern-Developer Same as above + X Window System
 [ ] 8 User            Average user - binaries and doc only
 [ ] 9 X-User          Same as above + X Window System
 [ ] A Minimal         The smallest configuration possible
 > > B Custom          Specify your own distribution set

                     OK          Cancel
            [ Press F1 for more information on these options. ]
```

Figure 3-13: The Menu for Choosing Distributions to Install

Here are guidelines for making a choice on the Choose Distributions menu:

- If you have 1GB or more for FreeBSD, choose 5, X-Developer. You get full source code.
- If you have 500MB to 1GB, choose 7, X-Kern Developer. You get kernel source, not full source.
- If you have 200MB to 500MB, choose 9, X-User.
- If you have less than 200MB, choose A, Minimal.

You make the choice this way:

1. **Move the highlight with the arrow keys to the choice you want.**
2. **Press the spacebar to get `[X]` next to your choice.**

3. **Press** Enter **if you're not taken immediately to the next dialog.**

Secret Handwriting

Before version 4.2 of FreeBSD, cryptographic software had its own menu because of various export-import restrictions. (In 4.2 and later, installation of software for encryption is automatic.) You see:

```
Do you wish to install cryptographic software?
```

1. **Press** Enter.

   Your screen displays the menu shown in Figure 3:14.

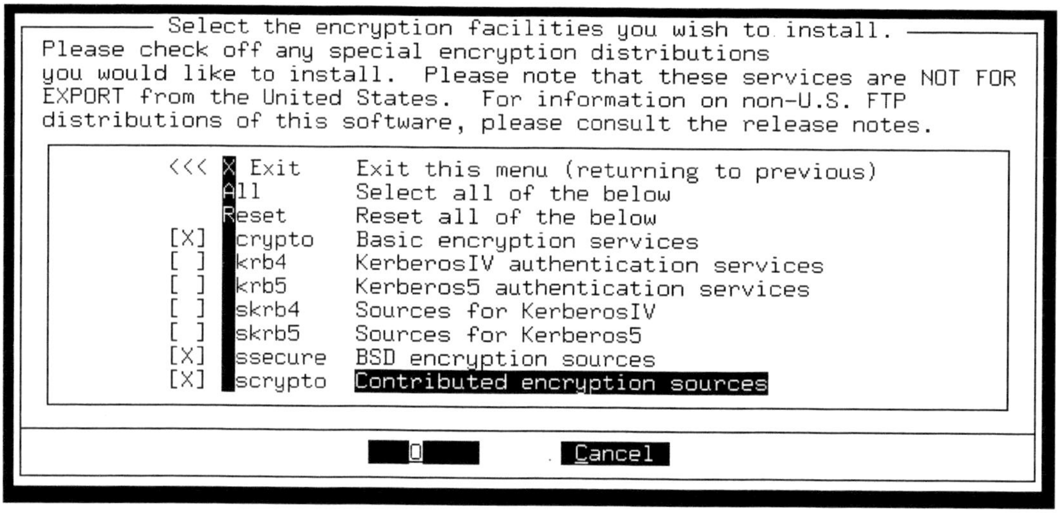

Figure 3-14: Selecting Encryption Software

2. **Use the arrow keys to highlight an item you want.**

3. **Press the spacebar to select it.**

   You want `crypto`. You probably don't want any of the Kerberos stuff (`krb4`, `krb5`, `skrb4`, `skrb5`). But you want `ssecure` and `scrypto`, if they appear on the menu.

4. **Press** Enter.

5. **Press** Enter **(if you are a U.S. resident) or** Tab+Enter **if you're not.** As of October 2000 or so, the patents that restricted the use of some cryptographic software in the United States expired, so you can claim you're not a U.S. resident without violating any laws.

The Ports Collection

The FreeBSD ports collection makes it easy to find out about and install third-party software. Figure 3-15 shows the dialog box.

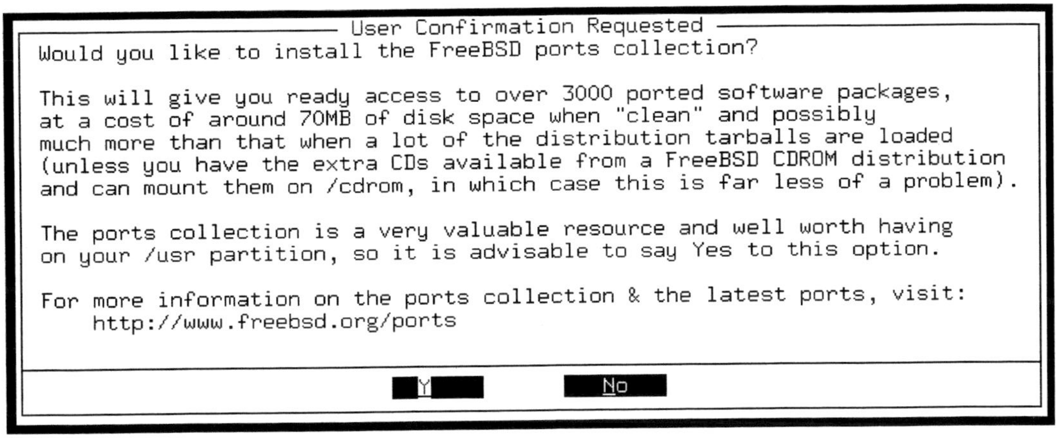

Figure 3-15: Ports Collection Dialog

- **Press** Enter **to install the ports collection. Unless your space is very limited, you want it.**

The X Window System (GUI)

If you chose to install X, the graphical user interface, you see a menu for selecting more or less of it. The defaults are likely to be acceptable for all three parts of the menu—Basic, Server, and Fonts—unless your video card is manufactured by ATI (then you want to use the Server menu to install a `mach` server as well as the default servers).

1. **Select with the arrow keys the option that exits from the menu,**

returning you to the previous screen.

2. **Press** Enter.

Choosing Installation Media

FreeBSD can be installed not only from a FreeBSD CD-ROM, but over the Internet (by FTP, or using File Transfer Protocol), from a DOS partition, and other ways.

You see on your screen the display shown in Figure 3-16.

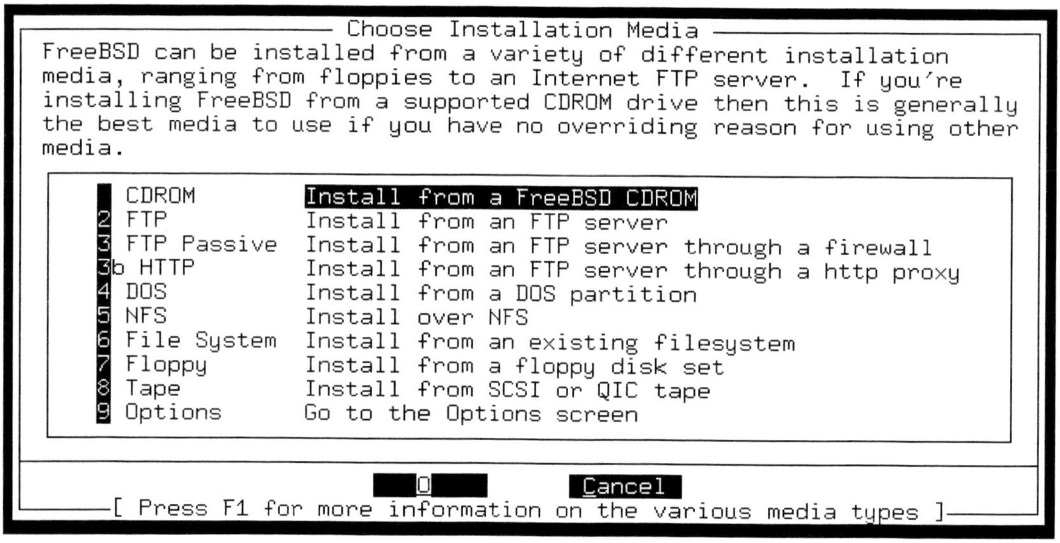

Figure 3-16: Install Media Dialog

You could simply press Enter here—the CD-ROM is the first choice and it will be highlighted when the installation media dialog appears.

But you might want to take this opportunity to look at the Options screen, the last choice on the list. It's where you go if your choice of media produces an error message like this:

```
No CDROM devices found!
```

If this happens to you, do this:

1. **Press** Enter **to get rid of the error message.**
2. **Use the arrow keys to highlight** `9 Options`.
3. **Press** Enter.

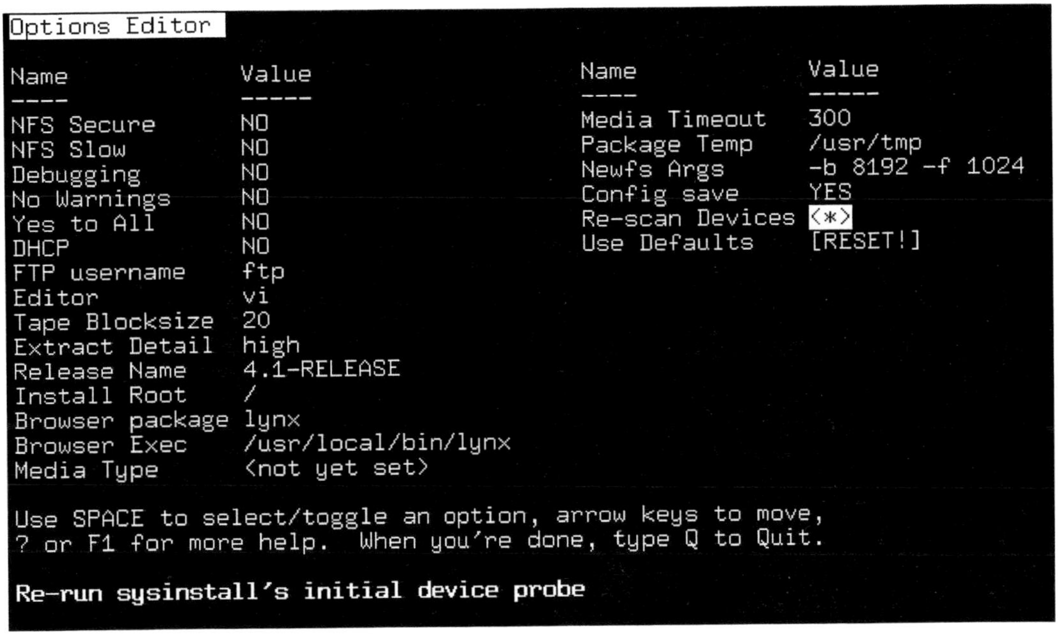

Figure 3-17: The Options Editor

Figure 3-17 shows the Options Editor. You seldom need to do anything on this screen. But if you get an error message like the failure to find your CD-ROM, you will want to use the Options Editor to re-scan your hardware.

1. **Use the arrow keys to move through the list until the highlight is the right-hand column on** `Re-scan Devices`.
2. **Press the spacebar.**

   You will see a message on your screen about probing for devices, and soon you will be returned to the Options Editor.

3. **Press** `Q` **to leave the Options Editor and return to the previous**

menu.

4. **Use the arrow keys to highlight the CDROM choice.**

5. **Press** Enter. If your CD-ROM still isn't found, you'll need to look at troubleshooting documents like `TROUBLE.TXT` on the CD-ROM and the FreeBSD FAQ on www.freebsd.org.

X-REF

Installing by FTP involves a few more choices. You can do so over an ethernet connection or a `ppp` (dial-up) connection.

Chapter 4's Networking section describes how to set up a network card. The information you need to provide and the form you fill out for installing by FTP over ethernet is just about the same as described there.

Installing by FTP over a `ppp` connection involves making a connection to your Internet service provider that's similar to a Windows Dial-Up Networking connection. The sections in Chapter 12 on What You Need for Dial-Up and Making Your First Connection may be helpful. The installer tells you to press Alt+F3 and not return to Alt+F1 until your connection is established.

If you install by FTP over a slow connection and you're worried about losing the connection, you can choose the Minimal distribution or X-User (see Figure 3-13) and get additional distributions later.

The Final Choice

When the installation media selection finishes, you see:

```
User Confirmation Requested
Last Chance! Are you SURE you want to continue the
     installation?
If you're running this on a disk with data you wish
     to save then WE STRONGLY ENCOURAGE YOU TO MAKE
     PROPER BACKUPS before proceeding!
We can take no responsibility for lost disk
     contents!
          [YES]              No
```

Until you press Enter with the highlight on `[YES]`, you can back out. If you have doubts:

- **Press** Tab.
- **Press** Enter.

You can also get out of the installer any time by rebooting the machine—either by turning it off or pressing Ctrl+Alt+Del.

But screw your courage to the sticking point (as Lady Macbeth said while goading her husband to murder). The highlight is on [YES] by default. You just:

- **Press** Enter.

  You see:

```
          Extracting bin into /directory . . .
```

This is going to take a while— half an hour, maybe more. How long depends on how much stuff you picked. You deserve a break. Eat, walk, read, sleep. Get away from the screen.

If you want to watch, press Alt+F2 to see messages flash by on what's happening (and any error messages). Press Alt+F1 to get back to the installation menu screen, which will continue to tell you what the installer is doing.

When the installer finishes you see this message:

```
Congratulations!  You now have FreeBSD installed on
     your system.
We will now  move on to the final configuration
     questions.
For any option you do not wish to configure, simply
     select No.
If you wish to re-enter this utility after the
     system is up, you may do so by typing:
     /stand/sysinstall.
                  [  OK  ]
```

- **Press** Enter.

And go on to Chapter 4, which tells you how to finish up the install and configure FreeBSD.

Chapter 4

Polishing Your Installation

You've installed FreeBSD! The installer congratulates you but goes right back to work, offering more menus and submenus.

The installer is smart, knowing just what you need to do next to get the system going. (Or maybe it's Jordan Hubbard, one of the founders of the FreeBSD Project and the main author of the installation program, who's smart.) It's called *configuration*. What will it be, the leather jacket or the silk bomber jacket? One earring or two?

This chapter tells you about your choices and how to make them:

- setting up your networking connection
- configuring your mouse
- adding software and a desktop
- adding users and passwords, and finally,
- rebooting.

You can come back to these menus any time after the system is up and running—and you get a chance at the end to revisit the menu and do anything that didn't get done on the first round.

The Setup Dialogs

FreeBSD's installer always seems to be asking questions. Don't worry if you don't know the answers—you can come back later.

WARNING

You answer the questions by pressing Enter when the highlight is on the answer you want. Some of the "right" answers (and the defaults—that is, what happens if you just press Enter instead of Tab Enter) are a little different in different versions of FreeBSD (4.3 versus 4.1, for example), so read the screen and make sure the highlight is where you want it before you press Enter.

Networking

The net wouldn't be the net without networking. FreeBSD's first post-install dialog asks:

```
Would you like to configure any Ethernet or
     SLIP/PPP network devices?
```

Highlight `[Yes]` **or** `[No]` **and press** Enter.

You may have an ethernet card in your computer that connects to a cable modem or to other computers, or you may connect to an ISP by dialup modem—that's usually `ppp`, or point-to-point protocol. The dialog box will look like Figure 4-1, with a list of network interfaces FreeBSD found on your system.

The first one in the example in Figure 4-1 is `dc0`, which is the name of the software driver that runs the ethernet card in my computer. If an ethernet card is listed in your display, it means you've got one and FreeBSD found it. Further down the list are a couple of `ppp0` options, which means only that FreeBSD found a couple of serial ports.

1. **Highlight the interface you want to configure.**
2. **Press** Enter. **You see:**

   ```
   Do you want to try IPv6 configuration of the
   interface?
   ```

   You probably don't, so **highlight** `[No]` **and press** Enter.

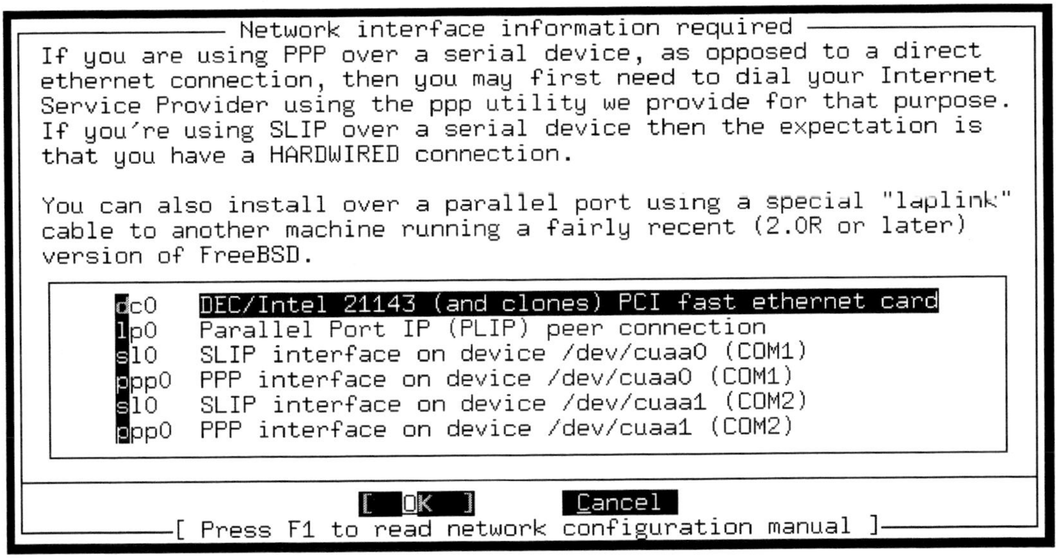

Figure 4-1: Network Interfaces

`Do you want to try DHCP configuration of the interface?`

With DHCP (Dynamic Host Configuration Protocol), you get assigned an IP address—the four numbers separated by dots that identify your computer when you're connected to the Internet—from a server to which you're already connected. If you have it, you probably know from setting up Windows connections. For this option, just **highlight** `[Yes]` **and press** Enter.

If you have either a fixed IP address or get assigned one after you dial up, you **highlight** `[No]` **and press** Enter to reject DHCP.

You see a dialog box like the one in Figure 4-2, but blank (unless you installed by FTP over the Internet). You can move around the box with the Tab key and the right and left arrow keys (backwards, too).

TIP

What you wrote down (Chapter 2) about your Windows dial-up networking connection will come in handy here.

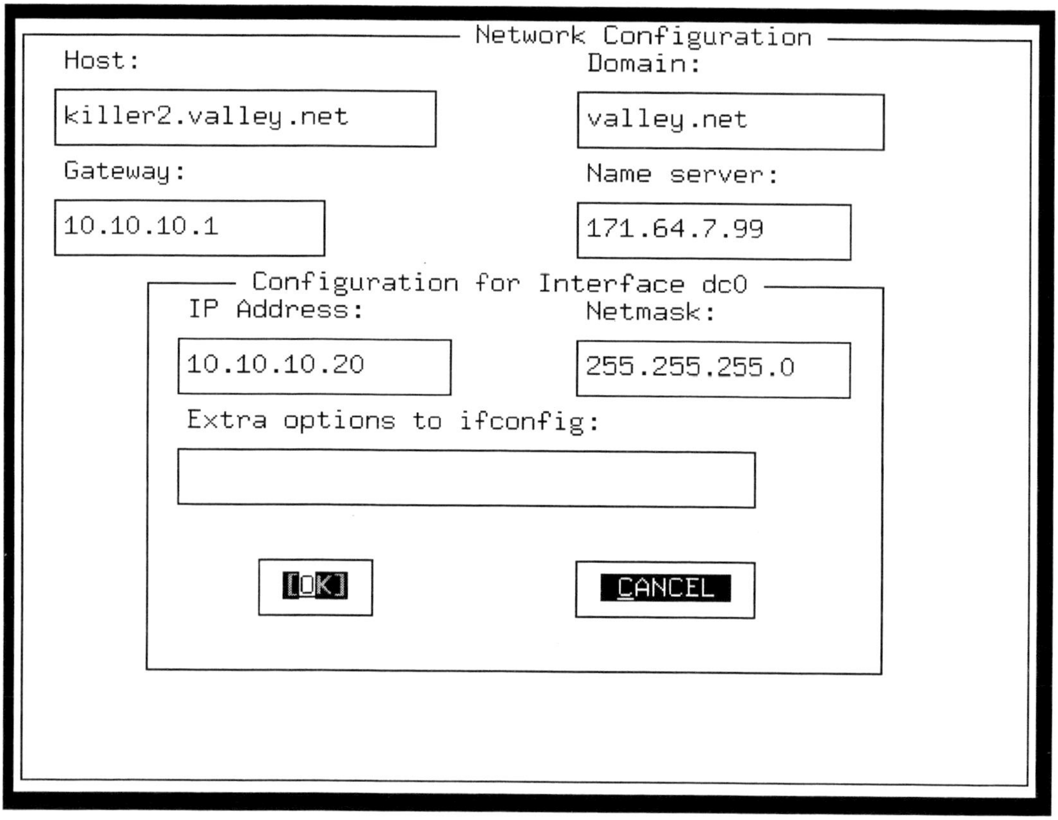

Figure 4-2: The Fill-Out Form for a Network Connection

Host is the name of your computer. A host is any computer on the Internet, and you set yours up to get on the Internet (assuming you have an Internet service provider, or ISP) in this dialog box. Name it anything you like (you can change the hostname later), and include the domain.

Domain is either the domain to which the computer belongs, if it is part of a domain (like stanford.edu, or mindspring.com) or you invent a domain name for your personal network—like valley.net, or wanderer.org. When you connect to an ISP, your connection will have its own name temporarily assigned for the life of the connection.

Gateway is the computer through which your computer will send stuff—email messages, requests to view a web page with your browser, and so forth. My computer at the office has a specific IP (internet protocol) address (of another computer) to which outgoing packets (which is what they're really called) are sent. In an organization, the system administrator tells people what number to use for the gateway. The gateway IP address is four one- to three-digit numbers separated by dots. You've seen them before.

Checking Out Error Messages

Press **Alt+F2** (where F2 means the function key) to see messages from the FreeBSD installer—including trouble messages about things it can't find. Press **Alt+F1** to get back to the install screen. You can do this whenever you like, and more than once.

For a computer on an internal network (at home, for example) the gateway is the IP of the computer through which your computer sends messages. If you have a network at home (computers connected with ethernet cards) the gateway is the number of the home computer that connects to the Internet. In the example, killer2 connects to the Internet over a home network by sending messages through another computer at home, which has an IP address of 10.10.10.1.

If you connect to the Internet by dial-up modem (and are setting up a ppp connection with this dialog box) you can leave **Gateway** blank. The address will be completed when you dial up. This is the same as a dial-up networking Windows setting under TCP/IP (see Chapter 2) that has a check in the box for "Use default gateway on remote network."

Name server is an IP address you get from your Internet service provider or the organization where your computer is located. The name server is a computer that specializes in converting computer hostnames to numerical IP addresses (and the other way around, too). Without a valid number in this box, your computer won't be able to figure out where yahoo.com or ftp.freebsd/org is. If your Windows dial-up networking TCP/IP box uses the "Specify name server address" radio button and you have a number in the box for Primary DNS, that's what you want here, dots and all—something like 207.69.188.185, but the right one for your ISP.

IP address can be the internal IP address of your computer on an internal network, a fixed IP address if you've been assigned one, or left blank for your ISP to fill in when you connect. Leaving it blank is like the Windows TCP/IP selection of "Server assigned IP address."

Netmask is likely to be 255.255.255.0, and will be filled in by default. You can change it if you know you should.

3. **Press** Tab **until** [OK] **is highlighted, and press** Enter. **You see:**

```
Would you like to bring the dc0 interface up
right now?
```

4. **Press** Enter **for Yes**.

You see a dialog box asking one of these questions (they're the same—the computer will either be a leaf node or a gateway).

```
Will this machine be a leaf node (e.g., will
not forward packets between interfaces)?
```

or

```
Do you want this machine to function as a
network gateway?
```

5. If you plan on connecting *another* computer to the Internet *through* this computer, it won't be a leaf node—it will be a gateway. If it will be a gateway, you want **[No]** as the answer to the first question, and **[Yes]** if the second question is asked. If you're not sure, make it a gateway and not a leaf node.

Checking Out Network Interfaces

If FreeBSD can't find your modem or you have an ethernet card that doesn't show up in the list of network interfaces, you look at what FreeBSD found when it booted by doing this:

Press ScrollLock

Press the up arrow to see the boot messages that are still there above the install screen. Your serial ports (your modem is attached to one of them) start with `sio`.

Press ScrollLock again to get back to the install screen.

Anonymous FTP

The next dialog box asks whether you want to limit FTP access to normal users (people who have an account on the machine) or whether you want to allow anonymous users to have FTP access. Right now, you don't want to give everyone in the world FTP access.

If the question is:

```
Do you want to grant only normal users FTP access
     to this host (e.g., no anonymous FTP
     connections?
```

the answer is **`[Yes]`**. You, as a user on your own FreeBSD computer, will be able to access it from other computers (when it's on the Internet or a local network) and transfer files using FTP, or File Transfer Protocol. If you change your mind and want to offer *anyone* access to some of your files and possibly the privilege of uploading files to your computer, you can easily do it later.

If the question is:

```
Do you want to have anonymous FTP access to this
     machine?
```

the answer is **`[No]`**.

NFS

FreeBSD now asks you two questions about NFS—whether you want this machine to be a server, and whether you want it to be a client. NFS is the network file system, and is used to make files on one UNIX-style computer available to another. Unless you have another computer running Linux or FreeBSD or some other UNIX flavor, you want to choose **`[No]`** for both. **Highlight** `[No]` **before pressing** Enter **on these two screens.**

The Console

You now see a screen asking if you would like to customize your computer's console settings—the keyboard and the screen. Unless you want a keyboard layout for a foreign language or want a screensaver, you can say **No**.

Security

In versions 4.2 and later of FreeBSD, you see a question about security—something like:

```
Do you want to select a default security profile
     for this host (select No for "medium"
     security)?
```

Medium security is just what you want, so **press** Enter **with** `[No]` **highlighted** as the best choice here. Higher levels of security make it difficult to change stuff, and a security level can't be lowered without some special techniques. If you choose Yes, you'll still have an opportunity to select Medium security if you're installing 4.3.

The Time Zone

Next you see:

```
Would you like to set this machine's time zone now?
```

You would. Press **Enter**. You see:

```
Is this machine's CMOS clock set to UTC? If it is
     set to local time or you don't know, please
     choose NO here.!
```

UTC is the Universal Time Convention (which used to be called Greenwich Mean Time) and your computer's CMOS clock (its built-in clock) is probably not set to UTC—not if the time shows up in Windows as local time. You probably want **`[No]`**.

You see a screen on which you use the arrow keys to select your region. The second choice is `America -- North and South`, but every place in the world is available. Press **Enter** when the highlight is on your choice.

Next you see the list of countries in your region. You can use **Page Down** to move through the list faster than the arrow keys would take you. When the highlight is on your country, press **Enter**.

You see time zones for your region.

1. **Use the arrow keys to highlight your time zone.**

2. **Press** Enter.

You see a screen like Figure 4-3, asking you if the time-zone abbreviation looks reasonable.

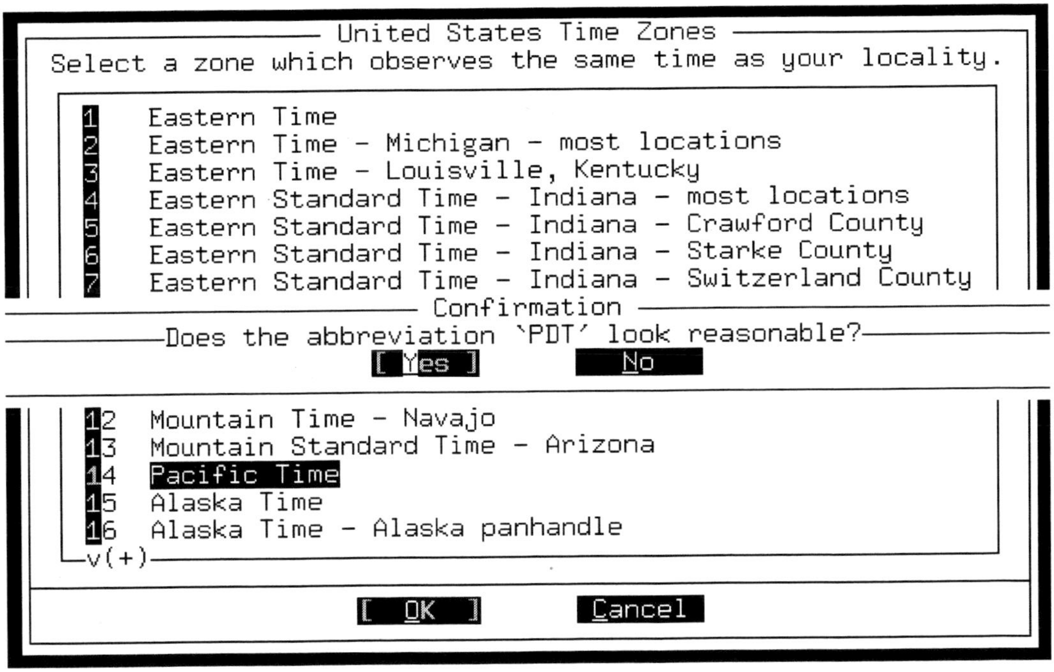

Figure 4-3: Does the Time Zone Look Reasonable?

PDT looks reasonable to me since my time zone is Pacific Daylight Time (at least in the summer). Press **Enter** to accept your choice or press **Tab Enter** to reject it and try something else. FreeBSD will handle changes between standard and daylight time when they occur without your intervention.

Getting Friendly with Linux

Installing the capability to run Linux programs that can't otherwise be run on FreeBSD is a one-line dialog, but it has consequences—it takes about 60MB.

The StarOffice suite, a Microsoft Office work-alike that's free for individual users, needs Linux support. So does WordPerfect, also free for individuals. The Linux versions of Netscape can be run if you enable Linux support, as can Adobe's Acrobat Reader, which reads PDF files. *PDF* stands for portable document format—a common format for some documents (technical manuals, government reports) you might want to download from the Internet. (Then again, maybe you'd rather watch paint dry.)

VMWare, a commercial program that makes it possible to actually install another operating system on FreeBSD, needs Linux compatibility. And some graphics programs need linux, although there are usually FreeBSD versions as well.

Unless you're cramped for space, when you see:

```
Would you like to enable Linux binary
     compatibility?
```

Press Enter **for** `[Yes]`.

The installation occurs immediately.

Mouse Matters

FreeBSD will let you use your mouse to copy and paste even when the X Window System isn't running. All it takes is a daemon. A daemon is software that runs in the background ready to jump into action—in this case, at the click of a mouse button. If you have a mouse and you want mouse support, this dialog is for you. When you see:

```
Does this system have a mouse attached to it?
```

1. **Press** Enter **for** `[Yes]`.

   You see a screen like Figure 4-4.

2. **Press the down arrow to highlight**

```
2 Enable      Test and run the mouse daemon
```

3. **Press** Enter.

   You see a request to move the mouse to see if it works. It won't work very well here and the mouse buttons won't work at all, but if the mouse pointer on the screen moves, things are set up right. Eek, a mouse! FreeBSD has detected your kind of rodent and where it's attached to the computer—probably a PS/2-style mouse on the mouse port, that little connector that's easy to confuse with the keyboard connector on newer computers.

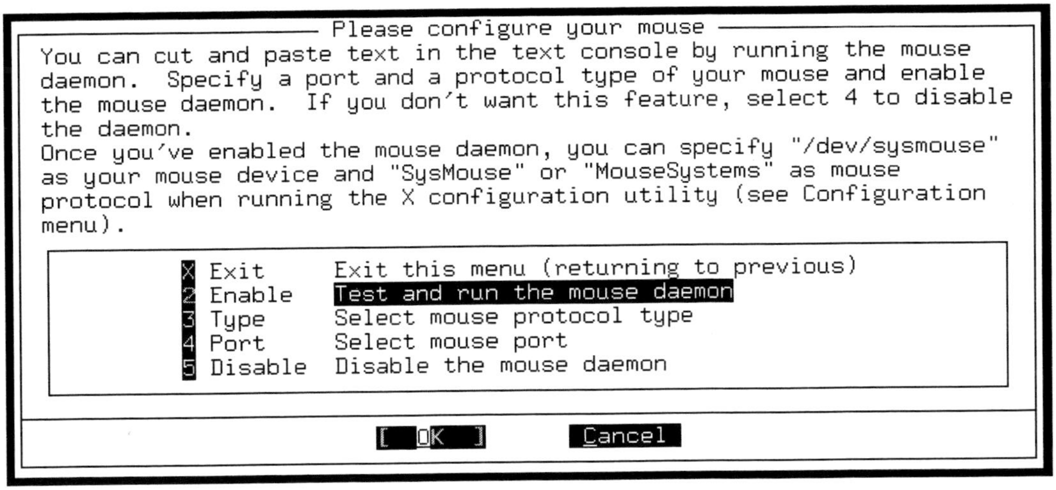

Figure 4-4: The Basic Mouse Dialog

4. **If the mouse pointer moves, press** Enter **with** `[Yes]` **highlighted.**

5. **Press the up arrow to highlight:**

```
X Exit    Exit this menu (returning to previous)
```

6. **Press** Enter; **you're done.**

If the mouse pointer doesn't move, **press** Tab Enter **to choose** `[No]`.

You see again the basic mouse dialog shown in Figure 4-4. Since your mouse is not the most typical of rodents, you experiment with item 3 on the menu, `Type`, and item 4, `Port`, choosing one from each, until you get a combination that works (the mouse pointer moves).

TIP

Turn your mouse over and see what its underside says. It should tell you what `Type` it is and what kind of `Port` it uses—PS/2, Serial, or BusMouse. Your Windows device print-out (see Chapter 2) should also tell you what Windows knows about your mouse.

Press the down arrow key to highlight:

```
3 Type        Select mouse protocol type
```

You see the screen shown in Figure 4-5.

On this screen you **press the down arrow** to highlight a mouse protocol so FreeBSD knows what kind of mouse you have. **Press the spacebar to get an asterisk next to the one you want to try.** For a first go-around, Auto (the default selection) remains your best choice.

Press Enter **to return to the basic mouse dialog**

Press the down arrow to highlight:

```
4 Port        Select mouse port
```

The menu looks like Figure 4-6.

```
─────────── Select a protocol type for your mouse ───────────
If your mouse is attached to the PS/2 mouse port or the bus mouse port,
you should always choose "Auto", regardless of the model and the brand
of the mouse.  All other protocol types are for serial mice and should
not be used with the PS/2 port mouse or the bus mouse.  If you have
a serial mouse and are not sure about its protocol, you should also try
"Auto".  It may not work for the serial mouse if the mouse does not
support the PnP standard.  But, it won't hurt.  Many 2-button serial mice
are compatible with "Microsoft" or "MouseMan".  3-button serial mice
may be compatible with "MouseSystems" or "MouseMan".  If the serial
mouse has a wheel, it may be compatible with "IntelliMouse".

   (*) 1 Auto           Bus mouse, PS/2 style mouse or PnP serial mouse
   ( ) 2 GlidePoint     ALPS GlidePoint pad (serial)
   ( ) 3 Hitachi        Hitachi tablet (serial)
   ( ) 4 IntelliMouse   Microsoft IntelliMouse (serial)
   ( ) 5 Logitech       Logitech protocol (old models) (serial)
   ( ) 6 Microsoft      Microsoft protocol (serial)
   ( ) 7 MM Series      MM Series protocol (serial)
   ( ) 8 MouseMan       Logitech MouseMan/TrackMan models (serial)
   ( ) 9 MouseSystems   MouseSystems protocol (serial)
   ( ) A ThinkingMouse  Kensington ThinkingMouse (serial)

                      [  OK  ]        Cancel
```

Figure 4-5: Selecting a Mouse Protocol

```
─────────── Select your mouse port from the following menu ───────────
The built-in pointing device of laptop/notebook computers is usually
a PS/2 style device.

       (*) 1 PS/2       PS/2 style mouse (/dev/psm0)
       ( ) 2 COM1       Serial mouse on COM1 (/dev/cuaa0)
       ( ) 3 COM2       Serial mouse on COM2 (/dev/cuaa1)
       ( ) 4 COM3       Serial mouse on COM3 (/dev/cuaa2)
       ( ) 5 COM4       Serial mouse on COM4 (/dev/cuaa3)
       ( ) 6 BusMouse   Logitech, ATI or MS bus mouse (/dev/mse0)

                      [  OK  ]        Cancel
```

Figure 4-6: Selecting a Mouse Port

If the mouse is attached to a serial port, it has an external 9-pin D-shaped connector instead of a little round one. If you have a card in your computer to which you attach the mouse to a round connector, it may be a BusMouse.

Press the down arrow to highlight a mouse port. Press the spacebar to get an asterisk next to the one you want to try.

Press Enter **to return to the basic mouse dialog.**

Use the arrow keys to highlight:

```
2 Enable     Test and run the mouse daemon.
```

If it still doesn't work, try different combinations of `Type` and `Port` until it does work.

Press Enter **when it works.**

Press the up arrow to highlight Exit **and go on to the next configuration step.**

TIP

Whether or not you enable console mouse support in the basic mouse dialog matters when you get to setting up the mouse for the X Window System. If mouse support is enabled for the console, the right choice for a mouse in X `/dev/sysmouse`. Otherwise `X` needs one of the other mouse ports that show up on Figure 4-6, like `/dev/psm0`, `/dev/cuaa0`, or `/dev/mse0`.

Configuring XFree86

X-REF

The next question is whether you want to configure your `X` server for the X Window System at this time. See Chapter 14 if you want to do this now. It's covered there.

Whenever you choose to do it, you can do it from a graphical interface or from a text interface. Why wait? Because it's a fairly long process that you need to do carefully, and if you use the graphical interface, it might hang the machine and force you to reboot without getting to the other configuration stuff.

Unless you really want to do it now, choose **`[No]`** ; it's not the default.

Adding Packages

Packages are ready-to-run software. Adding packages is the quickest way to install a lot of software on a new system.

When you choose software, other required software is automatically installed—but you get advance warning and a chance to revise your selections. And at the end of the installation you get an invitation to revisit the configuration menus. The space hogs are graphics programs and programs that need Linux support. Linux support will get added to the list of packages to install if it's not already installed.

The sidebar **All Spaced Out?** tells you how to figure out how much space you have left while you're in the install program, so you can add packages of your choice if you have space.

TIP

Chapter 11 tells you more about software and what different packages do.

Right now, I show you how to install a couple of important packages—one central to maintaining FreeBSD (`cvsup-bin`) and one that will make it lots easier (`bash`).

The Package Selection menu is shown in Figure 4-7. I step through the process below, but here's an overview of what happens:

The menu lists categories of packages, such as Communications utilities. Submenus list the software packages themselves. You highlight a category, press Enter to get the list of packages, highlight a package you want, and press the spacebar to select it for installation.

You can select as many packages as you like (and have space to install). Pressing Enter accepts your selections and takes you back to the list of categories so you can select packages from other categories. Pressing Tab to highlight [Install] and then pressing Enter gives you a last chance to accept or reject your choices. Another Enter and it's off and running.

All Spaced Out?

When the installer started writing files to the disks, you probably noticed a message flashed on the screen:

```
Starting an emergency holographic shell on VTY4.
```

Any time after you see this message, you can **press Alt+F4** to go to `VTY4` (virtual terminal number 4). You see only:

```
#
```

That's just a shell prompt. At this prompt type:

```
# df -k
```

to see a display like this:

Filesystem	1K-blocks	Used	Avail	Capacity	Mounted on
/dev/md0c	2803	1769	810	69%	/
/dev/da0s3a	59519	24250	30508	44%	/mnt
/mnt/dev/da0s3f	809998	64571	680627	9%	/mnt/usr
/mnt/dev/da0s3e	59519	59	54699	0%	/mnt/var
/dev/cd0c	6411164	6411164	0	100%	/dist

In this display the partition ending with `a` will become your `/` partition, the one ending in `f` will become your `/usr`, and the one ending in `e` will become `/var`. In the example a 1,000MB slice was partitioned to 60MB for `/`, 60MB for `/var`, 60MB for `swap`, and the balance (about 800MB) for `/usr`. Thus far only a minimal distribution has been installed, so the `Used` column shows a total under 100MB (the swap space doesn't show up here).

Knock off the last three numbers from the amount `Avail` for the partition mounted on `/mnt/usr` (under `Filesystem`, in this example it's `/mnt/dev/da0s3f`) to get an approximation in megabytes of the space you have remaining to install more distributions or software.

The amounts under `Used` plus the amounts under `Avail` don't add to the total `1K-blocks` because FreeBSD reserves about 8 percent of file space for operations—like keeping a little something in the bank. A file system is "full" at 92 percent. The `Capacity` takes into account this reserve for operations.

The first entry in the list (`/dev/md0c`) is the file system mounted from the `mfsroot` floppy, and the last one (`/dev/cd0c`, which of course has no space available and is at 100% of capacity) is the CD-ROM.

Press Alt+F1 to get back to the install screen.

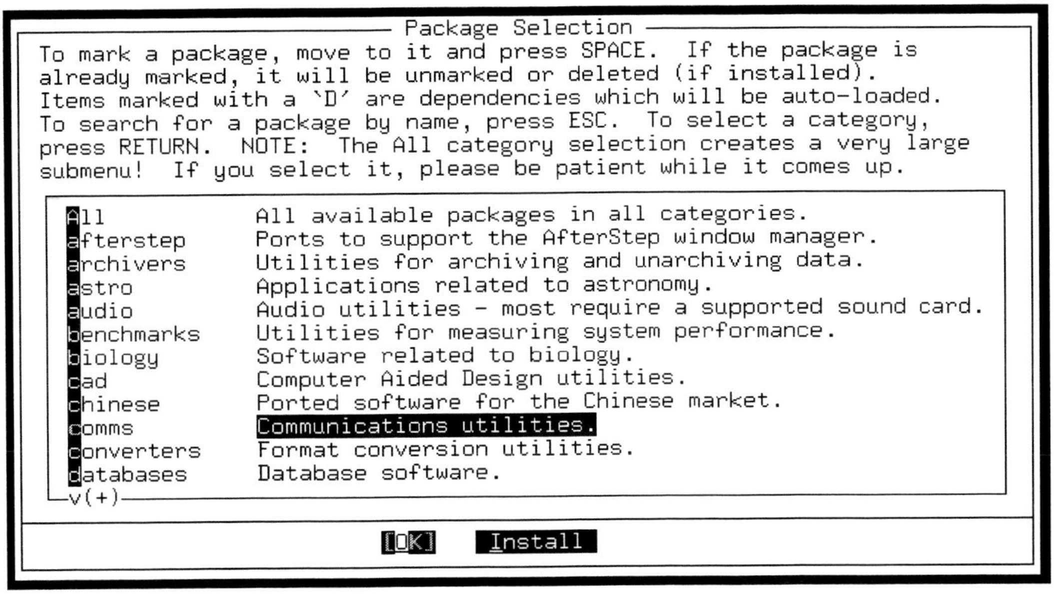

Figure 4-7: Selecting Packages

To install `cvsup-bin` and `bash`:

1. **Use the arrow keys to highlight the category** `net`
   `Networking utilities`

2. **Use the arrow keys to highlight** `cvsup-bin-16.1` (or whatever version number of `cvsup-bin` is offered).

WARNING

Note that the package you want is `cvsup-bin`, not `cvsupd-bin`.

3. **Press the spacebar to get an** `[X]` **next to** `cvsup-bin-16.1,` **as shown in Figure 4-8.**

   Select any other packages in the category you want with the arrow keys and the spacebar.

4. **Press** Enter **with the highlight on** [OK] **to finish the selection within the category.**

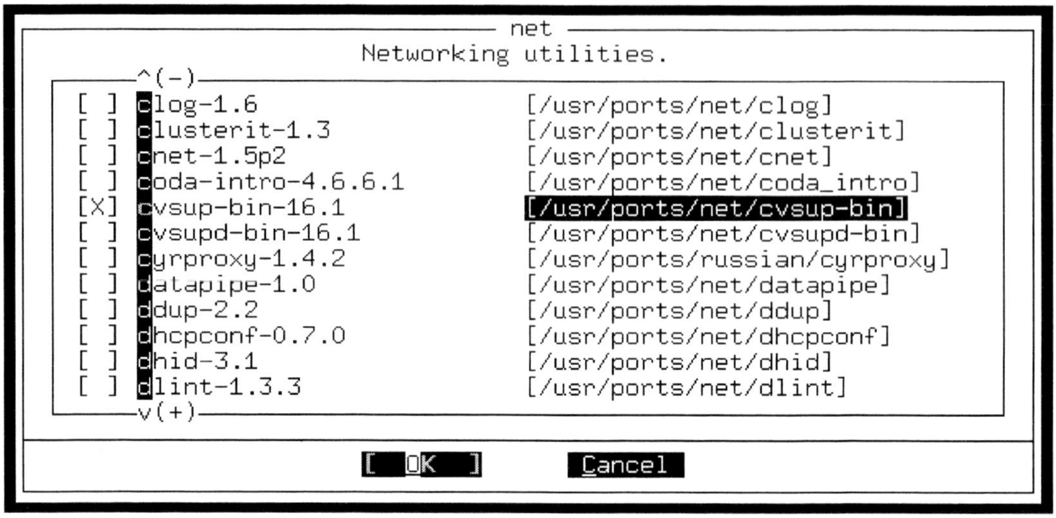

Figure 4-8: A Package Selected for Installation

5. **Use the arrow keys to highlight the** `shells     Various shells (tcsh, bash, etc).` **category.**

6. **Use the arrow keys to highlight** `bash-2.04`

7. **Press the spacebar to place an** `[X]` **next to** `bash2.`

8. **Press** Enter **to finish the selection in the** **`shells`** **category.**

   Repeat the process for other categories and packages you may want.

TIP

You can come back to the package selection menu after the system is installed, so don't worry about missing something good! But I recommend `links` or `w3m` in the `www` category. They're text-based web browsers that don't require a graphical user interface. You also might want to select `pine` in the `mail` category. `Pine` is a good text-based program for reading and sending electronic mail and comes with `pico`, a text editor that's easy to use.

9. **Highlight** `[Install]` **and press** Enter.

   You see a list of packages you selected like that in Figure 4-9, which shows `bash`, `cvsup-bin`, and two other packages selected for installation. (Your list will reflect your own choices.)

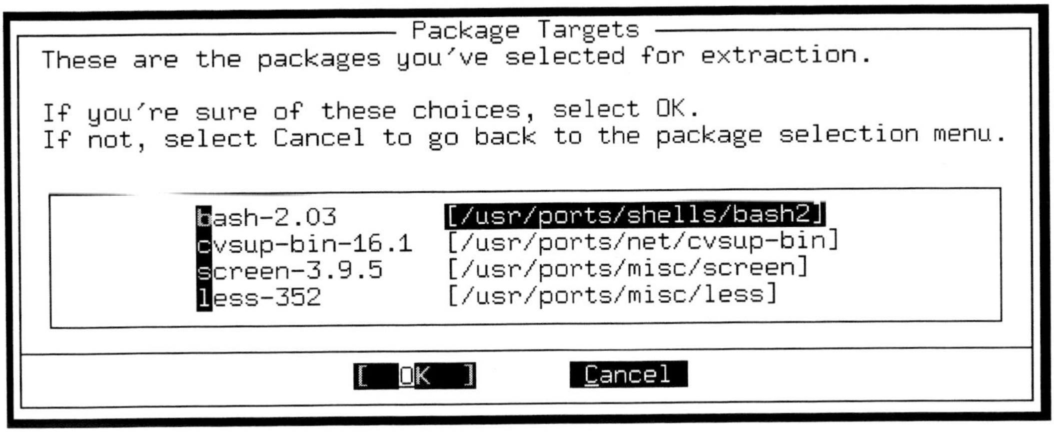

Figure 4-9: Selected Packages

10. **Press** Enter **to choose** [OK]. **The installation will begin, giving you updates on its progress.**

A Little Sysadmin

FreeBSD is going to be all yours—you get to run it. When someone says "Talk to your system administrator," that's you! When your packages are installed, you see an invitation to add user accounts to the system. Since FreeBSD is a multi-user operating system, it wants advance notice about users. It's not going to let just anyone use it. You see:

```
Would you like to add any initial user accounts to
     the system ....
```

Press Enter **for** `[Yes]`.

Highlight `User:  Add a new user to the system` **and press** Enter.

Figure 4-10 shows the form you see after it's been filled out. You move from box to box with the Tab or arrow keys (you can go backwards with Shift-Tab). You can delete text in a box with the Backspace key and enter what you like by typing. Here's what you enter in each box:

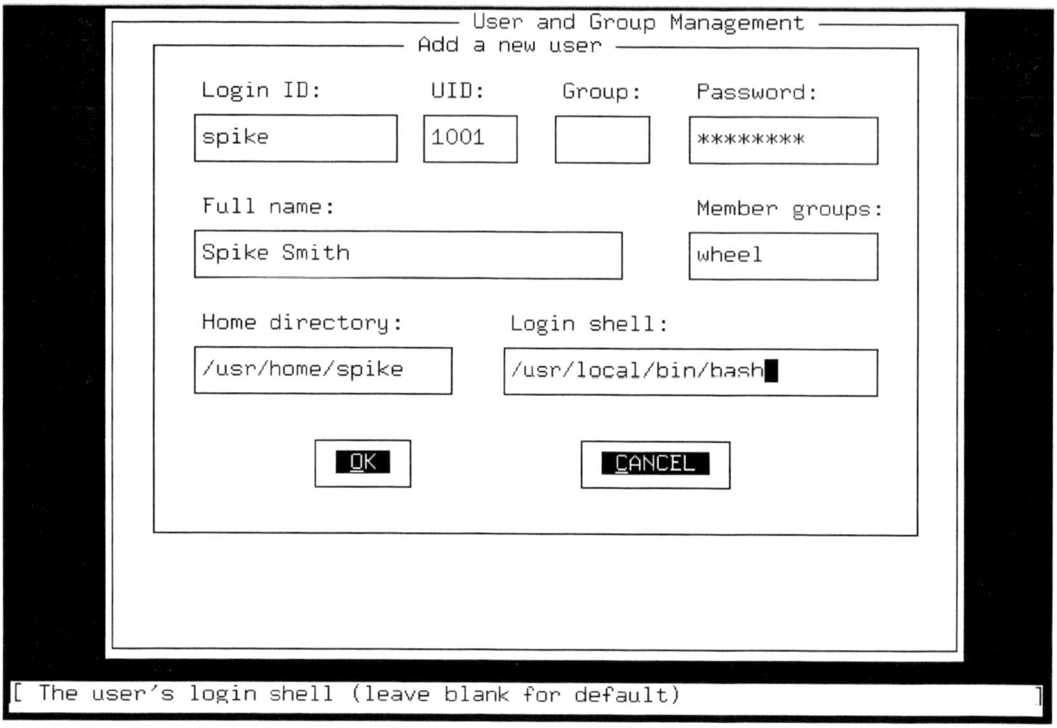

Figure 4-10: Creating a New User

Login ID: The user's login name. It can be a nickname, a first name, a last name, or some combination. It should be eight letters maximum, lower-case (not capitals), and easy to type. In Figure 4-10, a user `spike` is created.

UID: The user identification number. If the default of 1001 doesn't show up, put it in. The UID's should start with 1001 and go up from there. (Some of the lower numbers are used for other stuff.)

Group: The standard for a user's main group is to make it the same as the Login ID, so the group will be `spike`. It will be filled in by default (you don't type anything here).

Password: Enter a password for `spike`. It will show up as a series of asterisks. Remember it, or `spike` won't be able to log in! Passwords should be easy for you to remember (and not too hard to type) but hard for other people to guess. Bad choices: your pet's name; the street you live on; your nickname; your username; anything so complicated you have to write it down.

Good choices: take a phrase or saying you can easily remember. If you're a fan of the Doors you might use "Come on baby light my fire." Take the initial letters, giving you "coblmf". Turn one of the letters into a number, "c0blmf". And there you have a relatively easy to remember, but completely unguessable password—until now, because it's in this book.

Cracking programs exist to figure out users' passwords. They test words in both English and foreign language dictionaries. Good passwords can't be found in any dictionary, include lower-case and capital letters and symbols, and are usually five to eight letters and symbols.

Full name: The user's full name will be used by some electronic mail programs and other programs. It's useful if this is a real name, but it can be anything. In a stunning demonstration of creativity, the example gives `spike` the name `Spike Smith`.

Member groups: You can put your user into other groups here in addition to the user's main group. If you want this user to be able to become `root` easily—the user who can do anything on the system—put `wheel` in this box. Then the user will be able to become `root` by typing `su Enter` and typing `root`'s password. The `su` command stands for *superuser* or *substitute user*, depending on who's writing the history. (The UID for `root`, who has an account on the system automatically, is 0, and a wheel is round, like a zero—you get the idea?)

In Figure 4-10, `spike` is made a member of the group `wheel` and thus will be able to use the `su` command to become `root`—if he knows `root`'s password.

In FreeBSD, unlike Linux, users need to be a member of the group `wheel` to use the `su` command to become `root`.

Home directory: The home directory should be `/home/` with the addition of the user's login ID. So `spike`'s home directory is `/home/spike`. If the home directory isn't included by default or you've created a special partition for home directories, include the full path (one example is shown in Figure 4-10). The home directory is the user's playground and the place where his or her configuration files live. By default it's really located in `/usr/home`, with a symbolic link (like a shortcut) that goes from `/home` to `/usr/home`.

Login shell: The shell is a program that loads when a user logs in, the way

DOS's `command.com` loads when you click on the MS-DOS icon and go to the command line in Microsoft Windows. Remember `doskey`, a DOS feature that let you recall previous DOS commands? Several different shells with different features are available for FreeBSD and other varieties of UNIX.

FreeBSD comes with two shells, called `sh` and `tcsh` (or `csh`, which is the same as `tcsh`), by default. The login shell box will probably show `/bin/sh` for a user. Don't accept the default. The `sh` shell is hard to use. If you installed `bash` as a package (see above), you can make your new user's shell `bash`, which is like `sh` but has more features (nice features!). If you didn't install `bash`, `tcsh` is probably a better choice than `sh` (you put `/bin/tcsh` in the box to get the `tcsh` shell). I tell you more about `bash` in Chapter 6. FreeBSD needs to know exactly where to find the shell, so type carefully in the box:

```
/usr/local/bin/bash
```

Press Enter **for** [OK].

LINUX

Linux uses `bash` as the default shell, so Linux users will almost certainly want `bash` as their shell. In Linux `bash` is located in `/bin`, but in FreeBSD it will be in the `/usr/local/bin` directory. Get the path right in this box!

You find yourself back at the menu for adding users. You add another user (a hot spare) in case you damage or delete `spike`'s home directory or files. For example:

Login ID: `vicki`

UID: `1002`

Group:

Password: ********

If `vicki` is going to be your account, you could give `vicki` the same password you gave `spike`.

Full name: `Queen Victoria`

Member groups: `wheel`

Home directory: `/usr/home/vicki`

Login shell: `/usr/local/bin/bash`

When done, **use the arrow keys to highlight** `Exit` **and press** Enter.

You see:

```
Now you must set the system manager's password.
     This is the password you'll use to log in as
     "root".
```

Press Enter **to continue**. You see, at the bottom left of your screen:

```
Changing local password for root.
New password:
```

Type a password for `root` and press Enter. The password won't echo. It's even more important to choose a good password for `root` than for ordinary users, because `root` can go anywhere and do anything on your system. You see:

```
Retype new password:
```

Retype it. Again, it won't echo.

Last Options

Finally—you see this:

```
Visit the general configuration menu for a chance
     to set any last options?
```

Press Enter **for** `[Yes]` **here**. In spite of a state of advanced exhaustion, you want to see this menu, because you can retrieve it any time after the system is installed by typing `/stand/sysinstall` and choosing, with the arrow keys and Enter:

`Configure Do post-install configuration of FreeBSD.`

You can always get back here so you can install more packages, add users, set the time, or whatever you want to do later.

The menu, called the FreeBSD Configuration Menu, looks like Figure 4-11.

As you can see, you have a second bite at the apple on just about everything.

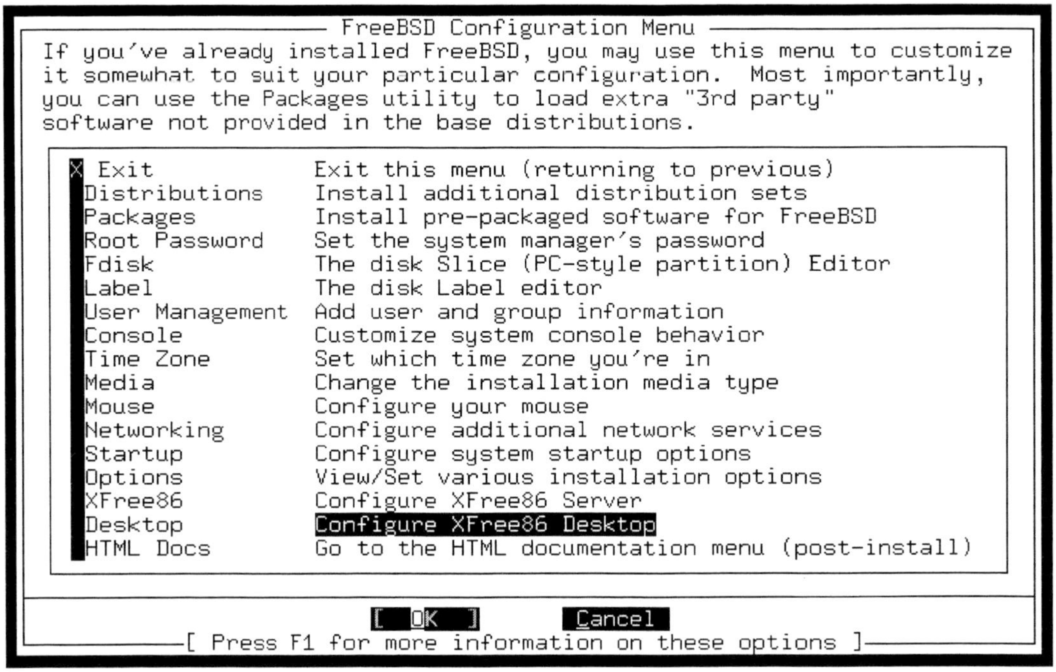

Figure 4-11: The Post-Install FreeBSD Configuration Menu

Your Desktop

The real gem on the Post-Install Configuration Menu is:

`Desktop          Configure XFree86 Desktop`

Use the arrow keys to highlight it.

Press Enter **to see the desktop menu, as shown in Figure 4-12.**

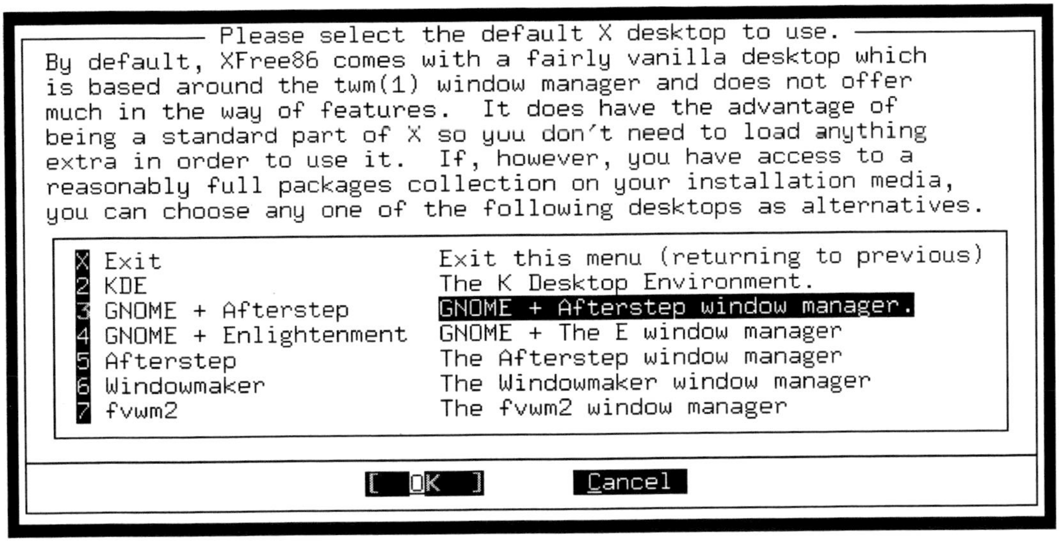

Figure 4-12: The Desktop Menu

This menu is a great way to get a good desktop for the X Window System. What you end up liking here is a matter of personal preference.

X always needs a window manager. The default, `twm`, is about as feature-free as you can get—but it doesn't take much space on your hard drive or in memory. The other window managers listed on this menu are `afterstep`, `enlightenment`, `windowmaker`, and `fvwm2`.

KDE and GNOME are called "desktop environments"—they're not window managers, although KDE has its own built-in window manager, and so can be installed without a separate window manager. GNOME has to work with a window manager, so it's listed with `afterstep` and `enlightenment`.

TIP

Chapter 14 tells you a little about GNOME and `afterstep`. If you have space (about 40MB of hard drive space), I recommend installing GNOME and `afterstep`. My own choice is GNOME and `enlightenment`, but `enlightenment` takes quite a lot of memory too, so GNOME and `afterstep` are a good combination and are available on the CD-ROM. If space is at a premium, `afterstep` alone is a good window manager. The choice of gurus would probably be `fvwm2`, also not covered in this book.

1. **Use the arrow keys to select a desktop choice.**

2. **Press** Enter **to install your choice.**

   Your choice will be installed for the use of the `root` account, but before you use it you have to get X running, as described in Chapter 14. You can arrange later for users to have the same configuration.

3. **Use the arrow keys to highlight** `Exit` **and press** Enter.

Startup Options

You see again the FreeBSD Configuration Menu:

1. **Use the arrow keys to highlight:**

```
Startup          Configure system startup options
```

2. **Press** Enter.

   You see a screen like Figure 4-13. The boxes next to some options will be checked already. Leave the checked boxes alone—they're suboptions for unchecked options (and have no effect) or are something you want, like the `[X]` startup directories.

3. **Use the arrow keys to highlight any additional option you want and press the spacebar to enable it.**

   Options you might want are:

```
[X] lpd   This host has a printer and wants to
run lpd.
[X] linux This host wants to be able to run
linux binaries.
```

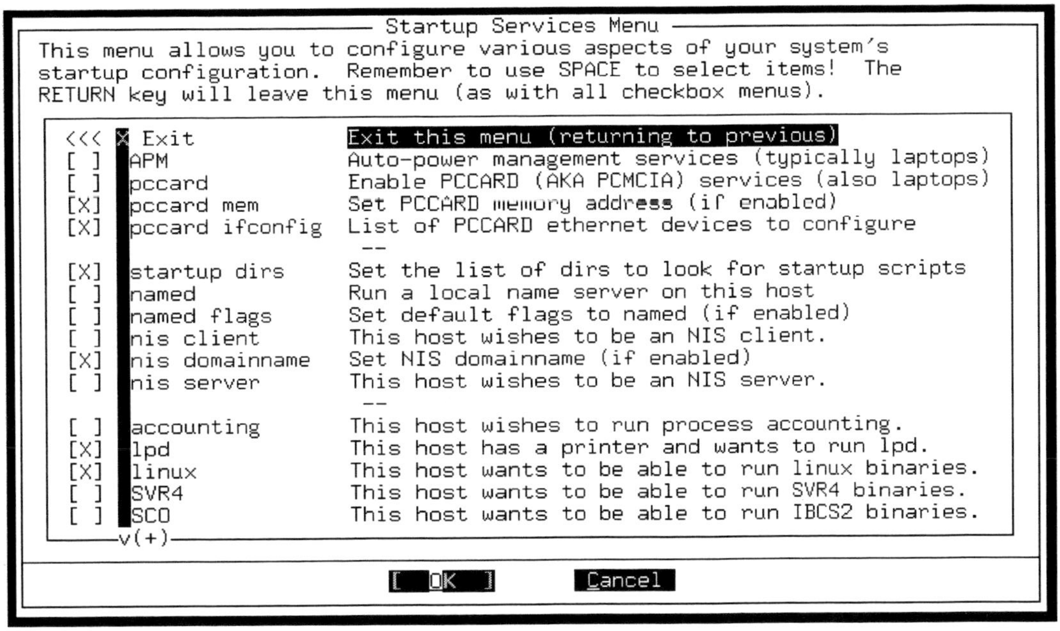

Figure 4-13: Startup Options

4. **Use the arrow keys to highlight** `Exit` `Exit this menu (returning to previous)`

5. **Press** Enter.

Rebooting

If you left some things undone, use the FreeBSD Configuration Menu to do anything else you want to do. When you finish, use the arrow keys to choose Exit, press Enter, press Tab to highlight Exit Install, press Enter, and finally, you're done! Take the disks out of the drive and pray.

Chapter 5

Running FreeBSD

FreeBSD is installed! A message on the screen tells you that the computer will reboot. You take the disks out of the drives. It reboots—to your boot manager or directly to FreeBSD if it's the only operating system on your computer.

You see `login:`

What do you do now? This chapter tells you how to:

- log in and get out when you want to
- create new users from the command line (with `root` privileges, if you like)
- use FreeBSD's Easy Editor
- get around, find files, and use the system's own on-line help
- use the most useful UNIX commands, get the floppy and CD-ROM drive working, and print from DOS/Windows.

This is the magic moment. You will probably never again sit in front of a computer with such a powerful operating system about which you know virtually nothing. After you read this chapter, that won't be true any more. Prepare to lose your virginity. You may even enjoy it.

Logging in and Getting Out

When you see the `login`: prompt, type the name of the user you created when you installed, for example `spike`:

```
login: spike
```

You see:

```
Password:
```

Type `spike`'s password and press Enter. The password won't echo on your screen.

You can also log in (if you didn't create a user) as `root`. Your FreeBSD installation always has a `root` account—the administrative account that can go anywhere and do anything (and delete anything, so be careful!)

```
login: root

Password:
```

You see a command prompt ending with a symbol—a `$`, `%`, or `>` , or a `#` if you log in as `root`.

To log out (and get a new `login:` prompt) type:

```
$ exit
```

as often as necessary. Press Enter after commands, and remember that UNIX is case-sensitive. It won't cry if you type `EXIT` instead of `exit`, but it will say something like:

```
EXIT: Command not found.
```

This UNIX sensitivity about upper-case and lower-case is a disaster if your `CapsLock` key gets stuck. Otherwise it can be useful.

To shut down the computer, type:

```
# /sbin/shutdown -h now
```

Or to reboot type:

```
# /sbin/reboot
```

TIP

You can also reboot with the three-finger salute: **Ctrl+Alt+Del.** This is equivalent to `/sbin/reboot` (except in older versions of FreeBSD). And you can do this as an ordinary user—you don't have to be logged in as `root`. Give it a little time to do its work. What it's doing is *syncing* the disks—something like what Windows does when it says "Please wait while the computer writes unsaved data to disk."

WARNING

Try never to just hit the reset button—FreeBSD will probably recover but it will take it quite a while when it next boots to make sure its files and disks are in good working order.

Adding a New User

If you didn't create any users when you installed (see Chapter 4) and are logged in as `root`, you should create a user now with:

```
# adduser
```

The first time `adduser` runs, it asks you for defaults to save. These defaults are saved in a file called `adduser.conf` in the `/etc` directory. It's an editable file and it doesn't exist until you run `adduser` for the first time. Here's what you see (and what you do) when you run `adduser`, assuming the `bash` shell is installed and you want to create a user named `vicki`:

```
# adduser

/etc/adduser.conf: No such file or directory
Use option ``-silent´´ if you don't want to see all
    warnings and questions.
```

```
Check /etc/shells
Check /etc/master.passwd
Check /etc/group
Enter your default shell: bash csh date no sh zsh
    [sh]: bash
Your default shell is: bash -> /usr/local/bin/bash
Enter your default HOME partition: [/home]: Enter
```

```
Copy dotfiles from: /usr/share/skel no
     [/usr/share/skel]: Enter
Send message from file: /etc/adduser.message no
[/etc/adduser.message]: Enter
Create ``/etc/adduser.message´´? (y/n) [y]: Enter
Use passwords (y/n) [y]: Enter
```

```
Write your configuration to /etc/adduser.conf?
     (y/n) [y]: Enter

Ok, let's go.
Don't worry about mistakes. I will give you the
     chance later to correct any input. [not true!]
Enter username [a-z0-9_-]: vicki
Enter full name []: Victoria Empire
Enter shell bash csh date no sh zsh [bash]: Enter
Enter home directory (full path) [/home/vicki]:
     Enter
Uid [1000]: 1003
Enter login class: default []: Enter
Login group vicki [vicki]: Enter
Login group is ``vicki´´. Invite vicki into other
     groups: guest no
[no]: wheel
Enter password []: [it doesn't echo]
Enter password again []: [it doesn't echo]

Name:        vicki
Password: ****
Fullname: Victoria Empire
Uid:   1003
Gid:   1003 (vicki)
Class:
Groups:      vicki wheel
HOME:      /home/vicki
Shell:       /usr/local/bin/bash
```

```
OK? (y/n) [y]: Enter
Added user ``vicki´´
Send message to ``vicki´´ and: no root
     second_mail_address
[no]: Enter

Victoria Empire,

your account ``vicki´´ was created.
Have fun!

See also chpass(1), finger(1), passwd(1)

Add anything to default message (y/n) [n]: y
Use ``.´´ or ^D alone on a line to finish your
     message.
hi there vicki
.
Send message (y/n) [y]: Enter
Copy files from /usr/share/skel to /home/vicki
Add another user? (y/n) [y]: n
Goodbye!
```

The only tricky part of `adduser` is that it starts with 1000 as a user id number, not knowing whether users have already been created during the install process. It will complain, however, if you try to give a user an existing number, and it will increment the number it offers by default each time it's run to completion.

TIP

After you've run `adduser` the first time and have therefore created the `/etc/adduser.conf` file, you can run `adduser` like this:

```
# adduser -silent
```

so you don't get asked for defaults.

You can quit `adduser` any time by typing **Ctrl+c**, and at the end you have a chance to approve your new user or simply type **n** for no. You might want to create an extra user so that you have a hot spare in case something goes wrong.

Another way to add a user is to type:

```
# /stand/sysinstall
```

and use the `User Management` option from the `Configure` menu. Chapter 4 tells you how to use the menu.

Once you have created one or more user accounts, type:

```
# exit
```

to exit from the `root` account and get a login prompt. Log in as the new user you created.

TIP

In general, it's a good idea to do as much work as possible as an ordinary user who doesn't have the power—and risk—of `root`.

Deleting a User

To delete a user, use the `rmuser` command. For example, you delete user `jack` by typing:

```
# rmuser jack
```

Actually `jack` will continue to exist—he just won't have an account on your computer anymore. The `rmuser` command deletes the entries for the user in the password and group files and deletes the user's home directory and mail directory.

Got Root? Becoming the SuperUser

If you're logged in as an ordinary user, you can become `root` with the `su` command:

```
$ su
Password:
```

```
#
```

If you get the message:

```
su: you are not in the correct group to su root.
```

the user is not in the group `wheel`.

Making a User a Big Wheel

If you want a user, say `spike`, to have `root` privileges, you can log in as `root` and edit the file `/etc/group`, adding `spike` to the first line (the group `wheel`). The first line of `/etc/group` looks like this with users `spike` and `vicki` added to the group `wheel` (notice the users are separated with a comma and no spaces):

```
wheel:*:0:root,spike,vicki
```

The next section tells you about using FreeBSD's Easy Editor, `ee`, to edit a text file.

Changing Your Password

You can change your password any time with the `passwd` command. (If you want to change `root`'s password, you should type `passwd root`, and of course you have to be logged in as `root` to do that.)

```
$ passwd

Changing local password for spike.
Old password:
New password:
Retype new password:
passwd: updating the database...
passwd: done
$
```

FreeBSD's Easy Editor

FreeBSD comes with `ee`, a simple text editor with all its commands on-screen.

WARNING

When you edit an important file, like `/etc/group`, you should back it up first. You need to be logged in as `root`.

Backing Up A File

To back up a file, you copy it to a new name with the `cp` command:

```
# cp /etc/group /etc/group.orig
```

Better yet, move it to a new filename with the `mv` command and copy it back, like this:

```
# cd /etc
# mv group group.orig
# cp group.orig group
```

Now if you need to get the original file back because your editing went awry, you type:

```
# mv group.orig group
```

The `mv` command preserves the original date and ownership of the file (files in UNIX systems have owners!), so you can always put things back just as they were.

Editing a File with ee

You start `ee` by typing:

```
$ ee <filename>
```

and you can then erase text with the Backspace key and add text by typing it in. You can move around with the arrow keys.

The top panel of your screen displays `ee`'s commands. The `^` symbol stands for the **Ctrl** key, so **Ctrl+y** is the key combination for starting a search for text. **Ctrl+x** searches again for the same text.

Ctrl+c opens a line at the bottom of the screen that says:

```
command:
```

and puts the cursor there. The top of the screen changes to show commands you can type in. The `read` command is useful if you want to insert another file into the file you're editing at the location where the cursor is. If you wanted to add the file `notes.txt` to `file.txt`, for example, you type:

```
$ ee file.txt
Ctrl+c
command: read notes.txt
```

You can save the file you're editing to a new name of your choice with the `write` command:

```
Ctrl+c
command: write newfile.txt
```

You can go to a specific line in a file, like line 257, like this:

```
Ctrl+c
command: 257
```

When you're finished making changes, press **Esc**. You see this menu:

```
a) leave editor
b) help
c) file operations
d) redraw screen
e) settings
f) search
g) miscellaneous
```

```
press Esc to cancel
```

You choose among them with the arrow keys and Enter. Choosing `(a) leave editor` will bring up another menu to save changes or exit without saving changes. Choosing `(c) file operations` gives you a menu that includes the option to write (save) with another name.

Looking Around

Logged in as an ordinary user, look around and try out some UNIX commands. You run a UNIX command by typing its name and pressing **Enter**. Here are some commands for finding out who you are (that's important!) and where you are—not where in the universe, but where in the file system—and commands for moving around the system and for looking at files.

The `id` command tells you who you are. As user `spike` I see:

```
$ id
uid=1001(spike) gid=1001(spike) groups=1001(spike),
     0(wheel)
```

But as `root`:

```
# id
uid=0(root) gid=0(wheel) groups=0(wheel), 2(kmem),
     3(sys), 4(tty), 5(operator), 20(staff),
     31(guest)
```

The `pwd` command shows you the present working directory—where you are right now. FreeBSD like other operating systems has directories with files and subdirectories, and the subdirectories can in turn have files and other subdirectories.

```
$ pwd
/usr/home/spike
```

The `ls` command lists files in a directory. It has many options or switches to list different kinds of information. You can combine options. You can also list files by name and use a * as a wild card.

Table 5-1 Listing Files

Command	*What It Does*
ls	lists files in the current directory
ls -F	lists files with a * after executables (runnable commands), a / after directories, and an @ after symbolic links (file names linked to another file)
ls -G	instead of symbols for kinds of files, color!
ls -l	lists files in the long format—size, date last modified, and permissions
ls -a	lists hidden files—like .cshrc—along with others. If you're root, the dot files show up without the -a switch
ls -d x*	all the files beginning with x—but not those in subdirectories starting with x
ls -lrt	a long-form file listing ordered by reverse time—the last ones modified at the end

The `cd` command changes directories.

`$` **`cd /var/log`** goes there.

`$` **`cd ..`** backs up one level; if you start in `/var/log`, it takes you to `/var`. Note the space after `cd`.

`$` **`cd`** goes straight to the home directory of the logged-in user.

`$` **`cd -`** goes to where you were before, so you could switch back and forth between two places without damaging your carpal tunnels. Look at this:

```
$ pwd
/usr/home/spike
```

```
$ cd /usr/local/bin
$ pwd
/usr/local/bin
$ cd -
/usr/home/spike
$ cd -
/usr/local/bin
```

Looking at Files

Looking at files is a great way to find out about your system. UNIX has many ways to look at files. Three places with interesting files are `/etc`, `/var/log`, and your home directory.

If you've done a few `ls` commands here and there, you've probably noticed that very few of the files seem to have extensions that tell you what kind of a file is what. No `.exe` files or `.com` files. UNIX doesn't use extensions the same way DOS/Windows does—to identify file types.

Instead UNIX looks into the file itself, no matter what its name is. And you don't want to splatter a binary file—one that can be understood only by the computer—all over the screen; it might ring bells, mess up the display, and maybe even hang the computer.

Not All Files Are Created Equal

UNIX does have a cool command for finding out about files, called (drum roll, please) `file`.

You use the `file` command by typing **`file`** *`<filename>`*.

Table 5-2 gives a few examples (if you use the full path name, you don't have to `cd` to the directory where the file lives).

Table 5-2 Kinds of Files

Command	*What FreeBSD Tells You*
file /etc/fstab	/etc/fstab: English text
file /etc/rc	/etc/rc: Bourne shell script text
file /usr/bin/adduser	/usr/sbin/adduser: perl commands text
file /etc/termcap	/etc/termcap: symbolic link to /usr/share/misc/termcap
file /usr/share/misc/ /termcap	usr/share/misc/termcap: English text
file /etc/ssh	/etc/ssh: directory
file /var/log/wtmp	/var/log/wtmp: data
file /usr/bin/file	/usr/bin/file: ELF 32-bit LSB executable, Intel 80386, version 1 (FreeBSD), dynamically linked, stripped
file /kernel	/kernel: ELF 32-bit LSB executable, Intel 80386, version 1 (FreeBSD), dynamically linked, not stripped
file /dev/ad0s1	/dev/ad0s1: character special (116/131074)

You can look at files that are English (or ASCII) text or scripts. Scripts are like DOS batch files (those with a `.bat` extension)—a series of commands to be run. They are written using the commands of a shell, like the `sh` (Bourne) shell, or some other scripting language like `perl` or `awk`.

The `/etc/termcap` file is a *symbolic link*—a file that points to another file, just as a Windows shortcut points to another file.

The `/etc/ssh` file is a directory. It doesn't do any harm to try to look at a directory, but it doesn't do anything for you, either.

The `/var/log/wtmp` file is data—not directly readable by humans, but useful information for some other program. The `wtmp` file keeps track of logins to the system and provides data for the `last` command.

The /usr/sbin/file file is the command used above, and is an *executable* file that's been *compiled*. That means it's been converted from the human-readable code a programmer wrote to a form comprehensible by FreeBSD but not readable on your screen. The /kernel file—the basic file that runs the system and allows communications with the hardware and with users—is also an executable file. Most of the files in directories whose names end in bin or sbin are binary executable files. If they were DOS/Windows files they'd have extensions like .exe or .com.

The /dev/ad0s1 file is a special device file. You definitely don't want to try to display this one on your screen.

You display a file on the screen with:

```
$ cat <filename>
```

The file is printed to your screen. For example:

```
$ cat /etc/rc.conf

# This file now contains just the overrides from
     /etc/defaults/rc.conf
# please make all changes to this file.

# -- sysinstall generated deltas -- #
ifconfig_dc0="inet 10.10.10.20  netmask
     255.255.255.0"
hostname="killer.stanford.edu"
moused_port="/dev/psm0"
moused_enable="YES"
gateway_enable="YES"
defaultrouter="10.10.10.1"
linux_enable="YES"
lpd_enable="YES"
```

The /etc/rc.conf file holds some of the information FreeBSD saved during the installation process—information (the values of variables, with the variable on the left and its value, in quotes, on the right) it uses when the system boots. Yours will look different, of course.

Just a Screenful, Please

If a file (like `/etc/defaults/rc.conf`) is too big to display on one screen, all but the end of it just scrolls off the screen when you `cat` *<filename>*.

One way to see what's scrolled off the screen is to press ScrollLock and use the arrow keys to move up and down in the saved buffer. Press ScrollLock again to get back to the command prompt.

LINUX

Looking for Shift-PageUp and Shift-PageDown to scroll the screen buffer? The equivalent in FreeBSD is ScrollLock plus the up and down arrow keys.

You get a screenful at a time by *piping* it to `more`, like this:

```
$ cat /etc/defaults/rc.conf | more
```

The vertical bar—it's usually on the key above Enter on your keyboard—is the pipe, just like a vertical lead pipe. Think of it as a hollow pipe, though, through which you can send something—not smoke but the output of what's on the left side of the pipe.

TIP

You can pipe the output of just about any command to `more`—like a long directory listing: `ls -l | more`.

You look at files with `more` directly by typing:

```
$ more <filename>
```

With `more` in action, you move forward and backward in the file with the arrow keys. You move forward a screen with Ctrl+f (or just tap the spacebar), and backward with Ctrl+b.

You search for text by typing a / and the text you want to find:

```
/text
```

You can search for the next instance of `text` just by typing `n`. If the word or phrase you want is above your location in the file, it won't be found. You search in the opposite direction with `N` (a capital `N`—remember UNIX is case sensitive).

You search backwards by using a ? instead of a /. So ?sendmail would search backwards for sendmail. When you start with ?, an n repeats the backwards search, and N goes forward.

You go back to the first line of the file by typing

```
1G
```

(that's the number one before the G) or to any line number you like followed by G.

A G by itself goes to the end of the file, and since more exits when it gets to the end of the file, that's one way out. Or just type q to quit.

More is called a *pager*; the other pager that comes with the system is less, and many people think less is more.

Viewing Files

Another command to look at a file is:

```
$ view <filename>
```

You use the same commands (except for the spacebar) for getting around and searching with view that you use with more, but view won't exit when it gets to the end of the file.

With view you can also type:

```
:se nu
```

That's shorthand for setting line numbering on. It doesn't change the file—it just numbers the lines on the screen for you. To save part of a file when you're using view to look at it, find the consecutive line numbers you want to save. Say you want to save lines 24 through 28. Type:

```
:24,28w myfile
```

Lines 24 to 28 will be saved (written) to myfile in the directory where you started the `view` command. At least `view` will try. If you're not `root` (and just for exploring, you shouldn't be—no need to risk doing damage) you won't be able to save the file if your starting directory was one in which ordinary users don't have the right to write! FreeBSD will let an ordinary user look at most files, but not change files that don't belong to the user. But you can always save a file to your home directory:

```
:24,28w ~/myfile
```

The ~/ means the user's home directory—it's just shorter than typing `/usr/home/spike.`

If you don't want to look at a file or a directory listing, the `wc` (word count) command may be enough. You can pipe output to `wc` to count lines:

```
$ ls | wc -l
     56
```

You count the words in a file, such as `/etc/motd` (message of the day—you saw it when you logged in) by typing:

```
$ wc -w /etc/motd
     161 /etc/motd
```

Finding Text in a File

You find text in a file (just the lines with the text) *without* calling the whole file to your screen with the `grep` command. To see what there is about the mouse in `/etc/defaults/rc.conf`, type:

```
$ grep mouse /etc/defaults/rc.conf
```

You see:

```
moused_enable="NO"        # Run the mouse daemon.
moused_type="auto"        # See man page for
     rc.conf(5) for available settings.
moused_port="/dev/psm0" # Set to your mouse port.
```

```
moused_flags=""          # Any additional flags to
    moused.
```

But to see what `/etc/rc.conf` has to say about the mouse, which has the settings that override `/etc/defaults/rc.conf` and were created when you installed, you type:

```
$ grep mouse /etc/rc.conf
```

You see something like the following, if you configured the mouse when you installed:

```
moused_port="/dev/psm0"
moused_enable="YES"
```

The `grep` command is very powerful and has many options. Piping long output to `grep` is especially useful. If you have lots of files in a directory but you only want to see a listing of the ones that include *text* in the filename, you do this:

```
$ ls -la | grep text
```

You see output only if you have files including the string *text.*

Getting Help and Information

FreeBSD, like all UNIX systems, has scads of built-in help.

Finding Files: The Setup

To find a file called `rc.conf`, type:

```
$ locate rc.conf
```

`Locate` will tell you the location (full path and filename) of any file whose name includes *rc.conf.* If you have just installed FreeBSD, you are likely to see:

```
locate: database too small: /var/db/locate.database
```

The `locate` database hasn't been built. The `locate` command and its cousin, the `whereis` command, depend on databases built, by default, once a week, on Saturday at 3:30 a.m. You don't have to be there, but the computer has to be turned on and running FreeBSD. (It's `/etc/crontab` that tells FreeBSD to do this,)

You build the `locate` database yourself with these commands:

```
$ su
Password:
# cd /etc
# periodic weekly
```

(You can also type, as `root`, `/usr/libexec/locate.updatedb` if you like.)

The database takes a while to build—how long (maybe 20 minutes) depends on how much stuff you've got installed and the speed of your computer. So press **Alt+F2** to go to another *virtual terminal* and log in again. (You see a `login:` prompt.) After all, FreeBSD is a multi-user system, and there's no reason why two (or more) of *you* can't use it at the same time. You press **Alt+F1** to get back to your original screen. FreeBSD can run many of these virtual terminals at once, and comes with eight of them, named `ttyv0` through `ttyv7`, turned on by default. The eighth is set up for running X.

When the database is built, you can see how big it is with:

```
$ ls -l /var/db/locate.database
-r--r--r--  1 nobody  wheel  1745970 Jun 30 23:38
     /var/db/locate.database
```

The size is less than 1 percent of total file space used, so it's well worth having around.

FreeBSD also runs daily and monthly maintenance. If your computer isn't going to be turned on in the middle of the night or at 5:30 a.m. on the first of the month, run these commands yourself now and then with:

```
# cd /etc
# periodic daily
# periodic monthly
```

With the `locate` database set up, you type:

```
$ locate <text>
```

The `locate` command finds all the paths where the string *text* is found. It will find, for example, a file called `mytextfile` and display the full path and filename, because the string *text* is part of `mytextfile`.

Useful Commands

Here are a few useful commands for getting some help:

```
$ which <command>
```

The `which` command finds the first place in your path where *<command>* is found. Your path is set up in your home directory, in files read by your shell when you log in. You can see what your path looks like any time by typing:

```
$ echo $PATH
```

You see (if your username is `spike`):

```
/sbin:/bin:/usr/sbin:/usr/bin:/usr/games:/usr/local
     /bin:/usr/X11R6/bin:/usr/home/spike/bin
```

These directories are where FreeBSD will search for *<command>*.

The `echo` command itself is in `/bin`:

```
$ which echo
/bin/echo
```

Which Bin?

If you're in you home directory and you type `cd bin`, you go to the `bin` directory that's in your home directory—`/usr/home/spike/bin`, if you're `spike`.

But if you type `cd /bin`, you go to `/bin`, because the opening / takes you to the root of the file system.

The `whereis` command tells you more—all the places where a specific command exists (including your path) and the manual page (more about manual pages below) for the command. And `whereis` takes a wild card. Suppose you've forgotten where that command to rebuild the `locate` database lives. Type:

```
$ whereis locate*
```

You see:

```
locate.bigram: /usr/libexec/locate.bigram
locate.code: /usr/libexec/locate.code
locate.concatdb: /usr/libexec/locate.concatdb
locate.mklocatedb: /usr/libexec/locate.mklocatedb
locate.updatedb: /usr/libexec/locate.updatedb
     /usr/share/man/man8/locate.updatedb.8.gz
```

Most of that output is not very useful—but the last one in the list is a hit.

The power finder, though, is the `find` command. It doesn't depend on a data base. You tell `find` a least three things: where to start searching, what kind of a search to make, and what to look for:

```
$ find / -name "somename"
```

searches for a file by name (the `-name` option) named `somename` in / and all of its subdirectories (which is everything). You use * as a wild card within the quotes:

```
$ find / -name "some*"
```

If you want to start `find` in the directory you're in and search it and its subdirectories, you use a dot:

```
$ find . -name "filename"
```

Man Oh Man

On-line manual pages, called man pages for short, are the main source of documentation for UNIX systems. And that's usually what they are—documentation rather than how-to style help, although some of them have a few examples or paragraphs, usually near the end, on steps you might take to actually accomplish something.

You read a man page by typing `man` <*command*>. To see the manual page for `which`, type:

```
$ man which
```

You see:

```
WHICH(1)                 FreeBSD General Commands
     Manual

WHICH(1)
NAME
     which - locate a program file in the user's
     path
SYNOPSIS
     which [-as] [command] ...
DESCRIPTION
     Which takes a list of command names and
     searches the path for each executable file
     that would be run had these commands actually
     been invoked.
     The following options are available:
     -a       List all instances of executables
              found (instead of just the first one
              of each).
```

```
     -s      No output, just return 0 if any of the
             executables are found, or 1 if none
             are found.
     Some shells may provide a builtin which
     command which is similar or identical to this
     utility.  Consult the builtin(1) manual page.
HISTORY
     The which command first appeared in FreeBSD
     2.1.
SEE ALSO
     builtin(1),  csh(1),  find(1),  locate(1),
     perl(1),  whereis(1)
AUTHORS
     The PERL script for this more modern version
     of which was written by Wolfram Schneider
     <wosch@FreeBSD.org>.
FreeBSD                  January 26, 1995          1
```

You move around a man page just like you move around a file read with `more`. The same commands work—Ctrl-f to go forward, Ctrl+b to go backward, or just Enter to move through the text. A tap on the spacebar moves you down a screen. You can search with / or ?. Use `q` or Ctrl+c to quit.

TIP

But suppose you don't know the name of the man page or quite what you're looking for. Try a little French! The `apropos <text>` command shows you everything in the `whatis` database (which got built or updated when you ran `/etc/periodic weekly`) that contains the string *text*:

```
$ apropos cron

cron(8) - daemon to execute scheduled commands
     (Vixie Cron)
crontab(1)                  - maintain crontab files
     for individual users (V3)
crontab(5)                  - tables for driving cron
cx(4), if_cx(4)             - asynchronous/synchronous
     Cronyx-Sigma adapter driver
```

You see two man pages for `crontab`, (1) and (5). You read the first with `man crontab` or `man 1 crontab`. You read the second with `man 5 crontab`.

Altogether there are nine sections of manual pages. Those in sections 1 and 8 (and possibly sometimes 5 and 7) are relevant to giving orders at the command line; sections 2, 3, and 4 have to do with programming; 6 holds the man pages for the games installed by default; and 9 has information for programmers developing code for the FreeBSD kernel.

The `apropos <text>` command and the `whatis <text>` command both use the same database, but `whatis` searches only for whole words. So `apropos` may give you too much, including some irrelevancies. Both commands tell you the names of man pages that might be useful. Looking through the output of `apropos network` could be a little long but might reveal just what you're looking for.

The `whatis` command is especially useful in the directories with binaries—those ending in `bin`, like `/usr/sbin`.

```
$ cd /usr/sbin
$ whatis *
```

will produce a lot of output on what's in `/usr/sbin`.

And `man hier` will tell you about the layout of the FreeBSD file system itself.

Even More Info

The other major source of information on UNIX systems is GNU info. You get to it by typing:

```
$ info
```

You see an introductory screen with some info on `info` itself. You search with `/text`. The `bash` shell is one of the topics that shows up with a search. A listed item with a `*` next to it can be read when the highlight is on the item by pressing Enter. Then you use (among many options for moving around) the following:

```
?     list commands
h     help tutorial on how to use info
n     next topic in the section
p     previous topic in the section
u     up
t     top
```

Floppies, CD-ROM Drives, and DOS

FreeBSD (and other UNIX systems) *mount* file systems to make them accessible.

You can see what's mounted (and where) with the `mount` command. Another command, `df`, shows free space and mount points as well. The file systems created when you installed FreeBSD are automatically mounted because they're listed in `/etc/fstab.` (Chapter 6 tells you more about `df` command and `/etc/fstab.)` Additional file systems need to be mounted by `root` to be accessible.

To use a floppy disk with a DOS file system on it, put the floppy in what DOS/Windows calls the `A:` drive and type (as `root`):

```
# /sbin/mount -t msdos /dev/fd0 /mnt
```

This command mounts the file system on your floppy. The type (`-t`) of file system it will try to mount is `msdos` (the default is `ufs`, and can be left out). The mount command will try to mount this file system from the device (or device node, to be really nerdy) `/dev/fd0` on the mountpoint `/mnt,` which must exist (as a directory) in `/`.

You can now use UNIX commands—like `cd`, `ls`, and `cp`—to move around, list files, and copy stuff from your hard drive to the floppy and vice versa. For example, `ls /mnt` lists the files on your floppy.

To get the floppy out of the drive you dismount the file system:

```
# /sbin/umount /mnt
```

Yes, the command is really `umount`, not `unmount`. Now you can put in another floppy, mount it, and transfer a few more files.

You mount your CD-ROM, if the CD-ROM is included in `/etc/fstab`, with:

```
# /sbin/mount /cdrom
```

If it's not in `/etc/fstab`, you have to tell it more—the file system type and the device name. For a SCSI CD-ROM:

```
# /sbin/mount -t cd9660 /dev/cd0c /cdrom
```

For an IDE CD-ROM:

```
# /sbin/mount -t cd9660 /dev/acd0c /cdrom
```

If it doesn't work, try substituting `acd1c` for `acd0c`.

TIP

You mount only file systems—not music CDs. And you don't mount the FreeBSD CD-ROM (the one that came with this book) when you use `/stand/sysinstall` to install more stuff (like software) because `/stand/sysinstall` mounts it for you.

The two mountpoints FreeBSD creates for you when it installs are `/mnt` and `/cdrom`. If you want more, type (as `root`):

```
# cd /
# mkdir dos-c
# mkdir dos-d
```

You can call the directories whatever you like.

Now you can mount the DOS partitions on your hard drive. Where are they, anyway? One of them is probably the first DOS partition (FreeBSD slice) on your drive. For an IDE drive, you type:

```
# /sbin/mount -t msdos /dev/ad0s1 /dos-c
```

For a SCSI drive:

```
# /sbin/mount -t msdos /dev/da0s1 /dos-c
```

LINUX

To mount a Linux file system, you need to build a kernel with support for the Linux file system (compiling a kernel is covered in Chapter 16). Many Linux file systems are in extended partitions. Extended partitions in FreeBSD start with the number 5. The command for mounting a Linux file system (assuming the support is in the kernel and an empty directory exists in / called `lin` to use as a mountpoint) would be something like:

```
# /sbin/mount -t ext2fs /dev/ad0s5 /lin
```

depending on where in the extended partition the Linux file system is.

Printing Files from DOS

Setting up printers in FreeBSD—or any variety of UNIX—isn't the easiest task in the world (Chapter 15 tells you about it). Meanwhile you print files (if you want to) from DOS/Windows.

In FreeBSD you direct the output of a command to a file instead of the screen like this:

```
$ cat /etc/rc.conf  > rc.conf.txt
```

Manual pages need a little more processing. Suppose you want a print-out of the manual page for `chmod`, the command that changes file permissions:

```
$ man chmod | col -b > chmod.txt
```

Instead of appearing on your screen, the `chmod` man page will be piped through to another command (`col -b`) that will remove formatting codes. It will then be sent to the file `chmod.txt`. You can copy `chmod.txt` to a floppy disk or to a DOS partition that's mounted while you're in FreeBSD.

When you reboot to Windows, you can open these files with the Windows accessory `WordPad` or another Windows editor or word processor and print them as you normally would in Windows. From the MS-DOS command prompt you type:

```
C:\> write chmod.txt
```

The file appears on your screen and you can set it up to print using the `WordPad` menus.

Many man pages are 80 columns wide and need to be printed with narrow margins or 10-point type to avoid wrapping.

Just clicking on the file names causes them to be opened with the `Notepad` editor, which usually doesn't work very well.

Chapter 6

Shell Wars

A shell is your interface with your operating system—like the buttons on your phone or the panel on your microwave. Between you, the thinking human being with plans and goals, and the machine standing ready to do what you tell it to do, is the shell, the medium through which you transmit your messages.

A UNIX shell is like DOS's `command.com`, the program that, in some versions of Windows, interprets the commands you type in an MSDOS window. Because in UNIX you work more at the command line, a shell, or command interpreter, is more important than it is in DOS. A shell that's easy to use can make your life at the command line much easier.

One of the modern UNIX shells is `bash`. This chapter covers:

- finding out whether the `bash` shell is installed
- setting up `bash`, and
- using `bash` features.

Choosing a Shell

UNIX users are often passionately committed to a favorite shell.

You would think the best shells would float like cream to the top and the lesser or passé offerings would fade gracefully into history where they belong. The truth is that UNIX systems have an embarrassment of riches—too many good shells. The CD-ROM offers at least ten shells as installable packages, including `bash`, `pdksh`, and `zsh`, in addition to the two that come with FreeBSD, `sh` (the Bourne shell) and `tcsh` (a shell with syntax similar to the C programming language). Even more are available.

Although most shells can be set up to behave the way you want them to, modern shells have more built-in features and are easier to configure than older shells.

You can choose whatever shell you like, of course. And each user (or you as the real human being behind more than one user) can experiment and pick a favorite shell.

This book uses `bash` for two reasons:

- `Bash` is a superset of `sh`. That makes writing shell scripts (for which `sh` is the preferred shell) easier, because the scripts use the same commands you use at the command line.

- `Bash` has all the bells and whistles you want for both routine and sophisticated operations at the command line of a modern computer—a prompt that's easy to set to show who and where you are, command line recall and editing, and Tab completion of file names.

LINUX

Because Linux uses `bash`, using `bash` is easy for Linux users and easy for FreeBSD users who might want to try Linux.

Installing Bash

Is `bash` installed? The command:

```
$ which bash
```

should tell you. (Your prompt may be a `%` or a `>` instead of a `$`.) If it's installed, you see:

```
/usr/local/bin/bash
```

That's where `bash` lives on FreeBSD—in `/usr/local/bin/bash.`

X-REF

If you see `file not found`, or a similar message, it's not installed. Chapter 4 tells you how to install `bash` as a package as part of installing FreeBSD. You can go right back to the installer and do it now if you didn't do it then. Chapter

9 tells you about installing packages from the CD-ROM after FreeBSD is installed. It uses `bash` as an example. If `bash` isn't installed, this is the time to do it.

WARNING

Check the installation with the command `which bash` again when you're done.

Setting Up Bash

To see your default shell, type:

```
$ echo $SHELL
```

You might see `/bin/sh` or `/bin/tcsh` instead of what you want, which is:

```
/usr/local/bin/bash
```

You use a text editor to make `bash` your default shell.

To see your default editor, type:

```
$ echo $EDITOR
```

You may see:

```
$ vi
```

If you're not happy with what you see—you want to use the Easy Editor, `ee`, instead of `vi` to edit files—what you type to change it depends on your shell.

For the `sh`, `bash`, and `zsh` shells (and cousins) type:

```
$ EDITOR=ee
$ export EDITOR
```

For the `csh` and `tcsh` shells, type:

```
$ setenv EDITOR ee
```

With the EDITOR environmental variable set to your favorite editor, vipw, which is the command you always use (all by itself) when you want to edit the master.passwd file (because it rebuilds the password database for you when you exit) will also use the editor of your choice.

TIP

Typing echo $SHELL and echo $EDITOR is a bother, isn't it? You see both of these (and a bunch of other stuff that's set, called environmental variables) by typing env. This is the environment for the shell you're in. When you su to root, you need to set these environmental variables again—unless you use su -m, which keeps the same environment and shell.

Changing Your Shell

You change your default login shell with the chsh command:

```
$ chsh
```

For user spike and the sh shell, you see:

```
#Changing user database information for spike.
Shell: /bin/sh
Full Name: Spike Smith
Office Location:
Office Phone:
Home Phone:
Other information:
```

The chsh command uses your default editor—the one that shows up with the echo $EDITOR command. It displays only the information the user is allowed to change. Change the second line of the file to:

```
Shell: /usr/local/bin/bash
```

and save the file. You're done. You see:

```
chsh: updating the database...
chsh: done
```

TIP

If you made a mistake and `spike` can't log in, log in as `root` and type `chsh spike.` Change the line beginning with `Shell.` `Root` has the power to change the shells of other users.

TIP

If you want to experiment with a shell without making it your default shell, you can simply type its name at the prompt (if it's installed).

Why You Shouldn't Change Root's Shell

You don't need to change `root`'s shell—and you risk (unless you know exactly what you're doing) making it impossible for `root` to log in. The `su -m` command (instead of plain old `su`) lets you keep your `bash` shell when you become `root`, and the next section tells you how to put that command in your configuration files so that it becomes the default.

WARNING

`Root`'s default shell on FreeBSD is `csh` (which is really `tcsh`), a fine shell. If you ever get in a situation where you only have the / file system available to you, you won't be able to use `bash` anyway because it needs other files from `/usr` to run.

Shell Start-up Files

FreeBSD's installation of the `bash` shell doesn't come with any start-up files, but it's not hard to create them. Start-up files are *dot* files in your home directory that a shell reads to set things up to your liking. They're called dot files because they begin with a period, and you need to type `ls -a` to see them (unless you're logged in as `root`). The basic set of dot files is copied from `/usr/share/skel` when the user's account is first created:

```
$ ls -d ~/.*

.cshrc                 .mailrc                .xinitrc
.login                 .profile               .xsession
```

```
.login_conf           .rhosts
.mail_aliases         .shrc
```

If they exist, `bash` will read `.bash_profile` when a user logs in and `.bashrc` for a new shell that's not a login shell, like the shell you get when you `su` to `root`. The `.login` and `.cshrc` files are for `csh` and `tcsh`; the `.profile` and `.shrc` files are for the `sh` shell.

Using `ee` or another text editor (Chapter 5 tells you about using `ee` and Chapter 7 tells you about using `vi`), edit `.bash_profile` (it will be created) by doing the following:

1. **In your home directory, type** `ee .bash_profile`
2. **Enter the following** (all lines starting with # are comments and each should be on one line; comment lines have no effect on what happens, but it's good to type them in for future reference).

```
# This is .bash_profile, read on bash login and
     similar to .profile:

# set prompt to display user@host and working
# directory, with # for root and $ for user;
# indent as shown.

PS1="\u@\h \w "
case 'id -u' in
        0) PS1="${PS1}# ";;
        *) PS1="${PS1}$ ";;
esac

# you may want to move /usr/local/bin to a place
# before /usr/bin
# make sure the PATH statement is all on one
# line

PATH=/sbin:/bin:/usr/sbin:/usr/bin:/usr/games:/u
     sr/local/bin:/usr/X11R6/bin:$HOME/bin;
```

```
     export PATH

# change the default editor from vi to ee if
# you like
#
BLOCKSIZE=K;      export BLOCKSIZE
EDITOR=vi;        export EDITOR
PAGER=less;       export PAGER

HISTFILE="$HOME/.bash_history"
export HISTFILE
# file permissions: rwxr-xr-x
#
umask   022

set -o ignoreeof
set -o noclobber
set -o nounset

# keep the user's environment when using su to
# become root
alias su=´su -m´
source $HOME/.bashrc
BASHENV=$HOME/.bashrc; export BASHENV

# search path for cd(1)
# CDPATH=.:$HOME
```

3. **Save the file.**

4. **Edit the `.bashrc` file, creating it and putting these lines in it:**

```
# this is .bashrc
# some useful aliases
alias h=´fc -l´
alias j=jobs
```

```
alias m=$PAGER
alias ll='ls -laFo'
alias l='ls -l'
alias ls='ls -F'
alias lt='ls -lrt'
alias g='egrep -i'

# # be paranoid--get warned before overwriting
     and deleting files
alias cp='cp -ip'
alias mv='mv -i'
alias rm='rm -i'
# the same lines for the prompt as .bash_profile
     uses
PS1="\u@\h \w "
case `id -u` in
        0) PS1="${PS1}# ";;
        *) PS1="${PS1}$ ";;
esac
```

5. **Save the file.**

6. **Type** `exit` **to exit from your shell. Log in again.**

Your `bash` shell should be all set up now. When you log in you can do this, if you're `spike` on the computer `killer`:

```
spike@killer ~ $ cd /etc
spike@killer /etc $ su
Password:
root@killer /etc # cd
root@killer ~ # pwd
/usr/home/spike
root@killer ~ #
```

Now you know who you are and where you are!

Because the PAGER variable is set to `less`, the `more` command will actually use `less`—a pager that has two benefits: it doesn't exit when it comes to the end of a file, and it doesn't read the entire file into memory at once, so it can handle really large files.

You can see the aliases set up in the shell—short-cuts you can type instead of the full version—by typing:

```
$ alias
```

You see in the list:

```
alias rm=´rm -i´
```

The `rm` (remove) command is aliased to `rm -i`, so when you type `rm <filename>` you get prompted (the `i` stands for interactive) for whether or not you really want to remove the file. That can get annoying when you want to delete a long list of files. You can get rid of this alias for the current session by typing:

```
$ unalias rm
```

You get rid of it for future logins by deleting it from your `.bashrc.` or putting a # at the beginning of the line that says `alias rm='rm -i'`.

Bash Features

Like other shells, `bash` has Tab completion. You type part of a filename following a command, press Tab, and `bash` finds the filename in your current directory or path and completes it for you—or as much of it as it can. You type `Esc?` to see all the files that are possible completions.

Suppose you want to edit `.bash_profile`. You type:

```
$ ee .b Tab
```

You see:

```
$ ee .bash
```

You type (without pressing Enter) `Esc?`

You see:

```
.bash_history  .bash_profile  .bashrc
```

Those are the three files starting with `.bash`. You can then type in the next few characters and press Tab again to complete the name, and press Enter.

`Bash` also has command line recall with editing. You press the up arrow to recall previous commands, and when the one you want shows up, you can edit it by moving backward and forward with the right and left arrow keys, deleting characters with Backspace, and entering characters at the cursor. When the command is right, you press Enter to run it.

Making History Work for You

You can see the commands you've run with the `history` command.

```
$ history
```

You see a numbered list of commands. If you want to run a command again, you type a `!` (a bang) and its number. The following command would rerun the command numbered 5 in the list:

```
$ !5
```

You tell `bash` more about how you want it to behave by entering more lines in your `.bash_profile.` `Bash` has some built-in shell options that use `shopt`. If you put this line in `.bash_profile`:

```
shopt -s histverify
```

when you type `!5` `bash` offers the fifth command for your editing instead of running it right off the bat.

You tell `bash` not to record some commands in its history list by using the

HISTIGNORE variable. This line in .bash_profile would make bash ignore ls, cd, and exit:

```
HISTIGNORE="ls:cd:exit"
```

You get bash to reread your .bash_profile without logging out and logging in again by typing:

```
$ source .bash_profile
```

Controlling Jobs

Bash has job control. Jobs are what your shell (not the whole computer) is running. If you press Alt-F2 to get another login prompt on another virtual terminal, you get a new shell—not the same shell you were in before.

Controlling jobs means suspending them, putting them in the background, and recalling them to the foreground where their output displays on your screen. You can see the jobs your shell is running with the command:

```
# jobs
```

A command like:

```
root@killer ~ # /usr/libexec/locate.updatedb
```

can take a long time. It writes to the screen when run in the foreground, although it does not produce a lot of output. But you don't have your command prompt. If you type Ctrl-c, it will kill it altogether. You want to put it in the background. First you suspend it and then you background it. You type Ctrl-z to stop a job.

```
^Z
[1]+  Stopped   /usr/libexec/locate.updatedb
root@killer ~ # jobs
[1]+  Stopped   /usr/libexec/locate.updatedb
```

You put job 1 in the background with:

```
root@killer ~ # bg %1
[1]+ /usr/libexec/locate.updatedb &
root@killer ~ # jobs
[1]+ /usr/libexec/locate.updatedb &
```

Your command to update the `locate` database is still working, and so can you—you've got your prompt back!

You can recall a job (say it's job 2) to the foreground that's in the background with:

```
# fg %2
```

TIP

If you want to start a job that takes a long time and you want to log out of the computer (but leave it turned on), you start the job by preceding its name with `nohup` (for no hangup). Then it continues to run until it's finished, even after you log out.

Bash Help

You get on-screen help in `bash` with the help command:

```
$ help
```

You ask for help on something specific like aliases by typing:

```
$ help alias
```

Perhaps most comprehensive is:

```
$ info bash
```

X-REF

Chapter 5 offers a few basics for using `info`.

A Simple Script

Shell scripts are a common way to make your UNIX life easier. The best shell for writing scripts is sh, because the sh shell is available on all flavors of UNIX. You can write an sh shell script regardless of which shell you use.

Writing a script sounds hard—but a script is just a collection of commands to the shell like the ones you type at the command prompt. If you wish you didn't have to type that long command to mount your DOS partition every time you log in—you don't. Put the command in the shell script and run the script by typing its name. Here's the process for writing a shell script called dosup that mounts your DOS partition:

1. **Log in as** root **and type** cd /etc **(which is where this script should probably live).**
2. **Open a file for your script with your favorite editor by typing (for example)** vi dosup
3. **Enter as the first line of the script the text::**

```
#!/bin/sh
```

That's the line that tells the system your file is a script and should be run using the sh shell.

4. **Enter on the next line (with a full path) the command you use to mount your DOS partition, e.g.:**

```
/sbin/mount -t msdos /dev/ad0s1 /dos
```

5. **Save the file.**
6. **Type** chmod 755 dosup **to make the script executable or runnable.**
7. **Test the script by typing** /etc/dosup **or, while in the** /etc **directory,** ./dosup.

TIP

You make a shell script run when the computer boots by putting the script file in the /usr/local/etc/rc.d directory and adding an .sh extension to its name. You can move dosup there and change its name at the same time with the command:

```
/etc # mv dosup /usr/local/etc/rc.d/dosup.sh
```

LINUX

You can add a line to the above script to mount a Linux partition. A script in `/usr/local/etc/rc.d` is a good way to mount a Linux partition on boot because if it fails (because the Linux partition is not clean), the system will still boot. If you put Linux partitions in `/etc/fstab` and they're not clean, you get forced into single-user mode and have to boot Linux to `fsck` (clean up) the file system, which can't be done from FreeBSD.

You don't have to be logged in as `root` to create or run a shell script. But if it contains commands for doing something that can only be done by `root`, it will fail if it's user-owned and run.

Chapter 7

What's Happening

Often you want to find out how things are going—what FrecBSD found when it booted, what's running, how much space is available, who's logged in, and so forth. This chapter tells you how to:

- explore your FreeBSD system
- find out what's running (and kill it if necessary)
- manage file access
- run programs automatically, and
- speed up the file system.

In other words, this chapter gives you a bird's eye view of the FreeBSD tiger and how to catch it by the tail, so you can tell what it's doing and poke it and pacify it to perform even better for you.

Your FreeBSD System

Now that you have some good tools to work with, you can find out more about what's going on. The commands you use to find out about the system and what it's running have many options. You can always find out more by reading the man pages with **man** ***<command>***. But what's covered here will get you a long way.

What UNIX Is This?

The `uname` command tells you what version of UNIX is running on your computer. Adding `-a` (for "all") shows you everything: the hostname, the version of the operating system (from the kernel's viewpoint), and when the kernel was compiled (and even who compiled it).

```
$ uname -a
```

You see something like this:

```
FreeBSD  4.3-RC3 FreeBSD 4.3-RC3 #0: Tue Apr 10
     20:20:52 GMT 2001
     jkh@narf.osd.bsdi.com:/usr/src/sys/compile/GEN
     ERIC  i386
```

What FreeBSD Knows

FreeBSD has several ways to keep track of what it knows about your hardware and the operating system running on it, and with a little effort you can find out what it knows.

File Systems and Space

TIP

You use the `df` command to find out about free space, as well as what's mounted—the file systems to which you have access—and where:

```
$ df

Filesystem  1K-blocks   Used  Avail Capacity Mounted on

/dev/da0s3a     59519  27024  27734    49%    /
/dev/da0s3f   1736543 770140 827480    48%    /usr
/dev/da0s3e     69407   2253  61602     4%    /var
procfs              4      4      0   100%    /proc
```

You see the device name of the file system in the first column and where it's mounted—which is where you go (with the `cd` command) to get at the files—in the last column. The space `Used` and the space `Avail` don't add to the total `1K-blocks`, because FreeBSD reserves about 8 percent of disk space for operations. (The `procfs`, or process file system, is always at 100% of capacity, so don't panic.)

TIP

The file systems created when you installed FreeBSD are automatically mounted (the CD-ROM drive is only mounted if there's a CD in the drive) because they're listed in `/etc/fstab`:

```
$ cat /etc/fstab
```

You see a display like the following, which shows FreeBSD installed on SCSI disk 0 in slice 3 (the third DOS-style partition on the physical hard drive):

```
# Device       Mountpoint   FStype  Options      Dump Pass#
/dev/da0s3b    none         swap    sw           0       0
/dev/da0s3a    /            ufs     rw           1       1
/dev/da0s3f    /usr         ufs     rw           2       2
/dev/da0s3e    /var         ufs     rw           2       2
/dev/cd0c      /cdrom       cd9660  ro,noauto    0       0
proc           /proc        procfs  rw           0       0
```

The `du` command (disk usage) shows you the disk space used by the directory you're in and its subdirectories. Adding `-s` tells `du` to display only summaries (not a listing for each file) and a `-h` tells `du` to make the output more readable to ordinary mortals. The following summarizes disk space used in the `X11R6` directory (where `X Window` is installed) and the home directories:

```
root@pninety /usr # du -sh X11R6 home
 71M     X11R6
 43M     home
```

If you wonder what's taking up so much space in `/usr`, the command:

```
$ du -sh /usr/*
```

would be useful, or if you're in `/usr`, just `du -sh *`.

While you consider space, consider moving the tmp directory in / to somewhere with more space, like /usr. Make a tmp directory in /usr, move everything in /tmp to that directory, delete the tmp directory in /, and create a symbolic link from tmp in / to /usr/tmp, with these commands:

```
# mkdir /usr/tmp
# mv /tmp/* /usr/tmp
# cd /
# rmdir tmp
# ln -s /usr/tmp tmp
```

An ls -l in / should show (among other files and directories, and leaving out the date to show it on one line):

```
lrwxr-xr-x  1 root  wheel [date] tmp@ -> /usr/tmp
```

Boot Messages

TIP

What FreeBSD found when it booted is shown by the dmesg command. This is what scrolled across your screen during boot.

```
$ dmesg
```

The output of dmesg could be 90 lines long, so I show you parts of it here (the messages from the last boot are saved in /var/run/dmesg.boot, a file you can look at any time).

```
$ dmesg | grep FreeBSD
Copyright (c) 1992-2000 The FreeBSD Project.
FreeBSD 4.0-STABLE #14: Tue Jul 4 20:53:44 PDT 2000
```

TIP

If the boot messages in the system message file are no longer available because other messages have replaced them, you can use grep FreeBSD /var/run/dmesg.boot instead of the above command, and comparable commands for the following dmesg commands.

The CPU and the Memory

Your central processing unit, or CPU, and your installed memory are the two most critical factors in how fast your computer does its work, so if things are slower than you expect you can check up on them.

```
$ dmesg | grep CPU
```

You see information about your CPU—how fast it's running and the class to which FreeBSD assigned it:

```
CPU: AMD-K7(tm)Processor (704.94-MHz 686-class CPU)
```

You find out about memory with the following command, and you see two lines about memory. This example shows a computer with 256MB of RAM:

```
$ dmesg | grep memory
real memory  = 268369920 (262080K bytes)
avail memory = 257310720 (251280K bytes)
```

Grepping Around

The `grep` command is a basic UNIX command—one of the most useful. It shows you the lines in a file that have the text you're looking for. It has many options, including `-v` to tell it to show you the lines that *don't* have the specified text.

Many UNIX commands produce a lot of output, but you're only interested in part of the list—which is why piping the output of a command to `grep` is so useful and so frequently used. That's how it's used in this chapter in several different ways.

You can find all the files in a directory that have particular text in them with `grep text *`.

Useful Hardware

FreeBSD can tell you about the hardware it found installed on the motherboard of your computer and the add-on cards installed.

```
$ dmesg | grep fd
```

You see the floppy controller and drive:

```
fdc0: <NEC 72065B or clone> at port 0x3f0-
     0x3f5,0x3f7 irq 6 drq 2 on isa0
```

```
fdc0: FIFO enabled, 8 bytes threshold
fd0: <1440-KB 3.5" drive> on fdc0 drive 0
```

```
$ dmesg | grep "sio[0-3]"
```

Here the expression we want to find is in quotes so that the square brackets are not read literally, but rather as enclosing a range of digits, any one of which can come after `sio`. This shorthand searches for `sio0`, `sio1`, `sio2`, and `sio3`—four possible serial ports (your modem or a mouse may be attached to one of them). Just `sio` would have worked too, with some unwanted output like lines with the word *revision* in them. In this case the output shows two serial ports (DOS would call them COM1 and COM2):

```
sio0 at port 0x3f8-0x3ff irq 4 flags 0x10 on isa0
sio0: type 16550A
sio1 at port 0x2f8-0x2ff irq 3 on isa0
sio1: type 16550A
```

TIP

The `-i` option to `grep` makes `grep` ignore case and treat capitals and lowercase letters the same. So the following command finds two lines and tells me my mouse is using the `psm0` driver:

```
$ dmesg | grep -i mouse
psm0: <PS/2 Mouse> irq 12 on atkbdc0
psm0: model Generic PS/2 mouse, device ID 0
```

Ethernet Cards and Your Network

Whether FreeBSD found your ethernet card is pretty important when you want to connect to a cable modem or other computers on a local network. It's tricky because different ethernet cards produce different kinds of output.

TIP

If your ethernet card was found by FreeBSD and FreeBSD succeeded in setting up a driver for it (the software that runs it), the following command will show it to you:

```
$ dmesg | grep address
```

Searching for the word *address* finds the following line on the computer `killer`:

```
dc0: Ethernet address: 00:a0:cc:58:d7:cc
```

But on the computer `pninety`, which has a different kind of ethernet card, the `dmesg | grep address` command produces this:

```
ed0: address 00:40:33:97:0d:44, type NE2000 (16
     bit)
```

In both cases I find out what I need to know—the name of the driver (`dc0` and `ed0`) for the ethernet card FreeBSD found on each computer. The numbers separated by colons are hex numbers (hex numbers use `a` to `f` as well as 0 to 9) and are the hardware or MAC addresses of the cards. These numbers come from the card itself.

Additional lines of `dmesg` start with `dc0` on `killer` and `ed0` on `pninety`, and I see them on my screen if I type `dmesg | grep dc0` (on `killer`) or `dmesg | grep ed0` (on `pninety`). But grepping for `dc0` will give me output I don't want—like lines with `fdc0`—so I can ask only for lines beginning with `dc0` by using `^`:

```
$ dmesg | grep "^dc0"
dc0: <82c169 PNIC 10/100BaseTX> port 0xc000-0xc0ff
     mem 0xefffff00-0xefffffff irq 5 at device 16.0
     on pci0
dc0: Ethernet address: 00:a0:cc:58:d7:cc
dc0: supplying EUI64: 00:a0:cc:ff:fe:58:d7:cc
```

If an ethernet card (or some other hardware) is in the computer and isn't being found, the reason could be an `irq` conflict, since each device needs its own `irq` (FreeBSD is pickier about that than Windows). A useful command is:

```
$ dmesg | grep irq
ncr0: <ncr 53c810 fast10 scsi> port 0xd100-0xd1ff mem
      0x21000000-0x210000ff irq 11 at device 1.0 on pci0
fdc0: <NEC 72065B or clone> at port 0x3f0-0x3f5,0x3f7
      irq 6 drq 2 on isa0
```

```
atkbd0: <AT Keyboard> irq 1 on atkbdc0
psm0: <PS/2 Mouse> irq 12 on atkbdc0
sio0 at port 0x3f8-0x3ff irq 4 flags 0x10 on isa0
sio1 at port 0x2f8-0x2ff irq 3 on isa0
ed0 at port 0x280-0x29f iomem 0xd8000 irq 10 on isa0
sbc0: <Soundblaster 16> at port 0x220-0x22f irq 5 drq 1
     flags 0x15 on isa0
sbc0: setting card to irq 5, drq 1, 5
```

If I had an ethernet card set for IRQ 3, it probably wouldn't be *configured* or set up on boot because a serial port had already grabbed IRQ 3. I would have to change the IRQ the card uses with jumpers or software (probably DOS software) or disable `sio1` by configuring the kernel on boot. (See Chapter 16 for more about configuring the kernel on boot.) Another useful command for finding out the IRQs in use is `vmstat -i`.

Two other commands tell you about your network connections.

```
$ ifconfig -a
ed0: flags=8843<UP,BROADCAST,RUNNING,SIMPLEX,MULTICAST>
          mtu 1500
     inet 10.10.10.7 netmask 0xffffff00 broadcast
          10.10.10.255
     ...
lp0: flags=8810<POINTOPOINT,SIMPLEX,MULTICAST> mtu 1500
sl0: flags=c010<POINTOPOINT,LINK2,MULTICAST> mtu 552
ppp0: flags=8010<POINTOPOINT,MULTICAST> mtu 1500
lo0: flags=8049<UP,LOOPBACK,RUNNING,MULTICAST> mtu 16384
     inet 127.0.0.1 netmask 0xff000000
```

This shows a network card (`ed0`) up and running with an IP address, a parallel port (`lp0`), a serial line interface (`sl0`), the `ppp0` device for dial-up Internet connections, and `lo0`, the loopback interface so the computer can communicate with itself. The `-a` switch to `ifconfig` shows all interfaces, and is optional in FreeBSD 4.3. The `-u` shows only those that are up.

```
$ netstat -rn
Routing tables
```

```
Internet:
Destination    Gateway            Flags   Netif Expire
default        10.10.10.1         UGSc      1        2   ed0
10.10.10/24    link#1             UC        0        0   ed0 =>
10.10.10.1     0:a0:cc:63:44:5f   UHLW      4     8344   ed0
                                                         1189
127.0.0.1      127.0.0.1          UH        1       29   lo0
```

The netstat command shows you the status of your network. Here you see the default route configured for the computer (10.10.10.1); FreeBSD has discovered its hardware (MAC) address. The details about setting up your network are in Chapter 12.

The Drives

This command:

```
$ dmesg | grep "cd[01]"
```

should find not only `cd0` and `cd1` (possible SCSI CD-ROM drives) but also `acd0` and `acd1`, IDE CD-ROM drives. The output might look like this:

```
cd0 at ahc0 bus 0 target 4 lun 0
cd0: <PIONEER DVD-ROM DVD-303 1.10> Removable CD-
     ROM SCSI-2 device
cd0: 20.000MB/s transfers (20.000MHz, offset 8)
cd0: Attempt to query device size failed: NOT
     READY, Medium not present
```

That last line looks like an error message. It's not. FreeBSD has tried to find out how big the disk in the CD-ROM drive is ("query device size") but it didn't work ("failed") because there was no disk in the drive ("Medium not present").

Here finally are the hard drives, and the name of the device from which the kernel was mounted. If you have trouble booting (maybe because another operating system trashed your boot manager), that's information you'll want.

```
$ dmesg | grep "da[0-3]"
```

```
Mounting root from ufs:/dev/da1s1a
da1 at ahc0 bus 0 target 1 lun 0
da1: <IBM DNES-309170W SA30> Fixed Direct Access
     SCSI-3 device
...
da0 at ahc0 bus 0 target 0 lun 0
da0: <IBM DNES-309170W SA30> Fixed Direct Access
     SCSI-3 device
...
```

TIP

If your drives are IDE instead of SCSI, use:

```
$ dmesg | grep "ad[0-3]"
```

How FreeBSD Boots

When FreeBSD boots, it starts the kernel and then runs the `/etc/rc` script, which in turn runs other `rc.*` scripts in `/etc`. In these scripts it uses the default values in `/etc/defaults/rc.conf`, a file that you never edit.

WARNING

Don't copy `/etc/defaults/rc.conf` to `/etc/rc.conf`. It may be tempting, but it can be a disaster.

The defaults in `/etc/defaults/rc.conf` are overridden by the settings in `/etc/rc.conf`, a file that was created when you installed FreeBSD to hold the specfic information you provided at that time. You can edit the `/etc/rc.conf` file directly—or you can run `/stand/sysinstall` (as `root`) and return to the various dialogs, and it will save the information you provide in `/etc/rc.conf` or other appropriate files.

If you edit `/etc/rc.conf` directly, you can find the syntax you need in `/etc/defaults/rc.conf`. The manual page lists the many variables you can set in `/etc/rc.conf` to override the defaults, but if you polished up your installation as described in Chapter 4, most of what you need to do is already done.

When you read /etc/defaults/rc.conf, you notice a line starting with local_startup. It tells FreeBSD where to look for scripts that you want the system to run on boot: in /usr/local/etc/rc.d, which is a directory that's initially empty. Scripts in that directory that end with an .sh extention (like myprog.sh) run on boot if you make them executable (more about that later).

Topping Up

The top command is your quickest way to see what's running. Most people think of what's running as *programs*, but UNIX calls them *processes*, which makes sense because a software program often does more than one thing. Some processes are run by users; others are run by the system, ready for action if called on.

```
$ top
```

You see a display like that shown in Figure 7-1.

The top display updates continually. It tells you in its headers the *last pid*—the process id of the last process run. The PID is the identification number the kernel has given the process to keep track of it. The display also tells you how many processes have been running (load averages), how long since the computer last booted (over two days, in this case), how many processes are loaded and how many of them are actually doing something (running), and how much of the cpu is in use.

The memory on this particular computer is 96MB, and almost all of it is in use, with very little (less than three megabytes) listed as Free. Often people find this worrisome, as though it's about to run out of memory and couldn't load another program (or run another process). But this really isn't the case—FreeBSD always tries to use the available memory if only to cache (hold for quick recall) stuff you looked at and might want to see again soon.

```
last pid: 12820;  load averages:  0.00,  0.00,  0.00        up 2+21:48:49  18:12:28
43 processes:  1 running, 42 sleeping
CPU states:  3.8% user,  0.0% nice,  1.9% system,  1.2% interrupt, 93.1% idle
Mem: 16M Active, 24M Inact, 14M Wired, 4488K Cache, 6709K Buf, 2420K Free
Swap: 120M Total, 32K Used, 120M Free

  PID USERNAME PRI NICE  SIZE    RES STATE    TIME   WCPU    CPU COMMAND
12820 xanne     28   0  1832K  1016K RUN      0:01  5.47%  1.81% top
11729 xanne      2   0  5152K  4416K select   0:32  1.42%  1.42% Xvnc
12819 root       2   0  1832K  1016K select   0:01  0.05%  0.05% top
  164 root       2   0   844K   328K select   0:14  0.00%  0.00% moused
  129 root       2   0  1392K   708K select   0:07  0.00%  0.00% sendmail
  122 root      10   0   920K   504K nanslp   0:06  0.00%  0.00% cron
   80 root       2   0   876K   452K select   0:04  0.00%  0.00% syslogd
11733 xanne      2   0  1824K  1224K select   0:03  0.00%  0.00% fvwm
  128 root      10   0   888K   412K nanslp   0:03  0.00%  0.00% lpd
12549 root       2   0  1968K  1156K select   0:03  0.00%  0.00% telnetd
11741 xanne      2   0  2896K  2112K select   0:02  0.00%  0.00% xterm
  180 xanne      3   0  1640K  1120K ttyin    0:02  0.00%  0.00% bash
11743 xanne      2   0  2308K  1484K select   0:01  0.00%  0.00% xclock
12550 xanne     10   0  1636K  1276K wait     0:01  0.00%  0.00% bash
12624 root      10   0  1636K  1268K wait     0:01  0.00%  0.00% bash
11747 xanne      2   0  2852K  2044K select   0:01  0.00%  0.00% xterm
  181 xanne      3   0  1628K  1240K ttyin    0:00  0.00%  0.00% bash
11744 xanne      2   0  1596K   944K select   0:00  0.00%  0.00% FvwmPager
  120 root       2   0  1020K   500K select   0:00  0.00%  0.00% inetd
11739 xanne      2   0  1664K  1008K select   0:00  0.00%  0.00% GoodStuff
11745 xanne     10   0  1628K  1248K wait     0:00  0.00%  0.00% bash
11748 xanne      3   0  1628K  1248K ttyin    0:00  0.00%  0.00% bash
  184 root       3   0   892K   380K ttyin    0:00  0.00%  0.00% getty
  183 root       3   0   892K   380K ttyin    0:00  0.00%  0.00% getty
  182 root       3   0   892K   380K ttyin    0:00  0.00%  0.00% getty
```

Figure 7-1: Output of the Top Command

If I load a memory hog like Netscape, FreeBSD will just pushes something out of the way. The real tip-off that memory is adequate is Swap: only 32 kilobytes are being swapped to disk.

The first column of `top` lists the process id, or PID. The last column of the display gives the name of the process. The ones in between provide information on the total size (SIZE) and resident memory (RES) of the process, and the percentage of the CPU it's using.

When you want `top` to quit, you press `q`.

The `swapinfo` command also shows you swap spacc available and in use:

```
xanne@killer ~ % swapinfo
Device          1K-blocks     Used    Avail Capacity  ...
/dev/da1s1b        130944        0   130944     0%
/dev/rda1s4b        65408        0    65408     0%
```

```
Total              196352        0   196352        0%
```

Killing a Process

If you want to kill a process, you run `top`, find the PID, press `k` (without quitting from `top`) and enter the PID (process id) number from `top`'s first column.

If you don't want to kill it dead but just want it to reread its configuration files because you've changed them (not all processes support this), after you quit `top` you can type at the command line:

```
# kill -HUP <PID>
```

WARNING

HUP stands for *hang up*. You could type `kill -1 <PID>`, but it's easy to make a mistake and kill `init`, which always had PID 1. FreeBSD won't run without `init`. Type `man kill` (how could you resist?) to see the names of the signals `kill` takes and their corresponding numbers.

If you want a process to end so you can restart it yourself, `kill -15 <PID>` will do the trick. The strongest form of kill is:

```
# kill -9 <PID>
```

This is the FreeBSD equivalent of the CIA's legendary "terminate with extreme prejudice." Use it in emergencies. A better way to terminate a process and a very convenient one is with `killall`, which sends the process a signal 15 (software termination) but uses the name of the process instead of its PID, for example:

```
# killall ppp
```

Finding Out If a Process Is Running

A command with many options and output similar to `top` is `ps` (short for process). In fact, `ps` is the standard utility for finding out about processes, and it exists in one form or another on all UNIX systems. It shows all loaded processes and is therefore especially good for finding out whether a particular one is running. The short form:

```
$ ps ax
```

shows you processes running by all users and the system. For more information, try:

```
$ ps aux
```

This form shows more information about CPU time and so forth, with a header line to give you an idea of what the columns mean.

TIP

You add the `w` (or even two of them) to the other `ps` options to make the output wrap—otherwise the process (like `sendmail`) you're looking for might be off the screen:

```
$ ps auxw | grep sendmail
```

You see:

```
root      134  0.0  0.5  1420 1208  ??  Ss   12:08AM
     0:00.02 sendmail: accepting connections on
     port 25 (sendmail)
```

`Sendmail` runs by default on most versions of FreeBSD.

LINUX

Linux uses the SysV (non-BSD) form of `ps`, which has different letters for the options. If you use `ps -elf` on Linux, use `ps aux` on FreeBSD.

Kernel Info

The FreeBSD kernel has loadable modules—kernel add-ons you can load on the fly (and unload) after the computer has booted. The `kldstat` command shows you what the kernel has loaded:

```
root@killer ~ # kldstat

Id Refs Address    Size     Name
```

```
1     3 0xc0100000 27cffc    kernel
2     1 0xc1328000 11000     linux.ko
3     1 0xc134c000 12000     fire_saver.ko
```

Besides the kernel itself (that better be there!), the display shows that `killer` has two kernel modules loaded—`linux` and `fire_saver`. The `linux` module provides kernel support for Linux programs and `fire_saver` is a console screensaver (your roommate may think your monitor's burning up). Kernel modules are kept in the `/modules` directory and always have a .ko extension.

Listing some files in `/modules` shows several screensavers available:

```
root@killer ~ # ls /modules/*saver.ko
/modules/apm_saver.ko*       /modules/logo_saver.ko*
/modules/blank_saver.ko*     /modules/rain_saver.ko*
/modules/daemon_saver.ko*    /modules/snake_saver.ko*
/modules/fade_saver.ko*      /modules/star_saver.ko*
/modules/fire_saver.ko*      /modules/warp_saver.ko*
/modules/green_saver.ko*
```

To unload `fire_saver` and load `star_saver`, type:

```
root@killer ~ # kldunload fire_saver
root@killer ~ # kldload star_saver
```

Check out your work:

```
root@killer ~ # kldstat | grep saver
4     1 0xc15ab000 2000     star_saver.ko
```

Kernel modules also exist for adding sound drivers to the kernel. Because they're pre-compiled, they may not do precisely what you need, but it's worth giving them a try before you recompile your kernel. Try this command to load sound services into the kernel:

```
# kldload snd
```

You also need to type (as `root`) `sh /dev/MAKEDEV snd0`. If that doesn't make sound work, see Chapter 13—and Chapter 16 for how to load a kernel module on boot.

More Messages

FreeBSD keeps track of what's going on and sends messages about problems and reports on what it runs, like its scheduled maintenance routines. Emergency messages are also sent to the console and flash on the screen.

All messages are saved in `/var/log/messages`, which is a readable file that gets rolled over every now and then. The old messages are compressed and saved. You might want to send the files of old logs right down the river, and that's exactly what happens to them—although UNIX-types would say they're sent to the bit bucket. The old sets of messages are eventually deleted so the file system doesn't run out of space.

To read `/var/log messages`:

```
$ cd /var/log
/var/log $ view messages
```

You see all the message files by typing:

```
/var/log $ls -la messages*

-rw-rw-r--   1  root  wheel  9315 Jul  9 01:22
    messages
-rw-rw-r--   1  root  wheel  9366 Jul  4 22:00
    messages.0.gz
-rw-rw-r--   1  root  wheel  9950 Apr 22 17:00
    messages.1.gz
```

TIP

You can look at a file that's been compressed with the `gzip` utility (they usually end with `.gz`) by using a variant of the `more` command—of course, it's the `z` that does it:

```
/var/log $ zmore messages.0.gz
```

If you use `grep` to search for text in a gzipped file, you need the `-a` option to get it to read what it considers a non-text file. You can also use the following to decompress a gzipped file and display it on your screen without changing the original file (the `-d` decompresses and the `-c` sends it to `stdout` (your screen):

```
$ gzip -dc <filename> | more
```

Setting Up a Log

The `/var/log` directory has many more log files. The `/etc/syslog.conf` configures logging and is usually where you put the instructions for how to log the output of new software you install. Software usually comes with information (somewhere!) on how to set up its logging. Here are steps you take as `root` for logging `ftpd`—the file transfer protocol daemon—and thus making a log of files transferred to and from the system by FTP:

1. **Edit /etc/syslog.conf, adding the lines:**

```
!ftpd
*.*                  /var/log/ftpd/log
```

2. **Save the file.**

3. **Find the PID of syslogd by typing** `ps auxw | grep syslog`

   You see a line like:

```
root       110  0.0  0.5   904  632  ??  Is
        1:28AM    0:00.11 syslogd -s
```

   The PID is 110, the second column in the output.

4. **Type** `kill -HUP <PID>` **substituting 110 (in this case) for <PID>.**

5. **Type** `touch /var/log/ftpd.log`

TIP

The `touch` command creates a file without putting anything in it—a necessary step here because `syslog` can't write to non-existent files. If you `touch` an existing file, it changes its date to the current date.

The `newsyslog.conf` file in `/etc` controls how often logs are rolled over and how long they're kept. You can edit this file as `root` and change the defaults if you like, but they're usually satisfactory.

You can add a line to `/etc/newsyslog.conf` for a new program (like your `ftpd` log) if you want the log file rolled over and compressed (and eventually discarded) by copying a line for another program (for example, `ppp.log`) and changing `ppp.log` to `ftpd.log`. The new line would look like:

```
/var/log/ftpd.log                    600  3      100   *       Z
```

This line will cause the log file `/var/log/ftpd.log` to be rolled over to a file with permissions 600; three old files will be kept (then discarded); a roll-over will occur whenever the basic log file reaches 100 kilobytes (rather than on a time schedule, which is why the next column has a *); and `gzip` (indicated by the Z) will be used to compress them.

Mail Messages

Some messages about system happenings are mailed to `root` and go to `/var/mail/root`. In fact, each user has a mail file in `/var/mail`. To see the mail files type:

```
$ ls -la /var/mail

-rw-------   1 root   wheel  98316 Jul  8 03:38 root
-rw-------   1 spike  spike      0 Jun 11 16:46 spike
-rw-------   1 vicki  vicki    498 Jun 25 15:47 vicki
```

You can read the mail with the simple mail program that comes with FreeBSD called `mail`. If you type `mail`, it lists the user's mail messages in `/var/mail`. You read them by pressing a message number at the & prompt, or you move around the list with the arrow keys and press Enter to read a message, or `n` for the next message. A `d` will delete a message; an `r` will start a reply. Mail you read will be sent to the user's `mbox` in his or her home directory; unread mail is kept in the `/var/mail/<user>`.

The `mail` program is a minimal utility, though, and you will want to install a mail program with more features. FreeBSD has lots of good programs for reading and sending mail mentioned in Chapters 9, 10, and 11.

Instead of using the `mail` program, you can read the mail the same way you look at other files—with `more` or `cat` or `view`. The superuser (`root`) can read anyone's mail this way.

If you give accounts on your machine to people other than yourself, you face your first decision of principle as a system administrator. It's unethical (and possibly illegal) to read other people's mail or their files. If they abuse the privileges you give them, take the account away. But don't read their mail. If you can't offer privacy, don't offer an account.

TIP

You set up `root`'s mail (while you are logged in as `root`) to be forwarded to you as a user by placing a `.forward` file in `root`'s home directory, which is `/root`. In this file you put the user to whom you want to forward `root`'s mail, say `spike`, with a \ in front of `spike`'s name:

1. **# cd /root**
2. **# ee .forward**
3. **Enter** `\spike` **in the file.**
4. **Save the file and exit.**

The `\spike` line in the file means that a copy of `root`'s mail will go to local user `spike`. Read `man forward` for information on other mail forwarding options.

You test your handiwork by typing as user `spike`:

```
$ mail -s "for root via spike" root
hi there spike
.
```

This sends mail with the subject *for root via spike* to root. You can enter as many lines of text as you like (although you can't edit a line once you press Enter to go on to the next one), ending with a `.` on a line alone to say "I'm done!"

```
spike@pninety ~ $ mail
Mail version 8.1 6/6/93.  Type ? for help.
"/var/mail/spike": 1 message 1 new
>N  1 spike            Tue Jul 25 13:39  14/397
    "for spike via root"
& q
Held 1 message in /var/mail/spike
You have mail in /var/mail/spike
```

Who's Playing—and With What

The `last` command shows you who logged in to the system when. Why do you care? Because once your computer is on the Internet, it becomes a target of attack. So it's good to be able to see who's logged in, even though an attacker might try to conceal his (or her) presence.

The most recent information on who logged in is at the top of the output of the `last` command and it can get long, so pipe it to `more`. Or do something new; pipe it to `head` and look at the first six lines:

```
xanne@pninety ~ $ last | head -6
vicki  ttyp2             Sun Jul  9 15:52   still
    logged in
xanne  ttyp2  andrsn3    Sun Jul  9 15:34   still
    logged in
xanne  ttyp1             Sat Jul  8 02:29   still
    logged in
xanne  ftp    10.10.10.20 Sat Jul  8 00:57 - 00:57
    (00:00)
xanne  ttyv0             Fri Jul  7 23:12   still
    logged in
reboot         ~           Fri Jul  7 23:12
```

A couple of commands—`w` and `who`—show you who's logged in to the system and what they're doing, but w tells you the most:

```
$ w

3:11AM  up 3:04, 2 users, load averages: 1.00, 1.00,1.00
USER     TTY      FROM        LOGIN@   IDLE WHAT
xanne    v0       -           12:09AM  3:02 -bash (bash)
xanne    p0       andrsn3     3:06AM      - w
```

Being Less (or More) Permissive

When you do a long (`ls -l`) directory listing, you see more than just filenames—you see the permissions on the files, the owners, the size of the files, and their date last modified as well.

The ownership and permissions on files determine, in combination, who can read them, who can change the content (write to them or delete them), and who can run (execute) them, if they're runnable. The ownership and permissions can be changed by their owners and by `root`, and sometimes they need to be changed to make things work right.

```
spike@killer ~/ $ ls -l dmesg.txt
-rw-r--r--  1 root spike 4707 Jul 2 16:21 dmesg.txt
```

The very first column of the long file listing reveals whether the file is a directory (`d`), a regular file (`-`), a character (`c`) device (found in `/dev`), or a symbolic link (`l`).

The next nine columns or slots show permissions: three slots for the user-owner, three for the group-owner, and three for all others (the world). Here are their meanings and numerical values:

```
r    read        4
w    write       2
x    execute     1
```

The most permissive gives read, write, and execute rights across the board:

```
-rwxrwxrwx
```

Expressed in numbers, this file has mode (permissions) 777, because each of the three sets of slots sums to seven.

The dmesg.txt file (-rw-r--r--) has permissions 644, because the user-owner slots, rw- (allowing user-owner root read and write) sum to six; the second set of slots, for the group-owner spike, is r--, allowing read permission, as is the third set. Anyone can read this file, but only owner root can alter its contents (write). The right to write includes the right to delete.

Changing Ownership

Changing ownership of a file is a lot easier than transferring the ownership of your car. But you can't sell a car you don't own. Because root owns dmesg.txt, even though spike is the group-owner, only root can change its ownership:

```
-rw-r--r--  1 root spike 4707 Jul 2 16:21 dmesg.txt
```

This file in spike's home directory was probably created root-owned while spike was logged on as root. As root the ownership can be changed with the chown command:

```
/usr/home/spike # chown spike:spike dmesg.txt
```

The first spike is for the user-owner, and the second spike (after the colon) is for the group-owner and doesn't make any difference here, as spike was already the group-owner. To see the results type:

```
/usr/home/spike # ls -l dmesg.txt
-rw-r--r--   1 spike   spike    4707 Jul  2 16:21
     dmesg.txt
```

The exception to the rule that only the owner can change ownership is that root can change the ownership (and permissions on) any file.

A la Mode

The mode (the read, write, and execute permissions) can be changed two ways—in one fell swoop with numbers, or by adding or subtracting a permission for the user-owner (u), the group-owner (g) or the rest of the world (o). Both use the chmod command.

With numbers, you change a file's mode by giving new permission numbers for all three sets of slots. Because spike now owns the file, user spike can change its permissions. A mode of 660 gives read (4) and write (2) permissions to the user-owner and group-owner, and nothing to the rest of the world:

```
$ chmod 660 dmesg.txt
$ ls -l dmesg.txt
-rw-rw---- 1 spike spike 4707 Jul 2 16:21 dmesg.txt
```

Owner spike can add or subtract permissions. The following command subtracts write permissions for the group-owner (g) and adds read permissions for the world (o):

```
$ chmod g-w o+r dmesg.txt
$ ls -la dmesg.txt
-rw-r--r-- 1 spike spike 4707 Jul 2 16:21 dmesg.txt
```

Default Permissions

You might think that default permissions are no fault of your own, but they are—they depend on your umask, and you can change the umask in your shell initialization files. If your shell initialization files don't set a umask, you'll still have umask 022 because that's what FreeBSD gives all users by default. This default and others are set in the /etc/login.conf file.

The umask gives the permissions that are *not* provided on new files.

You can see your umask with the umask command:

```
$ umask
022
```

A `umask` of 022 means new directories will be created with permissions 755. Write permission, which has a value of 2, is denied to all but the user-owner, but read and execute, summing to 5, are provided for the group-owner and, in fact, all others.

New regular files will be created with permissions 644. Again, write permission is denied to all but the user-owner, so the only permission granted to the group-owner and others is read permission.

These permissions, 755 for directories and 644 for files, are usually just what you want, with a couple of exceptions.

First, when you create a file you want to be able to run, like a shell script with commands in it, the file needs to be executable. Regular files are never created with executable permissions. To make it executable you change its permissions to 744 (so the owner can run it) or 755 (so anyone can run it). Suppose it's called `myscript`:

```
$ chmod 755 myscript
```

or

```
$ chmod ugo+x myscript
```

makes it executable by all. A long directory listing will show `-rwxr-xr-x` for the file.

Second, your home directory was created (as they all are) with 755 permissions on the directory. On a directory, an `x` gives the ability to traverse the directory. That means you, as the owner, can read, write, and move across the directories (`cd` to subdirectories), but the group-owner (which is, by default, the same as the user-owner) can too, and so can the rest of the world. Your home directory is readable by any user on the system.

```
xanne@pninety /home $ ls -l
total 5
drwxr-xr-x   6 root   wheel   -   512 Jun 25 15:51 ./
drwxr-xr-x  19 root   wheel   -   512 Mar 20 15:03 ../
drwxr-xr-x   2 spike  spike   -   512 Jul  3 17:29 spike/
drwxr-xr-x   2 vicki  vicki   -   512 Jul  9 03:21 vicki/
drwxr-xr-x  11 xanne  xanne   -  1024 Jul  7 23:12 xanne/
```

So users spike and vicki can cd to xanne's home directory and read anything that's world readable—and execute any scripts that are world executable.

Luckily a quick chmod fixes this problem:

```
xanne@pninety /home $ chmod 711 xanne
xanne@pninety /home $ ls -la
total 5
drwxr-xr-x   6 root   wheel   512 Jun 25 15:51 .
drwxr-xr-x  19 root   wheel   512 Mar 20 15:03 ..
drwxr-xr-x   2 spike  spike   512 Jul  3 17:29 spike
drwxr-xr-x   2 vicki  vicki   512 Jul  9 03:21 vicki
drwx--x--x  11 xanne  xanne  1024 Jul  7 23:12 xanne
```

Now spike can cd to xanne's home directory, but he won't be able to list the files. He will still be able to read the world-readable files, but only if he knows their names.

Going to the Library

Not everyone needs to own a copy of *The Moon Is a Harsh Mistress* to be able to read it, and not every program needs to have built into it the capability to do something like displaying characters on the screen. Instead, the programs depend on files they share with other programs, called libraries.

I hope you never have to worry about them.

When your system boots, it prepares lists of libraries and where they can be found. A list is created for each of the two kinds of binaries on the system—aout binaries and elf binaries (most are elf). These lists of libraries save a lot of search time, since a program knows just where to find the files it needs that aren't part of it. They're called *hint* files.

The /etc/defaults/rc.conf file tells the system where the libraries are located. You should not need to change this.

But sometimes—when a program can't find a library—you want to know what's in the hints file. The command to read what's in the hints file for `elf` libraries (it reads the file `/var/run/ld-elf.so.hints`) is:

```
$ ldconfig -r or ldconfig -elf -r
/var/run/ld-elf.so.hints:
        search directories:
    /usr/lib:/usr/lib/compat:/usr/X11R6/lib:/usr/l
    ocal/lib
        0:-lcom_err.2 => /usr/lib/libcom_err.so.2
        1:-lscrypt.2 => /usr/lib/libscrypt.so.2
        2:-lcrypt.2 => /usr/lib/libcrypt.so.2
        3:-lm.2 => /usr/lib/libm.so.2
        ...
```

If you want to see the lists for `aout` libraries, the command, which reads the `/var/run/ld.so.hints` file, is

```
$ ldconfig -aout -r
/var/run/ld.so.hints:
        search directories:
    /usr/lib/aout:/usr/lib/compat/aout:/usr/X11R6/
    lib/aout
        0:-lresolv.1.1 =>
    /usr/lib/compat/aout/libresolv.so.1.1
        1:-lgnumalloc.1.1 =>
    /usr/lib/compat/aout/libgnumalloc.so.1.1
        2:-lrpcsvc.1.1 =>
    /usr/lib/compat/aout/librpcsvc.so.1.1
        3:-lskey.1.1 =>
    ...
```

After you install a few programs you might have over a hundred libraries on the system, so it's a good idea to pipe the output of these commands to `more`.

The `ldconfig -m` command will merge the libraries listed in a particular directory into the hints file. If you want to update the hints file with what's in `/usr/local/lib`, you type:

```
# ldconfig -m /usr/local/lib
```

The ldd command shows you the libraries on which a binary depends:

```
$ ldd /usr/local/bin/lynx
/usr/local/bin/lynx:
        libz.so.2 => /usr/lib/libz.so.2 (0x2814d000)
        libncurses.so.5 => /usr/lib/libncurses.so.5
    (0x2815a000)
        libc.so.4 => /usr/lib/libc.so.4 (0x2819b000)
```

Giving Orders in Advance

The file /etc/crontab is the system's crontab—a table of orders to FreeBSD about programs to run as scheduled. Those already in the table should be left alone except for changing their times if you wish.

As an example, if you wanted to add an entry to the table to run a script in the bin directory of spike's home directory once a week at 4:20 a.m., this line in crontab would do it:

```
20  4  *  *  4  spike  /usr/home/spike/bin/myscript
```

The column header in the file looks like this:

```
#minute hour mday month wday who command
```

The # at the beginning of the line means the line is a comment and not a command line. The columns don't have to line up in the file, although making them do so makes it easier to read.

Using the column headers as a guide, the first column of the new command orders cron to run this command at 20 minutes after the hour. The second column tells it which hour (24-hour clock). There's a * in the next two columns since mday (day of the month) and month are not at issue here, only wday or weekday. The column for who runs the command must be filled in, as well as the command—that's what `cron` will run.

TIP

A command in `crontab` needs a full path name; the executable file is in a path `cron` doesn't know about.

The `/etc/crontab` file is reread every minute or two, so nothing need be done to activate a change except editing and saving the file.

WARNING

FreeBSD and other BSDs also allow user crontabs in `/var/cron/tab`. To create or edit these crontabs (and `root` as a user can have a crontab there too) the `crontab` *command* is used. The format of these files is identical to that of `/etc/crontab` except for the absence of a *who* column. Don't use the `crontab` command to edit the `/etc/crontab` file or you'll risk getting a copy of it in `/var/cron/tab` with unpredictable results.

Three man pages cover all of `cron` and the `crontabs`: `cron`, `crontab (1)`, which is about the command, and `crontab(5)`, which explains the syntax for `crontab` files.

Speeding Up the File System

FreeBSD 4.1 and later versions come with *soft updates*, thanks to its inventor, Kirk McKusick, a major figure in the development of Berkeley UNIX. Soft updates makes the file system faster, which means it can read from and write to the hard drives more quickly. It also makes an unexpected shutdown from the dog pulling the power cord out of the wall less risky.

It's up to you to enable soft updates on each file system. You don't want to run in on / (not very much gets written there anyway, so there's little point). To enable soft updates on `/var` and `/usr`, follow these steps:

1. **Boot into single-user mode (you might want to do this at other times too, so it's useful to know how) by doing this:**

2. **Shut down the computer with** `/sbin/shutdown -h now`

3. **On reboot, just as the baton starts twirling, press the spacebar.**

   You see `boot:`

4. **Type** `/kernel -s`

   If you don't press the spacebar soon enough, you get a message that the kernel is already loaded or can't be found (the prompt will be an **ok**). Type **`unload kernel`** and then **`boot /kernel -s`**

5. **Press Enter when it asks for a default shell, or type** `tcsh` **for the** **`tcsh`** **shell.**

6. **Type** `cat /etc/fstab` **to see your file systems. At the left of the display you see something like this:**

```
# Device          Mountpoint        FStype
/dev/da1s1b       none              swap
/dev/da1s1a       /                 ufs
/dev/da1s1f       /usr              ufs
/dev/da1s1e       /var              ufs
```

7. **For each** **`ufs`** **(FreeBSD) file system other than** **`/`,** **type** `tunefs -n enable <device>`. **For the file systems mounted on** **`/usr`** **and** **`/var`**, **type (substituting the device names on your system):**

```
# tunefs -n enable /dev/da1s1f
# tunefs -n enable /dev/da1s1e
```

   For each device name, you see a message telling you soft updates have been enabled.

8. **Type** `exit` **to leave single-user mode and continue booting.**

You can check that soft updates are working with the command:

```
$ mount
```

You see a display that shows you soft updates enabled on `/usr` and `/var`, but not on `/`:

```
/dev/da1s1a on / (ufs, local, writes: sync 2547
     async 7544, reads: sync 946 async 11)
/dev/da1s1f on /usr (ufs, local, soft-updates,
```

```
    writes: sync 32 async 9343, reads: sync 45549
    async 211)
/dev/da1s1e on /var (ufs, local, soft-updates,
    writes: sync 308 async 8762, reads: sync 2878
    async 58)
```

This change is permanent—you only have to do it once. The command to undo soft updates is `tunefs -n disable` <*device*>.

Chapter 8

Editing Files

Getting connected to the Internet, setting up sound, configuring `X`, and writing up for your chile receipe for your web page means you have to edit (or even create) files. For that you need a text editor. FreeBSD comes with a couple of text editors already installed. You can add others, and even a whole office suite. This chapter covers:

- choosing an editor
- using `vi`, the universal UNIX editor
- a better `vi`: `vim`, and
- the `pico` editor.

FreeBSD's Easy Editor, `ee`, is your first friend—easy to get to know, but a bit shallow. I tell you about using `ee`—what there is of it— in Chapter 5.

The other editor included with FreeBSD is `vi` (call it vee-eye if you dare to talk about this stuff out loud). It can do amazing things and exists on virtually every version of UNIX around the world—so if you can handle `vi`, you can handle anything. This chapter shows you some `vi` basics so you can begin to use `vi` right away and describes a few nifty things you can do with this editor.

I also mention some other options—including `vim` (an improved `vi`), `pico`, `emacs`, and the full-fledged word processors you can install on FreeBSD.

Editors: Your Choice

FreeBSD comes with two full-screen text editors, `ee` (see Chapter 5) and `vi`. Many other editors can be installed easily. Most of them offer a few more features than `ee` and are easier to use but less powerful than `vi`. A few other editors, like `vim`, are `vi` variants—`vi` with added features and conveniences. Some are `vi` stripped down a bit so that they take less space and memory.

The `emacs` editor does much more than just edit—you can use it to read and send mail, read USENET news, manage files, and much more. It takes longer to learn, but it may be worth it. It's a favorite program for many people, especially programmers, and is available in a text version and an X version with many add-ins. Not covered in this book, `emacs` is a space hog and a memory hog, but a very versatile pig. It's supposedly self-documenting, and if you believe that, I have some jewelry you might be interested in.

TIP

The `pico` editor gets installed when you install the `pine` mail program. Chapters 9 and 10 tell you about installing third-party software

Three word processors, all requiring the X Window System, are:

- AbiWord. Abi-Word (you run it by typing `abiword` after you install it) is open-source, free software.

- StarOffice from Sun Microsystems is a full-fledged office suite with a word processor, spreadsheet, database, and presentation manager. Free for individual users, it's the closest of the three to a Microsoft Office work-alike.

- WordPerfect is Corel's word processor, and it works just like the Microsoft Windows version. It's free for individual users.

All three also have versions available for Windows, and all three can read Microsoft Word 97 documents. StarOffice also handles spreadsheets and presentation software. Chapters 10 and 11 have more information on installation.

Vying with vi

TIP

The `vi` editor is a wretched thing, frustrating and confusing (only at first, I hope). It's worth learning for two reasons:

- `vi` is a very powerful editor—you can do things with it you can't do with anything in Windows.

- `vi` is the universal UNIX editor, probably available on any UNIX machine you'll ever log in to anywhere in the world.

The `vi` editor has so many commands that no one (no one I know, anyway) uses them all, so each person's `vi` is a little different. You don't have to learn it all at once— in fact you can't—but you can begin using it knowing just a few commands.

Giving Basic vi Commands

You edit a file in `vi` by typing:

```
$ vi <filename>
```

You move through the text with the arrow keys. Pressing **Esc** puts `vi` in command mode. In command mode you're talking to `vi` and telling it what to do instead of entering text into your document.

Table 8-1 lists some basic `vi` commands. `Vi` starts in command mode. Once you type **`a`** or **`i`**, you can insert text (you're in insert mode, not command mode). Pressing one of the arrow keys completes an insert and lets you move elsewhere in the file to insert text (except in `vim`, where you have to press Esc before you move around).

TIP

Pressing **Esc** always puts you back in command mode, where you can save the file with **`:w`**, save and exit with **`:wq`**, or exit without saving changes with **`:q!`**.

That doesn't sound so hard, does it? Every editor or word processor needs to know, when you type something, whether it's receiving instructions from you or whether it's just supposed to put what you type in the document.

When you press **Esc**, `vi` knows that what comes next are instructions, not text. Some of the commands start with **`:`** (a colon) and some don't.

Table 8-1 Basic vi Commands

Command	*What It Does*
x	deletes the letter under the cursor
dd	deletes the entire line (even if it wraps on the screen)
i	lets you insert text at the cursor
a	lets you insert text after the cursor
:w	saves the file to disk and lets you continue working
:wq	saves to disk and exits
:q!	exits without saving changes
u	undoes the last edit; press `Esc` first
:help	gets on-screen help

Undoing Disaster

WARNING

What makes `vi` tricky is that the commands that don't start with `:` don't show up on the screen, so you can't be quite sure what you've told `vi` to do. Is this really so odd? When I use shortcut keys in Microsoft Word, like Ctrl-s to save my document, I don't see anything on the screen.

Suppose you try to insert a number in your text and call your airplane a 747 Boeing. You try to type 747 and nothing happens because you're in command mode. You press `i` for insert, type `747 Boeing`, press an arrow key to move somewhere else, and you get `747 Boeing` repeated on your screen 747 times! That's a lot of airplanes.

What to do? Press **Esc u** and it will undo the mess.

You can also press **`:q!`** to exit without saving; but that discards all your changes since you last pressed **`:w`** (for write to disk).

Disaster Protection

Whatever surprises you get from `vi`, you can protect yourself by:

- Saving often with **`:w`**
- Pressing **Esc** once or twice (or until `vi` rings a bell to tell you you're already in command mode) to cancel any previous commands whenever you're unsure about what's going on.

The single-letter commands are `vi` commands. The ones that start with `:` are also part of `ex`, a line editor that comes with FreeBSD and graces, if you can call it that, virtually all UNIX systems, since `vi` is really just a full-screen visual interface to `ex`. Why would you want to know? Sometimes the available help makes a distinction.

TIP

Another line editor, called `ed`, is difficult to use but is the only editor available when you get in trouble and are limited to what's in the `/` partition of your drive. I tell you how to use `ed` in such dire situations in Chapter 19.

Getting Help

In most versions of `vi` (FreeBSD actually uses `nvi`) typing **`:help`** will show you some commands.

TIP

You can install `vilearn`, a `vi` tutorial, if you like a more systematic rather than experimental approach to learning. It's available as a port or a package (see Chapters 9 and 10).

Going Places with vi

`Vi` has more ways to move around than a go-go dancer. You probably already know some of them ways to move around because they're the same as the commands used by `more` and `less` and the commands used to move around man pages:

- **Ctrl+f** takes you forward a page.
- **Ctrl+b** goes back a page.

- **1G** goes to the beginning of the file.
- **G** goes to the end of the file.
- ***n*G** goes to the *n*th line of the file.

Ctrl+g shows you information about the file—its name and number of lines.

Searching for Lost Causes

Searching is not only a good way to find something; it's also a good way to move around. Searching is just like searching a man page or a file you're looking at with `more`:

```
/some text
```

searches forward for *some text* and goes right to the start of it. A **?** searches backwards:

```
?some text
```

TIP

Typing **n** repeats the search in the same direction, and **N** repeats it in the opposite direction.

Searching, like UNIX in general, is case-sensitive. Sometimes it helps to leave off the first letter of a word, which might or might not be capitalized. Typing **:se iclower** will make searching case-insensitive if what's typed is all lower case.

Substituting the Good for the Bad and the Evil

You can turn Republicans into Democrats and boys into girls (and the other way around!) without much trouble in `vi`. You don't even have to send out a brochure.

TIP

The text you want to change (the bad stuff) always comes first.

The basic command to make a substitution is **:s**. It works on the line the cursor is on (even though the command shows up at the bottom of the screen) and only on the first instance of the text you want to change—unless you tell it to do more.

Table 8-2 summarizes substitution commands.

Table 8-2 vi Substitutions

Command	*What It Does*
:s/bad/good/	substitutes good for bad in the line you're on, but only for the first "bad" it finds
:%s/bad/good	substitutes good for bad on all lines of the file but only the first "bad" in each line The % is what tells `vi` to do it on all lines.
:%s/bad/good/g	substitutes good for bad on all lines of the file and all instances of "bad"
:%s/bad/good/gc	substitutes good for bad on all lines of the file and all instances of "bad"—and asks for confirmation of each change
:s/^/#/	inserts a # at the beginning of the line
:8,10s/^/hi there /	puts the text "hi there " at the beginning of lines 8 through 10
:11,13s/$/bye/	puts the text "bye" at the end of lines 11 through 13
:.,+3s/bad/good/	substitutes "good" for "bad" (first instance in each line) on the line you're on (that's what the dot stands for) and the three following lines
:%s/$/Ctrl+vCtrl+M//	substitutes nothing for ^M all though the file
:%s/ //	substitutes nothing for eight spaces (the first block of eight it finds) in the line the cursor is on

Here are the hieroglyphics:

- **%** stands for the entire file
- Line numbers on which to operate are separated with a comma, so **5,7** stands for lines 5 through 7 of the file.
- **$** stands for the end of the line
- ^ stands for the beginning of the line.
- **.** —a dot—stands for the line where the cursor is located.
- **g** stands for global and means "not just the first one, all of them!"
- **c** stands for confirm and lets you say yes or no to a substitution.

TIP

You separate the bad text and the good text with a `/`, although you could use something instead of a `/` as the separator. Try the + sign instead if the text you want to replace has a slash mark within it. Or put a backslash (\) in front of a `/` within the text to tell `vi` the `/` is part of the text, not a separator.

TIP

You put line numbers on your screen with the **:se nu** command, which is short for set line numbering on. You turn off line number with **:se nonu**.

TIP

When you transfer a text file from DOS/Windows, sometimes it ends up with a `^M` (which stands for carriage return-line feed, or the Enter key) at the end of every line. This isn't what UNIX systems use, and you want to get rid of it. A **Ctrl+v** is the message to `vi` to treat the next thing you type literally, even if it's a control key. **Ctrl+v** works in both insert and command mode.

Exports and Imports

You can export and import entire files around the world with email, but sometimes you just want to export part of a file to a new file or import an entire file into the one you're editing.

Exporting All or Part of a File

You can save the file you're editing to a new filename with this command:

```
:w newname
```

and continue to edit the original file.

To save lines 55 to 65, you type:

```
:55,65w newname
```

To add more text to the file `newname`, you use a command like this:

```
:75,80w >>newname
```

and lines 75 through 80 get added to `newname`. It's the >> symbols that get the text appended to the file.

Inserting a File

To incorporate `file2` into `file1`, you use the **`:r`** command. While you're editing `file1`, you command `vi` to read `file2`:

```
:r file2
```

and all of `file2` will be inserted after the line the cursor is on.

Getting a Date

This date won't pay for dinner or the movie, but at least it will be there for you.

TIP

The **`:r`** can read in a file, but that's not all it can read. If you follow it with a **`!`** (called a bang in everyday Unixspeak) and a UNIX command, it will put the output of the command into the file. Say you want to put the date in your file. You command `vi`:

```
:r !date
```

and the current date is inserted into your document. You can insert the output of commands like `df` the same way.

When the Arrow Keys Don't Work

If the arrow keys don't work in command mode because of terminal problems, you can move around (in command mode) with:

j to go up a line

k to go down a line

h to go left

l to go right

Cutting and Pasting

You cut the line the cursor is on with **`dd`**, and you paste it with **`p`**. To cut four lines, the command is:

```
4dd
```

and the paste command is still **`p`**. You can paste those four lines as often as you like. They get pasted after the line to which you move the cursor. `Vi` can't paste within a line.

If you want to copy (not cut) and paste, the commands are **`yy`** and **`p`**. Thus, **`yy`** copies a line, and **`3yy`** copies three lines, all of which get pasted with **`p`** after the line to which you move the cursor. Table 8-3 summarizes some of these commands.

But that's not enough, is it? You want to copy a line (or more) in `file1` and paste it into `file2`. Here are the steps:

```
$ vi file1
```

Use the arrow keys to go to the line you want to copy. Type:

```
yy
```

If you made any changes to `file1`, save it with **:w.** Type:

```
:e file2
```

Use the arrow keys to go to the line before the place where you want to put the line. Type:

```
p
```

Table 8-3 Some vi Specifics

Command	*What It Does*
yy	Copies the line where the cursor is.
p	Pastes the copied line or lines to the line after the cursor (`vi` can't paste within a line)
r	Replaces the character the cursor is on with the character you type next
R	Replaces multiple characters—you can keep on typing and overwriting
J	Joins the next line to the current line

A Few vi Tricks

You can do some editing with `vi` right in command mode—with the **r** and **R** commands.

You press **r** while the cursor is on a letter you want to change, and then press the replacement. It's a one-shot deal.

You press **R** and you can replace not only the letter the cursor is on, but the letters following it.

You can do some more dramatic deleting, too. Pressing **x** deletes the character under the cursor—but **5x** deletes five characters (and so forth!). A **dd** will delete a line—but **10dd** deletes 10 lines.

- **d$** deletes from the cursor to the end of the line
- **dG** deletes from the cursor to the end of the file

You can insert a non-printing character in a file (in insert mode) with **Ctrl+v<*character*>**. For example, if you want a real Esc character, you:

1. **Press** `i` **for insert mode**
2. **Press** `Ctrl+vEsc`

An Esc character in your file looks like `^[`, but when you move over it with the right arrow key, you'll discover it's only one character (if it's not, you didn't get the Esc character in there).

TIP

`Vi` will repeat the last editing command you gave her if you press (in command mode) `.` (dot).

You can repeat the last search-and-replace command with **&**.

TIP

The **:set all** command shows you all the variables you can set in `vi`. You can set any of them with **:se**. Say you want tab stops of four spaces instead of eight. You type:

```
:se tabstop=4
```

This setting is just for the current session—tabstops go back to the default when you exit. When `vi` loads, it reads the file `.exrc` in your home directory. You can create this file (with `vi`, of course!) and put into it:

```
set tabstop=4
```

to always give you tab stops of four instead of eight spaces, and similarly with other variables.

vim: A Better vi

`Vim` does a few tricks `vi` hasn't learned. The most useful is editing two or more files on the screen at the same time, making it easy to copy and paste between them.

You install `vim` as a port or package (Chapters 9 and 10) and then type:

```
$ vim -o file1 file2
```

and press Enter a second time when `vim` tells you what it's going to do. Then `vim` comes up with a split screen and shows you both files. To switch from one to the other, type:

```
Ctrl+ww
```

You can use **yy** to copy a line in one file, switch to the other file, and press **p** to paste the lines into the second file. This is especially convenient when you're working on a kernel configuration file (Chapter 16).

The Pico Editor

The `pico` editor is a favorite with new users. `Pico` comes with the `pine` mail program, so you install `pine` as a package or as a port to get `pico` (see Chapters 9 and 10). `Pine` itself uses `pico`.

`Pico` comes, as does `pine`, with a display of on-screen commands—letters preceded by a ^ symbol, like ^R. That means you press **Ctrl+r** (it doesn't have to be a capital R) and you'll be prompted for a file to insert into the file you're editing. Help comes with **Ctrl+g**, or ^G. You cut a line with **Ctrl+k** (or a series of lines) and paste them back in, if you want them, with **Ctrl+u**.

Pico Problems

WARNING

`Pico`'s biggest disadvantage is that when you start it the normal way, with `pico <filename>`, it wraps the text at about 83 characters, puts a hard carriage return in the file, and starts a new line. That's OK for mail messages, but it's a problem with configuration files. You insert text, `pico` wraps—and you've got a new line. The new line will be read as part of the configuration file and will be misunderstood, and your file won't work.

TIP

When you edit a file that has configuration information—anything in the `/etc` directory or any of the files beginning with a `.` (a dot) in your home directory, your kernel configuration file, script files, and lots of other files, you should start `pico`, if you use it, like this:

```
$ pico -w <filename>
```

That turns off wrapping. The line just continues, and `pico` puts a `$` sign at the end of the line on the screen to show you that there's really more text there. You can see it by scrolling to the right with the right arrow key.

`Pico` doesn't seem to have any way to insert the output of a command in a file (no dates here!) or to insert a control character (like Esc) in a file. Nor does it have search-and-replace. It can't do everything `vi` and `vim` can do, but it's easier.

The Pilot Bonus

With `pine` you get not only `pico`, but also `pilot`, a text-based file navigator that makes it possible to move around the directory structure with the arrow keys and the Enter key to look at a file. Like `pico`, it has on-screen commands.

With the cursor on a filename, you can press **E** to edit it (it opens the file with the editor assigned to the `EDITOR` variable in your shell configuration files). If you're already looking at a file because you pressed Enter, you edit it by pressing **v**.

Chapter 9

Ready-to-Run Packages

More than 5,000 third-party software applications, ready to install and run, are available for FreeBSD. They are not really part of FreeBSD, but FreeBSD helps you get and install this software. And more software applications become available virtually every day.

You wouldn't want to install all these applications—you'd end up with a bunch of text editors and a slew of programs to read your mail, and duplicates of quite a few of them in Japanese, Russian, and several other foreign languages. But in addition to just plain useful programs, there are some real gems here—like a free counterpart to Adobe's PhotoShop, software to burn CD-ROMs, office suites, and much more.

Most of these applications come in two forms: a package and a port. Although some software comes in only one form, either a package or a port, you can install most software either way—the result is the same.

Packages are ready-to-run software. You install a package with a simple one-line command and the software is ready to go and in the right place on your hard drive. Packages are the quickest way to get the software you want onto your computer.

This chapter tells you:

- how to install packages
- how to find out what files the package installed and how you run the software, and
- how to delete a package.

Packages versus Ports

Packages and ports are different ways to get the same software. The difference between packages and ports is that packages are already *compiled* or *built*—they are *binaries*. Packages don't come with their source code—the human-readable files that the programmers wrote. Ports do. A port gets the source code from the Internet, builds the software right on your computer, and installs it.

The computer engineers (like Satoshi Asami) who create FreeBSD make the packages from the ports collection—a tip-off that what gets installed really is the same.

Why Packages Are Better Than Ports

Sometimes packages are better than ports, and sometimes ports are better. Here are the advantages of packages:

- Packages are quicker. Because the software is already in binary form, it's ready to install—it doesn't have to be built first. This is especially nice if your computer doesn't have much RAM (memory). If it has 32MB or less, some software takes a long time to build.

- Packages take less space. Whether you get a package from a CD-ROM or over the Internet, the only space it takes is the space for the software application itself.

  Ports need the ports collection—files on your hard drive that tell FreeBSD where to get the source code for an application and how to build it and install it. Hard drive space is also needed to actually do the building, and sometimes the build process itself requires some software that isn't necessary later.

- Packages are easier—with less chance for error and fewer puzzles.

Why Ports Are Better Than Packages

Sometimes ports can be better than packages.

- Installing the ports collection on your hard drive (more about that in Chapter 10, if you haven't already done it) gives you information about the software you can install—what it does, where it will get installed, and whether there's a version of a port more recent than the one you have installed. (The ports collection isn't the application software itself; it's just the installation framework.)
- Because ports get built, you have an opportunity to select special features.
- Some applications are only available as ports.

Installing Packages

You can install packages from a CD-ROM or by FTP. Installing from the CD-ROM is quick—and essential if you aren't connected to the Internet. Installing by FTP gives you a wider choice of packages.

Installing Packages from the CD-ROM

The easiest way to install packages is from the installation CD-ROM (the other CDs also have packages). Chapter 4 tells you how to install packages while you install FreeBSD.

ON CD-1

Put the CD-ROM in the drive (don't mount it) and type:

```
$ su
Password: [it won't echo]
# /stand/sysinstall
```

You see the `/stand/sysinstall Main Menu`, shown in Figure 9-1.

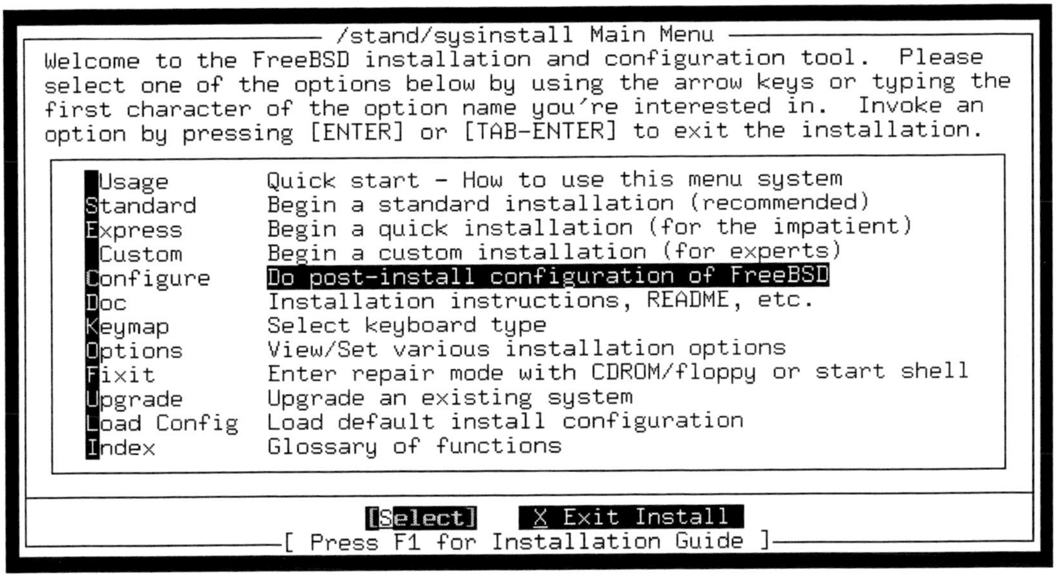

Figure 9-1: Configuring FreeBSD After Installation

1. **Use the arrow keys to select** `Configure  Do a post-install configuration of FreeBSD`

2. **Press** Enter.

   You see the `FreeBSD Configuration Menu`.

3. **Use the arrow keys to select** `Packages  Install pre-packaged software for FreeBSD`

4. **Press** Enter.

5. **Press** Enter **to select** `Install from a FreeBSD CDROM`

   You see the `Package Selection` menu.

TIP From this menu you can select any number of packages in any categories. In this example, you go to the `shells` category and select `bash` for installation.

6. **Use the arrow keys to select** `shells  Various shells (tcsh, bash, etc)`

7. **Press** Enter.

8. **Use the arrow keys to select** `bash` **(the first item) and press the spacebar so an** X **shows up next to** `bash`**:**

```
[X] bash-2.03        [/usr/ports/shells/bash2]
```

9. **Press** Enter **to accept your choice.** You see the `Package Selection` menu.

   Select additional packages in other categories if you like.

   WARNING

   Packages already installed will have an X next to them. Pressing the spacebar when the highlight is on an installed package clears the X; the package will be deleted (you get a chance to confirm this action).

10. **Press** Tab **to highlight** `[Install]` **and press** Enter. You get a chance to accept the list of packages you've selected.

11. **When your packages are installed, press** Tab **to highlight** Cancel **and return to a previous menu—eventually the one that allows you to highlight** `[X Exit Install]`**. Press** Enter **to exit!**

12. **Even if you select no packages, you have to choose** `[Install]` **to continue if the** `[Cancel]` **option isn't available. Just press** Enter **when it says** `no packages selected for extraction`

    If the list is not to your liking, press Tab **to select** `[Cancel]`**.** You see the `Package Selection` menu again, and must select the category for the package you don't want and clear the X next to it by using the spacebar.

    TIP

    If things get so confused and mixed up you don't know what will be installed or uninstalled, press Ctrl-c and then Enter to get out of `/stand/sysinstall` without doing anything. Usually you can exit from `/stand/sysinstall` by choosing `[Cancel]` on one menu after another until you get to `[X Exit Install]`.

When you select a package, FreeBSD automatically selects other packages necessary to install or run the package you choose. You don't have to worry about that.

The CD-ROM has about 1,800 packages on it, but almost three times that many exist. The set of four CD-ROMs from BSDI-Walnut Creek (now owned by Wind River Systems) includes the other packages, and you install packages from them the same way (you press Enter to say that you really do want to use the CD in the drive if necessary).

TIP

The package files are actually located on the CD-ROM in `/cdrom/packages/All` in compressed form and have a `.tgz` extension. From the command prompt, you can mount the CD-ROM with `/sbin/mount /cdrom`. Then type `cd /cdrom/packages/All` and look at the file listing with `ls -l`. The size of the files are shown in kilobytes in the fifth column. The command `ls -l netscape*` shows you a line like this, among others:

```
-rw-r--r--  1 root  wheel   9321038 Mar 18 03:38
    netscape-navigator-4.72.tgz
```

The compressed package for this version of Netscape is over 9MB. Rule of thumb: the installed package will be about three times the size of the compressed package, not counting other "helper" software it might install.

Installing Packages by FTP

FTP stands for File Transfer Protocol. Protocols are just a set of conventions for computers to talk to each other—but when computers talk, you can get what they've got. If you have an Internet connection, you can install packages by FTP.

You follow the same steps for installing packages from a CD-ROM listed above, except you don't have to put the CD-ROM in the drive, and you choose `FTP Install from an FTP Server` from the `Choose Installation Media` menu. When the packages install, you see a screen like that shown in Figure 9-2.

```
Adding packages/All/wget-1.5.3.tgz
from ftp://ftp.freebsd.org/pub/FreeBSD/releases/i386/
```

Figure 9-2: A Package Being Installed by FTP

TIP

One hitch (it couldn't be that simple, right?). When you choose FTP, FreeBSD looks at the name of the FreeBSD release that's installed, and tries to get the packages for the right version. If your FreeBSD installation has been upgraded since you installed it, the release name might not match anything available by FTP. You can either change the release name temporarily as described in the last section of this chapter, Installing Packages After Upgrading, or install the package by hand.

Installing Packages by Hand

If your only Internet connection is from a computer that isn't running FreeBSD and what you want isn't on the CD-ROM, you can get a package

FTP Mirrors

The ftp.freebsd.org ftp site is mirrored (copied) on other servers in the United States and around the world.

You'll notice in the FTP example at the end of the chapter that I used a FreeBSD mirror, ftp9.freebsd.org, rather than ftp.freebsd.org. This mirror keeps its FreeBSD files in a subdirectory of `/pub` called `os`. FTP servers may be different (and every now and then, like failing government agencies, they get reorganized). You may have to look around to find the FreeBSD directory (case-sensitive). Once you find it, though, the arrangement of subdirectories of FreeBSD should be the same on all servers.

Often one of the mirrors will be faster than ftp.freebsd.org, either because it's closer to you or because it's less busy. Only the primary site, ftp.freebsd.org, is likely to have the latest ISO images, in case you want to burn an ISO to a CD-ROM.

by hand, move it to your FreeBSD box, and install it. Once you get it to FreeBSD, install it by typing (as `root`)

```
# pkg_add <packagename>
```

To get a package by hand you follow these steps:

1. **Log in as `root`.**
2. **Type `ftp ftp.freebsd.org`**
3. **Log in to the server by typing `ftp` when it asks for `Name:` and your email address as your password.**
4. **Type `cd /pub/FreeBSD/ports/i386`**
5. **Type `ls` to get a listing of the packages for different versions of FreeBSD.**

WARNING

You see a list like the following. Notice `packages` is linked to `packages-stable`, which is in turn linked to yet another file, in this case to `packages-4-stable`. That's probably what you want, but always check it out. If you have an earlier version of FreeBSD, get packages compiled for your version—and don't be seduced by "current"—it's the experimental version of FreeBSD.

```
lrwxrwxrwx  ...  Sep  3  2000 packages -> packages-
     stable
...
lrwxrwxrwx  ...  Sep  3  2000 packages-4-current ->
     packages-4-stable
drwxrwxr-x   ... Apr 13 22:59 packages-4-stable
lrwxrwxrwx   ... Sep  3  2000 packages-4.0-current ->
     packages-4-current
dr-xr-xr-x   ... Mar 13  2000 packages-4.0-release
lrwxrwxrwx   ... Sep  3  2000 packages-4.0-stable ->
     packages-4-stable
dr-xr-xr-x   ... Jul 22  2000 packages-4.1-release
lrwxrwxrwx   ... Sep  3  2000 packages-4.1-stable ->
     packages-4-stable
dr-xr-xr-x   ... Sep 23  2000 packages-4.1.1-release
lrwxrwxrwx   ... Sep 23  2000 packages-4.1.1-stable -
     > packages-4-stable
drwxrwxr-x   ... Nov 20 09:06 packages-4.2-release
lrwxrwxrwx   ... Nov  4 16:05 packages-4.2-stable ->
     packages-4-stable
```

```
lrwxrwxrwx   ... Mar 14 11:09 packages-4.3-release ->
     packages-4-stable
lrwxrwxrwx   ... Mar 25 19:51 packages-4.3-stable ->
     packages-4-stable
drwxrwxr-x   ... Mar 30 16:59 packages-5-current
lrwxrwxrwx   ... Sep  3  2000 packages-5.0-current ->
     packages-5-current
lrwxrwxrwx   ... Sep  3  2000 packages-current ->
     packages-5-current
lrwxrwxrwx   ... Sep  3  2000 packages-stable ->
     packages-4-stable
```

6. **Type `ls` to see the list of packages, or `ls x*` to see the list of packages starting with the letter `x`.**

   One of the benefits of looking at the list is that you see the size of the packages (in kilobytes). Even though they're compressed, you get an idea of which ones are monsters and which are minor matters.

7. **Type `get` *`<packagename>`* to download the package to your computer.**

   TIP: Most FTP clients let you press Tab to complete a filename.

8. **When the package is downloaded, log in as `root` and type `pkg_add` *`<packagename>`* in the directory where you put the package.**

TIP: The packages always have a `.tgz` extension, which means that they're a compressed collection of files. The `t` is for `tar`, or tape archive—a term left over from the days when the `tar` program was used primarily to back up files to tape. The `gz` is for `gzip`, a program for compressing files so they take less space, similar to DOS `zip`. Don't try to decompress or extract these tarballs yourself—`pkg_add` won't know what to do with them then.

WARNING: Not all files that have a `.tgz` extension are FreeBSD packages; some are just compressed collections of files. A FreeBSD package is special because it includes information used by `pkg_add` when it's installed.

Finding Out About Packages

If the FreeBSD ports collection is installed on your hard drive, you have a great source of information about add-on software right at hand. There's also an overview of software and specifics on some programs in Chapter 11.

If the ports collection isn't installed, you can use the Internet to find out about software available for FreeBSD.

Use your browser to go to http://www.freebsd.org/ports/

About three screens down, there's a list of the same categories of software on the CD-ROM and the FTP sites and, of course, applications within the categories. Happy browsing! The applications are in alphabetical order within the categories. UNIX sorts capital letters before lower-case letters (and numbers come before letters). You want to keep this in mind if you're looking for something like `Abi-Word` and it's not in the `a`'s.

Each software application has a link called `Long description` (a page or less) you can click on to read about it.

Each application also lists the other software it requires—a tip-off on how much stuff will get installed to help it run if it isn't already installed.

WARNING

The `Package` link lets you download the package right from the web, but the package links may be to packages for a different version of FreeBSD than the one you have installed. The FTP site is safer, so you know what you're getting.

The link to `Sources` is a link to the sources FreeBSD needs to build and install the port. If you download from there, the sources go in `/usr/ports/distfiles`. See Chapter 10.

TIP

On the http://www.freebsd.org/ports web page, the link `Download a gzip'd tar file of all 5,045 ports` is the up-to-date ports collection itself. (The number may be different.) It's one way to install the ports collection. You move the file to `/usr` after you download it and type:

```
/usr # tar xzf ports.tar.gz
```

to install it. The `x` is for extract, the `z` decompresses it, and `f` stands for the file on which you want to perform this operation—the one you downloaded, `ports.tar.gz`.

Using the ports collection is the topic of Chapter 10, but you can install packages from `/usr/ports/`*<category>* by typing `pkg_add -r` *<portname>*, just as the port name appears in the listing in the `/usr/ports/`*<category>* directory.

Finding Your Software

Finding your software after you install it can be worse than hunting down your car after a football game when you didn't bother to notice where you parked it. Unfortunately you can't hang around the parking lot until everyone goes home because those other files aren't going anywhere.

You find out about software you installed with the `pkg_info` command:

```
$ cd /var/db/pkg
/var/db/pkg $ pkg_info -L <packagename>
```

The `-L` switch to `pkg_info` produces a list of the files the package installed. You can run `pkg_info` from anywhere, but you can use Tab to complete the package's name when you're in `/var/db/pkg`.

Since you run a UNIX command by typing its name, you need to know the names of the binaries (the runnable programs) the software package installed. Maybe you also want to read the documentation that came with the program or find a configuration file.

The `which` command will tell you where in your path a binary is located. In some shells, you need to type `hash` or `rehash` to update the listing of files in your path so that new files will be found.

X-Based Software

Here's the listing for an `X` program called `xv`, a program with which you can display and edit image files in various formats:

```
xanne@killer /var/db/pkg $ pkg_info -L xv-3.10a/
Information for xv-3.10a:

Files:
/usr/X11R6/man/man1/bggen.1.gz
/usr/X11R6/man/man1/vdcomp.1.gz
/usr/X11R6/man/man1/xcmap.1.gz
/usr/X11R6/man/man1/xv.1.gz
/usr/X11R6/man/man1/xvpictoppm.1.gz
/usr/X11R6/bin/xv
/usr/X11R6/bin/bggen
/usr/X11R6/bin/vdcomp
/usr/X11R6/bin/xcmap
/usr/X11R6/bin/xvpictoppm
/usr/X11R6/lib/X11/xv_mgcsfx.sample
/usr/X11R6/share/doc/xv/README
/usr/X11R6/share/doc/xv/README.PNG
 ...
```

With the `-L` switch `pkg_info` shows you the full path names of the files installed, so you know exactly where they are. The `xv` program is an X program and everything is underneath `/usr/X11R6`, which is where `X` lives and keeps its files.

You see on the list five manual pages (readable with, for example, `man xv`), five entries in the `bin` subdirectory which are likely to be runnable binaries, a file under the `lib` subdirectory which is likely to be used by the program rather than directly by you, and, in `share/doc/xv`, a bunch of READMEs (only two of many are shown)—another place to go for information.

Text-Based Software

Text-based programs that aren't part of the base system usually install under `/usr/local`, as you can see from this output from `pkg-info` for `bash`.

```
xanne@killer /var/db/pkg % pkg_info -L bash-2.03/
```

```
Information for bash-2.03:

Files:
/usr/local/man/man1/bash.1.gz
/usr/local/man/man1/bashbug.1.gz
/usr/local/bin/bash
/usr/local/bin/bashbug
/usr/local/info/bash.info
/usr/local/share/doc/bash/article.ps.gz
/usr/local/share/doc/bash/bashref.ps.gz
/usr/local/share/doc/bash/article.txt
```

You see here manual pages, runnable binaries, and an `info` file that you can read with the command `info bash.`

The two files ending with `ps.gz` are compressed postscript files. You uncompress a file compressed with `gzip` (the tip-off is the `.gz` extension) with:

```
# gunzip <filename>
```

or, to take one example,

```
/usr/local/share/doc/bash/ # gunzip article.ps.gz
```

If you are not in the directory where the file is located, you provide a full path name. What's left is `article.ps,` which is ready to be sent to a postscript printer or can be viewed (in X) with `ghostview,` an installable program.

It's a pretty safe bet that `article.ps.gz` and `article.txt` are the same document in different formats. Reading `article.txt` with a text editor produces a lot of `^H` symbols on the screen; such documents display normally when read with a pager (`more` or `less`).

The Permanent Record

You get a description of a package (and sometimes hints on running it) with:

```
/var/db/pkg $ pkg_info <pkgname>
```

TIP

Package names are long and complicated because of the version numbers. Type the first few letter of the package name and press Tab to get your shell to do the rest of the work.

If you want to find out about all your installed packages, this command will do it for you:

```
/var/db/pkg $ pkg_info -a
```

and `pkg_info -av` will be more verbose—maybe more than you wanted to know!

How big is an installed package? This command tells you how big `wine` is:

```
/var/db/pkg # pkg_info -s wine-99.11.14/
Information for wine-99.11.14:

Package Size:
34205   (1K-blocks)
```

At 34MB, `wine` (a Windows emulator) is rather hefty, and this doesn't included other installed software it needs to run.

All this great information comes from the permanent record FreeBSD keeps about software you installed. It's stored in `/var/db/pkg`. Each package has its own subdirectory with the information on the package itself and the other packages that depend on it.

TIP

Software that's installed as a port (details are in Chapter 10) gets recorded in exactly the same way as software installed as a package. Once installed, they're all packages as far as FreeBSD is concerned.

Deleting a Package

You delete a package (as `root`) with the command:

```
/var/db/pkg # pkg_delete <packagename>
```

If you try to delete a package required by other software, FreeBSD will refuse. FreeBSD's record of interdependencies among packages is a safety feature that prevents you from deleting software other software needs. You can override this feature and force the package to be deleted, if you really want to, with `pkg_delete -f` *<packagename>*.

WARNING

Software you install all on your own—without the benefit of the packages and ports mechanisms—doesn't get recorded in `/var/db/pkg` and can't be deleted with the `pkg_delete` command.

If you download a package called `newpkg.tgz` and want to delete the old versions and install the new one at the same time, the `pkg_update` command is a possibility; `pkg_update`, first appearing in FreeBSD 4.3, claims to update dependency records as well. The example shows it with the `-n` switch, designed to tell you what it would do if you ran it.

```
# pkg_update -n newpkg.tgz
```

Installing Packages After Upgrading

If you've upgraded your FreeBSD system and try to install packages by FTP using `/stand/sysinstall`, FreeBSD uses the release name of your installed version to find the right packages on the FTP server. If it can't find a match, you get an error message:

```
Warning:  Can't find the '4.3-STABLE'
distribution on this FTP server. You may need
to visit a different server for the release
you are trying to fetch or go to the Options
menu and set the release name to explicitly
match what's available on ftp.freebsd.org (or
```

```
    set to "any").
```

You see the release name of your installed version by selecting `Options` (with the arrow keys and Enter) from the FreeBSD Configuration Menu after you start `/stand/sysinstall`. (See Chapter 3, Figure 3-17 for a screen shot of the `Options Editor`). In the Options Editor you see a list including, about half-way down the first column:

```
    Release Name   4.3-RELEASE
```

If it says `4.3-stable` (which it might after an upgrade), you need to change it to a release name FreeBSD can find on the FTP server. The FTP server looks in its `FreeBSD/release/i386` directory for a match with your `Release Name`. You can find out what will match by using the `ftp` program on FreeBSD to go to the server and look around. Here are the steps (from the command line, not from `/stand/sysinstall`):

```
$ ftp ftp9.freebsd.org
Connected ...
Name (ftp9.freebsd.org:xanne): ftp
331 Guest login ok, send your complete e-mail address as
    password.
Password: [doesn't echo]
...
ftp> cd /pub/os/FreeBSD/releases/i386
```

```
250 "/pub/os/FreeBSD/releases/i386" is new cwd.
ftp> ls
...
drwxrwxr-x  ...  Dec 20  1999 3.4-RELEASE
lrwxrwxrwx  ...  Sep  7  2000 3.4-STABLE -> 3.x-STABLE
lrwxrwxrwx  ...  Sep  3  2000 3.5-STABLE -> 3.x-STABLE
drwxr-xr-x  ...  Mar 17 06:06 3.5.1-RELEASE
drwxrwxr-x  ...  Jun 23  2000 3.x-STABLE
drwxr-xr-x  ...  Sep 26  2000 4.1-RELEASE
lrwxrwxrwx  ...  Sep  3  2000 4.1-STABLE -> 4.x-STABLE
```

```
drwxr-xr-x  ...  Nov 20 17:50 4.1.1-RELEASE
drwxr-xr-x  ...  Nov 20 17:49 4.2-RELEASE
drwxr-xr-x  ...  Apr 18 12:31 4.3-RC4
drwxr-xr-x  ...  Apr 19 08:44 4.3-RC5
drwxr-xr-x  ...  Apr 21 18:00 4.3-RELEASE
drwxr-xr-x  ...  Aug  7  2000 4.x-STABLE
drwxrwxr-x  ...  Feb 11 07:25 5.0-CURRENT
drwxrwxr-x  ...  Apr 23 08:35 ISO-IMAGES
226 Listing completed.
```

The list you see in the directory `/pub/FreeBSD/releases/i386` when you type `ls` is the list of acceptable entries (except for ISO-IMAGES) in `Release Name`. Make note of the one closest to what you have installed (just the part before the `->` symbol, if there is one).

Back in `/stand/sysinstall`, you change the `Release Name` in the `Options Editor` by highlighting the entry and pressing the spacebar. You can then type in the dialog box that comes up, press Enter, and press `q` to leave the `Options Editor`. You then go back to the steps for selecting packages and choosing installation media. You have to make this change every time you restart `/stand/sysinstall`.

Chapter 10
Build-It-Yourself Ports

FreeBSD offers over 5,000 software applications that are not part of the operating system itself, but are add-on programs ready to install and run. Each one can usually be installed as a package (ready to run) or as a port.

Chapter 9 tells you about packages. This chapter describes the FreeBSD ports collection and how you use it:

- finding the ports collection
- searching the ports collection
- installing a port, and
- running your new software.

Grokking the Ports Collection

The FreeBSD *ports collection* makes it easy to discover, install, and run software applications.

The *ports collection* is a collection of files on your FreeBSD hard drive that tells FreeBSD how to install each application (it's not the applications themselves!). The port for each application is smart enough to know just what files need to be downloaded, where to get them, how to turn them into software that runs on FreeBSD, and where to put them.

Most of these applications are for UNIX in general rather than FreeBSD in particular. They need a little special tweaking for each flavor of UNIX, perhaps merely information of where FreeBSD keeps certain files.

Jordan Hubbard, one of the founders of the FreeBSD Project and its release engineer (he puts new versions together), designed the ports collection because he wanted an easier way to install all the UNIX software that's out there on the Internet on FreeBSD. The ports collection is the result.

The ports collection uses *source code*—what the programmers actually wrote. That's what gets downloaded, along with any how-to help the programmers wrote.

To make it useful, the source code usually needs to be *compiled* or *built* (same thing)—transformed into *binary* form, something your computer understands. And put in the right place. The ports collection does all of this for you.

Finding the Ports Collection

If the ports collection is installed, finding it is a lot easier than finding a port in a storm. Simply type:

```
root@killer # cd /usr/ports
cd: /usr/ports: No such file or directory
```

ON CD-1

Oops, not installed. You can install it quickly from the CD-ROM. Remember the ports collection is just the framework for installing software—not the applications themselves. It eats up about 70MB. Here are the steps for installing it from the CD-ROM:

1. **Log in as** `root`.
2. **Put the CD-ROM in the drive** (don't mount it—i.e., *don't* type `mount /cdrom`).
3. **Type** `/stand/sysinstall` **to start the** `sysinstall` **program**.
4. **From the menu, highlight (with the arrow keys)** `Configure: Do post-install configuration of FreeBSD` **and press** Enter.
5. **You see the** `FreeBSD Configuration Menu.` **Highlight**

`Distributions: Install additional distribution sets` **and press** Enter.

6. **You see the menu for selecting distributions sets. Use the arrow keys to highlight** `ports: The FreeBSD ports collection`. **Press the spacebar to get an** `[X]` **next to** `ports`. **Press** Enter.

7. **You see the** `Choose Installation Media` menu. **The highlight will be on** CDROM, **so just press** Enter.

8. **Answer any confirmation prompts by pressing** Enter; **the installation will proceed. Press** Tab+Enter **to return to the menu with** `[X Exit Install]` **at the bottom, press** Tab **to highlight it if necessary, and press** Enter. **You return to the command prompt.**

You can also install the ports collection from a link to `ports.tar.gz` on http://www.freebsd.org/ports. Chapter 9 explains how.

And you can also install the ports collection by FTP, from the directory `/pub/FreeBSD/releases/i386/<release version>/ports`. This file is called `ports.tgz` (it's not a small matter). Get `install.sh` from the same directory and run `install.sh` as `root` to install the ports collection. You want to run `install.sh` from the directory where you put `ports.tgz`. You type:

```
# chmod 755 install.sh
# sh install.sh
```

Once the ports collection is installed, type `cd /usr/ports` to change to that directory. Type `ls` to get a list of what's in the directory. You see a screen like that shown in Figure 10-1.

Almost everything in this list that doesn't start with a capital letter is a software *category*—a directory stuffed with the names of software programs for you to install. It's a good bet the `pine` program for reading and sending mail is in—you guessed it, `mail`. Sometimes, though, it's not so obvious.

```
root@killer /usr/ports # ls
./               benchmarks/      german/          print/
../              biology/         graphics/        russian/
.cvsignore       cad/             hebrew/          security/
INDEX            chinese/         irc/             shells/
LEGAL            comms/           japanese/        sysutils/
Makefile         converters/      java/            textproc/
Mk/              databases/       korean/          vietnamese/
README           deskutils/       lang/            www/
README.html      devel/           mail/            x11/
Templates/       distfiles/       math/            x11-clocks/
Tools/           editors/         mbone/           x11-fm/
YEAR2000         emulators/       misc/            x11-fonts/
archivers/       french/          net/             x11-servers/
astro/           ftp/             news/            x11-toolkits/
audio/           games/           palm/            x11-wm/
root@killer /usr/ports #
```

Figure 10-1: The `/usr/ports` Directory

Searching the Ports Collection

Sifting through some 5,000 software programs to try to find what you want is like wandering around a huge department store. There's lots of stuff that's OK but you wouldn't want to own it, some real gems, and a few clunkers. But the ports collection is searchable if you have a glimmer about the name of what you're looking for.

You search the ports collection from `/usr/ports`. Suppose you want the `pine` program for reading and sending mail. Just type at your prompt:

```
root@killer ~ # cd /usr/ports
root@killer /usr/ports # make search name=pine
```

You see a list of all the programs that have the string *pine* in their names.

Ports of Call

Port is another one of those words that deserves extra pay because it does so much work.

Carry Me, Please!

Your computer has serial ports with connectors in the back of the computer to which you connect serial devices like modems, which carry serial communications. Don't confuse serial ports with cereal ports, which is how you carry breakfast when you go backpacking. If you go on a canoe trip and hit a dry patch, you'll have to carry the whole canoe and the cereal—that's a *portage*.

Your computer also has a parallel port or two, with a connector on the back for connecting a printer to carry signals from your computer to the printer or to other parallel devices (like a scanner) you might attach to it.

Hardware often has an I/O (input/output) port—a hardware address—it uses for getting and sending information. If you have two ethernet cards, they need different ports.

Software "listens" on yet another kind of port for incoming messages. Sendmail listens on port 25 and web servers listen on port 80. It would be mass confusion if sendmail got those http:// messages and Apache (a web server) got your email messages. *Any port in a storm* just won't do.

It's Been Ported!

The add-on software available for FreeBSD has been ported to FreeBSD—carried from some other UNIX flavor or software written for UNIX in general—by providing a few changes that let it install and run without difficulty on FreeBSD or perhaps just a few changes to locate the files it installs in places consistent with FreeBSD's file system arrangement.

FreeBSD itself has been ported from the i386 architecture (what we call personal computers are all based on the i386 architecture) to the Alpha, which is made by DEC (now owned by Compaq). When you see i386, it doesn't mean the old PC's based on 386 chips (hey, the oldest thing you've got around is a 486, right?). Even Pentiums are included in the i386 machine architecture.

Becoming a Porter

Toting luggage may not be your idea of a way to make a living. But porting software is often the first way new users contribute to FreeBSD. If you have favorite software that runs on another UNIX variant and some programming skills, consider porting it to FreeBSD. The *FreeBSD Handbook* has an entire chapter on how to do it.

TIP

You don't have to be `root` to look around the ports collection. You can do that as an ordinary user, from the $ or % or > prompt (whatever your shell uses). But to install (or uninstall!) software, you need to be logged in as `root`.

So many `pines!` People the world over seem to be pining away, with all those foreign-language versions. Use `more` to get the output by the screenful by typing:

```
/usr/ports # make search name=pine | more
```

You see eight or nine listings like these two:

```
Port:    ja-pine-3.95
Path:    /usr/ports/japanese/pine
Info:    Program for Internet News and E-mail with
     Japanese Support
Maint:   max@FreeBSD.org
Index:   japanese mail
B-deps: ja-Canna-3.2.2
R-deps: ja-Canna-3.2.2

Port:    pine-4.331
Path:    /usr/ports/mail/pine4
Info:    PINE(tm) -- a Program for Internet News &
     Email
Maint:   pine@freebsd.org
Index:   mail news
B-deps: cclient-0104101757
R-deps: cclient-0104101757
```

You get a name (with version number), a brief description of the port on the `Info` line, and an email address to write to if it doesn't work. The `pine-4.331` port seems to be the English version. The last two lines tell you what the port needs to build (`B-deps` or *dependencies*) and what it needs to run (`R-deps`).

TIP

Most important, the listing tells you where the port is located: in `/usr/ports/mail/pine4`

You can also search the ports collection more broadly with the command:

```
root@killer /usr/ports # make search key=pine
```

You get much more output with `key` than you do from `make search name=pine`, because more than just the port names are being searched.

Finding Out What a Port Offers

You find out more about a port by looking at some of the other files in its directory. It's nice to know a little more before you invite it to take up residence on your hard drive. Will it do any useful work or just lie around waiting for you to feed it? Type at your prompt:

```
root@killer ~ # cd /usr/ports/mail/pine4
root@killer /usr/ports/mail/pine4 # ls
./              distinfo        pkg-descr
../             files/          pkg-install
Makefile        pkg-comment     pkg-plist
```

You see a `Makefile`, a `distinfo` file with a checksum in it (used by FreeBSD to make sure the file you get is the one you want and not a Trojan horse), and a directory called `files` that contains patches. Patches sometimes modify code to make the port build on FreeBSD; sometimes patches merely deal with file locations to maintain the consistency of FreeBSD's file structure.

The `pkg-install` file holds a message that will display on your screen when you start an installation. This one warns of security vulnerabilities. You have to be there (and say Yes) to this warning to proceed. Most ports don't have such a file.

The `pkg-comment` file is a one-liner. The `pkg-descr` file is usually one page, just about right for viewing on your screen with the `cat` command:

```
root@killer /usr/ports/mail/pine4/pkg # cat pkg-
     descr
Pine (Program for Internet News & Email) is a tool for
     reading, sending, and managing electronic
     messages. It was designed specifically with novice
     computer users in mind, but can be tailored to
     accommodate the needs of "power users" as well.
     Pine uses Internet message protocols (e.g. RFC-
```

```
      822, SMTP, MIME, IMAP, NNTP) and runs on Unix and
      PCs.
Besides Pine this package includes the Pico editor, the
      Pilot file browser and also the IMAPv4r1 daemon
      and POP2/POP3 servers (these daemons are not built
      by default -- please use the "imap-uw" port for
      this).
An optional set of configuration files can be put into
      /usr/local/etc to set system wide defaults. Have a
      look at the documentation installed in
      /usr/local/share/doc/pine/ for more details.
Also included in dot.pinerc.pgp.sample are example
      entries needed to add to your .pinerc to activate
      the pgp add on scripts pgpdecode, pgpencode, and
      pgpsign.
WWW: http://www.washington.edu/pine/
Adrian Penisoara (Ady)
pine@freebsd.ady.ro
```

Error: Your Port Uses an Old Layout . . .

In October 2000, the layout of the ports collection was changed. In the old layout, each port had a `Makefile` and three subdirectories: `patches`, `files`, and `pkg`. The `pkg` subdirectory contained `COMMENT`, `DESCR`, and and `PLIST`, three files that did what `pkg-comment`, `pkg-descr`, and `pkg-plist` now do. If your port uses the old layout when the ports collection expects the new layout, FreeBSD won't be able to find the files it needs.

Sometimes you get this error with one particular port because there's a leftover `pkg` directory. You can move or delete this directory—it probably has old stuff in it.

You can update your ports collection with `cvsup`, explained in Chapter 17. This approach may leave a few old files around (so you'll sometimes get the "old layout" error). The safest thing to do with an old ports layout is to delete the entire ports collection and install a new one (the software you've installed won't be deleted, just the ports framework). You delete the ports framework (as `root`) with:

```
# cd /usr
/usr # rm -rf ports &
```

The `&` makes the command run in the background, which is nice since deleting the ports collection takes a while.

You can install a new ports collection from the web or by FTP if the one on your CD-ROM is out of date.

TIP

The `pkg-plist` file has a list of files the port installs. Important notice! This is the only place on your hard drive to find out what a port (or a package, since the same software can usually be installed as a package) installs *before* you install it.

```
root@killer /usr/ports/mail/pine4/ # cat pkg-plist
@unexec %D/bin/pine -conf >%D/etc/pine.conf.tmp
@unexec if cmp -s %D/etc/pine.conf
     %D/etc/pine.conf.tmp; then rm -f
     %D/etc/pine.conf; fi
@unexec rm -f %D/etc/pine.conf.tmp
bin/pico
bin/pilot
bin/pine
bin/pgpencrypt
bin/pgpdecode
bin/pgpsign
etc/dot.pinerc.pgp.sample
@exec %D/bin/pine -P %D/etc/pine.conf -conf
     >%D/etc/pine.conf.tmp
@exec /bin/mv %D/etc/pine.conf.tmp %D/etc/pine.conf
%%PORTDOCS%%share/doc/pine/brochure.txt
%%PORTDOCS%%share/doc/pine/tech-notes.txt
%%PORTDOCS%%share/doc/pine/tech-
     notes/background.html
[more files in
     %%PORTSDIR%%share/doc/pine/technotes]
%%PORTDOCS%%@dirrm share/doc/pine/tech-notes
%%PORTDOCS%%@dirrm share/doc/pine
```

The `pine` port installs not only `pine`, but also `pico` and `pilot`, a default configuration file in `/usr/local/etc`, and more stuff than anyone really wants to read in `/usr/local/share/doc/pine`. (`%%PORTDOCS%%` here refers to `/usr/local`; most ports don't use this prefix.) The `pkg-plist` file never lists man pages that will be installed. The `@unexec` lines show the directories that will be removed if the port is deinstalled (or the package deleted). Some people like the `pico` text editor so much they install `pine` just to get `pico`, but `pico` is also available by itself.

TIP

Except for X Window System programs (they go in `/usr/X11R6/`), by default FreeBSD prefixes stuff you install with `/usr/local/`. So the full path for the `pine` binary would be `/usr/local/bin/pine`. You run it like any other UNIX program—by typing its name.

Why Ports? Aren't Packages Easier?

Packages installed from the CD-ROM are a wonderful, quick, easy way to get your FreeBSD system populated with the software you want to run. And you can usually install a package if a port won't install and keeps producing errors. Chapter 9 has more on ports versus packages—but in the end, ports win:

- The ports collection tells you about software, so you can find out ahead of time if you want an application. You can get this information from the FreeBSD web site—http://www.FreeBSD.org/ports.html —but having it on your hard drive is more convenient.
- The ports system is better at handling *dependencies*—getting the other stuff the software needs to work, and knowing if it's already installed.
- The ports system can be updated (so you get the latest versions) and saves you the worry about getting the right version of a package for your system.
- Some software isn't available as a package—either because it needs information from you or because the copyright owners won't allow it.
- If a port fails to install, what it downloaded is still on your hard drive in `/usr/ports/distfiles`. When a package fails, the downloaded package disappears.
- Because a port is built from original source code, you have complete flexibility in setting configuration options. With pre-compiled packages, all the choices have already been made.

LINUX

The ports collection and package capabilities are FreeBSD's counterpart to RedHat RPMs and the package managers in other Linux distros like Debian's dpkg, but no one-to-one correspondence exists. You'll find some things better (handling dependencies) some things you'll miss, but along with pkg_info and pkg_version, covered in Chapter 9, FreeBSD provides just about the same kind of information and functionality as other package managers.

Installing a Port

Installing a port is a piece of cake. You log in as root, type a couple of commands, and eat your cake while you watch.

REMINDER

To install a port using the ports collection, you have to be connected to the Internet.

Here are the commands for installing pine:

```
root@killer ~ # cd /usr/ports/mail/pine4
root@killer /usr/ports/mail/pine4 # make install
```

This is some of what you see on the screen—a somewhat long example because it shows the port finding and installing a dependency:

```
pine4.33.tar.gz doesn't seem to exist in
     /usr/ports/distfiles/.
>> Attempting to fetch from
     ftp://ftp.cac.washington.edu/pine/.

Receiving pine4.33.tar.gz (3333758 bytes): 100%

3333758 bytes transferred in 1113.8 seconds (2.92 kBps)
===>  Extracting for pine-4.33_1
>> Checksum OK for pine4.33.tar.gz.
===>   pine-4.33_1 depends on shared library: c-
     client4.8 - not found
===>    Verifying install for c-client4.8 in
     /usr/ports/mail/cclient
>> imap-2001.BETA.SNAP-0104101757.tar.Z doesn't seem to
     exist in /usr/ports/distfiles/.
```

```
>> Attempting to fetch from
     ftp://ftp.cac.washington.edu/imap/./.
fetch: imap-2001.BETA.SNAP-0104101757.tar.Z: size of
     remote file is not known
Receiving imap-2001.BETA.SNAP-0104101757.tar.Z: 1892897
     bytes
1892897 bytes transferred in 623.5 seconds (2.96 kBps)
===>  Extracting for cclient-0104101757
>> Checksum OK for imap-2001.BETA.SNAP-0104101757.tar.Z.
===>  Patching for cclient-0104101757
===>  Applying FreeBSD patches for cclient-0104101757
===>  Configuring for cclient-0104101757
>> The c-client shared library will be named libc-
     client4.so.8
===>  Building for cclient-0104101757
...
===>  Installing for cclient-0104101757
===>   Generating temporary packing list
===>   Running ldconfig
/sbin/ldconfig -m /usr/local/lib
===>   Registering installation for cclient-0104101757
===>   Returning to build of pine-4.33_1
===>  Patching for pine-4.33_1
===>  Applying FreeBSD patches for pine-4.33_1
===>  Configuring for pine-4.33_1
===>  Building for pine-4.33_1
Making Pico and Pilot
...
Making Pine.
...
Done
===>  Installing for pine-4.33_1
===>   pine-4.33_1 depends on shared library: c-
     client4.8 - found
...
===>   Generating temporary packing list
```

```
===>   Compressing manual pages for pine-4.33_1
===>   Registering installation for pine-4.33_1
```

That's it—`pine-4.33` is installed and ready to run. The command to install every port is the same: `make install`.

TIP

Every port also goes through the same steps you see reported on your screen: fetching, extracting, patching, configuring, building, and installing. If you like, you can do these six steps one by one (`make fetch`, `make extract`, `make patch`, `make configure`, `make build`, and `make install`) or you can do everything but the installation itself with the command `make all`. The port records tasks completed in the `work` subdirectory it creates, which is where it also puts the temporary packing list, in a file called `.PLIST.mktmp`. This file is more up-to-date than `pkg-plist` and will be available before you install the port.

Arggh! Stop: Error Code 1

Sometimes a port runs into problems and quits. It's very frustrating when you really want something. A message like this appears on your screen:

```
Stop in /usr/ports/www/w3m.
*** Error code 1
```

Just before this message appears you usually see a message that gives you a hint about why the port quit. If it has scrolled off the screen, you might be able to retrieve it by pressing ScrollLock and using the arrow keys to move backward through the messages.

If that doesn't work or you want to capture the message, here are some steps you can take:

1. **Logged in as `root`, rerun `make install` and capture the messages to a file by typing:**

```
# cd /usr/ports/www/w3m
# make install > make.out 2>&1&
```

If you're using the csh or tcsh shells, the second command is:

```
# make install >& make.out&
```

TIP

This peculiar looking command (whichever version works with your shell) redirects the output that usually appears on the screen, including error messages, to a file called make.out (you can call it whatever you like). The & at the end makes the command run in the background. You get your prompt back, so you can continue working and read make.out when you feel like it. It's a good idea to capture the output of anything you make.

Rerunning make install is quick because the port records tasks completed in its work subdirectory and doesn't redo them. It will also know if it has already successfully fetched the files it needs; it won't fetch again if it has.

2. **Read make.out with your favorite text editor or by typing:**

```
# more make.out
```

and try to figure out why it quit. Often the messages tell you what you need to do to fix it.

Fixing Errors

Ports can fail for so many reasons it's a wonder they work most of the time. Here are some of the reasons and what you can do:

- The port needs information from you. It might just want to know what parts of the software you want to install or (for printing software) what kind of printer you've got.
- The checksum failed. A message on your screen will tell you how to override the checksum with

```
make NOCHECKSUM=yes install
```

but do you want to? The failure of the checksum means the files the port downloaded don't match what was expected. It could be innocent—or not.

Port Distfiles

If you want to retrieve the files the port needs—known as the *distfiles*—by hand (with `ftp`) the `Makefile` for the port tells you their names and the sites where you can download them. You put them in `/usr/ports/distfiles`, which is where the port would put them. The port will take care of processing them further; in fact, if you do anything to them it won't even recognize them. These files are usually compressed archives with a `tar.gz` extenstion.

- The port itself went along fine, but one of the other programs it needed—a dependency—didn't work. One way to fix this is to install whatever failed as a package. You can use one of the ways I tell you about in Chapter 9, or you can try, as `root`:

```
cd /usr/ports/<category>
pkg_add -r <portname>
```

  If this works, you can return to the directory of the port that failed and type

```
make install
```

  again. It should work now!

- The port fails with a message of some kind that says "forbidden." Yikes, that's a strong word. You can fix this by editing the `Makefile` for the port (as `root`) and placing a # in front of the line or lines that say `FORBIDDEN`. That's called *commenting it out*—lines beginning with # are not acted on. They're just information, or comments.

WARNING

But one reason a port is forbidden is that it's a security risk. Often the risk exists only when you're running the software and only when you're connected to the Internet (that includes connections by modem to your Internet service provider). But it may be a risk just to have it on your computer if other people have accounts on your machine—they might be able to use it to get `root` privileges. Go for something else unless you're pretty sure you're not at risk, or wait. It will probably get fixed.

- The port requires that you download files yourself (usually because you need to accept licensing conditions). Often these are binary files; the port is just a framework for getting them properly installed. Follow the directions.

- The port spewed out some awful messages with lots of hieroglyphics. OK, it's broken (for now). Don't waste too much time on it. Try getting the package (as `root`) while you're still in the port's category directory with

```
cd ../
pkg_add -r <portname>
```

It doesn't always work, but it's your best shot right now. Otherwise, wait a few days, update your ports collection (see Chapter 17), and try again.

Makefile Magic

When you type `make install` to install a port, the port's `Makefile` (the one in the directory where you type the command) takes over. It holds instructions for how to build the port. It has to know how to make whatever you ask it to make. It's not warm and cuddly. (It doesn't do windows, either.) So if you type `make love`, this is what you get:

```
root@killer /usr/ports/mail/pine4 # make love
make: don't know how to make love. Stop
```

Makefiles are written in a rather peculiar language, but you can get good information from a makefile. The command

```
cat Makefile | more
```

from the port's directory (the one with the `Makefile`) puts the `Makefile` on your screen by the screenful.

Some makefiles include the line:

```
IS_INTERACTIVE= YES
```

which means that this isn't a good time to go to lunch. The port needs you to answer some questions—about residency, your printer, or what it needs to work with your hardware. Some ports ask questions but fail to say that they're interactive in the `Makefile`.

Some makefiles have lines saying "Uncomment this if you want . . ." You uncomment by deleting the # at the beginning of a line, which makes the line active. This gives you an opportunity to customize the port.

A port's `Makefile` also tells you the names of the manual pages it installs.

And it lists the port's dependencies—the other files it needs to build or run—and the sites from which it will try to download files. The original location for the files often has a helpful web page.

The `Makefile` in a port's own directory also has available to it the makefiles in `/usr/ports/Mk`, which apply to all ports. It accomplishes this through the `.include` statements you see in the file.

So if you want to read a port's `Makefile` before installing the port, go ahead! It's not entirely English, but at least some of it will make sense.

Running the Software

You can now run the `pine` software you installed by typing the name of one of the new files in `/usr/local/bin,` or you can read about them by typing `man pine` or `man pico` or `man pilot.`

`Pine` comes with manual pages and other documentation in `/usr/local/share/doc/pine`. Most of the help is, however, available from menus within `pine.` When you first run `pine`, it will create a configuration file called `.pinerc` in your home directory, which is where it will save the choices you make when you run `pine`'s configuration routine from its main menu.

TIP

Some software, like the Apache web server and Samba, installs files that run the software when the computer boots. The files are scripts located in `/usr/local/etc/rc.d` and have an `.sh` extension. You may have to copy a file like `apache.sh.default` to `apache.sh` and edit a configuration file as well (for Apache, probably `httpd.conf`) to get the software running. Configuration files are often placed in the directory `/usr/local/etc/`*<program>*.

Keeping Track of Your Software

The installation of a port is recorded in `/var/db/pkg/`*<packagename>* just as it is for software you install as a package. At this point, FreeBSD doesn't care how you installed it. Just as for packages, the information about installed ports recorded in this database can be read with `pkg_info`, like this (Tab stands for the key):

```
xanne@killer ~ $ cd /var/db/pkg
xanne@killer /var/db/pkg $ pkg_info -v pine Tab
```

The `-v` is for being very chatty—telling all, or in Unixspeak, verbose (noisy). It will give you basically the same information you got from the files in `/usr/ports/mail/pine4/`—a comment and a longer description, a list of files installed, and a list of the installed software that depends on this particular port or package. That's how FreeBSD knows what it needs to keep around even if you tell it to delete a package.

Chapter 9 tells you more about using `pkg_info`.

TIP FreeBSD's permanent record of installed ports and packages in `/var/db/pkg` means that you can delete your ports collection (you might need the space for something else!) and still have a record of what's installed.

Recovering Your Real Estate

Type `df`, and find out how your disk space is going. If it shows `/usr` filling up, you might have a lot of big files in `/usr/ports/distfiles` (where the ports system puts the files it downloads) and in the work directories for ports that have been installed.

Cleaning Up

Typing `make clean` in the port's directory will delete the work directory and other work directories the port created. Typing `make clean` in `/usr/ports` will systematically get rid of all work directories, but it takes a long time.

But `make clean` doesn't do distfiles. Go to `/usr/ports/distfiles` and delete the downloaded files for the software you've already installed, unless you think you may want to reinstall soon. They take up a lot of space. You can see just how much by doing `du -sh` in that directory.

Deleting a Port or Package

Oh, you don't like `pine`? You'd rather have `mutt`? Delete it! What you need to know is the name of the package. (Of course, you have to be logged in as `root`.) Do the following:

```
xanne@killer ~ # cd /var/db/pkg
xanne@killer /var/db/pkg # ls -d pine*
```

You see:

```
pine-4.33/
```

Type:

```
xanne@killer /var/db/pkg # pkg_delete pine-4.33
```

and it will be gone. So will `pico` and `pilot`.

TIP

You can also go to the directory in `/usr/ports` from which you installed the software (in this case `/usr/ports/mail/pine4`) and type `make deinstall`. It does exactly the same thing, but if you've updated your ports collection and `pine4` has a new version number, this method won't work.

The ports collection also has a `/usr/ports/sysutils/pkg_remove`, which is an alternative to `pkg_delete`.

Upgrading Installed Software

Upgrading your ports collection once it's installed is easy with `cvsup`, explained in Chapter 17. But upgrading a specific port to a new version is a little tricky. The ports process is good about not overwriting your configuration files for software, but the other files will get overwritten if you install a new version.

TIP

The `pkg_version` command is designed to tell you whether a new version of your software is listed in the ports collection on your hard drive. The `pkg_version -v` commands shows you the version numbers and tells you whether or not a port "needs" upgrading (if it ain't broke, don't fix it). The `pkg_version -c` command gives you commands (but see the warning in the next section) for upgrading.

```
xanne@killer ~ % pkg_version -v | grep xplanet
xplanet-0.60     <    needs updating (index has 0.70)
xanne@killer ~ % pkg_version -c | grep xplanet
#  xplanet
cd /usr/ports/astro/xplanet
make && pkg_delete -f xplanet-0.60
```

To Delete or Not to Delete

Should you delete or deinstall before you install the new version? Most people would say you should, because the old version may leave some files around that get in the way of the new version working properly.

Use `make all` in a port's directory when you want to upgrade. This does everything except the installation; you'll know that the new version built successfully. Then delete the old version and type `make install` in the port's directory to install the new version.

WARNING

If you install a new version of software that's a set of libraries for other programs, it's possible that the software you already have installed won't run because it's looking for the old versions of the libraries rather than the new versions. With some stuff it's safer not to delete the old version. The command recommended by `pkg_version` forces (the `-f` switch) deletion even if the software is needed by other programs. Doing that can make your other software unable to run. You may be able to create a symbolic link from the old names to the new ones, but this is a lot of work.

The port `/usr/ports/sysutils/portupdate` updates an installed package using the ports collection, and you may want to consider it.

Saving Your Precious Configs

Ports and packages are careful not to overwrite your configuration files. You might have worked long and hard to get a program to run the way you want it to. That's why configuration files come with extensions like `.sample` or `.default` and why you need to copy them to a filename without the extension. The new version of the software will overwrite the `.default` or `.sample` files, but not the file with your own handcrafted information.

WARNING

Remember the software in ports has been written by lots of different third parties with different views on what makes software (and parties) good. Backing up files, stashing them in another directory, or copying or moving them to a new name can be a worthwhile precaution.

That's How; Now What?

Searching through over 5,000 software programs trying to figure out what they do, or trying to find one that does what you want, isn't easy. The next chapter describes exactly where you find the software to burn your CDs, play your music, edit your photos, and display a map of the world on your screen while you do it.

Chapter 11

Software

This chapter tells you what specific software applications do so you can decide what you want to install.

With more than 5,000 software titles in 39 categories (not including foreign languages), you could go crazy trying to figure out what you wanted and you still might miss the cool ones.

The software is organized here just as it's listed in the ports collection (see Chapter 10) because that's the way you find it on your hard drive when you want to install an application. I've tried to identify the apps I think are especially good or useful for users, while also hinting at some of the system administration stuff. FreeBSD's many offerings for programmers are merely summarized, although they are extensive and make FreeBSD an excellent development platform.

Of the 5,000-plus applications, close to 600 are foreign language versions of programs available in English. If you want, say, a Russian email program, you don't need me to tell you about it. So this overview doesn't delve into the foreign-language categories—`chinese`, `french`, `german`, `hebrew`, `japanese`, `korean`, `russian`, `ukrainian`, and `vietnamese`—at all.

Software Descriptions on Your Hard Drive

TIP

The ports collection (see Chapter 10) on your own hard drive is the most convenient way to get information about what a software application will do for you, although Chapter 9 tells you how to get information from the FreeBSD web page.

Getting Short Descriptions

You see the short (one-line) summaries of what the different software packages in a category do by typing, in /usr/ports/<*category*>, make describe, like this:

```
xanne@killer /usr/ports/mail $ make describe
```

Getting Long Descriptions

TIP

One-line descriptions often aren't enough for deciding about a program. If you want to make a text file of the longer descriptions in a category, you cd /usr/ports, log in as root, and use your favorite text editor to create a file called getdescr (you can call it whatever you like) with the following text in it:

```
#!/bin/sh
for i in  $1/*  ; do
   if [ -d $i ]; then
   echo " "
   echo $i
   echo " "
   cat $i/pkg-descr
   fi
done
exit;
```

Save the file and exit the editor. Type chmod 755 getdescr to make the file executable. To create a file of the long descriptions of a category such as archivers, type (note the "dot slash" at the beginning of the command) ./getdescr archivers > archivers.txt.

When you view archivers.txt with more or a text editor, you see the names and descriptions of each of the software packages in the archivers category. You do this for any category where you want to see the descriptions so you can select software to install. Sometimes these descriptions include hints for running the software that aren't available elsewhere.

If you're interested in sound and want to find programs that record or play WAV files, you type `cd /usr/ports` (if you aren't there already) and type:

```
/usr/ports # ./getdescr audio >audio.txt
```

You then read `audio.txt` at your leisure or print it out for marking up.

If your ports collection uses the old layout (and you don't want to upgrade it), change the line in the script starting with `cat` to `cat $i/pkg/DESCR`.

Is It Right For You?

Some software is designed to work with other software. It might require X, the graphical user interface, or one of the fancier X environments, like GNOME or KDE.

A program might be an add-on utility for an office suite or the classic UNIX `emacs` system, which does (either in X or not) just about everything from reading your mail (or at least organizing it so you can read it) to reading news, managing files, and warning you about your next scheduled therapy session and whether it's time to rotate your tires.

Some software is specifically designed with foreign language support, so that if you happen to be regularly conversing around the world in Dutch, German, Japanese, and Russian as well as English, you can choose these utilities.

You get some clues, listed in Table 11-1, about what works with what from the software names, especially the first few letters.

Software that requires X usually has a name starting with `x`, like `xmms`.

More demanding are the programs or utilities for the KDE environment. You may or may not want to install and run this space-and-memory hungry Windows work-alike. If you want it, a `kde` at the beginning of a name is the tip-off that it's a KDE application.

Table 11-1 Clues—for What You Want or Don't Want

It's All in the Name	*What It Tells You*
x*	Software for the X Window System
gnome*	For GNOME, an X Window environment
kde*	For KDE, another X Window environment
*-i18n	A version with international language support
ja-*	Japanese support
ko-*	Korean support
ru-*	Russian support
as*	Sometimes for the afterstep window manager
e*	Sometimes for the enlightenment window manager
wm*	Sometimes for the windowmaker window manager

In the same way, a port name starting with gnome is a GNOME add-on or utility. The KDE and GNOME applications may work outside these environments (when you're not running KDE or GNOME).

Some software tells you it needs Linux support (all 60MB of it); maybe you already have it installed. It's like reading the shrink-wrapped boxes in the stores: you want to figure out what you want before you go to the time and effort not only of installing it, but of figuring out how it works. Sometimes you discover software works only with particular hardware.

Although some applications need a good deal of graphics support, once you've installed one of them, the others will use pretty much the same installed graphics helper software.

A Rundown on the Software

This section gives you a brief overview of the kinds of programs in the different software categories and tells you about a few good ones, most of which are for users rather than system administrators, programmers, or ISPs.

Software Categories

The software installable from the FreeBSD ports collection is organized by category. Each category is a subdirectory of `/usr/ports`; see Chapter 10 for more information about installing the ports collection if it's not installed already. My apologies for the many categories—but that's how you'll find them organized on your hard drive. Within each category are directories for the software applications themselves; those are the names for applications used in the text and tables in this chapter.

ON CD-1

A * next to a name indicates that the FreeBSD installation CD-ROM includes the package for the software, although what gets included varies a little with each release of FreeBSD.

Archivers

Archivers are the programs that compress and uncompress files or groups of files so they can be stored or transmitted more efficiently over a network. An archiver is usually installed automatically when other software needs it. But among more than 45, you might find of interest those in Table 11-2 .

Table 11-2 Archivers

Name	*Description*
* macutils	Handles a variety of Macintosh file formats
* unzip and zip	Compatible with MS-DOS pkzip

Astro

From the trivial to the serious to the gorgeous, from moon phases to satellite tracing to testing transmissions from outer space for aliens (`seti@home`), this category has more than 30 astronomy applications.

The `xglobe` application offers a satellite image of the earth (or other planets) as wallpaper.

Audio

Here are over 200 sound applications for a variety of hardware; some just organize your music. Table 11-3 lists useful favorites. Note that `burncd`, which burns ATAPI (IDE) CDs, is part of the base system, so you don't need a port.

Table 11-3 Audio Applications

Name	*Description*
bladeenc	A freeware MP3 encoder
cd2mp3	A front end to dagrab and bladeenc
* cdplay	A cd-player for the console (text mode)
cdrecord	Make your own CDs (SCSI)
dagrab	Reads audio tracks from a CD into wav sound files; requires an IDE CD-ROM drive
festival	Speech synthesis (get FreeBSD to read to you!)
linux-realplayer	The Linux version of RealPlayer 5.0
mpg123	Plays MPEG I and II from the console
* tosha	Reads digital audio and digital video and writes them to the hard drive; SCSI interface only
* xcd	A simple graphical interface to a CD player
xmcd	A good cdplayer for X
xmms	A multimedia player Winamp look-alike; a favorite

Benchmarks

As someone once said, there are lies, damn lies, and benchmarks. Is your CPU *really* running at 500 mhz? Here are 22 or so software packages for measuring and comparing everything from processors to web servers.

The `lmbench` software package includes `mhz`, which will tell you the speed at which your CPU is running.

Biology

Molecular biology applications (34 at last count) and, more conventionally, `* gperiodic`, an attractive periodic table of the elements.

Cad

These 30-some applications are for computer-aided design of electronic circuits and the like.

Comms

This category has applications (about 43 offerings) for use with modems—sending and receiving faxes; a few file transfer utilities; and communications programs (if you want something other than FreeBSD's `ppp` point-to-point protocol, which comes with the system). Table 11-4 lists a few of them.

Table 11-4 Communications Software

Name	*Description*
kermit	Historic file transfer program
* hylafax	Sending and receiving faxes
minicom	MS-DOS Telix clone
* seyon	Telecommunications software somewhat like ProComm

Converters

This is a collection of file format converters. Ports or packages that need converters will install one or more of these 53 or so applications without user intervention.

You might want to install `unix2dos` (which also installs `dos2unix`). They convert files from the DOS line endings (carriage return + line feed) to the UNIX format (line feed only) and vice versa. These differences in line feeds often destroy effective printing.

Databases

Here are two industrial-strength databases, `postgres` (originally from Berkeley) and `mysql` (client and servers), and a variety of software (close to 100 offerings altogether) for front-end access to and analysis of databases. Also `gnats`, a standard program for tracking bug reports.

Deskutils

Deskutils includes calendars, ledgers, calculators, appointment and address books, to-do lists, financial managers, and milestones among the 47 options.

Devel

This collection of over 500 offerings in the field of computer programming languages and tools supplements the Lang category and what comes with the FreeBSD system itself to make FreeBSD a superb development platform.

Editors

Of the almost 225 software applications in the Editors category, many (including all those with *mule* in the name) have to do with `emacs`—plug-ins, `emacs`-lite, multi-lingual support and the like.

Several of them are variants of `vi` (the default FreeBSD editor and the default UNIX editor).

* Especially useful is `vim`, which is `vi` with enhancements—among other bells and whistles, two or more windows. You type `vim -o file1 file2`, press Enter, and each gets loaded in its own window. You switch between windows with Ctrl+ww.

AbiWord

* `AbiWord` is a graphical word processor for X, and is probably your best chance to read Microsoft Word files without installing 70MB of software.

Applixware

Applixware is an office suite available for sale (about $100) from http://www.freebsdmall.com. Good interaction with Microsoft products. The runnable binary is installed in `/usr/local/applixware/applix`.

StarOffice

StarOffice is a sophisticated office suite now owned by Sun Microsystems. Its interaction with Microsoft Office is excellent. Read the `Makefile` to find out what to download to `/usr/ports/distfiles` if typing `make install` in the `/usr/ports/staroffice52` directory doesn't tell you, and then try `make install` again. Once installed, you run a setup program as a user to create configuration files in your home directory. StarOffice provides a full office suite, with a word processor like Word, a spread sheet like Excel, a presentation manager, a drawing application, a network calendar, and more. Free for single users, it requires Linux support.

WordPerfect

When you type `make install` for this port, you get a message about how to download the files from http://www.corel.com after filling in the licensing agreement (it's free for single users). WordPerfect is a big download, but it may be worth it. It requires Linux support. Documents created are readable on WordPerfect running on Windows.

Emulators

The emulators category offers about 75 utilities to enable you to run software from other platforms on FreeBSD—some for the Mac, some for Nintendo, some for DOS/Windows, some basic to Linux support. But if you want to run DOS/Windows programs—why not run DOS/Windows?

Table 11-5 describes a few especially interesting offerings.

Table 11-5 Emulators

Name	*Description*
* linux_base	The 60MB basic software that constitutes Linux support. Recommended. FreeBSD's installer gives you an opportunity to install it, or you can use the package from the CD-ROM.
* mtools	If you can't stand mounting and dismounting floppy drives the UNIX way, mtools provides a convenient package.
vmware2	What FreeBSD needs to run the commercial VMWare (http://www.vmware.com), in which you can install other operating systems like Windows NT or Windows 2000 and run them at the same time you're running FreeBSD. The guest operating system takes a good chunk of your total RAM, so both systems are slower as a result. But it works very, very well.
wine	Makes it possible to run some DOS/Windows programs. Still being developed, but on its way. You can play Halflife.

FTP

FTP is a collection of almost 50 programs in the File Transfer Protocol category among which you might locate a better FTP program, but `ncftp` installs with the base system and is pretty good. Other programs are designed for running FTP servers.

The user gem here is `wget`, which runs in text mode and lets you download files and entire subdirectories from ftp and web sites.

Games

The several hundred games here aren't the commercial variety you know and love. Nevertheless, they can be fun. Some of them are X-based, and a few are for the GNOME or KDE environments. Nethack is a favorite. The doom port makes it possible to run DOOM if you have DOOM data from a real copy of one of the DOOMs.

Loki sells Linux versions of commercial games. They claim that with Linux support installed, Soldier of Fortune, MindRover, Heroes of Might and Magic III, Sid Meier's Alpha Centauri, Eric's Ultimate Solitaire, Descent 3, Myth 2, Heavy Gear 2, Heretic 2, Unreal Tournament, and SimCity 3000 Unlimited run on FreeBSD. See http://faqs.lokigames.com/index.php3.

Graphics

The graphics category is an amazing collection of graphics support software. If you install a window manager like `enlightenment`, some basic graphics programs and libraries will get installed as necessary support without your direct intervention.

Once images are on your computer, many applications are available for manipulating, rendering, and presentation. Table 11-6 describes some of the top displayers.

Table 11-6 Graphics

Name	*Description*
* gimp1	The Gimp has many of the features of Adobe Photoshop; the manual is a separate port.
* ImageMagick	Another favorite for display and manipulation of images
* xv	A solid standard in imaging; you can get a manual
* Mesa3	A 3-D graphics library similar to that of OpenGL
* camediaplay	Data downloading tool for the Sanyo digital camera and others—some Olympus, Epson, and Agfa models

* cqcam	Color QuickCam frame grabber
* qcread	For color and B&W parallel-port Connectix QuickCam
qvplay	Downloading tool for Casio QV digital cameras
* dc20pack	Serial port control of your Kodak DC20 /25
dc3play	Serial port downloading for the Ricoh DC-3 digital camera
* gphoto	Download, save, and manipulate images from several different digital cameras
* photopc	For an Epson PhotoPC digital still camera
* flashplayer	An implementation of the Macromedia Flash standalone player
* fxtv	TV-in-a-window and capture capabilities for BT848/878 based tuner/capture cards (audio capabilities unconfirmed)
mtv	MpegTV Player—a realtime software MPEG-1 Video+Audio player and VCD player
* mpeg2codec	Converts uncompressed video frames into MPEG-1 and MPEG-2 video coded bitstream sequences and vice versa
mpeg2play	A player for MPEG-1 and -2 video bitstreams
* mpeg_play	View MPEG movies on X Window displays
xanim	Display animations in various formats
xine	Plays video CDs
xmovie	Quicktime movie player
netshow	The Microsoft NetShow video stream player for Linux
sane and xsane	Support for many scanners
* xdgagrab	For capturing screen shots with the mouse pointer
xfractint	The port to UNIX of fractint to generate fractal images

Several applications among more than 300 in the graphics category let you work with images in different formats (TIFF, PNG, GIF, XPM, Photo CD, and so forth); others work with digital cameras and videocam images, TV tuner/capture hardware, MPEG (digital movie) files, scanners, and QuickTime movies. Utilities let you arrange photos in albums.

Whatever your hardware, something in this collection may work with it.

IRC

Internet Relay Chat software connects you to networks of computers hosting channels where people join and chat in more or less real time on diverse subjects. Some of these 45-plus programs are text-based; some are graphical or graphical front-ends to text-based programs. A few offerings in this category are proxies (`bnc`, `muh`, `ezbounce`); `infobot` is a bot of sorts that collects information and answers questions as it sits in an IRC channel. Table 11-7 lists a few IRC clients.

Table 11-7 Internet Relay Chat (IRC)

Name	*Description*
EPIC	Possibly the pick among the text-based clients—an enhanced ircII, the classic
tkirc	A good graphical front end to ircII
* xchat	A recent favorite graphical client

Java

Here are about 60 offerings primarily of interest to programmers using java utilities and applications.

Lang

The Lang category has over 180 computer programming languages and libraries, diverse and complex—everything from `qbasic` to `fortran` to `modula3`.

Mail

The `biff` utility, which installs with FreeBSD as part of the base system, is almost as good as AOL at announcing that you've got mail if you enable it by typing `biff y` at your command prompt. Rumor has it that `biff` is named after a dog that belonged to a woman on the Berkeley staff while Berkeley UNIX was being developed. The dog barked when the mail came.

Other barking dogs, some graphical, are included in this collection of more than 200 programs. But most are alternatives for reading, composing, and answering your own mail. Some fetch your mail from your Internet service provider. Table 11-8 lists popular ones.

Table 11-8 Mail Applications

Name	*Description*
* cucipop	A POP3 mail server—a program your ISP might run to make it possible for you to fetch the mail that arrives for you there
* elm	An alternative to pine—a text-based mail reading and answering program
* fetchmail	An excellent choice for getting the mail from your ISP
* pine4	A full-featured text-based user mail program. It comes with the pico editor, pilot (for navigating directories), and reads USENET news, too.
postfix	An alternative to sendmail
procmail	For sorting your mail on arrival into different mailboxes; useful if you subscribe to mailing lists that you want to separate from personal mail
qmail	Another alternative to sendmail

Also included in this category are "I've been spammed" programs (auto-responders to unwanted email), programs for running and managing mailing lists, and other mail utilities for encryption or conversion of a mailbox from one format to another.

Math

The Math category includes more than 120 statistical, numerical, graphing, plotting, and calculating applications. Several spreadsheets, including `wingz` and `gnumeric` (for the GNOME environment) are offered.

Mbone

Here are about a dozen multi-user or user-to-user audio conferencing and other applications for the mbone.

Misc

Lots of fun stuff here. Everything (almost 200 things) that didn't fit anywhere else, including a beat-the-dealer program, an acronym database, a jargon file, zip codes, a count-down timer, stock-quote fetchers, computer control of X 10 devices (wireless home automation), enhanced (supposedly) versions of some standard UNIX utilities, and some seriously useful (really!) apps, like `figlet`. Install `figlet`, type **figlet FreeBSD,** and you see:

```
 _____              ____  ____  ____
|  ___| __ ___  ___| __ )/ ___||  _ \
| |_ | '__/ _ \/ _ \  _ \\___ \| | | |
|  _|| | |  __/  __/ |_) |___) | |_| |
|_|  |_|  \___|\___|____/|____/|____/
```

This category includes upgrades (starting with your FreeBSD version number without a period, e.g., 41) so the latest ports run (not necessary until your version gets out-of-date), and those listed in Table 11-9 .

Net

Some of these 400-plus network utilities are listed in Table 11-10. Among them are variations or enhancements of utilities included in the base FreeBSD system. Several are `mud` and `ICQ` programs. Much of this software is of interest primarily to administrators of large networks. `The samba` port and `sharity-light` (or `smbfs`) are the basic tools for sharing files between Windows and FreeBSD machines.

Table 11-9 **Miscellaneous**

Name	*Description*
Howto	Linux how-to's modified for FreeBSD. DNS (how to run a domain name server), NFS (how to set up mounting file systems from or to other UNIX computers), NIS (sharing a password database among computers). If you like the Linux version, you'll love the FreeBSD version.
* amanda	A sophisticated tape backup program
* bidwatcher	Tracks items you're interested in on eBay, the huge auction site. Lets you snipe: schedule a last-minute (really a last-second) bid. Of course, that works only if your computer is on and connected to the Internet.
magicpoint	An X program for doing something like what Microsoft's PowerPoint does (presentations)
mc	A Norton Commander clone for file management, but not with all of NC's features
* screen	If you log in remotely to your FreeBSD computer, screen lets you run a program and keep it running when you log out, open new windows, switch among them, and so forth.
* xtail	Watches the growth of files (or all files in a directory) you specify

News

USENET has tens of thousands of newsgroups on many topics. Newsgroups are like bulletin boards—everyone sees all the messages and can read everything and reply to the entire group or just to the writer. The postings are called articles.

Some of the software in this category of almost 70 items is for providers of USENET news rather than readers. A few programs help with posting or downloading the many binary files found on some newsgroups.

Table 11-10 Networking Utilities

Name	*Description*
* cvsup-bin	A must-have for FreeBSD; it's the binary installation (you don't want to build this one yourself) of cvsup
* cvsupit	Installs cvsup and helps you configure it to upgrade your system or ports from source
licq	One of the ICQ clones (not endorsed by Mirabilis). For messaging
* naim	Works with America Online Instant Messenger chat system
netatalk	For AppleTalk networks, to provide access to FreeBSD file systems from Macintosh computers running AppleShare
openldap	LDAP protocol clients, servers, and tools
* rsync	On two computers with rsync installed, rsync efficiently transfers files in one direction or the other. It can be used to clone a running system
samba	Makes FreeBSD file systems and printers available from a computer running Microsoft Windows, using the Microsoft SMB protocol
* sharity-light	The counterpart to samba—makes Windows file systems available on FreeBSD. Like smbfs for Linux
smbfs	An alternative (probably better) to sharity-light
* trafshow	Watch the traffic on your network. A way to display the output of tcpdump, which is part of FreeBSD. Once installed, you simply type trafshow -i <interface>, where <interface> is the device (e.g., ed0) your network card uses.
vnc	Installs vncserver and vncviewer. You run vncserver on the FreeBSD machine to start an X session that can be viewed from another computer using vncviewer. You need the appropriate version of vnc on the viewing machine from http://www.uk.research.att.com/vnc. It's all free, and it works wonderfully well over a fast network, very slowly over a modem.

Table 11-11 lists software for reading newsgroups and posting to them, if you want to. A threaded news reader can sort articles by topic. Besides those listed, the `pine` mail program can handle news.

Table 11-11 USENET News Application

Name	*Description*
* krn	A newsreader for KDE
* tin	An easy to use threaded news reader
trn and trn4	Threaded news readers many people like
* xvnews	OpenLook interface, a newsreader for X

Palm

Here are utilities (28 of them) for communicating with your Palm Pilot, if you're lucky enough to have one. `Coldsync` may be the pick of the litter.

Print

Table 11-12 tells you about some of the more than 250 printing utilities. See Chapter 15 for installing and setting up `apsfilter`.

Security

The 200-plus software applications, mostly for system administrators trying to maintain security, include password crackers, port scanners and detectors of port scans, packet sniffers, and other tools, like `tripwire`, to determine if anything on your system has been altered.

`Openssh` comes with FreeBSD, which enables you to use encrypted logins on systems that support `ssh`, so you don't need any of the `ssh` ports. You may find those in Table 11-13 interesting.

Table 11-12 Printing Software

Name	*Description*
* a2ps-letter	Formats files for printing on a postscript printer
* acroread4	Acrobat Reader, the PDF (portable document format) viewer
* apsfilter	The solution for printing on many non-postscript printers. The SETUP (in /usr/local/apsfilter) program lets you tell apsfilter about your printer.
cdlabelgen	Makes labels for CDs
* ghostscript	With ghostview, lets you view postscript files
* ghostview	X interface for ghostscript
* magicfilter	An alternative to apsfilter
* psutils-letter	Psbook, one of the many utilties in this set, lets you print postscript documents in signatures for making booklets.

Table 11-13 Security Applications

Name	*Description*
crack	Run crack to try to crack the passwords on your own system; if it works, they're not secure enough
* oidentd	An identd server that may solve some of the problems of pidentd trying to run IRC through natd
pgp	Pretty Good Privacy (encryption)
* pidentd	The standard identd program, required by some IRC servers
rsaref	You may need this to run ssh on older systems
tripwire	Builds a database of the size of your binaries, so you can detect changes made by intruders

Shells

Here's a score of alternatives to the shells—`sh` and `tcsh`—with which FreeBSD ships. Shells interpret the commands you type, and have different features.

The `bash2` shell (perhaps `bash1` in older versions) is the Linux default, and explained in Chapter 6. Many people like `zsh`, which, among other things, corrects your spelling on the command line. It's more important to get familiar with one of them than switch around.

Sysutils

Listed in Table 11-14 are a few of 180 or so applications for monitoring computer hardware, system load and performance, and users. Some of these utilities are enhancements of utilities provided with FreeBSD.

Table 11-14 System Utilities

Name	*Description*
* lsof	Provides heaps of information about open files, but fstat, which is part of the base system, may do everything you need
mkisofs	Makes an image of a directory tree in ISO9660 format—what you need for creating a CD-ROM
* pib	A graphical ports index browser
pkg_remove	A package remover
portupgrade	Upgrades an installed package from ports
webmin	Administer your system from a browser

Textproc

These 200 applications are for processing text—converting it from one format to another, searching it, or spell-checking it.

Several of them (antiword, catdoc, mswordview, wv, xlhtml) try to convert various Microsoft Office files (Word, PowerPoint, Excel) to a format readable on a UNIX system. You'll have to experiment to see if they work better on the documents you might want to read than the office suite applications listed under Editors.

Spell-checkers include ispell and aspell, and are available for several languages. The spell-checkers and a few others are listed in Table 11-15. But don't forget dict, which is probably already on your hard drive.

This category includes all the applications used by the FreeBSD documentation project, headed by Nik Clayton, to produce one basic marked-up version of a document that can be used to output the document in many different formats. If you're interested in participating, you install docproj, and it takes care of installing everything else necessary.

Table 11-15 Text Processing

Name	*Description*
aspell	A spell checker
docproj	The metaport for FreeBSD's documentation project
glimpse	Indexes your files so you can search for specific text
isearch	Text search system that doesn't index
* ispell	The most commonly used spell-checker
wordnet	A lexical database with thesaurus and dictionary features from the Cognitive Science Laboratory at Princeton University (also available on-line)

WWW

Table 11-16 list some of the 350-plus programs for browsing the web (including a couple that blank out banner ads), running and managing a web server and analyzing log files, and creating content for web servers.

Table 11-16 World Wide Web Applications

Name	*Description*
* apache	A standard—and free—web server with many enhancements
bluefish	For creating and editing html
* links	Text-based browser
* lynx	The old favorite of text browsers
* netscape	Several versions—BSDI, FreeBSD, Linux—of both navigator and communicator
* w3m	Another text-based browser

X11

Here are some 170 utilities for the X Window System, including a little app that makes your screen look as if it has mold growing over it (`xmold`) and `bgrot`, which rotates the background image—mouse utilities, keyboard utilities, substitutes for the standard `xterm`, graphical login utilities, screensavers. Those of special interest are listed in Table 11-17.

The meta-ports for `GNOME` (`gnomecore` and `gnome`) and `KDE` (`kde11` and `kde2`) are found in this category, along with applications for these `X` environments.

X11-clock

Here are more clocks (over 30 of them) than anyone needs; `xalarm` lets you set alarms.

X11-fm

File managers for `X`—27 in number, with a variety of capabilities—include `filerunner`, `tkdesk`, and `xfm`. Some have drag-and-drop capabilities.

Table 11-17 X-Window Utilities

Name	*Description*
* XFree86-4	Version 4.0 of X, buildable as a port (it takes a long time)
eterm	Eye candy can be more important than stability. A substitute for the standard xterm, which gives your windows some spectacular backgrounds
* rxvt	A less memory-intensive xterm alternative
* tkgoodstuff	An easily configured button-bar for X, especially for the fvwm window manager, giving you some of the capabilities of the Windows taskbar
xloadimage	Utility for changing the background of X

X11-fonts

Some of these 50-plus font application programs are for XFree86-4 (version 4 of X).

X11-servers

This collection of almost 40 X servers offers substitutes for the standard X servers, but with support for TrueType fonts.

X11-toolkits

These 125 applications are primarily for X programmers.

X11-wm

Here are more than 60 window managers and related applications for X. It's the window manager you choose that determines how X looks—the window decoration, switching among windows, icons and how you load, minimize, and recall applications.

Windows managers manage windows—and a couple of the applications in this category manage the window managers, in case you want to go back and forth among them.

The default window manager in X is `twm`, which is small and quick but a little awkward, and lacking in features. Once you go beyond `twm`, it's personal preference and resources—some window managers are slow if you've got limited RAM and a slow processor.

Table 11-18 X Window Managers

Name	*Description*
* afterstep	Based on NeXtStep
* blackbox	Small and clean; not good with GNOME; themes
* enlightenment	Memory intensive, but pretty; many themes
* fvwm2	The classic; not good with GNOME
* windowmaker	Another popular window manager

Unlike Microsoft Windows, with most X window managers you can have multiple desktops with different applications running. Several of those listed in Table 11-18 also have alternative themes (backgrounds and window design), some installed by default and some downloadable over the Internet.

Other Software

The software installable on FreeBSD as a package or a port isn't the only software available. Other applications are being written every day for one UNIX flavor or another, and their writers usually try to make them work on all UNIX variants. You install them on FreeBSD simply by following the instructions. If you really want something, at least give it a try. A good source for software that may not yet have been ported to FreeBSD is http://freshmeat.net. See Dan Langille's http://freshports.org information on the latest FreeBSD ports.

Chapter 12

Connecting to the Internet

You want to surf the web, search the Internet, send (and get) electronic mail, download files, chat with people who share your interests, shop, and maybe even book an airline flight or a hotel room or sell the collectibles you no longer care about at auction. This is what the Internet is for, no matter who invented it.

FreeBSD is great for connecting to the rest of the world, whether you do it by dial-up modem, cable modem, or ethernet. This chapter tells you how to get on-line by dialing up or connecting by ethernet and how to use FreeBSD as a gateway.

Connecting by Dial-Up

Most homes and many offices connect to the Internet using a serial modem and an ordinary telephone line. The modem dials and converts computer output to signals that can be carried over phone lines. At the other end is your Internet service provider's modem, which converts the signals back to what computers understand.

On FreeBSD or Windows Dial-Up Networking, these connections are made with PPP: the point-to-point protocol. The PPP connection is capable of carrying Internet traffic.

What you Need for Dial-Up

For dial-up, you need:

- **An Internet service provider (ISP).** Some ISPs have millions of customers; others have a few hundred. You want to be able to make a toll-free phone call—probably on a phone line that has flat-rate service for local calls if you plan to spend a lot of time surfing. You may spend more time on-line than you expect. Think about it: only two industries call their customers "users." And the ISP should have enough modems for the number of customers it serves, so you don't get busy signals when you dial.

ISP's computers are run by hamsters on treadmills, and every now and then they need to sleep. You want an ISP with enough hamsters so you can connect when you want to.

If you travel, you want to be able to access your ISP from other cities, either through a local phone number or an 800 number.

- **The phone number to connect to your ISP.**
- **A login name (or username) and password given to you by your ISP.**
- **The IP address of the ISP's domain name server (DNS).** You get this too from your ISP. (It's good to know it, even though it may be entered automatically in FreeBSD when you connect.)
- **A modem.** Your modem can be internal (on a card you put in your computer) or external, sitting outside the computer with its own power supply.

WARNING

What won't work is a WinModem—a modem that uses the computer's resources instead of its own. WinModems come in many varieties, and some laptops have WinModems.

- **The name of the serial port used by your modem** (whether the modem is internal or external). If your modem uses the first serial port, which FreeBSD calls `sio0`, the related device the modem uses to dial out is called `/dev/cuaa0`. Windows would call it COM1. The FreeBSD device for the COM2 of Windows is `/dev/cuaa1`.

X-REF

If you already have an ISP and can connect to your ISP in Windows, you can get the information you need from Windows. Chapter 2 tells you how to do this.

Your First Connection

TIP

Your first connection should be made by hand, so you see the responses from your ISP. With the username, password, and phone number from your ISP, you follow these steps:

1. **Log in as** `root` (with `su`, as Chapter 5 explains).
2. **Type** `cd /etc/ppp`
3. **Type** `ppp`

   You see (if your computer's name is `killer`):

```
Working in interactive mode
Using interface: tun0
ppp ON killer>
```

You are now at the `ppp` prompt, `ppp ON killer>`. If your modem is on COM1 and not COM2, you type the following:

```
ppp ON killer>  set device /dev/cuaa0
```

ISDN Modems

Not very many people have ISDN modems. They're usually not as fast as a cable connection, but quite a lot faster than an ordinary serial modem.

For an ISDN modem, edit your `/etc/rc.conf file` and add the line `isdn_enable="YES"` and reboot. Within `ppp`, use the command `set device /dev/i4brbch0` if you have an ISDN card. You also need to recompile your kernel with `isdn` support (see Chapter 16).

4. **Enter terminal mode (where you're sending commands directly to the modem) with the** `term` **command, dial the modem (you type** `ATDT` **before the number) and enter your** `username` **and** `password` **when asked.**

   You see something like this, with differences depending on your ISP, of course:

```
ppp ON killer>  term
deflink: Entering terminal mode on /dev/cuaa0
Type '~?' for help
ATDT6180177
CONNECT 26400/ARQ/V34/LAPM/V42BIS
Welcome to MindSpring Dialup Service
arc-9b.oak login: xxx123@mindspring.com
Password: [doesn't echo]
Packet mode enabled: ppp ON killer>
PPp ON killer>
PPP ON killer>
```

When `ppp` turns to `PPP`, you're connected!

5. **Switch to another virtual terminal with `Alt-F2` or `Alt-F3`, log in as a user, and test your connection.** The `ping` command is the basic test for whether you're connected to the outside world. Here's how you use it:

```
$ ping -c 2 www.yahoo.com
```

If you see something like this, you have a good connection:

```
PING www.yahoo.akadns.net (204.71.202.160): 56
     data bytes
64 bytes from 204.71.202.160: icmp_seq=0 ttl=243
     time=3.463 ms
64 bytes from 204.71.202.160: icmp_seq=1 ttl=243
     time=3.951 ms
--- www.yahoo.akadns.net ping statistics ---
2 packets transmitted, 2 packets received, 0%
     packet loss
round-trip min/avg/max/stddev =
     3.463/3.707/3.951/0.244 ms
```

WARNING

Without `-c 2` (or `-c 4`, if you like) the `ping` command will go forever. If you use it that way, stop it with Ctrl+c.

Now you can run X (and Netscape) or ftp or whatever you like.

6. **Exit** ppp **by switching back to the virtual terminal on which you started it with** Alt-F1 **and type** bye at the PPP ON killer> prompt. It takes a few seconds for the modem to hang up and reset itself.

If you're lucky, that should be it.

Automating Your Connection

You don't have to type in your phone number, username, and password (or change the device ppp uses) every time you connect. The computer can do this for you.

To automate your connection, you edit /etc/ppp/ppp.conf.

1. **Type** cd /etc/ppp **to change to that directory and back up** ppp.conf **by typing** cp ppp.conf ppp.conf.orig

2. **Use your favorite text editor to open** /etc/ppp/ppp.conf.

   Everything in the file preceded by a # (called a hash mark) in the file is a comment—a line that doesn't do anything but provide information.

   TIP

   The ppp.conf file has labels, like default: and papchap:, at the left hand margin. The lines under each label must be indented with one or more spaces or a tab. Everything under the default: label is read every time you start ppp—it's always in effect. So this is where you want to change the line set device /dev/cuaa1 to the right device for your modem. For a modem on sio0 (COM1), change this line to set device /dev/cuaa0.

3. **Under the** papchap: **label, replace the words** PHONE_NUM, USERNAME, **and** PASSWORD **with the correct values for you and your ISP. Don't leave any spaces in the phone number.**

4. **Save the file.**

5. **Test your setup by typing** ppp papchap **as** root. **When the**

`ppp` prompt comes up, type `dial`. The modem should dial and you should be connected without having to enter a username or password.

You can create new labels in the `ppp.conf` file and call them anything you want. The easiest way to create a new label is to use your text editor to copy a label and everything under it (until the start of the next label) and change the values. (The `vi` and `pico` editors do this easily, but `ee` doesn't.)

The `set phone` entry in each label can be longer than seven digits and use whatever special symbols your modem understands. Usually a comma is a pause of two seconds, so if you need an outside line (because you're dialing from a hotel) you can put 9,5551212 (or even credit card numbers) into `set phone`.

FreeBSD's `ppp` is different from the Linux `ppp`, so Linux users should expect some new commands and methods—and capabilities. FreeBSD's `ppp` is mostly the work of Brian Somers, who regularly gives it new capabilities.

FreeBSD's `ppp` can be told to dial whenever your computer has something to send out over the Internet (with the `-auto` switch) or to open the connection and bring it up again whenever it goes down (with the `-ddial` switch). For example, to use `-ddial` with a label `myisp:` you type `ppp -ddial myisp`.

Troubleshooting Your Connection

If your attempt to connect to your ISP doesn't work, you need to figure out what's going wrong. Using terminal mode (type `ppp` and then `term` at the `ppp` prompt) is the best way to test possibilities.

At the ppp prompt you use the `show` command to see what's happening. For example, `show route` shows you the routes established and whether there's a default route. The `show ?` command gives you a list of items you can ask about with the `show` command.

The `ppp` program is set up on install to log information—it has an entry in `/etc/syslog.conf`. The log file is `/var/log/ppp.log`. You read this file to find out what might be wrong.

Modem Problems

Modem problems are the most common reason for `ppp` not working. Check a working Windows Dial-Up Networking connection for the modem port, if you have one.

If you type `AT` after entering terminal mode, your modem should respond with `OK`. `ATE0` might be necessary to turn on the modem's echo to the screen. If nothing happens, do a cold reboot (leave the computer off for a few seconds) and try again.

X-REF

If it still doesn't work, use the command `dmesg | grep sio` to find out if the serial port you're using is being found by the computer. If the computer has more than two serial ports and the modem is on the third or fourth one, you may have to enable `sio2` and `sio3` in the kernel with `UserConfig` when you boot your computer. Chapter 16 tells you how to use it.

In terminal mode you're connected directly to the modem, and any `AT` commands your modem understands should work. `ATI4` will give you information about how the modem is set up if your modem understands this command. If you want it set up differently, you use `AT` commands described in your modem manual.

Problems Logging In

You may be using the wrong kind of authentication for your ISP; consult their literature or web page. Sometimes your login requires the full email address your ISP has assigned to you; sometimes it's just your username without a domain.

Resolver Problems

If your modem dials but you get "host not found" or "no route to host" errors and can't connect to any Internet sites after you log in, your ISP may not be responding when asked for domain name server information. Look at the file `/etc/resolv.conf`. If you've connected, your ISP's `DNS` server numbers should be in this file in the form `nameserver nnn.nnn.nnn.nnn`. where the `nnn`'s are the "dot quad" IP address of the nameserver.

If the file doesn't exist, create it and enter the domain and nameservers, each on a separate line. It might look something like this:

```
domain          mindspring.com
nameserver      207.69.188.185
nameserver      207.69.188.186
```

Routing Problems

Another reason for failure to reach the Internet is that a default route hasn't been set. You can type at the ppp prompt:

```
> add default HISADDR
```

or

```
> add! default HISADDR
```

TIP

Don't substitute anything for HISADDR in this command—just type it as is. The ppp program knows what HISADDR is (the IP your ISP is using for this connection). If this solves the problem, you add the same line to the label you use when you invoke ppp with a label (don't forget to indent it).

The best, most complete description of FreeBSD's ppp, its options, and what might be wrong is the manual page (man ppp). It's long but it goes right through all the possibilities with explicit instructions on how to deal with problems.

Connecting over Ethernet

More and more, we're connecting our computers to the Internet without the benefit of telephone lines. And what a blessing it is.

If you have a cable modem, your computer probably has an ethernet card in it that connects to the cable modem. That's one situation. Or—this is the nicest—your computer is connected to the network directly, as might be the case in an office or a college dormitory or classroom.

No matter how you connect, your computer needs an IP address and (probably) a name that goes with it. The IP address and name can be fixed (given to you in advance, and not subject to change) or assigned dynamically.

TIP

Once your FreeBSD computer is set up to connect to the Internet, you can route other computers in your house or dorm or office through it, using it as a gateway. FreeBSD is an ideal operating system for use as a gateway or a router.

But the first step is to get the FreeBSD computer connected to the Internet.

Chapter 4 tells you how to set up your host, domain, gateway, and nameserver when you install FreeBSD. You can do the same thing after installation by running `/stand/sysinstall` as `root` (you select `Configure` > `Networking` > `Interfaces` and press the spacebar to get the list of network interfaces available to configure).

When you use `/stand/sysinstall` to help you set up your Internet connection, `/stand/sysinstall` edits files in `/etc` for you. This chapter tells you how to edit these files directly and how to use the command line.

Using a Fixed IP Address

If you're in the rather nice situation of having a fixed IP address and host-name—because you're part of an organization that has a block of IP addresses to give out, and you've been given one—you need to know six things:

- The name assigned to your computer
- The domain your computer is part of
- The IP address assigned to your computer
- The netmask you should use, probably 255.255.255.0
- The nameserver your computer should use (an IP address)
- The gateway your computer should use—where it should send stuff (call them packets when you're chatting with gurus) that isn't for your own computer or one your computer knows about. This should also be an IP address, although the gateway will also have a name.

X-REF If you've been running Windows and it connects to the Internet by ethernet card, you can explore Windows to get this information. See Chapter 2.

In this situation, your organization—your school or company—is your Internet service provider. With this information in hand, here's what you do:

1. **Find out if your computer has a hostname:**

   You can check to see if your computer already has a hostname (if it says `Amnesiac` when it boots, it doesn't) by typing:

```
$ hostname
```

   If it has a hostname, it will be printed out on the screen.

   The *hostname* is the name of your computer (e.g., `hunter`) plus the name of the domain your computer is part of—like `myschool.edu` or `greatmerchandise.com`. For example, the computer at my office at Stanford University is part of the `stanford.edu` domain.

2. **Change or assign the hostname by editing `/etc/rc.conf` and adding a line that says (if you're in the `myschool.edu` domain and you've been given the name `hunter` for your computer):**

```
hostname="hunter.myschool.edu"
```

   Save the file. When you reboot the computer, the new `rc.conf` will be read (but don't reboot yet, because there's more to do).

   At the command prompt (and as `root`) type:

```
# hostname hunter.myschool.edu
```

   to make the hostname effective before you reboot.

3. **Put your organization's domain name server (DNS) in `/etc/resolv.conf`.** Your ISP in this case is your organization—your school or company. You need to know the DNS number (or numbers) which you get from your system administrator (it may be on your Windows setup, as explained in Chapter 2). (If you're at college, your college is your ISP). Here are the steps:

Edit `/etc/resolv.conf` (as `root`), creating the file if it doesn't exist. Enter the following text, using the domain your computer belongs to and replacing the numbers with those for your organization's name server:

```
domain myschool.edu
nameserver 172.16.0.1
nameserver 172.16.0.2
```

4. **Edit** `/etc/hosts`

The `/etc/hosts` file has a lot of comments in it and, before you edit it, just a couple of other lines:

```
127.0.0.1    localhost localhost.my.domain
     myname.my.domain
::1          localhost localhost.my.domain
     myname.my.domain
```

In these two lines, change "`myname`" to the name of your computer ("`hunter`" in the example) and "`my.domain`" to your own domain, "`myschool.edu`" in the example. But don't change the numbers—127.0.0.1 is always the number of the local host, which is the computer on which the file lives.

Add a line starting with your own IP address and followed by your computer name and the full name (the name with the domain after it). If your IP address is 192.168.0.11, you add:

```
192.168.0.11   hunter hunter.myschool.edu
```

TIP

You can add any other hosts you know about; FreeBSD will use this file to find out the IP addresses of hosts (computers) quickly and easily, so it doesn't always have to go to the nameserver to look them up.

WARNING

Don't delete the lines beginning with a #—they have useful information you may need later.

Save the file.

Routable IP Addresses and Private IP Addresses

IP addresses—the numbers by which computers (or their interfaces) are known—come in two varieties: routable IP addresses that work on the Internet, and private IP addresses for internal networks.

Routable IP addresses need to be assigned to human owners (or organizations) that in turn give them to computers and connect them with computer names, so that when you tell your browser to look at a web page, it can figure out how to find it.

Three blocks of addresses have been reserved for internal use on private networks—like a network inside a company or a home network. These IP addresses don't work in the outside world—the computers that route packets just throw away packets destined for these addresses, because they don't belong to any computer on the Internet and they are used by hundreds of thousands of computers on private networks. You can use them, too.

The private addresses are 10.0.0.0–10.255.255.255, 172.16.0.0–172.31.255.255, and 192.168.0.0–192.168.255.255. The examples in this chapter use addresses beginning with 192.168 and 172.16 as if they were real ones (like using 555–1212 for a phone number), and use addresses beginning with 10.10.10 for internal (private) examples.

5. **Configure your network interface.**

   You find the name of your network interfaces with the command:

```
$ ifconfig
```

   You see output like the following—a list of interfaces with information about them. The first one (or two, if you have two ethernet cards) is your ethernet interface (it could be `dc0` or `fxp0` or whatever). That's what you want to work with. In this output, the ethernet card (and its hardware address) has been found, but it hasn't been given an IP address and the interface isn't up.

```
ed0: flags=8802<BROADCAST,SIMPLEX,MULTICAST> mtu
     1500
        ether 00:40:33:97:0d:44
sl0: flags=c010<POINTOPOINT,LINK2,MULTICAST> mtu
     552
ppp0: flags=8010<POINTOPOINT,MULTICAST> mtu 1500
lo0: flags=8049<UP,LOOPBACK,RUNNING,MULTICAST>
     mtu 16384
```

Bring up the network by typing the following command, substituting for `ed0` your own ethernet interface and your own IP address and netmask:

```
# ifconfig ed0 192.168.0.11 netmask 255.255.255.0
```

Now `ifconfig` (the `-a` is optional in FreeBSD 4.1 and later) should show you something like this for `ed0`, or your own interface:

```
ed0: flags=8843<UP,BROADCAST,RUNNING,SIMPLEX,
     MULTICAST> mtu 1500
   inet6 fe80::240:33ff:fe97:d44%ed0 prefixlen
     64 scopeid 0x1
   inet 192.168.0.11 netmask 0xffffff00
     broadcast 192.168.0.0
   ether 00:40:33:97:0d:44
```

It's not important right now to know what every single thing means here—but notice the UP in the first line, and the IP address assigned to the `ed0` interface. The `ifconfig -au` command shows you all the interfaces that are actually up (hey, the u stands for up!) and running.

To make your network come up on boot (so you don't have to retype this stuff every time you boot the computer), edit `/etc.rc.conf` and add this line, adjusted for your own network card, IP address, and netmask:

```
ifconfig_ed0="inet 192.168.0.11 netmask
     255.255.255.0"
```

WARNING

Watch out for capitalization and punctuation, keep it all on one line, and notice that what you type at the command line is a little different (although the information is the same) from what you put in `/etc/rc.conf`.

TIP

You look at `/etc/defaults/rc.conf` for the nitty-gritty of what to put in `/etc/rc.conf`. But don't copy `/etc/defaults/rc.conf` to `/etc/rc.conf` or you could be in trouble. See Chapter 19 for getting out of this kind of trouble.

6. **Add a gateway—also known as a default route.**

Edit /etc/rc.conf and add the following line (if it doesn't already exist), substituting the number you were given (or found in Windows) for the gateway your computer should use:

```
defaultrouter="172.16.0.100"
```

To make this effective before rebooting, type at the command line:

```
# route add default 172.16.0.100
```

If you get a message saying "File exists" you already have a default route. You can delete it with the command:

```
# route delete default
```

You can then use the route add default command to add the gateway.

7. **Check up on your work with netstat -rn. The netstat -r command shows you routes, and the -n switch does it in numbers. The first few lines should look something like this:**

```
Routing tables

Internet:
Destination    Gateway            Flags    Netif
default        172.16.0.100       UGSc       0
     0       ed0
192.168.0/24   link#1             UC         0
     0       ed0 =>
172.16.0.100   0:a0:cc:63:44:5f UHLW       2
     127       ed0   1160
127.0.0.1      127.0.0.1          UH         0
     0       lo0
```

Testing Your Connection

These basic tools are useful for checking and testing your connection:

- `ifconfig -au`
- `netstat -rn`
- `ping` *<hostname>*
- `traceroute` *<hostname>*
- `nslookup` *<hostname>*

If your ethernet card has been detected and you have assigned an IP address to your ethernet interface, `ifconfig -au` will show the interface UP with an IP address. The `netstat -rn` command should show you a default route, and you should be able to ping a computer on the Internet and trace a route to it. If `ping`, `traceroute`, and `nslookup` work with IP addresses but not names, you have a resolver problem (what you put in `/etc/resolv.conf` isn't right). If `ping`, `traceroute`, and `nslookup` work, so will your browser, `ftp`, and `telnet`.

Using a Dynamic IP Address

Your Internet service provider—whether it's an organization like a school or a company, or an ISP that's offering a connection over a cable modem—may dynamically assign you an IP address from a pool.

If you have a cable modem and your ISP uses DHCP (Dynamic Host Configuration Protocol), you put this line (substituting your own network interface for `ed0`) in `/etc/rc.conf`:

```
ifconfig_ed0="DHCP"
```

When you reboot, the boot process will run `dhclient` and get the information it needs from your ISP—your IP address, netmask, nameserver to use, and gateway.

To run `dhclient` without rebooting, type (substituting your own network interface):

```
# dhclient ed0
```

The commands for checking and testing your connection (`ifconfig`, `netstat`,`ping`, `traceroute`, and `nslookup`) should work for you now.

TIP The `/etc/dhclient.conf` file can be edited (it's empty by default) if you want to use specific options or override the information your ISP sends. See the manual page for more options than you should ever need. It tells you just what to put in it to accomplish your aims.

Setting Up an Internal Network

Connecting computers to each other by ethernet is not something done just by big organizations. The hardware (and the software) for connecting computers is getting cheaper and better, and you can do it at home or in a college dormitory or office.

Why would you want to do this? Here are a few reasons:

- You've got a desktop and a laptop, and you want to transfer files—fast and easily—or get to files on one computer from another.

- You've got one computer with a high-speed connection to the Internet—maybe through a cable modem—and you want your other computers to be able to get to the Internet using that computer as a gateway. (Then you and your sister can be on the Internet at the same time.)

- You've got one great printer, and you want to be able to print to it from all your computers.

What You Need

To connect your computers—that is, set up a *LAN* or local area network—you need:

- **An ethernet card for each computer** (sometimes ethernet is built in to a computer, especially a laptop—otherwise a laptop uses an ethernet device on a pccard). Cards can come with three different kinds of connectors; the RJ-45 connector, which looks like an RJ-11 telephone connector but is larger, is becoming standard.

Cards are either capable of only 10 mbs (megabits per second) or both 10 mbs and 100 mbs.

- **An ethernet hub**, capable of 10 mbs or both 10 mbs and 100 mbs. Hubs need to be plugged into an electric outlet. Hubs are different sizes. Small ones allow you to connect four computers, larger ones eight or more.

- **Cables to connect each computer to the hub.** It's called category 5 *patch* cable, or cat 5 for short. If you connect two computers to each other without a hub in between, you use category 5 *crossover* cable. You tell the difference by comparing the colors of the wire covers in the connectors. If they're arranged the same at both ends, it's patch cable. If the colors are in a different order, it's crossover cable. Cables come in a variety of lengths and external colors. Don't be caught with patch cable that doesn't match your decor!

- **A second network interface for the gateway computer.** The gateway computer—the one through which all the others connect to the Internet—needs not only the ethernet card that connects it to the hub, but another interface that connects it to the outside world—a modem that connects to the phone line or another ethernet card that connects to a cable or adsl modem.

Using FreeBSD as A Gateway

To use FreeBSD as a gateway, you first set up your Internet connection from FreeBSD so it works (see above)—whether you're using `ppp` or an ethernet connection. You should be able to ping computers on the Internet, surf the web with Netscape or `lynx` (or `w3m`), and use `ftp` and other Internet utilities. If the FreeBSD computer can't get to the Internet, your other computers aren't going to be able to get there by going through it.

Then you set up your internal network. And finally you arrange for the internal network to reach the Internet.

Setting Up FreeBSD

Plan your internal network. Select a domain name for it (say, `valley.net`) and names for your computers, and an internal IP address and netmask (all the computers should be on the same subnet) for each computer. For example:

```
10.10.10.1      lion.valley.net
10.10.10.2      tiger.valley.net
10.10.10.3      jaguar.valley.net
10.10.10.4      puma.valley.net
```

The netmask will be 255.255.255.0. This will allow you to have 254 computers (or other devices, like a printer) on your network. The 10.10.10.0 address is the network, and 10.10.10.255 will be the broadcast.

Naming Your Computers

Geeks worry a lot about naming their computers. You can name yours after the moons of Jupiter, your favorite rock groups, higher order elements in the periodic table, or dead pets.

It's traditional to give computers in a group related names. But you shouldn't anthropomorphize computers by naming them after people (like famous World War II generals, infamous dictators, your aunts and uncles, historic stars of "Saturday Night Live," or the members of the FreeBSD core group) because computers don't like that.

You add the entries above to your `/etc/hosts` file on your FreeBSD computer. You don't change your default route (either permanently entered in `/etc/rc.conf` or assigned when you connect to your ISP), nor do you change your nameserver in `/etc/resolv.conf`, which also comes from your ISP.

The FreeBSD gateway connects to the Internet with its external interface; its ethernet card for the internal network will have the address of 10.10.10.1.

You set up your internal ethernet card (after you physically install it in the computer) just like you set up an ethernet card for a connection to a cable modem, by adding this line (assuming your network card for the internal network uses the `dc0` driver, so it's distinguished here from your external interface, either `ed0` or `tun0`) to `/etc/rc.conf`:

```
ifconfig_dc0="inet 10.10.10.1 netmask
    255.255.255.0"
```

You can of course use the command line to make these commands effective before reboot, but remember to put them in `/etc/rc.conf` so they take effect automatically when the computers are rebooted.

Setting Up Another UNIX Computer

You set up another computer running FreeBSD or some other UNIX variant (maybe Linux) the same way. You install the ethernet card in the computer and give the computer a hostname of `tiger.valley.net` and an IP address of 10.10.10.2, and a default route of 10.10.10.1—the internal address of the gateway computer. Whenever the other UNIX computer doesn't know where to send something (like a request to look at a web page), it will deliver it to the FreeBSD gateway. You should also fill out the other computer's `/etc/hosts` file.

For now we'll postpone talking about how the traffic gets from the other UNIX machine to the Internet. But if you've got it set up right, the FreeBSD computer and the Linux computer should be able to ping each other by internal IP address and by hostname. You should be able to use `ftp` to get from one to the other (logging in with `username` and `password`) and `telnet` from one to the other. And they should show up in the output of `netstat -rn`.

Don't forget to install the hub and plug the ethernet cards into it. If you don't have a hub, you can connect two computers with crossover cable.

Setting Up A Windows Computer

Getting a computer running Windows on your internal network is a little trickier, but in concept it's the same. You install the ethernet card according to the instructions that came with it and connect it with the cable to your hub. Don't forget to connect each ethernet card to the hub (and plug in the hub's power supply).

Whether it's Windows 95/98 or Windows NT, you use Settings->Control Panel->Network to look at and change settings. (In Windows 2000, which is based on NT, it's Settings->Control Panel->Administrative Tools->Computer

Management).

The following lists show the settings you want to check (or change) so your Windows computers can use FreeBSD as a gateway.

TIP

If you want to be able to share some files or printers on your Windows machines, while you're setting up the network you might also want to include the settings Samba will need if you install it on FreeBSD. Without Samba (and settings for it), you'll be able to use the FreeBSD machine as a gateway but your FreeBSD directories won't show up in your Windows Network Neighborhood. You will be able to print to a network printer from each computer, though.

Windows NT/2000

In Windows NT under Settings->Control Panel->Network, you see a bunch of tabs, listed below. Click on the listed tabs and fill out the boxes or click the checkboxes as indicated.

Identification (use the Change button if necessary)

- Computer name: Enter the computer's name (without the domain)—`jaguar`, in this example.
- Workgroup: Specify a workgroup (the same for all your computers)—`MYGROUP` in this example.

Services

- The Workstation service should be listed here because it's installed by default; if it's not there, click the Add button and install it.

Protocols

- TCP/IP needs to be listed; if not, click Add and install it.
- Highlight TCP/IP and click Properties
    - On the IP Address tab add the IP address of the computer (10.10.10.3) and the gateway (the internal address of your FreeBSD machine, 10.10.10.1 in this example)

- On the DNS tab fill in the host name (`jaguar`) and the domain (`valley.net`) of the computer you're working on and list the DNS servers your ISP has given you by number

- On the WINS Address tab list your FreeBSD computer as the Primary WINS server (for later enabling when you install Samba) or use the Windows computer as the Primary WINS server. Check the box Enable DNS for Windows resolution.

Click OK and reboot.

Windows 95/98

In Windows 95/98 under Settings->Control Panel->Network, you see a bunch of tabs as listed below. Click on each in turn and fill out the boxes or click the checkboxes as indicated.

Configuration: If Client for Microsoft Networks and TCP/IP are not installed, click on Add and install each in turn. When installed, TCP/IP shows up with your ethernet card listed next to it. Click Properties and look at these tabs:

- **IP Address:** Click the Specify an IP address radio button and fill in the IP Address for the computer you're working on (10.10.10.4) and the Subnet Mask (255.255.255.0).

- **DNS Configuration:** Click the Enable DNS radio button and fill in the Host (`puma`) and the Domain (`valley.net`). Enter your ISP's domain name server number or numbers under DNS Server Search Order.

- **WINS Configuration:** Click the Enable WINS Resolution check box. Under WINS Server Search Order, enter the IP address of your FreeBSD computer—10.10.10.1—or your NT computer, if you've decided to use it for WINS resolution.

- **Bindings:** Under this tab Client for Microsoft Networks and File and Printer Sharing for Microsoft Networks should be checked.

Identification: Enter the computer name (`puma`) and the Workgroup (`MYGROUP`).

Click OK and reboot.

Reaching the Internet—The Final Step

At this point you have achieved two goals:

- The FreeBSD computer can reach the rest of the world.
- The other computers on your LAN can talk to each other in some way.

With all the computers on your local network set up properly, each should be able to `ping` the others. All of them should be able to `telnet` and `ftp` to FreeBSD or any other UNIX-type system you have running if these services are enabled on the UNIX-style computers. Windows machines usually have telnet and ftp clients but not telnet and ftp servers, so you can `telnet` from them to another machine but you can't `telnet` to them.

TIP

If your FreeBSD computer can't reach the Internet and your other computers can't communicate with the FreeBSD computer internally, you won't be able to get one of the internal computers to reach the Internet.

The final step depends on whether the FreeBSD machine uses `ppp` to connect to the Internet or an ethernet card that goes to a cable modem (or is directly connected to an organization ethernet).

Whichever one you use, your FreeBSD computer needs to be a gateway.

You enter the following in `/etc/rc.conf`:

```
gateway_enable="YES"
```

It becomes effective on reboot; or see the sidebar, "Talking to the Kernel."

Talking to the Kernel

To check whether your computer is already set up as a gateway, ask the kernel using `sysctl`. Type:

```
#sysctl -a | grep forward
```

You see:

```
net.inet.ip.forwarding: 1
net.inet.ip.fastforwarding: 0
net.inet6.ip6.forwarding: 0
```

If the first line has a 0 instead of a 1 at the end, forwarding (the gateway function) is not enabled. As `root` type:

```
# sysctl -w net.inet.ip.forwarding=1
```

You see:

```
net.inet.ip.forwarding: 0 -> 1
```

Be sure to put `gateway_enable="YES"` in `/etc/rc.conf` to make forwarding effective on reboot.

The PPP Internet Connection

If `ppp` is the way you reach the Internet—with a dial-up connection—just start `ppp` with the `-nat` switch:

```
# ppp -nat papchap
```

The `-nat` switch tells `ppp` to do network address translation. If you run a browser like Netscape from `tiger` or `jaguar`, the requests will be sent to `lion` (because `lion` is their gateway) and rewritten so they look like they're coming from `lion`. The response will come back to `lion`, and the `ppp` program on `lion` will send them where they should go—to `jaguar` or `tiger`. It keeps track of which computer sent a request with a table so that it knows where to send the response.

The Internet Connection

If your external interface (how you get to the Internet) is an ethernet card, you also need to enable a firewall. The loadable kernel module, `ipfw.ko`, that exists in FreeBSD 4.3 doesn't provide the services you need for this purpose, so you need to recompile the kernel with `ipfw` support.

The `natd` manual page gives a good summary of what you need in a kernel capable of sending packets from internal machines to the outside and getting a response back, and what else you have to do. Here are the steps, as `root`:

```
# cd /usr/src/sys/i36/conf
```

If no such directory exists (and kernel source isn't installed), see Chapter 16 for how to install it).

```
/usr/src/sys/i386/conf # cp GENERIC NEWKERN
```

Edit `NEWKERN` (or whatever you choose to call it), adding the following lines at the end of the file:

```
options         IPFIREWALL
options         IPDIVERT
```

You can also add, if you like, the following (the first is recommended), and other options displayed in the sample `LINT` file that you find in the same directory as `GENERIC`:

```
options         IPFIREWALL_DEFAULT_TO_ACCEPT
options         IPFIREWALL_VERBOSE
options         IPFIREWALL_VERBOSE_LIMIT=100
```

The following commands build and install your kernel:

```
/usr/src/sys/i386/conf # config NEWKERN
/usr/src/sys/i386/conf # cd ../../compile/NEWKERN
/usr/src/sys/i386/conf # make depend
/usr/src/sys/i386/conf # make
/usr/src/sys/i386/conf # make install
```

You reboot to run the new kernel, but first add some lines, as follows, to `/etc/rc.conf`:

```
enable_firewall="YES"
firewall_type="open"
natd_enable="YES"
natd_interface="<external interface>"
```

Be sure to substitute your external interface, for example `ed0`, for *`<external interface>`* above.

WARNING

A firewall is a security device—it lets you set rules for what's allowed to come into your computer (and go out). When you enable a firewall in `/etc/rc.conf`, rebooting will automatically use the firewall rules for the kind of firewall you have requested from `/etc/rc.firewall`. An open firewall doesn't restrict anything. It's no different from a regular Internet connection without a firewall. But you can change the firewall type or add rules to your firewall later.

If the `natd` lines aren't in `rc.conf`, you can run `natd` from the command line:

```
# /sbin/natd -n ed0
# /sbin/ipfw add 100 divert natd all from any to
     any via ed0
```

or (in place of the last line):

```
# /sbin/ipfw add 100 divert 8668 ip from any to any
     via ed0
```

TIP

Notice that the interface on which `natd` runs is the *external* interface—the one that connects to the outside world—not the ethernet card for the internal network, which in the example uses `dc0`.

Can you use `natd` with `ppp`, instead of `ppp -nat`? It will probably work, but you have to start `ppp` first so that you can type `/sbin/natd -n tun0`. The `tun0` interface, on which `ppp` runs, doesn't come up until `ppp` starts, so until then there's nothing for `natd` to work with.

LINUX

The `natd` program does the same kind of work Linux calls *ipmasquerading*.

Checking Your Firewall

Enabling a firewall is necessary to running network address translation when you're using an ethernet card, even if it's not walling off any fire.

Your firewall, `ipfw`, works with rules, and you can look at them any time (as `root`) with the command:

```
# ipfw list
```

For an open firewall, you see a display like the following:

```
00100 divert 8668 ip from any to any via ed0
00150 allow ip from any to any via lo0
00200 deny ip from any to 127.0.0.0/8
65000 allow ip from any to any
65535 deny ip from any to any
```

The packets crossing your ethernet hit each rule until one of them works on it. You can't change the last rule (unless you recompile the kernel), but you can add or delete rules above it.

The rules above are what you get with an open firewall. If you want to read more about `ipfw` firewall rules and `natd` (many options exist), see their manual pages.

Chapter 13

FreeBSD Can Be a Blast

You probably have a CD player, a tape player, an MP3 player, a stereo system on your desk and in the car, and a portable radio. The ideal companion to all this audio hardware is, of course, a sound-capable computer. How could you do without it?

This chapter tells you how to get sound working in FreeBSD.

Listening to Your Sound Card

Find out what kind of sound card is in your computer. Maybe you have the box or a list of components or the motherboard manual, if your sound card is built in.

Windows might be able to tell you, too. See Chapter 2 for extracting information from Windows. Make a note of the resources it uses—the IRQ and DMA and the address resources--and the manufacturer.

As a last resort, take the cover off your computer, grab a flashlight, and look at it. It's the card the speakers plug into—oh, you knew that! Is it an ISA card, in one of the long black slots, or a PCI card, in one of the white ones?

FreeBSD supports a lot of sound cards—see Appendix A: Supported Hardware (the Sound Cards and Multimedia section) for as well as this chapter. Some cards that aren't specifically listed may also work.

Sounding Off with Your Kernel

You're going to sound off at this news: Except in FreeBSD 4.3 and later, and maybe even then, you need to recompile your kernel to make sound work in FreeBSD. Versions 4.3 and later have easily loadable add-ons to the kernel (modules, to be really elegant about it) for sound. See the sidebar for more information.

Rebuilding your kernel isn't as hard as it sounds (no pun intended!).

Here's what you do (details later):

- Make sure kernel source is installed.
- Edit a kernel configuration file to add a few lines for sound.
- Tell FreeBSD to rebuild and install the kernel.
- Make sound devices in `/dev`
- Reboot the computer, and
- Test your new setup.

Loadable Kernel Modules for Sound

If the loadable kernel modules for sound work for you, you won't have to recompile your kernel just to get sound.

As `root`, type `kldload snd` to load the sound modules. Kernel modules are located in `/modules` (they're the `pcm` sound drivers and all start with `snd`). They show up when you type `kldstat`.

Next, `cd /dev` and type `sh MAKEDEV snd0`.

That's all—if the kernel mods work for you, sound will be enabled. Add the line

```
snd_load="YES"
```

to the `/boot/loader.conf` file to load the kernel sound modules on boot.

Checking for Kernel Source

To check for kernel source, type:

```
$ ls /usr/src/sys/
```

ON CD-1

If you see a bunch of files, kernel source is installed. If you don't see files, see the section in Chapter 16, What You Need to Build a Kernel, to find out how to install it. It's on the installation CD-ROM and won't take long.

With kernel source installed, you can proceed.

Adding Sound to Your Kernel File

Kernel configuration files are located in `/usr/src/sys/i386/conf`. To change to that directory type:

```
$ cd /usr/src/sys/i386/conf
```

Log in as `root` (see Chapter 5 for how to do this).

Copy the file called `GENERIC` to `NEWKERN` (or any name you like) by typing:

```
# cp GENERIC NEWKERN
```

Your new file, `NEWKERN`, is the one you want to edit—but the sound lines to add to the end of `NEWKERN` are in the `LINT` file, which includes everything imaginable you could add to a kernel configuration file.

X-REF

Chapter 16 tells you about other options you might want to add or delete from your kernel configuration file. This chapter covers only sound options.

WARNING

The LINT file has two sets of drivers for sound cards: Voxware drivers (the old ones) and "`newpcm`" (or just `pcm`) drivers (the new ones, which work better for newer sound cards). You select from one set or the other—don't mix them. The Voxware drivers are no longer maintained and will not be available in version 5.0 of FreeBSD.

LINT is a long file, but opening it in your favorite editor and searching for the word *sound* takes you right to the beginning of the description of the drivers. Both Voxware and `pcm` are described, and then the actual lines are listed. You choose the ones for your sound card from the Voxware or `pcm` lines.

Using pcm Sound Drivers

The `pcm` sound driver supports the cards or codecs (sound chips) listed in Table 13-1 and most of the more common ISA/PnP `sb/mss/ess` compatible cards.

Table 13-1 Sound Cards or Chips Supported by pcm

SB16 (SoundBlasters)
CS423x (ISA)
OPTi931 (ISA)
Yamaha OPL-SAX (ISA; used in several PnP cards and also in non-PnP mode on motherboards and some laptops)
Trident 4DWave DX/NX (PCI)
ENSONIQ AudioPCI ES1370/1371 (PCI)
ESS and Avance ISA chips
Creative Labs Soundblaster PCI and ISA (PnP and non-PnP)
NeoMagic 256AV(av97)/ZX (PCI)
Gravis Ultrasound ISA (PnP and non-PnP)
Crystal Semiconductor CS461x/462x/428x PCI

If your card is Plug and Play or PCI, you put this line in `NEWKERN`:

```
device    pcm
```

If it's not a Plug and Play ISA or PCI (and has no bridge driver), you use this, possibly with a different IRQ (5 is often used for sound cards) matching the card:

```
device   pcm0 at isa? irq 10 drq 1 flags 0x0
```

For a Creative SoundBlaster ISA non-PnP and also ESS and Avance ISA chips, this line should also be added:

```
device   sbc0  at isa? port 0x220 irq 5 drq 1 flags
    0x15
```

For Gravis UltraSound ISA non-PnP, add:

```
device   gusc0 at isa? port 0x220 irq 5 drq 1 flags
    0x13
```

Copy the lines from the `LINT` file that are appropriate for your sound card to the end of `NEWKERN`, each on a separate line, and save the file. Don't let long lines get split in two. Since joy sticks are located on sound cards, if you have a joy stick you add this line too:

```
device        joy
```

Using Voxware Drivers

If you choose to try the unsupported (and soon to disappear) Voxware drivers instead of using `pcm`, you edit your kernel configuration file and add this line at the end:

```
device        snd0
```

You also select the lines appropriate for your sound card from the following ones, using Table 13-2 to decide what you need. (You may need more than one.) Keep them in order—sometimes it matters which comes first—and add them at the end of your file:

```
device sbmidi0 at isa? port 0x330
```

```
device awe0   at isa? port 0x620
device gus0   at isa? port 0x220 irq 12 drq 1
device gus0   at isa? port 0x220 irq 12 drq 1 flags
     0x3 # for a Gravis Ultrasound card with two
     DMA channels
device mss0   at isa? port 0x530 irq 10 drq 1
device css0   at isa? port 0x534 irq 5 drq 1 flags
     0x08
device sscape0 at isa? port 0x330 irq 9 drq 0
device trix0  at isa? port 0x330 irq 6 drq 0
device sscape_mss0 at isa? port 0x534 irq 5 drq 1
device opl0   at isa? port 0x388
device mpu0   at isa? port 0x330 irq 6 drq 0
device uart0  at isa? port 0x330 irq 5
```

Table 13-2 Voxware Sound Drivers

Driver	*What It's For*
sb	SoundBlaster PCM - SoundBlaster, SB Pro, SB16, ProAudioSpectrum
sbxvi	SoundBlaster 16
sbmid	SoundBlaster 16 MIDI interface
pas	ProAudioSpectrum PCM and MIDI
gus	Gravis Ultrasound - Ultrasound, Ultrasound 16, Ultrasound MAX
mss	Microsoft Sound System
css	Crystal Sound System (CSS 423x PnP)
sscape	Ensoniq Soundscape MIDI interface
sscape_mss	Ensoniq Soundscape PCM (requires sscape)
opl	Yamaha OPL-2 and OPL-3 FM - SB, SB Pro, SB 16, ProAudioSpectrum
uart	stand-alone 6850 UART for MIDI
mpu	Roland MPU-401 stand-alone card

Building Your Sound Kernel

To build and install your new kernel (and reboot with it), use these commands:

```
/usr/src/sys/i386/conf # config NEWKERN
/usr/src/sys/i386/conf # cd ../../compile/NEWKERN
/usr/src/sys/compile/NEWKERN # make depend
/usr/src/sys/compile/NEWKERN # make
/usr/src/sys/compile/NEWKERN # make install
/usr/src/sys/compile/NEWKERN # /sbin/reboot
```

You see a remarkable amount of stuff flashing across your screen. A kernel takes about ten minutes to build on a fast machine.

Making Device Nodes

After your computer reboots with the new kernel, you can use `dmesg` to see if it found your sound card:

```
# dmesg | grep pcm
```

or, instead of (or in addition to) `pcm`, whatever devices you tried in the kernel, like `sbc`.

You see something like this:

```
pcm0: <ESS 18xx DSP> on sbc0
```

TIP

Before you can use sound, you must make sound (`snd`) device nodes in `/dev`. These device nodes are for both sets of drivers—Voxware and `pcm`.

If `dmesg` shows sound devices (especially `pcm`) ending with `0`, you use the following commands (logged in as `root`):

```
# cd /dev
```

```
# sh MAKDEV snd0
```

If `dmesg` shows sound devices ending with `1`, you use:

```
# cd /dev
# sh MAKEDEV snd1
```

TIP

These commands don't create anything in `/dev` starting with `snd`—what they create are device nodes ending in `0` or `1` and symbolic links (with the same names but without a number) as follows:

```
/dev/audio
/dev/dsp
/dev/dspW
/dev/midi
/dev/mixer
/dev/music
/dev/sequencer
/dev/pss
```

These symbolic names will be linked to their counterparts (the real device nodes) ending in either `0` or `1` depending on whether you last made the `snd0` device nodes or the `snd1` device nodes. You see what links you have this way:

```
root@pitcher 4:32PM ~ # ls -l /dev/audio*
lrwxrwxrwx  1 root  wheel        6 Apr  5 00:20
     /dev/audio@ -> audio1
crw-rw-rw-  1 root  wheel   30,   4 Apr  5 00:14
     /dev/audio0
crw-rw-rw-  1 root  wheel   30,  20 Sep 23 15:45
     /dev/audio1
```

On this computer (`pitcher`, a VAIO Picturebook), both sets of device nodes have been created, but `audio` is linked to `audio1`, as are all the other device nodes. To get links to `audio0` and other device nodes ending in `0`, typing `sh /dev/MAKEDEV snd0` would accomplish it.

If you added support for a joy stick to your kernel, also issue this command:

```
# sh /dev/MAKEDEV joy
```

Testing the Results

In addition to using `dmesg`, you can see the configured sound devices with:

```
# cat /dev/sndstat
```

TIP

To see if sound is really working (be sure the speakers are plugged in), download a file with an `.au` or `.AU` extension (you might find one at http://www.sony.com). If it's called `DANCE.AU`, type as `root` in the directory with the file:

```
# cat DANCE.AU > /dev/audio
```

and it should play. If you don't have an `.au` or `.AU` file, you can send any non-text file to `/dev/audio` to hear sound. Play your kernel:

```
# cat /kernel > /dev/audio
```

It will sound awful (kernels aren't very musical), but at least all that static tells you the sound card is working.

If it doesn't work, you experiment with different options from the `LINT` file. There's some information in a file on your hard drive called `/usr/src/sys/i386/isa/sound/sound.doc`, but it deals with Voxware drivers. Documents like that—and web guides—tend to get out-of-date when technology moves quickly.

Three manual pages (for `pcm`, `sbc`, and `mixer`) have additional (and more up-to-date) information. Typing `mixer` shows you a list of values you can change.

If all else fails and you really want to find out if your sound card works, removing a network card and trying it again might help. Sometimes cards just don't like each other and it's hard to sort out.

As a special case, licensing restrictions prevent the Maestro3/Allegro driver from being compiled directly into the kernel. If you have one of these, compile `device pcm` in the kernel and add this line to `/boot/loader.conf`:

```
snd_maestro3_load="YES"
```

Ripping and Listening

FreeBSD has many third-party software applications, from CD players to programs for converting sound files from one format to another and organizing the music on your hard drive. See Chapter 11, Audio, for a rundown.

Chapter 14

The X Window System

The X Window System is the graphical user interface for FreeBSD (and other BSD and UNIX systems). Whether you call it the X Window System, X11, XFree86, or just plain X, it's where you run your office suites, surf the web, and process photos from your digital camera with The Gimp, which is as close as you can get to Adobe's PhotoShop with no damage to your wallet whatsoever.

This chapter explains how to get version 3.3.6 (or earlier) of X up and running. It doesn't cover version 4.

What X Needs to Know

When you set up X, you tell the setup program about your video card and your monitor. Getting this information right makes all the difference in the world.

Your Video Card

Windows is a reliable guide to your video card (or display adapter, another name by which it is known). Find out about your video card while Windows is running this way:

1. **Right-click on any free space on the desktop.**
2. **Click on** Properties **and then click on the** Settings **tab.**
3. **Click on** Display Type **(in NT) or** Advanced-->Adapter **in 98 or 2000 or** Change Display Type **in 95.**

   You see a display like that in Figure 14-1, telling you not only the name of your video card but how much RAM it has and some other items of information. Sometimes another screen of additional information is available. Write down the manufacturer, model, and amount of RAM.

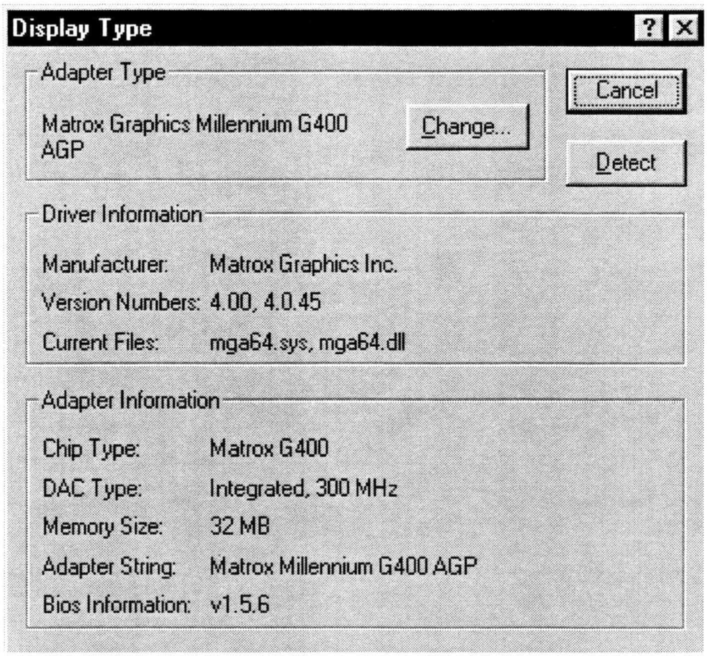

Figure 14-1: What Windows Can Tell You About Your Video Card

Windows knows less about your monitor (probably only what you told it yourself), but you may have an icon in the tray for video card settings that has a monitor tab with information about the available resolutions and refresh rates for your monitor. If so, write down this information too.

X itself has a program called `SuperProbe` you can run to tell you about your video card. It may hang your machine (type `man SuperProbe` to read all the dire warnings and see the many options), but if you don't know anything about your video card, it may be the way to go. Run it as `root` with the `-verbose` option, like this:

```
# SuperProbe -verbose
```

and write down what it tells you.

Your Monitor

Although Windows might be able to tell you something about your monitor, your best bet here is to look at the make and model (the model number should be on the back of it, if not the front) and either grab your manual or search the manufacturer's web site for the model number. You should be able to get some specs for the monitor that tell you the range of its horizontal and vertical refresh rates.

Your X installation on FreeBSD also has some information about monitors in `/usr/X11R6/lib/X11/doc/Monitors`, put together from actual experience.

Making Sure X Is Installed

X lives in `/usr/X11R6`. To find out if X is installed, type:

```
$ ls /usr/X11R6
```

You should see a bunch of directories. If you don't (you get a `"No such file or directory"` message), X is not installed. To install X, do the following:

1. **Put the CD-ROM in the drive.**
2. **Type** `/stand/sysinstall`
3. **From the main menu choose** `Configure > Distributions;` **use the arrow keys to highlight** `XFree86 The XFree86 3.3.6 distribution` **and press the spacebar.**

   You see the `The Xfree86 3.3.6 Distribution Menu.`
4. **Highlight** `Basic` **by pressing the arrow keys, press** Enter, **highlight each item you want and press the spacebar to put an** `[X]` **next to it (this X isn't related to** `X Window`, **it's just the marker for your selections). From the Basic menu you want** `bin`, `lib`, **and** `set`, **and optionally** `cfg` **and** `man`. **Press** Enter **(with** `[OK]`

highlighted) when you're done.

5. **Highlight** `Server` **by pressing the arrow keys, press Enter, highlight each server you want to install, and press the spacebar to get an** `[X]` **next to it.** `VGA16` runs any video card (and is necessary for running the graphical `XF86Setup`, which isn't described here). The `SVGA` server runs most recent video cards and is probably good to have installed. If you have something like an ATI Mach card, also install the server with the name that matches your card. Figure 14-2 shows you the list. **Press** Enter **(with** `[OK]` **highlighted) when you're done.**

```
─────────────────────── X Server selection. ───────────────────────
 Please check off the types of X servers you wish to install.
 If you are unsure as to which server will work for your graphics card,
 it is recommended that try the SVGA or VGA16 servers or, for PC98
 machines, the 9EGC or 9840 servers.

      <<< X Exit     Exit this menu (returning to previous)
          All        Select all of the above
          Reset      Reset all of the above
      [ ]  SVGA      Standard VGA or Super VGA card
      [ ]  VGA16     Standard 16 color VGA card
      [ ]  Mono      Standard Monochrome card
      [ ]  3DL       8, 16 and 24 bit color 3D Labs boards
      [ ]  8514      8-bit (256 color) IBM 8514 or compatible card
      [ ]  AGX       8-bit AGX card
      [ ]  I128      8, 16 and 24-bit #9 Imagine I128 card
      [ ]  Ma8       8-bit ATI Mach8 card
      [ ]  Ma32      8 and 16-bit (65K color) ATI Mach32 card
      [ ]  Ma64      8 and 16-bit (65K color) ATI Mach64 card
      [ ]  P9K       8, 16, and 24-bit color Weitek P9000 based boards
      [ ]  S3        8, 16 and 24-bit color S3 based boards
      [ ]  S3V       8, 16 and 24-bit color S3 Virge based boards
      [ ]  W32       8-bit ET4000/W32, /W32i and /W32p cards
      > >  PC98      Select an X server for a NEC PC98 [Submenu]

                       [  OK  ]        Cancel
```

Figure 14-2: X Servers

6. **Highlight Fonts by pressing the arrow keys, press** Enter**, and select the font distributions you want.** Fonts take a lots of space so you may not want anything but the Standard 75 DPI and miscellanous. **Press** Enter **(with** `[OK]` **highlighted) when you're done.**

7. **When you have selected the parts of XFree86 you want, choose**

Exit **and press** Enter **twice.** You see the Select Distribution Media menu. **Press** Enter **for the CDROM** (the first one on the list).

8. **Press** Enter **again if necessary.** Your selections will be installed. **Choose** `[Cancel]` **and** `[Exit Install]` **to exit from** `sysinstall` **(you can take the CD-ROM out of the drive now).**

Running xf86config

This section walks you through one of the two ways to configure X—the text-based method rather than the graphical method. The two do the same thing, and the text-based method is less likely to lock up your machine and more likely to succeed.

Either one should be run as the `root` user (see Chapter 5 for becoming `root`). Whichever you run, it does two things: it writes a configuration file in the `/etc` directory called `XF86Config`, and it makes a symbolic link from `X` to the `X` server you choose in `/usr/X11R6/bin`:

```
lrwxr-xr-x  1 root  wheel  24 May 28  2000 X@ ->
     /usr/X11R6/bin/XF86_SVGA
```

If you already have an `XF86Config` that's working but isn't quite what you want, back it up first by copying it with the commands:

```
# cd /etc
/etc # cp XF86Config XF86Config.bak
```

X always needs a server. The server you choose depends on your video card. If you don't have the right server installed when you run the configuration program, it doesn't matter. The `xf86config` program tells you what server goes with the video card you tell it you have. You can install the server later and make the link yourself.

You run a single command to configure X, and make choices from the menus. If you get something wrong, you can't go back, but you may be able to correct it easily later by editing `/etc/XF86Config`, where you can also add other options.

To start the configuration, type (as `root`):

```
# xf86config
```

You see some introductory information. Press Enter to continue.

You are first asked to specify a mouse protocol type. The `ps/2` mouse (number 4) is the most common, but yours may be different. (The mouse protocol is easy to change later.) The list looks like this, with some added explanation at the end:

```
 1.  Microsoft compatible (2-button protocol)
 2.  Mouse Systems (3-button protocol)
 3.  Bus Mouse
 4.  PS/2 Mouse
 5.  Logitech Mouse (serial, old type, Logitech
     protocol)
 6.  Logitech MouseMan (Microsoft compatible)
 7.  MM Series
 8.  MM HitTablet
 9.  Microsoft IntelliMouse
10.  Acecad tablet

Enter a protocol number: 4
```

If your mouse has only two buttons, you should type **y** when asked if you want to enable Emulate3Buttons. Enabling this option makes it possible to copy (with the left button) and paste with the combination of the left and right buttons. `X` is designed for a 3-button mouse with the middle button used for the paste function.

```
Do you want to enable Emulate3Buttons? y

Now give the full device name that the mouse is
     connected to, for example /dev/tty00. Just
     pressing enter will use the default,
     /dev/mouse.
```

TIP

You don't press Enter **here**—the default answer is wrong for FreeBSD. If you enabled the mouse on your console when you installed (so that your `/etc/rc.conf` file has `moused_enable="YES"` in it) what you want is `/dev/sysmouse`, no matter what kind of mouse you have. Type it in:

```
Mouse device: /dev/sysmouse
```

The next question asks about managing the keyboard layout; unless you have a good reason for not doing so, you want to use XKB:

```
Please answer the following question with either
     'y' or 'n'.
Do you want to use XKB? y
```

Next you see a question about setting the right Alt key different from the left Alt key, helpful for language specific characters. If you use foreign languages, say yes.

```
Do you want to enable these bindings for the Alt
     keys? y
```

WARNING

Here comes the hard part. Some monitors can be damaged by being run at refresh rates they can't tolerate. They just sort of go "poof" and little strands of smoke start curling out the back. As you can probably guess, this is not good. But most of the newer ones just turn off and aren't damaged.

Looking up on the web my old Sony monitor with its CPD-100VS designation, I find some specs that tell me its horizontal scan range is 31-65 kHz and its vertical scan range is 50-120 Hz, with a maximum resolution of 1280 x1024 @ 60 Hz. This is just what I need to know.

```
You must indicate the horizontal sync range of your
     monitor. You can either select one of the
     predefined ranges below that correspond to
     industry-standard monitor types, or give a
     specific range.
It is VERY IMPORTANT that you do not specify a
     monitor type with a horizontal sync range that
     is beyond the capabilities of your monitor. If
     in doubt, choose a conservative setting.
```

Here are your choices:

```
    hsync in kHz; monitor type with characteristic
     modes
 1  31.5; Standard VGA, 640x480 @ 60 Hz
 2  31.5 - 35.1; Super VGA, 800x600 @ 56 Hz
 3  31.5, 35.5; 8514 Compatible, 1024x768 @ 87 Hz
     interlaced (no 800x600)
 4  31.5, 35.15, 35.5; Super VGA, 1024x768 @ 87 Hz
     interlaced, 800x600 @ 56 Hz
 5  31.5 - 37.9; Extended Super VGA, 800x600 @ 60
     Hz, 640x480 @ 72 Hz
 6  31.5 - 48.5; Non-Interlaced SVGA, 1024x768 @ 60
     Hz, 800x600 @ 72 Hz
 7  31.5 - 57.0; High Frequency SVGA, 1024x768 @ 70
     Hz
 8  31.5 - 64.3; Monitor that can do 1280x1024 @ 60
     Hz
 9  31.5 - 82.0; Monitor that can do 1280x1024 @ 76
     Hz
10  31.5 - 95.0; Monitor that can do 1280x1024 @ 85
     Hz
11  Enter your own horizontal sync range

Enter your choice (1-11):
```

If you choose 11 instead of one of the pre-defined horizontal sync ranges, you enter 11 and you're then placed at the next question, where you put in the sync ranges.

```
Please enter the horizontal sync range of your
     monitor, in the format used in the table of
     monitor types above. You can either specify
     one or more continuous ranges (e.g. 15-25, 30-
     50), or one or more fixed sync frequencies.
```

For my monitor, I enter:

```
Horizontal sync range: 31-65
```

Next comes the vertical sync range:

```
You must indicate the vertical sync range of your
     monitor. You can either select one of the
     predefined ranges below that correspond to
     industry-standard monitor types, or give a
     specific range. For interlaced modes, the
     number that counts is the high one (e.g. 87 Hz
     rather than 43 Hz).


 1  50-70
 2  50-90
 3  50-100
 4  40-150
 5  Enter your own vertical sync range

Enter your choice: 5
```

I choose 5 because my numbers are a little different from any offered; I want 50-120, which I enter.

```
Vertical sync range: 50-120

You must now enter a few identification/description
     strings, namely an identifier, a vendor name,
     and a model name. Just pressing enter will
     fill in default names.
```

Giving the monitor some identification is worthwhile when you look through the file later and wonder what monitor it was for. It helps, then, for it to say it's the Old Grey Sony.

```
The strings are free-form, spaces are allowed.
Enter an identifier for your monitor definition:
     Old Grey Sony
Enter the vendor name of your monitor: Sony
Enter the model name of your monitor: CPD-100VS
```

The next section deals with the video card, reminding you that it's important to get it right but on the other hand not to worry. Over 800 video cards are listed. You cycle through them with Enter, and when you get to the end, they start over. So you can go through the list as often as you like, even though you can't move backward.

```
Do you want to look at the card database?
```

TIP

Answer **y**; you do want to look at it. Selecting the right video card (all you have to do is enter the number of the card) helps get X working right. You see:

```
  0  2 the Max MAXColor S3 Trio64V+   S3 Trio64V+
  1  3DLabs Oxygen GMX                PERMEDIA 2
  2  3DVision-i740 AGP                Intel 740
  3  3Dlabs Permedia2 (generic)       PERMEDIA 2
  4  928Movie                         S3 928
  5  ABIT G740 8MB SDRAM              Intel 740
  6  AGP 2D/3D V. 1N, AGP-740D        Intel 740
  7  AGX (generic)                    AGX-014/15/16
  8  ALG-5434(E)                      CL-GD5434
  9  AOpen AGP 2X 3D Navigator PA740  Intel 740
 10  AOpen PA2010                     Voodoo
     Banshee
 11  AOpen PA45                       SiS6326
 12  AOpen PA50D                      SiS6326
 13  AOpen PA50E                      SiS6326
 14  AOpen PA50V                      SiS6326
 15  AOpen PA80/DVD                   SiS6326
 16  AOpen PG128                      S3 Trio3D
 17  AOpen PG975                      3dimage975
   ...
```

and so forth for 800 and some video cards, so don't give up too soon.

```
Enter a number to choose the corresponding card
     definition.
Press enter for the next page, q to continue
```

```
    configuration.
```

WARNING

You don't want to press **q**—you want to find the right card. When you enter a number, you move on to server selection:

```
Now you must determine which server to run. Refer
     to the manpages and other documentation. The
     following servers are available (they may not
     all be installed on your system):


 1  The XF86_Mono server. This a monochrome server
     that should work on any VGA-compatible card,
     in 640x480 (more on some SVGA chipsets).
 2  The XF86_VGA16 server. This is a 16-color VGA
     server that should work on any VGA-compatible
     card.
 3  The XF86_SVGA server. This is a 256 color SVGA
     server that supports a number of SVGA
     chipsets. On some chipsets it is accelerated
     or supports higher color depths.
 4  The accelerated servers. These include XF86_S3,
     XF86_Mach32, XF86_Mach8, XF86_8514,XF86_P9000,
     XF86_AGX, XF86_W32, XF86_Mach64, XF86_I128 and
     XF86_S3V.
 5 Choose the server from the card definition,
     XF86_SVGA.
```

TIP

You should select 5, the server that goes with your card definition. If the server is one you did not install, make a note of it so you can install it later.

```
The server to run is selected by changing the
     symbolic link 'X'. For example, 'rm
     /usr/X11R6/bin/X; ln -s
     /usr/X11R6/bin/XF86_SVGA /usr/X11R6/bin/X'
     selects the SVGA server.
Please answer the following question with either
     'y' or 'n'.
Do you want me to set the symbolic link? y
```

```
Now you must give information about your video
     card. This will be used for the "Device"
     section of your video card in XF86Config....
 You must indicate how much video memory you have.
     It is probably a good idea to use the same
     approximate amount as that detected by the
     server you intend to use. If you encounter
     problems that are due to the used server not
     supporting the amount of memory you have (e.g.
     ATI Mach64 is limited to 1024K with the SVGA
     server), specify the maximum amount supported
     by the server.
```

```
How much video memory do you have on your video
     card:
```

```
 1  256K
 2  512K
 3  1024K
 4  2048K
 5  4096K
 6  Other
```

If you have more than 4MB of RAM on your videocard, you multiply the number of megabytes of RAM times 1024, enter 6 as your choice, and then enter the RAM in kilobytes (without the K after it). For 8MB RAM:

```
Enter your choice: 6
8192
```

You next have an opportunity to describe your card just as you described your monitor—useful for knowing later what's in the machine, although things will work if you just press Enter instead of typing something in.

```
Enter an identifier for your video card definition:
Enter the vendor name of your video card:
Enter the model (board) name of your video card:
```

The next sections are for Ramdac, Dacspeed, and ClockChip settings, and are becoming more and more unnecessary. Many of these settings are detected automatically if they are used at all. Unless you know that you need something specific, reject the offers:

```
Enter a number to choose the corresponding RAMDAC.
Press enter for the next page, q to quit without
     selection of a RAMDAC. q

Just press enter if you don't want a Clockchip
     setting.
What Clockchip setting do you want (1-12)? Enter

At this point I can run X -probeonly, and try to
     extract the clock information from the output.
     It is recommended that you do this yourself
     and if a set of clocks is shown then you add a
     clocks line (note that the list of clocks may
     be split over multiple Clocks lines) to your
     Device section afterwards. Be aware that a
     clocks line is not appropriate for most modern
     hardware that has programmable clocks.
You must be root to be able to run X -probeonly
     now.
Do you want me to run 'X -probeonly' now? n
```

When `X` starts, it runs with the number of colors you request (if it's capable). That's the color depth. I tell you how to request more colors in a later section. For each color depth (8, 16, 24, and 32 bpp), `X` starts at the first resolution (mode) listed and can be cycled through other resolutions by pressing Ctrl+Alt+Keypad+. These resolutions are the number of pixels on your screen—at higher resolutions, graphics are smaller and more stuff fits on the screen.

What you get now is an opportunity to change the starting resolution and the order of the resolutions. This order can be changed later by editing your `/etc/XF86Config` file (the order is listed in the Screens section of the file), which may be easier than doing it here.

```
For each depth, a list of modes (resolutions) is
```

```
     defined. The default resolution that the
     server will start-up with will be the first
     listed mode that can be supported by the
     monitor and card.
Currently it is set to:


"640x480" "800x600" "1024x768" "1280x1024" for 8bpp
"640x480" "800x600" "1024x768" "1280x1024" for
     16bpp
"640x480" "800x600" "1024x768" "1280x1024" for
     24bpp
"640x480" "800x600" "1024x768" for 32bpp
```

```
Note that 16, 24 and 32bpp are only supported on a
     few configurations.
Modes that cannot be supported due to monitor or
     clock constraints will be automatically
     skipped by the server.

 1  Change the modes for 8pp (256 colors)
 2  Change the modes for 16bpp (32K/64K colors)
 3  Change the modes for 24bpp (24-bit color,
     packed pixel)
 4  Change the modes for 32bpp (24-bit color)
 5  The modes are OK, continue.

Enter your choice:5
```

The next question asks if you want a virtual screen larger than the physical screen. X differs quite a lot from Windows in its behavior here, and running X with a virtual screen larger than the physical one may make you feel like you're driving on an oil slick. But you may like it.

```
Please answer the following question with either
     'y' or 'n'.
```

```
Do you want a virtual screen that is larger than
     the physical screen? y
```

```
I am going to write the XF86Config file now. Make
     sure you don't accidently overwrite a
     previously configured one.

Shall I write it to /etc/XF86Config? y
```

Enter **y** to write the file to `/etc/XF86Config`, which is where it should be. If you enter **n**, you are given an opportunity to write to `/usr/X11R6/lib/X11/XF86Config` or (if you say **n** to that as well) to a filename of your choice (you can use a full path). If you do that, you can move it later to `/etc/XF86Config`. If you enter **n** to all the prompts, the file is not written, `xf86config` exits, and your work is lost.

Running X

To run X, you type the following command as a user:

```
$ startx
```

If you want `X` to start with a higher color depth than the default of eight (only 256 colors), type:

```
$ startx -- -bpp 16
```

You can try 24 and 32 instead of 16. When you find one that works, you add it to the alias section of your shell initialization file (see Chapter 6).

The `startx` command starts your `X` server and reads a file in your home directory—the `.xinitrc` file. If no `.xinitrc` file exists, it will read `/usr/X11R6/lib/X11/xinit/xinitrc`. This is where it finds out that it should run `twm`, the default X window manager, and start up a few `xterms`—windows in `X` in which you can type commands.

If you don't have an `.xinitrc` file in your home directory, you might want to copy the default file with these commands:

```
$ cd
~/ $ cp /usr/X11R6/lib/X11/xinit/xinitrc .xinitrc
```

That copies the system default configuration file for `X` to your home directory as `.xinitrc`. The lines beginning with a hash mark (#) are comments, and most of the statements in the file tell it to read other files in your home directory if they exist. The end of the file has the real action:

```
# start some nice programs

twm &
xclock -geometry 50x50-1+1 &
xterm -geometry 80x50+494+51 &
xterm -geometry 80x20+494-0 &
exec xterm -geometry 80x66+0+0 -name login
```

The `twm` line starts the `twm` window manager (the X default window manager). This window manager doesn't take much space on your hard drive or in memory, but on the other hand, it doesn't have many features, either. The left mouse button held down outside a window (in the grey area) will give you a menu. Within an `xterm`, holding down the Ctrl key and a mouse button gives you other menus.

The `twm` window manager's slim pickings and slim size make it ideal for displaying X on one machine while X is actually running on another over a slow connection.

The default `.xinitrc` file also starts a little clock on your screen and three `xterms`—windows with a prompt where you can type the same commands you type at the console. The difference is that you can run graphics programs. If Netscape is installed, you type in an `xterm`:

```
$ netscape
```

to run it, or `gimp` if you've installed Gimp, the graphics program that lets you import and edit images much like Adobe Photoshop does.

You can always get out of X by typing Ctrl+Alt+Backspace. It's nice, though, to shut programs down before you do this so they have a chance to clean up after themselves.

Tuning Up Your X Display

If your display isn't centered properly on your screen or isn't the right size, you can tune it up using `xvidtune`. You run `xvidtune` as `root` while X is running simply by typing at the prompt:

```
# xvidtune
```

You see a dialog box with a Warning message (these folks aren't going to take responsibility for your washing machine overflowing or your monitor blowing up). Click OK in the lower left corner of the box. You see a display like Figure 14-3.

Click on `Auto` so that your changes get displayed immediately. Then use the boxes for Left, Right, Wider, Narrower, Up, Down, Shorter, and Taller to adjust the display.

As you adjust the display, the numbers change. When you get a display you like, click `Show` to copy the numbers in a format ready for your `XF86Config` file. In the `xterm` where you started `xvidtune`, you'll see a display like this:

```
Vendor: Sony, Model: CPD-100VS
Num hsync: 1, Num vsync: 1
hsync range 0:  31.00 -  65.00
vsync range 0:  50.00 - 120.00
"640x480"       45.80     640  692  788  852     480
     488  494  514 -hsync -vsync
```

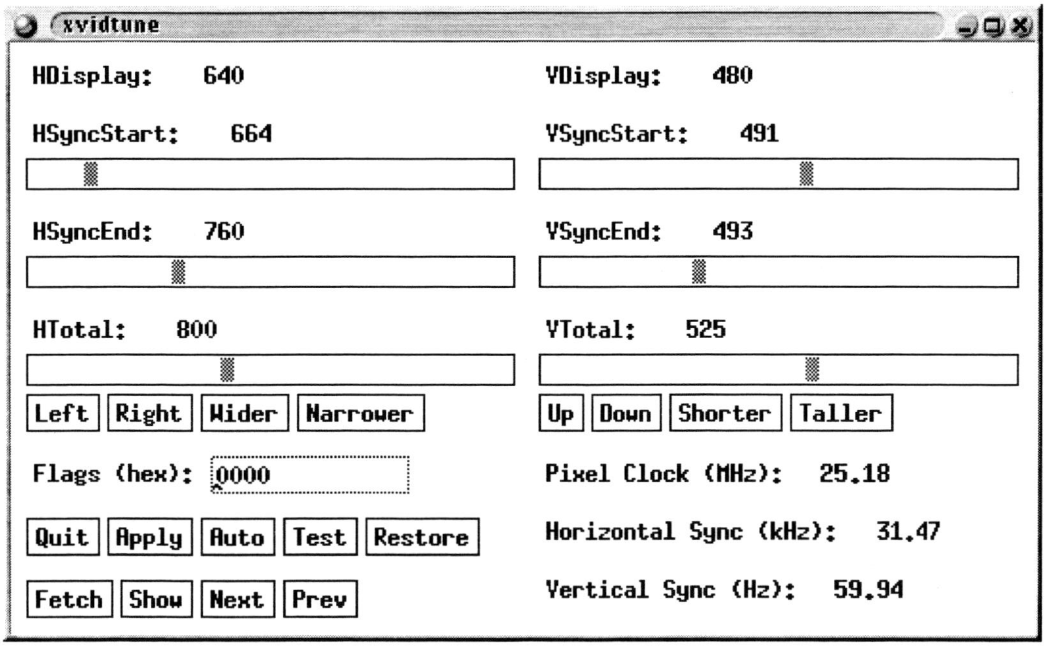

Figure 14-3: Tuning up your display with xvidtune

You can highlight the display with the left mouse button, open a file with your editor in another `xterm`, and paste the lines in the file with a middle mouse-click or the combination of the right and left mouse buttons. Or just grab a pencil and write them down.

You find the line in `XF86Config` that corresponds to the display being used. You know which one it is because the Vertical Sync in Hz and the Horizontal Sync in kHz match, as does the Pixel clock (the 25.175 below) although the numbers in `xvidtune` are rounded up. Then you substitute the new numbers from `xvidtune`, including the new number for the Pixel clock.

```
# 640x480 @ 60 Hz, 31.5 kHz hsync
Modeline "640x480"     25.175 640  664  760  800
     480  491  493  525
```

When the 640x480 mode (or whichever one comes up first) is done and you have new numbers, you click Next (or Prev, if you want to go backwards) to move to a new display resolution and repeat the process.

Tedious, isn't it? But once you get the right information into `/etc/XF86Config`, you won't ever have to do it again. (I'm beginning to remember why people like Windows.)

You can use your `XF86Config` file from Linux on FreeBSD if the version of X running on them is the same (and FreeBSD is running on the same computer on which you created the Linux `XF86Config` file).

Configuring Your Desktop

Everybody's X looks different—more different than their Windows, because with X you have more choices. You choose your window manager, and also—if you want it—an environment like KDE or GNOME.

KDE is a more comprehensive environment than GNOME and has its own window manager, although you can use other window managers with it. KDE (version 2) comes with its own browser, called `konqueror`, which some people prefer to Netscape.

The GNOME environment is a little less all-encompassing and works well with both the `afterstep` and `enlightenment` window managers. GNOME has menus that you can configure on-screen to call up your favorite programs.

You install GNOME and `enlightenment` (or GNOME and `afterstep`) if you haven't already done so from the CD-ROM:

1. **Put the CD-ROM in the drive (don't mount it).**
2. **Log in as `root` and type** `/stand/sysinstall`
3. **Choose** `Configure` > `Desktop` > `Gnome + Enlightenment`

   If you want `Gnome + Afterstep`, choose that instead.
4. **Press** Enter**; press** Enter **again if necessary to confirm your choice.**

   You see on the screen a report on files being installed.
5. **Press** Tab **to highlight Cancel; press** Tab **again to highlight X** `[Exit Install]`**; press** Enter.

When installed from the CD-ROM, GNOME is set up to be run from a `root` login. To run GNOME and `enlightenment` (or `afterstep`, if that's what you chose) as a user, edit the `.xinitrc` file in the user's home directory so it contains the line `gnome-session`; comment out (if you copied `xinitrc` to `.xinitrc`) everything from the `twm` line to the end.

The first time `gnome-session` runs, it will create a `.gnome` directory in the user's home directory and copy some GNOME files there. If you want a different window manager with GNOME (remember not all of them work well with it) edit the `default.wm` file to reflect your choice.

A nice addition to GNOME and `enlightenment` is `Eterm`, a substitute for the `xterm` application that lets you have backgrounds for each window. Figure 14-4 is an example. Notice the footprint at the bottom center of the screen—it's the equivalent of the Windows Start button.

As a user you can add items to your own menus, accessed through GNOME's `Settings > Menu Editor > Favorites (user menus)`. Except for the `User Menus`, only `root` can alter the menus. If you install `Eterm` from the ports collection (see Chapter 10), you can add `Eterm` as a new item and get it to use the galleon image by typing in as a command line:

```
Eterm -P /usr/X11R6/share/Eterm/pix/galleon.jpg
```

ON CD-1

Another GNOME enhancement you might want is `gnomemc` (a file manager), which can be installed from the CD-ROM as a package.

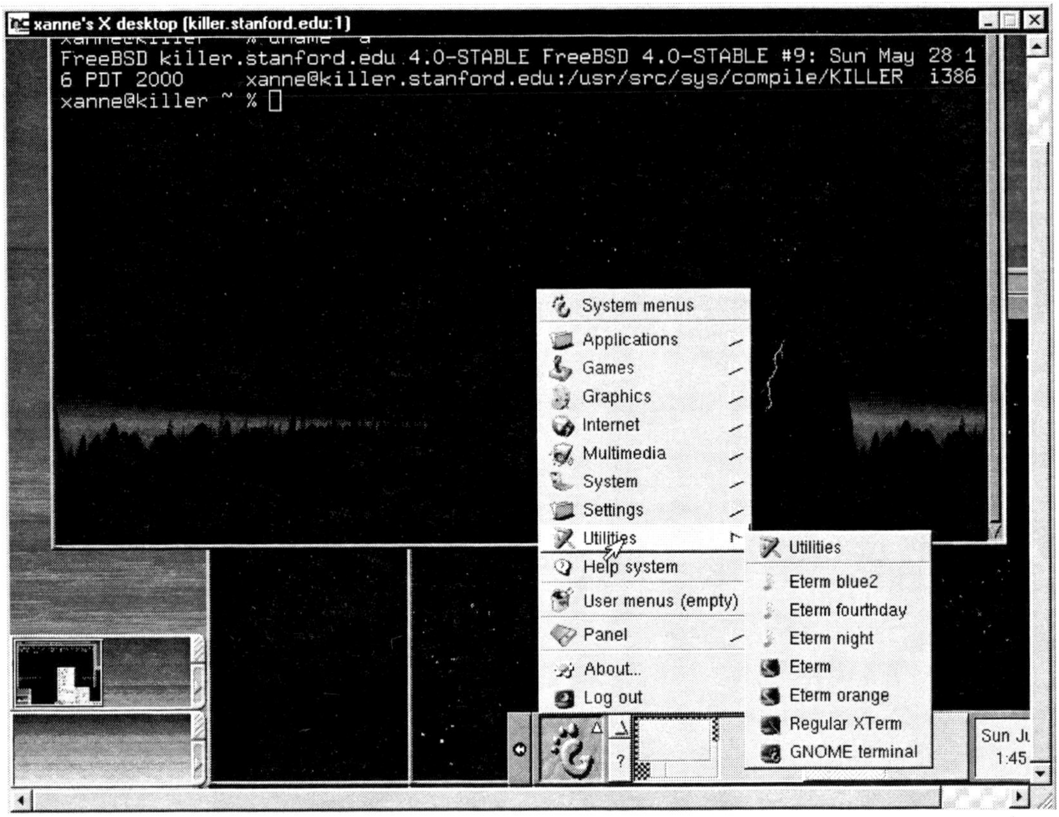

Figure 14-4: Gnome, Enlightenment, and a Couple of Eterms

If you decide you like the gnomadic life, you'll find entire books devoted to the topic in your local computer bookstore or on the web.

Figure 14-5 shows KDE running (only casually configured) with a background that isn't part of KDE, through `vnc`.

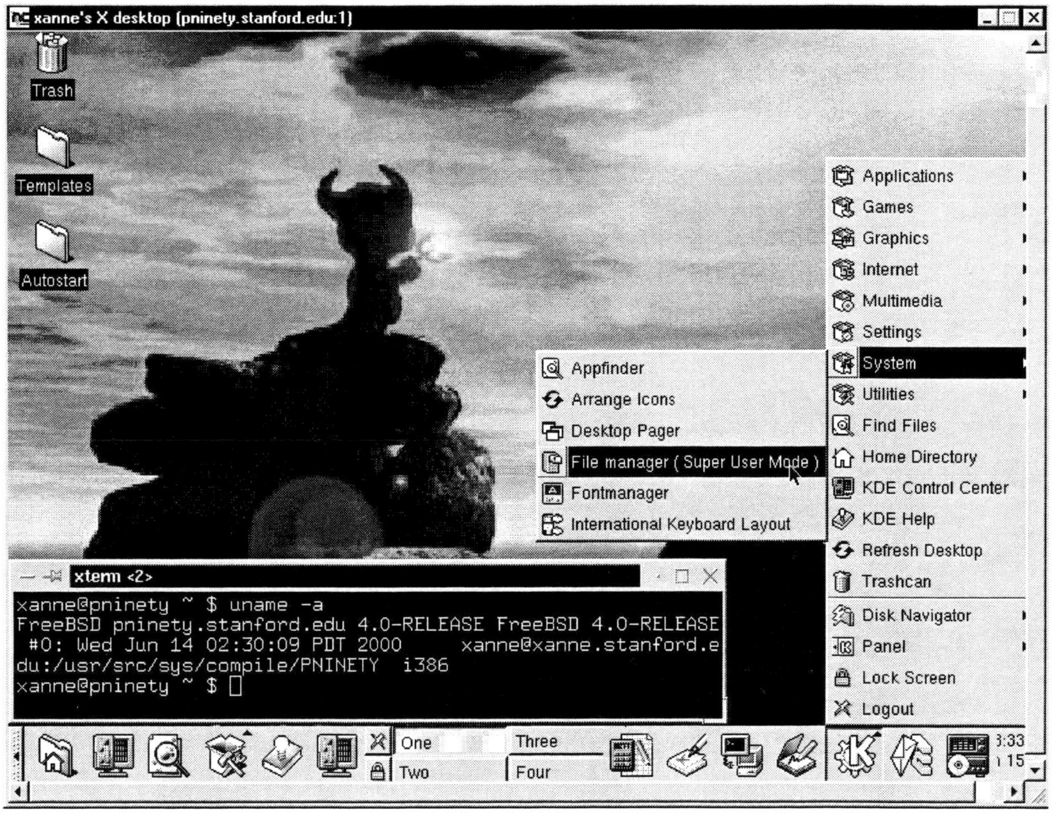

Figure 14-5: KDE Running on FreeBSD. Original artwork by Tatsumi Hosokawa.

Do We Need This Stuff?

`KDE` and `GNOME` attempt to provide the convenience of Microsoft Windows or a Mac operating environment. They're less all-encompassing—and you can always get to the command line by opening an `xterm`—but this is the goal.

It still takes some time to get acquainted with a new environment and to configure it to your liking. A window manager itself takes some learning and configuration.

Ultimately, however, the graphical environments and the window managers with more features hold out the promise that a standard `X` configuration could be installed on desktops throughout an office, giving everyone the same setup and making it possible for people who don't even want to know that they've got an `.xinitrc` file to use FreeBSD on their desktops.

Choosing a Window Manager

Choosing a window manager is right up there with choosing a shell for hot topics in the UNIX world.

What does a window manager do for you? It lets you click on a menu to open applications. It lets you minimize and restore applications. It lets you copy and paste among them. And of course it lets you run the graphics apps you can't run at the console, including word processors and spreadsheets.

Unlike Windows, you can have more than one desktop, and select among them. So you can be programming in C++ on one desktop (I know you want to get into that right away) and reading your electronic mail or surfing the net on another desktop. You can usually move an application from one desktop to another, or make an application (like a clock) appear on all desktops.

Some window managers (see a few brief comments about them in Chapter 11) have *themes*--different designs (backgrounds and icons and other decor) for your desktop. The eye candy can be stunning. Often you can select your own background, or a background for your `xterms`, or one for each of them.

Changing Your Window Manager

You change your window manager by editing the `.xinitrc` file in your home directory, commenting out the `twm` line and the lines starting `xterms` and adding a line for the window manager you want to run. If you don't use GNOME or KDE, but want `fvwm2`, you would add

```
fvwm
```

to your `.xinitrc` file.

Getting More Information

The `/usr/X11R6/lib/X11/doc` directory on your hard drive has documentation on many topics. You might find especially useful `QuickStart.doc`.

The XFree86 project also has a web page at http://www.XFree86.org. That's where to go for special configuration matters such as wheeled mice. Many window managers have web pages and sometimes mailing lists as well.

The `X -showconfig` command will show you the version of `X` that's installed along with other information.

Chapter 15

Printing

In spite of the wonders of the electronic world, we want hard copy—a printed version to hold in our hands, show to our grandmothers, scribble on, and provide a backup of those drafts of term papers and the electronic checkbook.

This chapter tells you how to get your printer working with FreeBSD. You don't have to sacrifice a goat, but you may need to sacrifice a little time. Once it's set up, it usually works very well.

How you set up printing depends on what kind of printer you have, how it's connected to your computer, and what kinds of files you want to print.

Your printer may be a PostScript printer, which is the kind most often used on Unix-style systems. It may be a printer that doesn't itself handle PostScript, but speaks another language like Hewlett-Packard's PCL (Printer Control Language), used by older HP LaserJets and DeskJets and emulated by many other printers. Or it could be a Canon Bubblejet or another brand that uses still another special language.

The files you want to print may be text files you've created, manual pages, PostScript files, files in PDF (portable document format), or files in any of a variety of graphical formats.

Printing with FreeBSD

Basic Printing Commands

TIP

Before you can print with FreeBSD, you need to start (as `root`) the printing daemon, which you do by typing `lpd` or:

```
# /usr/sbin/lpd
```

You can add the following line to `/etc/rc.conf` to start the `lpd` daemon on boot:

```
lpd_enable="YES"
```

TIP

The basic command for printing in FreeBSD (and other BSD systems) is:

```
$ lpr <filename>
```

This command sends the file you want to print to the default printer, which is named `lp`. More precisely, it sends the file, as processed for printing, to the printing queue for the `lp` printer, `/var/spool/output/lpd`. If you type:

```
# ls /var/spool/output/lpd
```

you see two files for each job in the queue, one beginning with `cf` and one beginning with `df`.

While you're setting up and testing printing, many files will probably fail to print, get stuck in the queue, and prevent new print jobs from printing. You clear the queues for all printers by typing:

```
# /usr/bin/lprm -
```

The `-` means all jobs from all users are to be cancelled and deleted from the queue. Deleting a print job from the queue does not, of course, delete the original file. The manual page for `lprm` provides options for deleting specific files, but for now, clearing the queue entirely is all you need.

The `lpc` command also allows you to see what's in the queues and to start and stop `lpd`. At the `lpc>` prompt, you type `status all` to see the status of all printers and their names. Type help at the `lpc>` prompt to see the commands `lpc` recognizes, and `help` <*command*> to get more information. You exit by typing `quit`.

Setting Up Printers

FreeBSD, like other UNIX systems, has a file called `/etc/printcap`, which defines the capabilities of the printers to which you can print. It's somewhat like the Printers folder in Windows, but instead of an icon, each printer definition has a name and a list of capabilities in the file. A physical printer can have more than one entry in the file, and thus more than one name. Before you edit it, `/etc/printcap` has two defined printers—the default printer called `lp` and another printer called `remote`.

Like many other files, all lines in this file beginning with a # are comments and have no effect.

The default printer definition in the file looks like this when each capability, defined with two letters following a colon, is put on a continuation line:

```
lp|local line printer:\
	:sh:\
	:lp=/dev/lpt0:\
	:sd=/var/spool/output/lpd:\
	:lf=/var/log/lpd-errs:
```

The second printer defined in `/etc/printcap` looks like this:

```
remote|sample remote printer:\
	:sh:\
	:rm=lphost:\
	:sd=/var/spool/output/lphost:\
	:lf=/var/log/lpd-errs:
```

Table 15.1 explains what the capabilities mean. The capabilities are separated by colons, and a \ means the list of capabilities is continued on the next line, which must be indented with a Tab. The last entry in the list ends with only a colon, and capabilities that take a numerical value, like baud rate or maximum size, are followed by a # instead of an = sign.

Table 15-1 Printer Capabilities

Capability	*What It Does*
sh	Suppresses a banner page
lp	The local port to which the printer is attached, usually `/dev/lpt0` (for a printer on the first parallel port) or `/dev/lpt1`
sd	The spooling directory for the defined printer; every printer needs a different one.
lf	The log file for the print queue; all defined printers can use the same log file.
rm	Used instead of `lp` for a "remote" printer—one attached for example, to your network or to a print server
if	Filters (changes) the file being sent to the printer to prepare it for printing
br	The bps rate for a serial printer
mx	Adds a maximum file size to limit the size of print jobs; :mx#0: allows any size

To add another printer definition to `/etc/printcap`:

1. **Copy the lines for the `lp` printer definition to another location in the file and edit them.**

   You replace `lp` on the first line with a new name and as many aliases, or alternative names, as you like, and a new description (which is also an alias). The name is important, because you use `-P`<*name*> as an argument to `lpr` to tell FreeBSD which printer definition you want to use; otherwise it uses `lp`.

   If your printer is on the second parallel port (LPT2 in Windows), you want `lp=/dev/lpt1` (here `lp` designates the parallel port, not the name of the printer). Specify the spooling device to use (each printer definition needs its own), and add the `mx` entry so you can print files of any size. Your new entry in `/etc/printcap` might look like this:

```
dj | deskjet | HP Deskjet 340 :\
```

```
    :sh:\
    :lp=/dev/lpt1:\
    :sd=/var/spool/output/deskjet:\
    :lf=/var/log/lpd-errs:\
    :mx#0:
```

If your printer is on a local network (and reached through a hub rather than directly attached to your computer—maybe it's an HP LaserJet 4100 you call `myps`) delete the `:lp=` entry or leave it explicitly blank (`:lp=:`). Add an `:rm` entry giving the IP address of the printer in "dot" notation. If the printer's IP address is 10.10.10.100, include `:rm=10.10.10.100:`

If your printer is attached to a serial port, set `lp=/dev/ttyd0` to communicate with the first serial port (COM1 in Windows) or `lp=/dev/ttyd1` for the second serial port (COM2 in Windows). Also determine the bps (bits per second) communication speed of the printer, and add a `br#9600` (for 9600 bps) to the printer definition (use a higher speed if your printer can handle it, and set up the printer physically for the same speed). See Chapter 7 for how to determine if FreeBSD found your serial ports. The device node for `sio0` (which is a driver) in `/dev is ttyd0`; don't expect to find an `sio` device node in `/dev`. See the *FreeBSD Handbook* (on your hard drive or the web) for more information if you need it.

2. **Create a spooling directory for your new printer definition with the following commands:**

```
# cd /var/spool/output
/var spool output # mkdir deskjet
```

The name of the spooling directory does not have to match the name of the printer, but it's useful.

3. **For a printer on a parallel port, check to make sure `/dev/lpt1` exists by typing `ls /dev/lpt*`, and if it doesn't, create it with these commands:**

```
# cd /dev
/dev # sh MAKEDEV lpt*
```

4. **Define additional printers in `/etc/printcap` for any other printers you may have.**

5. **Test your printer definition by trying to print a file.**

Printers on Other Computers

If you have a printer attached to another computer running some variety of Windows, you can print to it if it is shared as a resource (right-click on the icon for the printer and click Sharing; check the Shared box).

To print to such a printer, your computer running FreeBSD needs to be running programs from the Samba suite (installable as a port or package), your Windows computer needs to have Windows networking configured, and of course the computers need to be connected either directly to each other (via ethernet cards) or through a hub. Chapter 20 tells you where to get information on setting up Samba. But the basic command for printing to a computer running Windows from your FreeBSD computer is:

```
$ smbclient //WinBox/PrintShare -U user%pass
```

You are asked to log in (Windows 2000 seems to need a user with a registered password, which is what user%pass means here). You see the `smb` prompt, where you type:

```
smb:\> print <myfile>
```

Here WinBox is the name of your Windows computer as defined in Windows Networking and PrintShare is the name of the printer share—the "shared as" name on the Windows machine.

The `apsfilter` program on FreeBSD gives you more control over using such a printer because `apsfilter` uses the appropriate drivers for the files you want to print. It also installs an `smbclient.conf` file used for printing to that printer with information you give its `SETUP` program.

PostScript Printers

Printing PostScript files, which usually have a `.ps` extension, to a PostScript printer is probably the easiest FreeBSD printing task. If you installed the `doc` distribution when you installed FreeBSD, you have on your hard drive `/usr/share/doc/papers/jail.ps`. If your printer definition for your PostScript printer is called `myps`, you print with the command:

```
# lpr -Pmyps jail.ps
```

If you're not in the directory with the file you want to print, you provide its full path name.

Printing manual pages to a PostScript printer is also easy, with a pipe to `lpr`:

```
# man -t chown | lpr -Pmyps
```

Printing text to a PostScript printer, on the other hand, is a little trickier. The best utility for doing so, one version or another of `a2ps`, is installable as a package or a port (`/usr/ports/print`). (It will also get installed with `apsfilter`—more about that later.) Once installed, you can print a text file on a PostScript printer with:

```
# a2ps -Pmyps <filename>
```

The `a2ps` utility has many options—by default it prints two pages on one sheet. You can see some of the options with `a2ps --help`, or by reading the manual page.

PCL Printers

Printing to a printer that uses some version of Hewlett-Packard's Printer Control Language (PCL) (including Hewlett-Packard DeskJets) is more difficult than printing to a PostScript printer. A PCL printer expects a carriage return and line feed at the end of every line, which is how DOS text files are set up. UNIX files usually have only a line feed.

Changing Line Endings

Two little utilities, installable as ports or packages, convert text files from DOS line endings to UNIX line endings and back again. They're called `dos2unix` and `unix2dos`. If a file has DOS line endings, you see a ^M at the end of every line when you view it with a text editor. Otherwise it looks normal. These two utilities operate directly on the file, so the command to change file endings is simply:

```
~/ $ unix2dos .cshrc
```

or

```
~/ $ dos2unix .cshrc
```

which would change the line endings in the `.cshrc` file in your home directory first to DOS line endings and then back to UNIX line endings.

Having the DOS line endings prevents the text from creeping across the page. This is a good solution for printing a text file to a PCL printer (or another printer expecting DOS line endings) attached to a Windows computer.

You can print a text file with long lines by formatting it first with `fmt`, which has a variety of options for the width of lines and so forth (and then fixing the line endings if necessary):

```
$ fmt myfile >myfile.txt
```

WARNING

Samba's `smbclient`, when used to print, sends files with the line endings they have on your system. If you want to print a UNIX text document on a printer that needs a carriage return and a line feed at the end of every line, you should use `unix2dos` on it before printing it.

An Input Filter

TIP

More elegant than changing line endings, though, is an input filter. An input filter (the `if` capability) can be part of any printer definition. The filter processes the file on its way to the printer.

The following lines in a file called `hpif` are a shell script that's an input filter for a PCL printer. The filter first sends an Esc (`\033`) followed by an E to the printer, which resets it to its default values. It then tells the printer (`\033&k2G`) to convert a line feed to a carriage return + line feed, sends the text of the file to the printer (`/bin/cat`), and sends another Esc followed by an E to again reset the printer to its defaults. Substituting a 3 for the 2 also converts a carriage return to a carriage return + line feed, and you may find it works better for you.

Call the file `hpif`, put it in `/usr/local/libexec`, and make it executable with `chmod 755 hpif`. Like other files in that directory, make its ownership `root:wheel` with the command `chmod root:wheel hpif`.

```
#!/bin/sh
#hpif, a filter for PCL printers
printf "\033E\033&k2G" && /bin/cat && printf
    "\033E" && exit 0
exit 2
```

You add the following line (indented) to your printer definition for this printer (perhaps your `deskjet`):

```
    :if=/usr/local/libexec/hpif:\
```

You print manual pages to this printer by first creating a text file from the manual page:

```
$ man chmod | col -b > chmod.txt
```

The `chmod.txt` file, like any other text file with UNIX line endings, can now be printed on your PCL printer.

You can also print to a PCL printer using `apsfilter`, which is explained in the next section.

All Printers: apsfilter

The `apsfilter` program is the Swiss Army knife of printing. It arranges and does just about everything, but it doesn't do it alone. Its tools come from the wide range of other software it installs, and this software is going to take up residence on your hard drive. The centerpiece is `ghostscript`, which does most of the work of figuring out and converting different file formats so they can be printed, and possesses the actual printer drivers.

Installing apsfilter

When you type `make install` in `/usr/ports/print/apsfilter`, you see almost immediately the introductory screen, shown in Figure 15.1, which is an important one for what will get installed and how it will work.

You probably want to make some changes to the defaults (shown in Figure 15-1).

For standard U.S. paper, you want `LETTER` rather than `A4` (which is European-sized paper). If you do not have `X-Window` installed, you also want `GS_NO_X11`. `PSUTILS` is useful and you definitely want `A2PS`.

You may want to be able to read `PDF` files, but if Linux support is not installed and you don't plan to install it, you can dispense with `ACROREAD`. The `v` indicates there are options not viewable on the screen, so you want to scroll down to see them all.

Press the spacebar to toggle an X in a box.

Once `apsfilter` is installed (downloading the files it needs may take a long time) you can configure it at your leisure and one printer definition at a time; each printer definition adds something to your `/etc/printcap`.

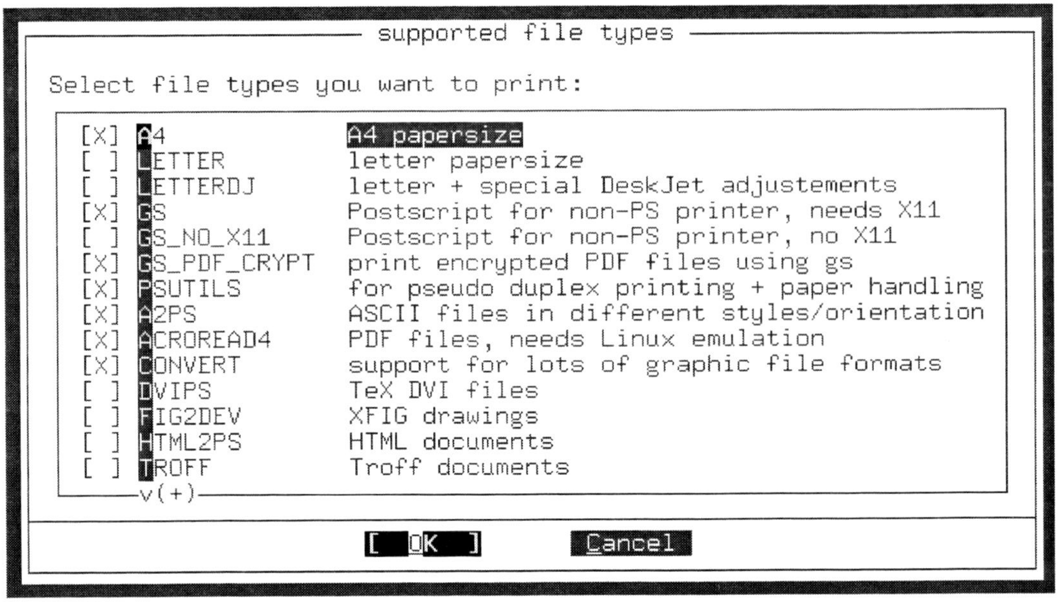

Figure 15.1: The Opening apsfilter Port Installation Screen

Configuring apsfilter

`Apsfilter` installs `SETUP` in `/usr/local/share/aspfilter`, which you run after `apsfilter` is installed. It should be run as `root`:

```
# /usr/local/share/apsfilter/SETUP
```

After opening screens, you press Enter to accept the default location for the configuration files, `/etc/apsfilter`. Press Enter again when `SETUP` checks permissions and the location of the spooling directory.

Note: if you rerun `SETUP`, you're given an option of adding to your previous selections or overwriting everything (starting over). You also get a warning if the version of `ghostscript` (which gets installed with `apsfilter`) should be updated.

```
Do you want to (a)dd another printer entry or
    to (o)verwrite the existing entries?
a/o?
```

You see the screen shown in Figure 15-2.

```
=================================================================
  A P S F I L T E R   S E T U P              -- MAIN MENUE --
=================================================================

                                              currently selected
-----------------------------------------------------------------
(D)     Available Device Drivers in your gs binary
(R)     Read Ghostscript driver documentation        (devices.txt)
(1)     Printer Driver Selection                     []
(2)     Interface Setup                              []

For printing the test page:
(3)     Paper Format (mandatory)                 []
(4)     Print Resolution in "dots per inch"      []
(5)     Toggle Monochrome/Color (1bpp=b&w)       []
(T)     Print Test Page, on local or Windows remote prt.(after 1-5)
(V)     View perf.log (times of print attempts)

(A)     Abort installation (don't do anything)
(I)     ==> Install printer with values shown above - repeat this
            step for installing multiple printers
(Q)     ==> Finish installation

Your choice?
```

Figure 15-2: The Opening apsfilter Setup Screen

The first two items on the screen are `D` (to see a list of drivers supported by `ghostscript`) or `R` (to see information about the capabilities of the drivers). If you have previously installed a printer using `SETUP`, the values for the previous printer will show up on the screen, which you can change for your new printer definition by selecting the appropriate number. You start doing something useful by pressing 1, which brings up the display shown in Figure 15-3.

You select a printer driver by entering a number. The first is for standard PostScript printers. The second is for emulating PostScript on other printers via `ghostscript`. This is likely to be the most useful if your printer isn't PostScript and isn't obviously identifiable as fitting in another category—like 4 and 5 for Hewlett-Packard DeskJets, and 7 for some color DeskJets—but other brands are listed also. Group 3 has a fairly wide variety of printers usually used for printing photos. Number 8 might let you print to "Windows" printers not otherwise usable.

```
===================================================================
                    PRINTER DRIVER SELECTION
===================================================================

    Please select the type of printer you want to install:

    1) PostScript printer
    2) printer driver natively supported by ghostscript

    3) gimp-print / stp
    4) hpdj
    5) pcl3 (successor to hpdj, experimental)
    6) IBM Omni
    7) cdj880, cdj970
    8) PPA printer, needs ghostscript "ppmraw" device and pnm2ppa

    0) return to main menu

Your choice: █
```

Figure 15-3: The Printer Driver Selection Screen

Whichever you choose, you see a long list of specific printers and their drivers. An example is shown in Figure 15-4.

When you find the one you want, which will have a name similar to that of your printer, you note its number and press `q`. You see:

```
Which driver do you want to choose?
[Hit RETURN to see the list again, enter 0 to
     choose new type.]
Enter number: 7
```

If you don't see a printer that looks right, press 0. Otherwise enter the number of the driver. You see a response—in the following example I've selected a PostScript printer (1) on the first menu and 7 on the second menu.

```
You selected driver: PS_600dpi

Driver PS_600dpi supports the following printer(s):
Generic Postscript, 600dpi (bypass
     ghostscript)|PS_600dpi
Do you want to use PS_600dpi? [Y|n] y
```

```
135 - HP DeskJet 660C [cdj550]
136 - HP DeskJet 660Cse [cdj550]
137 - HP Deskjet 690 Econo-Fast Gamma 2.0 [cdj690ec.upp]
138 - HP Deskjet 690 Normal Gamma 2.0 [cdj690.upp]
139 - HP DeskJet Plus [deskjet]
140 - HP DeskJet [deskjet]
141 - HP Deskjet 550c, 300x300DpI, Gamma=2 [cdj550.upp]
142 - HP Deskjet 690 Econo-Fast Gamma 2.0 [cdj690ec.upp]
143 - HP Deskjet 690 Normal Gamma 2.0 [cdj690.upp]
144 - HP LaserJet 3100 (with HP software) [lj3100sw]
145 - HP LaserJet 4 (defaults to 600 dpi) with duplex [ljet4d]
146 - HP LaserJet 4 with Floyd-Steinberg dithering [lj4dith]
147 - HP LaserJet 4, defaults to 600 dpi [ljet4]
148 - HP LaserJet 5 Color (new driver, old=cljet5pr) [cljet5]
149 - HP LaserJet 5 Color (old drv. with rotation hacks/flaws) [cljet5pr]
150 - HP LaserJet 5 Color Simple [cljet5c]
151 - HP LaserJet 5 family (PCL5 / PCL XL), bitmap [lj5mono]
152 - HP LaserJet 5 family, gray-scale bitmap [lj5gray]
153 - HP LaserJet 5L (not real LJ5), defaults to 600 dpi [ljet4]
154 - HP LaserJet 5M Color (new driver, old=cljet5pr) [cljet5]
155 - HP LaserJet 5M Color (old drv. with rotation hacks/flaws) [cljet5pr]
156 - HP LaserJet 5M Color Simple [cljet5c]
157 - HP LaserJet 5P (not real LJ5), defaults to 600 dpi [ljet4]
158 - HP LaserJet 6 family (PCL5 / PCL XL), bitmap [lj5mono]
159 - HP LaserJet 6 family, gray-scale bitmap [lj5gray]
Which driver do you want to choose?
[Hit RETURN to see the list again, enter 0 to choose new type.]

Enter number: █
```

Figure 15-4: A Partial List of Specific Printer Names and Drivers

If you press `n` instead of `y` here, you go back to driver selection. Otherwise you are returned to the main menu (Figure 15-2), where your selection of a printer driver is reflected. You can now redo item 1 or press 2 for Interface Selection—how your printer is connected to your computer. The interface selection looks like Figure 15-5.

You enter the number for your interface and answer remaining questions about it, and you are returned to the main menu. There you choose 3 for default paper size (you probably want letter if it isn't already selected). You can only choose one size. If you also want to be able to print on legal-size paper, you can create another printer definition identical except for paper size and the name of the printer definition.

You can now press T to print a test page, and if it doesn't work, make changes and test again. You then press I to install your printer definition or A if you really want to bail out. You get asked about creating a "raw" device and about a name for your printer and its spooling directory. If you have more than one printer or plan on creating more than one definition for a

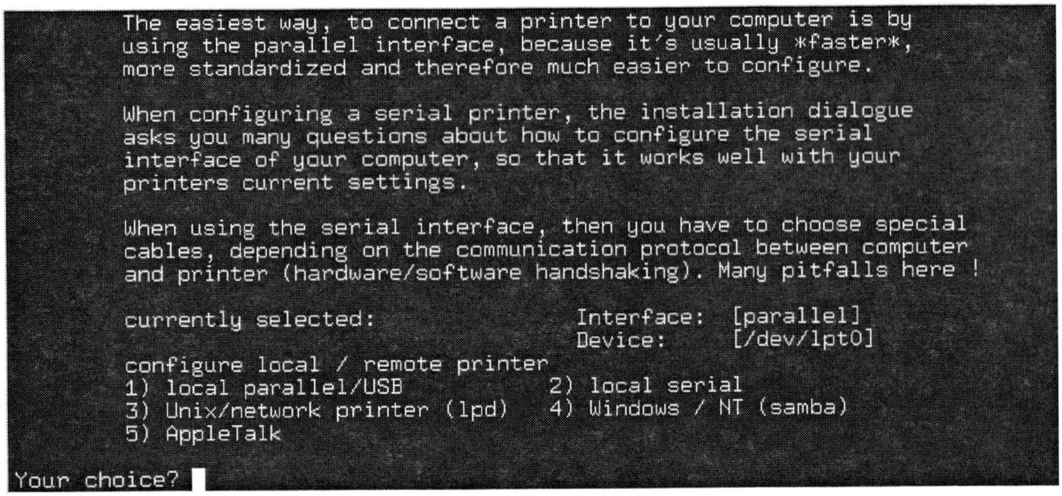

Figure 15-5: Interface Setup in apsfilter

physical printer, give your printer a descriptive name and a matching spooling directory so you know which is which.

You can now install another printer or press Q to finish up. You get quite a few informational messages (choose 0 on man page installation, as it's already done), but it's good to press Q to finish to get everything written and saved and to restart the printer daemon so it knows about your new printer definition.

After you install and configure `apsfilter`, you print PostScript files with `lpr` and text files with `a2ps`.

Other Information

The FreeBSD Handbook has a detailed chapter on printing that has more information on filters and on printing files created with programs specific to UNIX. The `apropos printer` command shows you FreeBSD utilities related to printing not described in this chapter (like `lpq`, which lists the files in the printer queues), and you may find useful utilities in `/usr/ports/print`. If you have a complicated network environment, *The FreeBSD Corporate Networker's Guide* by Ted Mittelstaedt is especially useful.

Printing from Netscape requires a PostScript printer or the PostScript emulation capabilities you get with `apsfilter`. You simply tell Netscape what your printer command is:

```
lpr -Pmyprinter
```

If you have one printer you usually use and you don't always want to type `lpr -Pmyprinter`, you can add `lp` as your favorite printer's primary name. (Be sure to comment out the standard `lp` definition in `/etc/printcap` so you don't have two printers with the same name, or replace `lp` with another name.

Another way to set your default printer is to set the PRINTER environmental variable at the command line or in your shell initialization files with:

```
PRINTER=myprinter
export PRINTER
```

or, in the `csh` or `tcsh` shells, with `setenv PRINTER myprinter`.

If your printer is attached to a parallel port (say, `lpt0`) and it prints but it seems to take forever, try putting it into polled mode with this command:

```
# lptcontrol -p /dev/lpt0
```

The log file for each printer is useful in determining why printing may be failing. Find it by looking at `/etc/printcap`. The `lf` capability for the printer will tell you where it is. My Epson Stylus printer attached to a Windows 2000 machine, with printer name `auto2`, failed to print after setting it up (with Samba programs properly installed) because the `smbclient.conf` that `apsfilter` installed was readable only by `root` (no doubt something I did wrong during installation), so I changed the permissions to make it world readable:

```
/etc/apsfilter/auto2 # chmod 644 smbclient.conf
```

Chapter 16

Configuring Your Kernel

The kernel is the big binary that runs your system. It communicates with the hardware, user programs (including your shell), and the file system , and starts up the operating system. FreeBSD keeps the kernel in sync with userland—the rest of the system—far more closely than Linux variants do.

This chapter covers:

- configuring your kernel on boot
- using kernel modules to add kernel capabilities on the fly, and
- compiling a new kernel for existing system.

Chapter 17 covers the method you use to recompile your kernel after you upgrade your system.

Of these three ways to modify your kernel, the first is the least important. Kernel modules are becoming more important and make it unnecessary to compile every option you might need into a kernel.

On-Boot Kernel Configuration

You make changes in your kernel when you boot into FreeBSD by using `UserConfig`, either when you install FreeBSD or when you boot the computer after FreeBSD is installed.

Why would you want to mess around with the kernel? After all, isn't this the most critical file of all, the one that runs everything else?

It sure is, but on the other hand it's not as smart as you might think. It knows how to run an `NE2000` compatible ethernet card with its `ed0` driver, but it looks for the card at port 280 and thinks IRQ 10 is the right interrupt to use. If your `NE2000` card is at port 300 and is set up to use IRQ 5, `UserConfig` is just what you need to get the kernel and the card communicating.

You can do three things in `UserConfig`:

- Disable a driver that may be conflicting with another driver.
- Change the resources (parameters) a driver uses so FreeBSD will find your hardware.
- Enable a disabled driver.

`UserConfig,` written by Mike Smith when it was desperately needed, is becoming much less important than it used to be when most cards were ISA cards, hardware was configured to use fixed IRQs and addresses, and the kernel had to know about these configurations.

To enter `UserConfig` when you install use the arrow keys when you see `Kernel Configuration Menu` to put the highlight on

```
Start kernel configuration in full screen visual mode
```

and press Enter.

If FreeBSD is already installed, do the following when you boot the computer:

1. **As soon as you see the first sign of the twirling baton (you have to be quick here) press the spacebar.**

   You see:

```
>> FreeBSD/i386 BOOT
Default: 0:da(0,a)/boot/loader
boot:
```

2. **Type** `kernel -c`
3. **You see** `config>`. **Type** `v` **`(for visual).`**

Either way, you see the `UserConfig` screen, with six categories of active drivers and the same six categories for inactive (disabled) drivers.

```
---Active-Drivers----8 conflicts----Dev---IRQ--Port
Storage:   (Collapsed)
Network:    (Collapsed)
Communications:    (Collapsed)
Input:    (Collapsed)
Multimedia:
Miscellaneous:   (Collapsed)
```

TIP

Only those drivers that can benefit from your attention by being disabled, changed, or enabled are shown in `UserConfig`,

You scroll among the categories of drivers with the arrow keys and press Enter to open the list. Then you scroll the list. (Keep scrolling if you don't see what you're looking for at first—the entire list may not fit on the screen.) If a driver uses the same resources as another driver, it will have CONF (for "conflict" next to it. You press Del (the Delete key) to inactivate (disable) a driver. The number of conflicts shown in the top line of the display will be updated so you can see how many are left.

WARNING

Don't disable a driver unless you're *sure* you don't have the hardware it supports. You can get rid of SCSI stuff if you don't have it and any ethernet card drivers once you know which driver you need for *your* ethernet card. Don't disable the console driver (`sco0`—the "syscons" driver for your screen), `npx0` (math co-processor), or your keyboard driver by mistake! It's better to have a few conflicts than not to have what you need.

Here's what's in each category:

- **Storage**: SCSI controllers, IDE (ATA/ATAPI) controllers (for your hard disks and CD-ROM drive, if they're not SCSI), and your floppy controller.
- **Network:** Ethernet card drivers. You can disable all of them if you don't have an ethernet card. See the list in Appendix A: Supported Hardware, Table A-1, for the description of the hardware supported by each of the drivers with those funny names. The names of the ethernet drivers you can disable are `cs0`, `ed0`, `fe0`, `ie0`, `le0`, `lnc0`, and `sn0`.

- **Communications:** Your parallel port and two serial ports (which is probably all you've got). Leave these alone unless your serial ports have some odd addresses or IRQs (they might, if the computer is a laptop.)

- **Input:** Keyboard, PS/2-style mouse, and the console driver. It's unlikely you need to change anything here. If you have a serial mouse, you can disable `psm0`; the driver for a serial device is already there. If you have a bus mouse, `UserConfig` can't help you.

- **Multimedia:** This category has no entries.

- **Miscellaneous:** One of the two pccard controllers (the other is disabled). If you have a laptop and are trying to install using a serial or ethernet pccard, you need this; otherwise you don't. If your pccard won't work, you may need to change the port or IRQ for your card. The other driver (`npx0`) is the math co-processor; leave it alone.

You change a driver's parameters—say, its IRQ—by pressing Enter when the highlight is on the driver. That puts you in the third section of the `UserConfig` screen (after the lists of Active and Inactive Drivers) where you can use the Tab key to move among the parameters. To change a parameter, backspace over it and type the new value. Press `Q` to get out of the third section.

TIP

On-screen help is at the bottom of the display, and tells you what commands are available depending on where you are in `UserConfig`.

You enable an inactive driver by using the Tab key to get to the Inactive Drivers section, pressing Enter to open a category of driver, scrolling to the driver you want, and pressing Enter to enable it. It shows up in the Active Drivers.

If you disable a driver, it moves to the Inactive Drivers section. You can re-enable it (either now or when you boot again at some later time) the same way you enable any inactive driver.

When you finish disabling drivers, changing driver parameters, and enabling drivers, press `Q` and then `Y` to keep your changes and proceed with booting.

When you install FreeBSD, the changes you make with `UserConfig` are saved to your hard drive in a file in the / directory called `kernel.config` because these changes may be necessary to get FreeBSD to boot. After installation, changes are not saved.

The command line interface for `UserConfig` is available both on install and afterward and has a help command.

Loading Kernel Modules

You can add capabilities to your kernel on the fly—if a module exists for what you want, and if it was compiled with the capabilities you need. Chapter 7's section on Kernel Info tells you how to find out what's loaded (with `kldstat`) and how to load modules (with `kldload` <*modulename*>) and unload them (with `kldunload` <*modulename*>).

Kernel modules are cool (in spite of that awful name that sounds like a cross between a mole and a nodule) because you don't have to recompile your kernel to use them—they're add-ons you can load and unload at will (or at least as `root`—this is another activity ordinary users aren't allowed to do).

The modules that exist on your system (fewer in 4.1 and 4.2) are listed in `/modules`. All have a `.ko` extension.

Besides the screensavers you can load and unload as modules, the `linux.ko` module is especially useful. Linux support requires software installation and also kernel support; it's the kernel support `linux.ko` gives you. You load it with this command:

```
# kldload linux
```

TIP

You don't have to be in the `/modules` directory to load a module. And many modules load automatically when they're needed.

Table 16-1 lists types of kernel modules. You load a kernel module on boot by editing the file (creating it if it does not exist) `/boot/loader.conf` and putting a line of the following form in the file:

```
linux_load="YES"
```

Table 16-1 Types of Kernel Modules

Type	*Comment*
Filesystem modules	md.ko is an example
Screen savers	*_saver.ko
Emulation modules	linux.ko is one of these
Networking modules	ipfw.ko and others
Network drivers	if_*.ko
Netgraph modules	netgraph.ko and ng_*.ko
Sound modules	snd.ko and snd_*.ko
USB modules	u*.ko and if_*ue.ko
Other	miscellaneous (no typical names)

Most of the file system , network driver, and USB modules are in the `GENERIC` kernel (the kernel installed by default with FreeBSD) and are useful only if you have removed drivers by recompiling your kernel and then discover you need them, perhaps because you get a new ethernet card. If you try to load a module whose capabilities are already in the kernel, the kernel will complain.

The file `/boot/defaults/loader.conf` lists many of the modules with a brief description; by default, they are not loaded on boot. If you want to load a module on boot, you use the syntax from this file, but change `"NO"` to `"YES"` and put the line in `/boot/loader.conf`.

If you upgrade your system and compile a new kernel (see Chapter 17), you'll probably get some new kernel modules at the same time.

Building A Lean and Mean Kernel

Some really cool things to do—hang a jury, design a cartel, break an embargo, land on the deck of an aircraft carrier, and compile a kernel. Only the last is dealt with here.

Compiling your own kernel is one of the joys of running your own FreeBSD system, and it's not that difficult. The hardest part is getting familiar with the short-hand names for stuff. Basically three major steps take care of it: creating a custom configuration file, building the kernel using that file, and installing the new kernel.

Why You Want a Cool Kernel

There are two reasons to compile your own kernel:

- To add stuff you want, and
- To get rid of stuff you don't use.

Adding stuff you want is important—to make your hardware (and some software) work. Most people probably compile a kernel to get support for a sound card, but that's not the only change you might want to make.

Getting rid of kernel support you don't need makes your kernel smaller (possibly by as much as one-third) and faster. That makes your whole system faster and gives you more memory for running software applications.

What You Need to Build Your Own Kernel

To build your own kernel, you need kernel source—the source code from which the kernel itself is built—a good text editor, and a little time.

WARNING

You want kernel source that's for the same version of FreeBSD as the sources that were used to build the rest of FreeBSD, known as *userland*. The kernel and userland work together. If they're different—out of sync—quite a few utilities, including `top` and `ps`, just won't work.

LINUX

The kernel is more closely related to the rest of the system in FreeBSD than it is in Linux and should be updated whenever you upgrade and rebuild the base system itself. The base system includes many utilities that in a Linux system come as packages.

To make sure kernel source is installed:

```
~/ # cd /usr/src/sys
/usr/src/sys # ls
```

You see output like Figure 16-1. Everything except the `Makefile` is a subdirectory of `/usr/src/sys`.

```
xanne@killer /usr/src/sys % ls
./              ddb/            msdosfs/        nfs/
../             dev/            net/            ntfs/
Makefile        fs/             netatalk/       nwfs/
alpha/          gnu/            netatm/         pc98/
boot/           i386/           netgraph/       pccard/
cam/            i4b/            netinet/        pci/
coda/           isa/            netinet6/       posix4/
compat/         isofs/          netipx/         svr4/
compile/        kern/           netkey/         sys/
conf/           libkern/        netnatm/        ufs/
contrib/        miscfs/         netncp/         vm/
crypto/         modules/        netns/
xanne@killer /usr/src/sys %
```

Figure 16-1: The /usr/src/sys Directory

You get kernel source from the CD-ROM or by FTP. If you installed FreeBSD from the CD-ROM, the kernel source will of course be in sync with the rest of the system. To install it if it's not installed, follow these steps:

1. **Put your installation CD-ROM in the drive (don't mount it) if you want to install kernel source from the CD.**
2. **As** `root` **type** `/stand/sysinstall`
3. **Choose** `Configure` **from the main menu (you can press** `C` **to get there quickly).**
4. **Choose** `Distributions`
5. **Highlight** `Sources for Everything` **and press the spacebar.**
6. **Highlight** `/usr/src/sys (FreeBSD kernel)` **and press the spacebar.**
7. **Press** Enter**; you see the screen for selecting media. Select CD-**

ROM or FTP if you installed by FTP, and answer the rest of the queries. Exit `sysinstall` when finished.

Creating Your Own Kernel Configuration File

Kernel configuration files live in `/usr/src/sys/i386/conf`. That's why they're lonely—no one can remember the address. There's a symbolic link in / from `/sys` to `/usr/src/sys`, so all you really have to type is `cd /sys/i386/conf`, and you'll be visiting.

The i386 doesn't mean this is for one of those old 386 computers that are slower than snail mail—it means the i386 architecture, which includes all Intel PCs (with Pentiums and so forth) as well as PCs that have AMD and Cyrus chips. One other architecture, or kind of computer, on which FreeBSD runs is the Alpha, made by DEC (now part of Compaq).

You know you're in the right place if the `ls` command shows you these files:

```
GENERIC     LINT
```

These files aren't kernels (yet)—they're just configuration files for kernels, although sometimes people talk about "the `LINT` kernel" when they mean the `LINT` configuration file.

You start with a copy of `GENERIC` and modify it, adding a few bells and whistles or a little fluff from `LINT`. `LINT` has everything but the kitchen sink and the Declaration of Independence. It's the candy store, so you pick and choose from it.

To create your own kernel configuration file, follow these steps:

1. **Log in as `root`.**
2. **Type** `cd /sys/i386/conf`
3. **Type** `cp GENERIC NEWKERN`
4. **Edit** `NEWKERN` **with your favorite text editor.**

   Comment out what you don't want by putting a # in front of the line.

Add what you want by uncommenting (removing the # in front of a line) or copying a line from the LINT kernel configuration file.

5. **Save the file (actually, save it often while you work) and exit.**

The difficult part is step 4, the editing—figuring out what to comment out and what to comment in, and what to pick up from the LINT file. It takes the most time, too. I'll go through the GENERIC kernel configuration section by section and explain what it all means so you can decide what to keep, what to trash, and what else you need. As a first experiment with building your own kernel, you might just want to add whatever you need—support for your sound card or a joy stick or a bus mouse, for example—or even compile your copy of GENERIC without making any changes.

Naming the Baby

You can name your baby—your own configuration file—anything you want; it doesn't have to be NEWKERN or MYKERNEL. Traditionally—and conveniently—kernel configuration files are named for the computer where they'll be put to work, so my configuration file is called KILLER (all caps is a tradition too). The configuration file name shows up when you type `uname -a`.

On my machine `uname -a` shows the following information—quite a lot about the system version, the hostname, and who compiled the kernel:

```
FreeBSD killer.stanford.edu 4.3-STABLE FreeBSD 4.3-STABLE #1:
Sat Apr 21 01:06:50 PDT 2001
xanne@killer.stanford.edu:/usr/obj/usr/src/sys/KILLER  i386
```

Nevertheless, when the kernel gets built and installed, it's just called `kernel`.

WARNING

Compiling a new kernel after upgrading your system often requires a special approach. See Chapter 17 for post-upgrade kernel building.

TIP

It's a good idea to back up GENERIC to GENERIC.orig with the command:

```
/sys/i386/conf # cp GENERIC GENERIC.orig
```

When you upgrade your sources, GENERIC (but not NEWKERN) will be overwritten with a new GENERIC file—and you can compare it to

GENERIC.orig to see if any changes have been made that you need to incorporate into your own config file.

Avoiding a Bad Wrap

FreeBSD thinks every line in the kernel configuration file that doesn't start with a hash mark (#) is part of the instructions for what to include in the kernel.

If a long line wraps and a new line is created, your kernel file won't work. You'll get error messages about unknown commands.

This is especially a risk with the `pico` editor. If you use `pico`, be sure to start it with the `-w` switch to turn off wrapping, like this: `pico -w NEWKERN`.

The `vi` editor has some good tricks for editing a file like this, where you want to add something at the beginning of a whole slew of lines. But `vim` is even better, because it lets you open two files at the same time and compare them, and copy lines from one to the other.

Open NEWKERN (or whatever you called your copy of GENERIC) with your text editor and let's rock 'n roll.

The file begins by telling you where in *The FreeBSD Handbook* you can find information about configuring your kernel. You can keep that in mind as another source.

TIP

Some people delete lines from their config file instead of just commenting them out. This makes it harder, though, to restore something—hey, you might decide to pop another floppy drive in there. Just commenting it out maintains a record of your changes.

Here's the first block of entries—live ones, with no # at the beginning of the lines:

```
machine          i386
cpu              I386_CPU
cpu              I486_CPU
cpu              I586_CPU
cpu              I686_CPU
ident            GENERIC
maxusers         32
```

Here's what you do:

1. **You leave `machine i386` alone; this is PC architecture. After all, your computer isn't an Alpha!**

2. **You pick one of the four `cpu` lines and comment out the others.**

   This is the identification of the main chip, the central processing unit, in your computer, and it cuts down a lot of overhead to get rid of the others, which are truly useless to you. But which one do you need? Your computer knows. The `dmesg | grep CPU` command will show you what CPU your computer found.

   On `KILLER, dmesg | grep CPU` says:

```
CPU: AMD-K7(tm) Processor (704.94-MHz 686-class
     CPU)
```

   so I comment out with a # at the beginning all the CPU lines except

```
cpu                I686_CPU
```

   If you have a dual-processor machine, you still only need one CPU line.

4. **In the `ident GENERIC` line, change `GENERIC` to the name you chose for your baby; mine says:**

```
ident     KILLER
```

5. **Increase `maxusers` to something higher.**

   The maxusers number has nothing to do with real humans who may or may not pound on your machine from different directions, and everything to do with how many files you can have open and how many processes you can run at one time, according to a formula someone cooked up (probably David Greenman, FreeBSD's principal architect, in `param.c`). For a machine with only a few human users but a fair amount of RAM, where you intend to run X and Netscape and maybe other stuff at the same time and even compile some ports, make it 96 or even 132.

The second block of entries from `GENERIC` starts with a commented-out line. Unless you're into kernel hacking, you can leave this commented out. Including it produces a huge kernel, maybe 9MB, and a debugging kernel can be built in any case with command-line options.

```
#makeoptions debug=-g
```

The series of options lines that come next relate to file systems and their use and some stuff to limit the effects of people trying to ping-flood your system—sending it so many messages it gets overloaded. All are worth having and accepting as written.

The third block is for `SMP`—simultaneous multi-processing—relevant only if you have a dual-processor motherboard. If you do, comment in (delete the # at the beginning of the line) the two required lines; leave the others alone, if they exist, as the default values are likely to be right.

```
options   SMP       # Symmetric MultiProcessor Kernel
options   APIC_IO   # Symmetric (APIC) I/O
```

The following block is best left alone. The first line is always needed, the second may be useful, and the third is needed for everything but old machines with no PCI slots. It's not worth a lot of sweat.

```
device          isa
device          eisa
device          pci
```

Next comes the floppy drives section—a floppy controller and two floppy drives. You can comment out the line with the second drive (`device fd1`) if you have only one floppy, so it looks like the following (neither here nor elsewhere should you replace the question marks):

```
# Floppy drives
device      fdc0    at isa? port IO_FD1 irq 6 drq 2
device      fd0     at fdc0 drive 0
#device      fd1     at fdc0 drive 1
```

The ATA and ATAPI devices section is everything for IDE disks and IDE CD-ROMS and some other devices. If your system is all SCSI, you can comment out everything here. Otherwise you comment out the devices you don't have—like a special floppy drive or a tape drive. (If your system isn't all SCSI, you probably have an ATAPI CD-ROM drive as well as ATA disk drives.) When in doubt, leave it in. The last option, to enable DMA on ATAPI devices, is commented out by default in 4.1 and 4.2, and has disappeared in 4.3 altogether. If it's there, leave it commented out. (Some lines are shown wrapping here, but they shouldn't wrap in your file.)

```
# ATA and ATAPI devices

device          ata0    at isa? port IO_WD1 irq 14
device          ata1    at isa? port IO_WD2 irq 15
device          ata
device          atadisk             # ATA disk drives
device          atapicd             # ATAPI CDROM drives
device          atapifd             # ATAPI floppy drives
device          atapist             # ATAPI tape drives
options         ATA_STATIC_ID       #Static device
     numbering
#options        ATA_ENABLE_ATAPI_DMA    #Enable DMA on
     ATAPI devices
```

If you have a SCSI system, include under `# SCSI controllers` only the controller you have. The command `dmesg | grep SCSI` will show you the SCSI controllers found on your system. On `KILLER,` I see (among other lines):

```
ahc0: <Adaptec 2940 Ultra2 SCSI adapter> port
     0xdc00-0xdcff mem 0xefffb000-0xefffbfff irq 10
     at device 14.0 on pci0
```

Thus, I include:

```
device          ahc
```

It's unlikely that you have two SCSI controllers, but on the chance that you do, of course you want both of them.

Under `# SCSI peripherals` you comment out everything if you don't have a SCSI controller (or host adapter). If you do have one, leave in all the peripherals. The peripherals are the disk drives, CD-ROM drive, and so forth.

TIP

Here, as elsewhere, keep things in order. One reason is that something specific (like a SCSI drive) expects to be preceded by a general SCSI controller, and otherwise may produce an error. For some hardware, the order in which it's probed, as they say, makes a difference.

RAID controllers treat several disks as one. Single-user systems are unlikely to have RAID controllers. If you have one, you'll know. Otherwise comment these out.

WARNING

The next block is for the keyboard, the PS/2 mouse (even if you don't have one, you could plug one in any time) and the basic display on your screen. Leave it all as it is.

```
#atkbdc0 controls both the keyboard and the PS/2
    mouse
device          atkbdc0 at isa? port IO_KBD
device          atkbd0  at atkbdc? irq 1 flags 0x1
device          psm0    at atkbdc? irq 12

device          vga0    at isa?
```

Leave the following as is if you want a screensaver to work in console mode:

```
# splash screen/screen saver
pseudo-device   splash
```

You need the console driver:

```
# syscons is the default console driver, resembling
    an SCO console
device          sc0     at isa? flags 0x100
```

The next few lines of the GENERIC kernel configuration file give you an opportunity to use an alternative console driver and suggest that you need it for IBM ThinkPads. Actually only a few ThinkPad models need this console driver; most are better with the standard console driver. If you enable these lines, you comment out the line above beginning with `device sc0`.

The following line always stays in:

```
device          npx0    at nexus? port IO_NPX irq 13
```

You leave in the following line, but notice the word "disable" in the middle of it—if you want advanced power management, you delete that word. The line is really important only on a laptop; and sometimes the laptop's built-in power management works better:

```
device          apm0    at nexus? disable flags 0x20
    # Advanced Power Management
```

The next batch of lines is for pccard (pcmcia) support. Comment them out unless you're creating a kernel for a laptop or you have a device that reads pccards on your desktop computer.

Ethernet Cards

Ethernet cards are also known as NICs, or Network Interface Cards. Comment out ethernet card (NIC) drivers other than your own. If your card is found by the installed kernel and works, `dmesg | grep address` will show you its driver.

Ethernet cards can be PCI cards (the ones that go in white slots on the motherboard) or ISA cards (in the old longer black slots), or ethernet support can be built into the motherboard. The odd-balls in the group are some PCI cards that use `ed0`, listed in the ISA category. If you have one of these, just include the `ed0` line.

If you have two identical NICs, you need to include the driver only once unless you have two ISA cards using the same driver.

WARNING

Most PCI cards need their own driver *and* the line that says:

```
device          miibus
```

so if in doubt, leave this line in. USB ethernet devices also need `device miibus`.

If you add an ethernet card after you've built a kernel, look at the kernel modules you can load instead of recompiling your kernel. That may be the easiest way.

Pseudo-devices

Pseudo-devices (the last big block of stuff) are various but useful. You want to keep most of these for use immediately or maybe a little later. The `tun` device is used by user `ppp`—your dial-up to your Internet service provider. Some people find kernel `ppp` works for them more easily. If you need more than 16 simultaneous logins or `xterms` in `X Window`, put a number higher than 16 (up to 256) next to `pseudo-device pty`.

The `gif`, `faith`, and `stf` pseudo-devices are for IPv6, Internet Protocol version 6, which isn't widely used yet (it increases the number of available IP addresses) but are used for tunneling more generally. These pseudo-devices are a little annoying as they greatly lengthen the display you get with the `netstat` command without offering any information you can use. You can comment these out unless your office or ISP is moving into IPv6.

The `pseudo-device bpf` (known as Berkeley packet filters) is essential to making `DHCP` work (Dynamic Host Configuration Protocol), and your ISP may use `DHCP`. But Berkeley packet filters are really Berkeley packet sniffers, so someone with `root` privileges can grab and read the traffic on the LAN (even traffic not for the particular machine). This is a violation of privacy unless you have a purpose in maintaining your network; it may also be illegal. Passwords sent in the clear can be read by someone with `root` privileges. If you give out accounts (as you might in a dorm, for example) you might want to build a kernel without this feature.

USB Support

Most newer computers offer a couple of USB ports, and some laptops depend heavily on USB. Kernel modules are available if you decide not to compile USB support into your kernel. If you include USB support and you want to include `device umass`, which is for a USB hard drive, you need to add back (if you took them out) the following lines from the SCSI peripherals section, because `umass` requires SCSI support:

```
device          scbus
device          da
```

Adding LINT Bells and Whistles

Once you've stripped your copy of `GENERIC`, it's time to look at the `LINT` configuration file. It's organized quite differently from `GENERIC` and is much longer, with a lot of detail. Most of it you don't want.

Here are some items from `LINT` that may be of interest:

You can include the kernel configuration file itself with the following line:

```
options    INCLUDE_CONFIG_FILE
```

You can then read the config file right from the kernel with a command that looks a little odd, ending as it does with three underscores, but works (`strings` reads text from a binary file).

```
# strings /kernel | grep ___
```

The following option (Appletalk communication protocols) might be useful if you want a Mac to communicate with your FreeBSD computer:

```
options    NETATALK
```

X-REF The basic sound option is `options    pcm`, but see Chapter 13 for more information:

If you have a bus mouse:

```
options    mse0 at isa? port 0x230 irq 5
```

LINUX

If Linux is installed on the same machine as FreeBSD, you probably want `options EXT2FS`, so you can mount your Linux partitions.

```
options          EXT2FS
```

If you have an `ISDN` modem you want to work with FreeBSD, see the `ISDN4BSD` section of the `LINT` file. Here too, you just copy the lines from `LINT` into your own configuration file.

X-REF

If you want FreeBSD to be a gateway for other computers on a local network, you need firewall options in the kernel (the loadable kernel module doesn't have what you need). Here is a set of workable entries from `LINT`— the same ones listed in Chapter 12, where the other steps for using FreeBSD as a gateway are described.

```
options    FIREWALL
options    IPFIREWALL_VERBOSE
options    IPFIREWALL_VERBOSE_LIMIT=100
options    IPFIREWALL_DEFAULT_TO_ACCEPT
options    IPDIVERT
```

Building Your Kernel

Building your kernel (actually, FreeBSD builds it—you just give the instructions) isn't hard; most of the work is editing your configuration file. If your configuration file is called NEWKERN, you stay right in the `/usr/src/sys/i386/conf` directory (where NEWKERN exists), which may appear just as `/sys/i386/conf` if you got there using the symbolic link:

1. **Type:**

```
/sys/i386/conf # config NEWKERN
```

You see:

```
Don't forget to do a ``make depend''
Kernel build directory is ../../compile/NEWKERN
```

2. **Change to the build directory, the full name of which is** `/usr/src/sys/compile/NEWKERN`, **with the command:**

```
cd ../../compile/NEWKERN
```

3. **Type:**

```
/sys/compile/NEWKERN # make depend
```

   You see a lot of messages on your screen. If `make depend` completes successfully, go on to step 4. If not, see the section on dealing with difficulties later in this chapter, especially making a log file so you can read the error messages.

4. **Type:**

```
/sys/compile/NEWKERN # make
```

   You see lots of messages on your screen as the kernel gets built, including messages about modules. It will take somewhere between four minutes (on a fast computer) to 30 minutes on a slow computer.

5. **Type:**

```
/sys/compile/NEWKERN # make install
```

   You see more messages; your existing `/kernel` will be moved to `/kernel.old`. Your new kernel will be installed as `/kernel`. New kernel modules will be installed in the `/modules` directory.

6. **Type:**

```
# /sbin/reboot
```

   when you're ready to reboot and try your new kernel.

If you want to build a kernel without building modules (they're time-consuming and there's no point in doing them unless your source code has changed), you type:

```
/sys/compile/NEWKERN # make -D_NOMODULES depend
/sys/compile/NEWKERN # make -D_NOMODULES
/sys/compile/NEWKERN # make -D_NOMODULES install
```

Alternatively you can copy the /etc/defaults/rc.conf file to /etc and uncomment the line that says #NO_MODULES= true to not build kernel modules when you build a kernel.

Dealing with Difficulties

Although building and installing a new kernel is a major system event, you're well-protected against disaster. Your kernel configuration file has to be correct at least in syntax or the kernel won't build, and you have other kernels on the system you can use if the new one doesn't work properly.

Build Failures

When a kernel file doesn't configure or build or install, you look for errors. The error messages on your screen are your best guide.

If the screen messages tell you something can't be found, you probably left something out of the kernel config file that's needed by something else in the file.

While doing make depend and later make, it's a good idea to keep a log file. You do this by redirecting the messages that usually go to the screen to a file, so your make depend command looks like this:

```
# make depend > depend.out 2>&1&
```

This sends errors messages (the 2) to the same file as status messages (the 1) and puts it all in the background (the second &). If you use csh or tcsh as your shell, the command is make depend >& depend.out &. With a log file you can examine errors carefully and quote from the log file if you need to ask about your problem.

Permission Denied

If you get a "permission denied" error when you try to install your new kernel, you may have your `securelevel` set to `1` or higher. Find out by typing:

```
sysctl kern.securelevel
```

If you see:

```
kern.securelevel: 1
```

your `securelevel` won't permit the installation of a new kernel. You can raise the `securelevel` but you can't lower it without rebooting. The setting is in `/etc/rc.conf`, where you want a `securelevel` of -1 (if you have any `securelevel`) to make it possible to install a new kernel. It should look like this:

```
kern_securelevel="-1"
```

If your `securelevel` is 1 or higher, change it to `-1` and reboot. You then rerun `make install` from `/usr/src/src/config/NEWKERN`.

Booting a Good Old Kernel

If the new kernel is installed, it's called `kernel` (just like the old one) and the old one is moved to `kernel.old`. At this point, `kernel.old` is a known good kernel. If you build and install another kernel, your "good old kernel" disappears, overwritten when the first kernel you built is moved to `kernel.old`.

If the first new kernel doesn't work, one trick is to preserve your original kernel by moving `kernel.old` to `kernel.good`. But if your new kernel doesn't boot, how do you get back into the machine? You boot `kernel.old`.

To boot a kernel with a name other than `kernel`, you interrupt the boot process just as it's starting by pressing the spacebar; then you type

```
boot:  kernel.old
```

If the boot process has already loaded a kernel, it will say so, and you have to type:

```
unload kernel
boot kernel.old
```

Another kernel, called `kernel.GENERIC`, is always installed in the / directory, and until you build and install a new kernel, this kernel is identical to the FreeBSD install installation kernel. You want to keep `kernel.GENERIC`, because if you pop a new drive in the box or add a new controller card (or whatever), it's the kernel most likely to have the stuff necessary to boot the new hardware.

If you move a drive from a computer with a 686 CPU to one with a 586 CPU, and you've configured the kernel for the 686 CPU, it won't boot on the 586—unless you either build a new kernel before you move it (which might be impossible if the old machine died) or you boot with `kernel.GENERIC`. And you can boot `kernel.GENERIC` in an emergency if neither `kernel` nor `kernel.old` works.

Installing a Kernel by Hand

If you want to replace an installed kernel with, say, `kernel.good`, you first delete the installed kernel. The problem is that a kernel is installed with a flag that prevents its deletion unless the flag is removed. You can see file flags with `ls -lo`:

```
/ # ls -lo kernel
```

You see the long listing for `kernel` and the flag— `schg`.

```
-r-xr-xr-x  1 root  wheel  schg 2700883 Apr 21
    01:10 kernel
```

To change the flag, type:

```
/ # chflags noschg kernel
```

Try `ls -lo kernel` again— you shouldn't see the `schg` flag. Now you should be able to do the following:

```
/ # rm kernel
/ # mv kernel.good kernel
/ # chflags schg kernel
```

The last line re-flags the kernel so it can't be deleted or moved accidentally.

Chapter 17

Upgrading FreeBSD

The ease with which you can upgrade FreeBSD is one of its great features.

You can upgrade your ports collection so you can install the latest third-party software.

You can also upgrade the entire system (and the kernel) whenever you like. It's not even very difficult. (Upgrading the system doesn't upgrade the ports collection.) This chapter tells you how to:

- upgrade your ports collection
- upgrade your system, and
- merge new start-up and configuration files.

Upgrading: How It Works

You do an upgrade in FreeBSD by getting the most recent *sources* for one or more collections and then doing whatever else may be necessary.

cvsup

The software that gets the sources for you is called `cvsup`. Thanks to John Polstra, who wrote it and maintains it, `cvsup` is wonderfully efficient. It just gets what's needed—the changes in updated files.

The `cvsup` program isn't part of the FreeBSD base system; you install it as a package or a port. It's one of the two add-on software programs (the other is your preferred shell, like `bash`) you should always install when you install FreeBSD.

Installing cvsup

You type:

```
$ which cvsup
```

If it's installed, you see:

```
/usr/local/bin/cvsup
```

ON CD-1

If it's not installed, install it as a port by typing `make install` in `/usr/ports/net/cvsup-bin`, or by installing the package using `/stand/sysinstall` (`Configure > Packages > Net > cvsup-bin`).

WARNING

Be sure you install `cvsup-bin` (on the advice of John Polstra himself) and not just `cvsup` or `cvsupd`. You want the binary; it just takes too long otherwise.

Using cvsup

The secret to running `cvsup` isn't reading the manual page (although I would never want to discourage you from such literary endeavors), but reading the files in `/usr/share/examples/cvsup`. These files are installed as part of the base FreeBSD system, so basic is `cvsup` to FreeBSD.

In this directory are *supfiles*, such as `ports-supfile` and `stable-supfile`. Each of these files is used to update a particular collection or set of collections on your hard drive. It doesn't update installed software; what `cvsup` updates is the source for the software or, in the case of the ports collection, the framework from which the software itself is built (see Chapter 10 for the full details).

Before you use a supfile, you edit it to tell it where to go to get what you want. Supfiles are like other files in FreeBSD in one way—the lines beginning with a hash mark (#) are comments. But in supfiles, the lines beginning with an asterisk (*) are action lines; they count.

The one line you need to change in a supfile is this one:

```
*default host=CHANGE_THIS.FreeBSD.org
```

You change `CHANGE_THIS` to `cvsup` or `cvsup2` or `cvsup9` (or anything in between) so it looks like this:

```
*default host=cvsup9.FreeBSD.org
```

This line determines where the source comes from. Some hosts will be closer to you than others, and some will be busier than others at different times. Usually `cvsup.freebsd.org` is a busy one, so try one of the others. To update a particular collection, the basic command is:

```
/usr/share/examples/cvsup # cvsup <supfile>
```

TIP

If you run `cvsup` from an `xterm` in `X`, you get a graphical interface unless you use the `-g` switch, which turns off the graphics. The other addition to the basic command is `-L 2`, which gives you a little more information on your screen as `cvsup` runs. The more complete command looks like this:

```
/usr/share/examples/cvsup # cvsup -g -L 2 <supfile>
```

It's a good idea to use one supfile for upgrading your ports (`ports-supfile`) and another one for upgrading your system (`stable-supfile`). It avoids errors and takes no more time. If you do this, you do not need to change the tag in the file.

When you update your entire system, you get updated versions of the files in `/usr/share/examples/cvsup`.

Upgrading Your Ports Collection

You can upgrade your ports collection regardless of the version of FreeBSD you're running, but when you try to install a port, if your installed system is old you may get a message that "your system is too old." The message will explain how to get an upgrade kit for your system; the upgrade kits are available as ports in `/usr/ports/misc`.

WARNING There's only one version—the current version—of the ports collection, so it's the same whether you have FreeBSD 4.0, 4.3, or 5.0. Do not change the line in your `ports-supfile` including `tag=.` (tag equals dot). It's right.

Upgrading the ports collection doesn't upgrade specific applications, just the framework for installing them.

The Ports Upgrade Command

The command for upgrading the ports collection is:

```
/usr/share/examples/cvsup # cvsup -g -L2 ports-supfile
```

You see on your screen:

```
Parsing supfile "ports-supfile"
Connecting to cvsup9.FreeBSD.org
Connected to cvsup9.FreeBSD.org
Server software version: REL_16_1
Negotiating file attribute support
Exchanging collection information
Establishing multiplexed-mode data connection
Running
Updating collection ports-archivers/cvs
 Edit ports/archivers/Makefile
  Add delta 1.51 2001.04.08.18.00.08 ijliao
  Add delta 1.52 2001.04.17.18.01.39 will
 Checkout ports/archivers/bitbox/Makefile
```

```
...
Edit ports/x11-wm/wmanager/Makefile
  Add delta 1.8 2001.04.03.08.14.33 will
 Edit ports/x11-wm/xwmm/Makefile
  Add delta 1.7 2001.04.03.08.14.33 will
Shutting down connection to server
Finished successfully
```

How long that takes depends on the speed of your connection and how different the updated ports collection is from what you have installed.

Variations on Ports

The file `/usr/share/examples/cvsup/ports-supfile` has a line that says:

```
ports-all
```

and other lines (around 40 of them) that begin with a hash mark (#):

```
#ports-base
#ports-archivers
....
#ports-x11-wm
```

The lines beginning with a # (commented out) are the individual collections that make up the ports collection. You can comment `ports-all` (put a # at the beginning of the line) and uncomment (remove the #) in front of the specific collections you want. But if you do so, be sure to get `ports-base`, because this collection has the up-to-date files for installing ports.

Unless you work in foreign languages, you can safely decide not to get `ports-japanese`, `ports-russian`, and so forth. See the description of software in different categories in Chapter 11 for other individual ports collections you may not need, but remember that a port in any category could need an application from another category like `ports-archivers`, `ports-lang`, or `ports-graphics`.

Commenting out `ports-all` and commenting in one individual collection is also a quick way to update a particular port category, but keep in mind those ports may have updated dependencies in other categories.

When you update the sources for your entire system, the files in `/usr/share/examples/cvsup` will also be updated. Your `ports-supfile` will get overwritten with a new one. The new one might have a new category in the list of individual ports collections. You should save your edited `ports-supfile` to another name:

```
# cp ports-supfile ports-mine
```

Upgrading FreeBSD from Source

Upgrading FreeBSD from one version to another means upgrading your entire base system. It doesn't include upgrading your ports collection or upgrading third-party software (the software you install as ports or packages). And it doesn't upgrade your installed version of `X-Window` or any additional `X` software you have installed.

You can upgrade your system two ways: from source or by doing a binary upgrade. Doing a binary upgrade means installing binaries over the binaries you installed as the original system and is discussed later in this chapter.

Upgrading from source (the files the programmers wrote) means getting the source and rebuilding the entire base system and installing the resulting binaries. This is the preferred method. It takes space for the source (300MB or so) and space for the binaries you build (another 300MB).

The FreeBSD source tree is depicted in Figure 17-1. The trunk is called the `-current` branch, and is experimental—the bleeding edge. When a set of new features works well and has settled down enough to be reliable in production work, a branch from the trunk, like the 4 branch, is created. The branch code continues to be developed and many improvements are made along the way. Sometimes features developed in `-current` are added to a `-stable` branch.

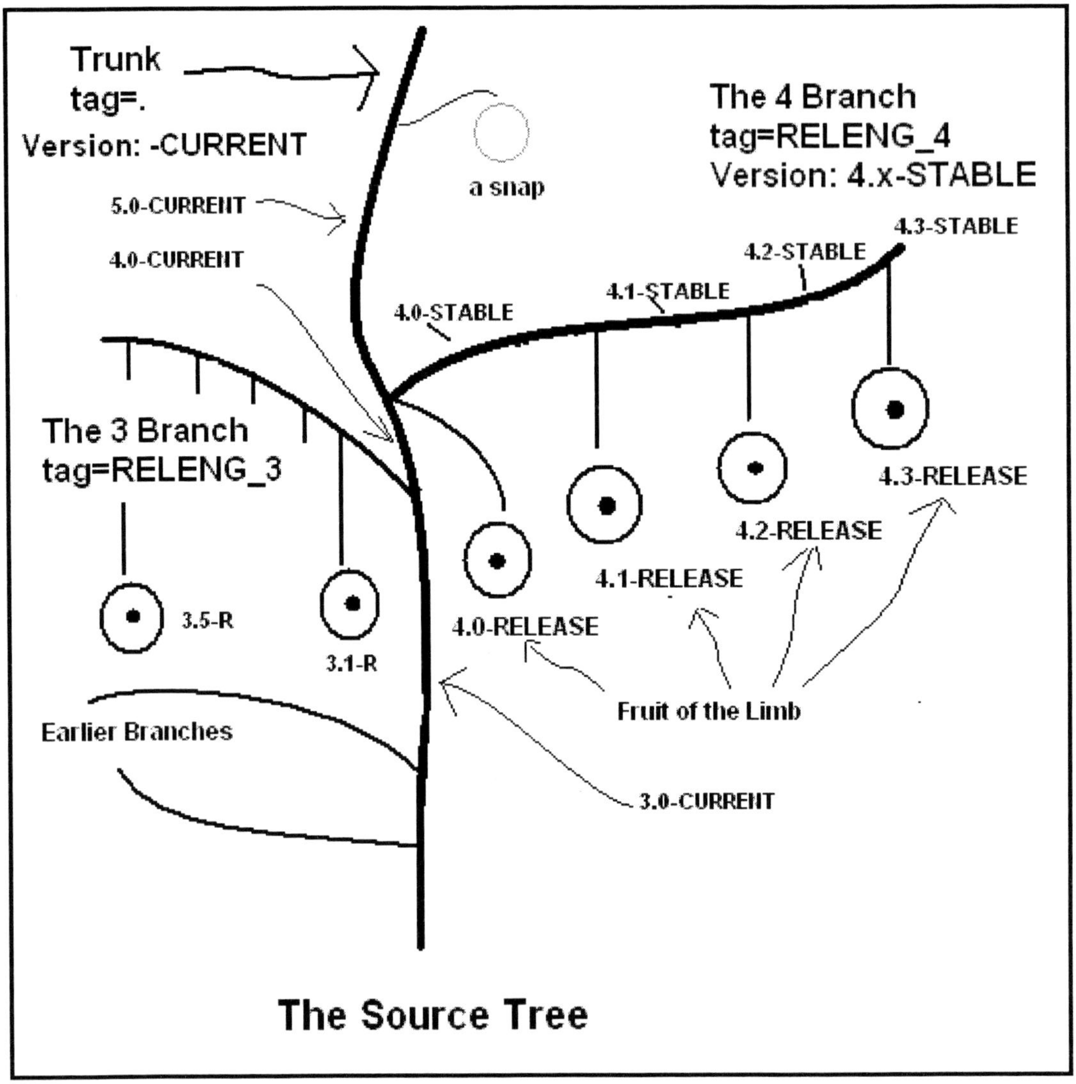

Figure 17-1: The FreeBSD Source Tree

From the branch come specific *releases* of the system at points in time—binary installable releases usually on CD-ROMs, one every three or four months and four or five over the active life of the branch.

In between the releases that reflect the branch at specific points in time, development continues and many improvements are made along the way. Usually no new major features are introduced, but sometimes good things developed in `-current` are brought into a branch.

The formal releases made along a branch have specific names (4.3-RELEASE, for example) and are available in binary form, but are part of the 4.x-STABLE branch. In the few weeks before a new release is produced from a branch, a few versions installable as binaries (by FTP or by downloading the ISO and creating a CD-ROM on your own hardware) may be available. They may be given special names (even though they're part of the branch) such as 4.3RC (release candidate). Thus 4.3-RC is binary-installable but is also part of 4.2-STABLE—as 4.2 morphs toward 4.3.

Before you begin, you should subscribe to the `freebsd-stable` mailing list, where new developments or problems in the `-stable` branch are reported and discussed. Send email to `majordomo@freebsd.org`, with the text `subscribe freebsd-stable` in the body.

What's important is the jump: what you upgrade *from* and what you upgrade *to*. A 4.2-RELEASE system can be upgraded to 4.2-STABLE or even to 4.3-STABLE, for example. Upgrades along a branch are usually straight-forward, although often a few special items must be addressed. These special items are listed in `/usr/src/UPDATING`, an invaluable reference on how to upgrade successfully maintained by Warner Losh.

A snap is like a release, but it usually isn't available on CD-ROM. You can install a snap by FTP in the same way you install a release. See Chapter 20.

Getting Source with cvsup

You get source—or update your installed source—with `cvsup`. If you have a CD-ROM, it helps to install that source using `/stand/sysinstall` (`Configure > Distributions > Sources for Everything > All`) if it's not already installed to minimize the `cvsup` download. The source is put (by default) in `/usr/src` and its various subdirectories.

You get or upgrade system source using the `stable-supfile` found in `/usr/share/examples/cvsup`. You edit only the line that says:

```
*default host=CHANGE_THIS.FreeBSD.org
```

to make it read, for example:

```
*default host=cvsup9.FreeBSD.org
```

You may also want to check to make sure the tag is right for the branch you want. The following is right all along branch 4, for the latest update (see Chapter 20 for updating to a specific release):

```
*default release=cvs tag=RELENG_4
```

Save your file (don't delete the initial * s) and run the following command (as `root`):

```
/usr/share/examples/cvsup # cvsup -g -L2 stable-supfile
```

You can use a form of the command that makes a log file and puts the output in the background instead of on your screen:

```
# cvsup -g -L2 stable-supfile >stable.out 2>&1&
```

The `stable.out` file logs what goes across the screen so you can look at it occasionally (with `tail -f stable.out`, exiting with Ctrl+c) or later.

WARNING

Don't use the `standard-supfile`. It sounds absolutely right—but it gets source for `-current`, the experimental version of FreeBSD, not the stable version. In `-current`, some things are likely not to be working and you're expected to help the developers solve problems, not get help yourself.

Making the World

When `cvsup` finishes you see:

```
Shutting down connection to server
Finished successfully
```

After a few hours, check your messages from the `freebsd-stable` mailing list for problems and read `/usr/src/UPDATING`. Re-run your `cvsup` command if problems are reported. You're ready to begin.

1. **Shut down any programs making large resource demands on your system if you want the process to go faster.**

2. **Type** `cd /usr/src` **and become** `root`

3. **Read** `/usr/src/UPDATING` **for information on recent events and changes.**

4. **Type:**

```
/usr/src # make buildworld >build.out 2>&1 &
```

The log file created here may be useful but is not essential (it will grow to over 7MB). The buildworld will take an hour on a fast machine and a lot longer on a slow one. (It took 14 hours on my P90). The object files (binaries) the process creates will be placed in `/usr/obj`. If you wish, you can also embellish this command to let the kernel start more than one process at a time (and thus speed things up) as follows:

```
/usr/src/ # make -j 4 buildworld
```

When it finishes, you prepare your kernel configuration file.

If make buildworld Fails

If your buildworld fails, check your `freebsd-stable` mail messages for reports of problems. Run `cvsup` again—the new code might correct it. Look at your log file for error messages.

Often you can re-start buildworld where it left off (if it quits with an error or was interrupted because of a power failure or whatever) with the command:

```
make -DNOCLEAN buildworld
```

5. **Type** `cd /sys/i386/conf` **and** `cp GENERIC MYKERN`**. Edit** this new copy of `GENERIC` called `MYKERN`**,** making the same kinds of changes described in the previous chapter—commenting out drivers for hardware you don't have and including special features you want. Kernel configuration files change in subtle ways, so it's best to start with a copy of the new `GENERIC` as a base rather than your old config file. (You can edit the config file while the `buildworld` is running.)

Whatever Happened to "make world"?

The `make world` command does two things: `make buildworld` and `make installworld`. As it has become more important to build a kernel and reboot in between these two steps, `make world` has fallen into disuse. In addition, using a `j` value in `make world` (e.g., `make -j4 world`) would be trouble, because it would be operative for both `make buildworld` and `make installworld`.

You would think the next step would be `make installworld`, but it's not. (See the Whatever Happened to "make world"? sidebar.) You have an old kernel, and to install the new binaries you just created in `/usr/obj`, you want (and may need) a new kernel, built with the new tools also residing in `/usr/obj`. Thus:

6. **Type** `cd /usr/src`
7. **Type**:

```
/usr/src # make kernel KERNCONF=MYKERN
```

This command both builds and installs a kernel using your new sources and your configuration file (which it knows how to find). You could have split it into two steps:

```
/usr/src # make buildkernel KERNCONF=MYKERN
/usr/src # make installkernel KERNCONF=MYKERN
```

If you get a "permission denied" message when your kernel tries to install, see Chapter 16 on checking and changing your `securelevel`.

8. **Reboot with `/sbin/reboot`, interrupting the boot process early by pressing the spacebar and typing `kernel -s` to go into single-user mode. Type `mount -a` to mount all your file systems (all those listed in `/etc/fstab`).**

Not everyone believes you always need to be in single-user mode to install your new system, especially if not much is going on. If you do upgrades on remote machines, single-user mode won't work for you (at least not without a serial console). But after all, not too many users are going to be left on the machine after you reboot.

9. **Type:**

```
# cd /usr/src
```

10. **Type:**

```
/usr/src # make installworld
```

WARNING

Don't use a `-j` value with `installworld` (it's dangerous). But if you like, create a log file.

11. **When** `installworld` **finishes, you can go on to merging with** `mergemaster` **(in multi-user mode if you like) or you can reboot first. You get into multi-user mode from single-user simply by typing** `exit`**.**

The next section, Merging, deals with merging files from `/usr/src/etc` and updating your device nodes. The Other Tasks section explains how to update `sysinstall` and update your `kernel.GENERIC`.

Merging

The `make installworld` command installs your newly built system, writing over the old files with the new ones, but doesn't install anything from the `/usr/src/etc` directory.

Installing what's in `/usr/src/etc` and its subdirectories is left for you because the files that would be overwritten are often files that you have edited or that have been edited by `sysinstall` or other utilities using information you or others have provided. Think about it: these include your password and group files; your `ppp` setup information; your network setup for your ethernet card, your host, your nameserver; and perhaps much else.

It's tempting to pay no attention to `/usr/src/etc`, but changes in the FreeBSD base system may require changes in the files in `/etc` and elsewhere. Here's an example: In January 2001, changes in the `openssh` program required some new lines in `/etc/pam.conf`. People who upgraded at this time without doing a merge from `/usr/src/etc` found that `ssh` no longer worked, and they couldn't figure out why (even though `/usr/src/UPDATING` gave them the information they needed).

As another example, your `/etc/group` file has changes you made directly or when using `sysinstall` or `adduser`. Users got added to the group `wheel` so they could use `su` to become `root`, and for each user you created, there's a group with the same name. But most of the groups in the file are system groups, and sometimes a new system group gets added, as did the `network` group a few years ago. If you don't update the `group` file in such a situation, some utilities won't work. If you just overwrite it, you wipe out the groups you have yourself created or edited.

WARNING

Merging the files from `/usr/src/etc` is important, but it needs to be done carefully. And before you start you want to back up your entire `/etc` directory with a command like this, which would make a copy of `/etc` and its subdirectories in your home directory:

```
# cp -Rp /etc ~/etc
```

Notice also that some of the files in `/usr/src/etc` are directories. Some of these directories have counterparts in `/etc`, such as `/usr/src/etc/defaults`. The `/usr/src/etc/etc.i386` directory, on the other hand, has files that are meant for `/etc` on a PC rather than a DEC Alpha computer (those are in `/usr/src/etc/etc.alpha`).

Some of the files aren't even meant for `/etc`. Consider the file `/usr/src/etc/MAKEDEV`. That's meant for `/dev`. It's the basic script for making the device nodes in `/dev`, and if `/dev/MAKEDEV` isn't up-to-date, you may be puzzled when not all the sound device nodes (just to take an example you might especially care about) get created.

TIP

One conclusion about the files in `/etc` is that it's a good idea to put as much stuff as possible in special configuration files rather than the basic files. This is why `/etc/defaults` exists—so the files there can be replaced without overwriting the configuration files in `/etc` that override them: `rc.conf`, `make.conf`, and `pccard.conf`. One way to tell which files you've changed is to print out (maybe even to paper) a long and recursive file listing in reverse time order with:

```
# ls -Rlrt /etc
```

You can do the merge by hand—comparing each file in `/usr/src/etc` and its subdirectories with those in `/etc` and its subdirectories, and putting other files in appropriate places—or you can use `mergemaster`, a script developed by Doug Barton especially for this purpose. It pulls in configuration files from places other than /etc, via `/usr/src/etc/Makefile`.

Using mergemaster

The `mergemaster` script creates a temporary directory with all files in their appropriate places in the hierarchy and proceeds to compare them with their installed versions. It gives you a choice of installing the new version, deleting the new version from the temporary directory, merging the two versions (and then installing or not), or leaving the file in the temporary directory for later action. It uses `sdiff` if you ask it to merge the two versions, which in turn gives you a choice of which lines from each file to include in the merged file.

The manual page for `mergemaster` suggests running it with `-v` (for verbose) the first time, which gives you more information about what it's doing and your choices. The `mergemaster` script is updated to take into account changes in FreeBSD, so reading its man page (and that for `sdiff` as well) before starting is a good idea.

When `mergemaster` compares two files, you press Enter to continue seeing lines of the two files. Identical lines are preceded by a space, lines from your installed file are preceded by a `-`, and lines from the new file have a `+`. When you've seen enough and want to take action, you press `q`, and then the action option comes up—install (`i`), delete the temporary new file (`d`), merge the two versions (`m`), or leave it for later. Leave anything you're not sure of for later by pressing Enter (it's the default).

If you choose merge, the left-hand side of the screen has the installed file and the right-hand side has the new version. Pressing Enter gives you a help list of commands `sdiff` uses. You press `l` to use the left-hand side and `r` for the right-hand side.

If you want to postpone making decisions, you can leave lots of stuff for later or bail out with Ctrl+c. You can use `mergemaster -rv` to run `mergemaster` again with the set of temporary files it created so that you have a chance to make decisions without having to look again at the ones you already decided about.

Updating /dev

`Mergemaster` installs (if you press `i` when asked) the new `MAKEDEV` file for `/dev`. You always want to install the new one because sometimes new device nodes come along. Most device nodes will be updated with the command:

```
# sh /dev/MAKEDEV all
```

Other Tasks

Once your upgraded system is running, you can delete `/usr/obj` with these commands:

```
# cd /usr
/usr # rm -rf obj
```

What Upgrading Doesn't Do

Upgrading your system from source doesn't do the following:

- It doesn't install anything from `/usr/src/etc`
- It doesn't update device nodes in `/dev`
- It doesn't upgrade the ports structure or installed third-party software.
- It doesn't upgrade X or any installed X software.
- It doesn't change the installed version of `sysinstall`
- It doesn't build or install a new `kernel.GENERIC`

The first two have already been taken care of with `mergemaster` and `sh /dev/MAKEDEV all`. The second two are handled through the ports structure.

You want to upgrade `sysinstall` if it's failing to recognize your drives and when it gets really out-of-date—when, for example, it's from a previous branch of FreeBSD. You upgrade `sysinstall` with these commands:

```
# cd /usr/src/release/sysinstall
# make clean
# make depend
# make
# make install
```

Before you do the final step—`make install`—you can run `sysinstall` from the `/usr/src/release/sysinstall` directory with `./sysinstall` to make sure it works.

Building a kernel you don't want to install as the main kernel for the system is a little different from building and installing a kernel in one step. Also, you don't want to build kernel modules again, as they're already freshly built and installed. Using the traditional method of building a kernel (as described in Chapter 16) is probably most convenient (copy your old `kernel.GENERIC` to a new name first, and recall that there's a symbolic link from `/sys` to `/usr/src/sys`):

```
# mv /kernel.GENERIC kernel.GENERIC.OLD
# cd /sys/i386/conf
/sys/i386/conf # config GENERIC
/sys/i386/conf # cd ../../compile/GENERIC
/sys/compile/GENERIC # make -DNO_MODULES depend
/sys/compile/GENERIC # make -DNO_MODULES
/sys/compile/GENERIC # cp -p kernel /kernel.GENERIC
```

If you build `GENERIC` from `/usr/src`, you use these commands:

```
# cd /usr/src
/usr src # make -DNO_MODULES buildkernel
     KERNCONF=GENERIC
/usr/src # cd /usr/obj/usr/src/sys/GENERIC
/usr/obj/usr/src/sys/GENERIC # cp -p kernel
     /kernel.GENERIC
```

You can build a kernel this way—from `/usr/src`—even if you've deleted `/usr/obj`, but the new kernel will end up out there in left field instead of in

/usr/src/sys/compile/GENERIC.

Doing a Binary Upgrade

A binary upgrade is not the only choice when you have limited disk space. A better choice may be reinstalling.

The document /stand/help/UPGRADE.TXT.gz, which explains binary upgrading, can be uncompressed by typing:

```
# cd /stand/help
# gunzip UPGRADE.TXT.gz
```

This document has many warnings. Doing a binary upgrade is riskier than upgrading from source. The document also refers to some transition problems that occurred when 2.x was the -stable branch, suggesting that it is not kept up-to-date.

Note that you need to boot from the version of /stand/sysinstall to which you intend to upgrade, so you need a new installation CD-ROM or new boot floppies.

In the /stand/sysinstall main menu, you choose:

```
Upgrade         Upgrade an existing system
```

and will be cautioned (and guided) from thereon. Read especially carefully the discussion of the handling of the files in /etc so you know where to look to merge the old and the new. The mergemaster program cannot be used when you do a binary upgrade.

Chapter 18

Other Tasks

This chapter is a miscellaneous collection from the sublime to the serious:

- getting color at the console
- booting from a floppy
- setting up your mail system
- keeping time
- using `tar`, and
- security—especially `ssh`.

Coloring Up Your Console

A couple of ports, `colorls` and `gnuls`, provide color at the console, but in versions 4.1 and later of FreeBSD, color is built in (duplicating the capabilities of the `colorls` port) with `ls -G`.

The `gnuls` port provides the capabilities with which Linux users will be familiar, and installs as `gnuls` so it won't conflict with `colorls` or `ls -G`.

You can type `ls -G`, or you can put one of the following (I prefer the first, as it's easier to turn off with `unalias ls`) in your `.bash_profile`:

```
alias ls=´ls -G´
CLICOLOR=yes
```

The `-G` switch to `ls` (however you invoke it) causes files of different types to be displayed in different colors. The terminal type needs to be capable of displaying ANSI colors. By default, the console terminal type is `cons25` and is so capable. Over a remote connection (perhaps you use SecureCRT to connect to FreeBSD) you need to set your terminal emulator to use ANSI colors and set the terminal type on the FreeBSD machine with `TERM=xterm-color`. In an `xterm` in X, typing `TERM=xterm-color` will make your `xterm` color-capable. (In the `csh` and `tcsh` shells, you use `setenv TERM xterm-color` instead.)

The trick is that `ls -G` uses as *its* defaults the background color set by `vidcontrol` and displays regular files (and your prompt) in the foreground color set by `vidcontrol`. And `vidcontrol`'s defaults are a white foreground and a black background. Until you change them, all regular files and your prompt will show up in white, and the background will be black, although files of other types (like directories) will have color.

Table 18-1 Console Colors with LSCOLOR (ls -G)

Default	*File Type*
4x	directory
5x	symbolic link
2x	socket (uncommon)
3x	pipe (uncommon)
1x	executable
46	block special (usually in `/dev`, but rare)
43	character special (most of the files in `/dev`)
01	executable setuid (a warning)
06	executable setgid (a warning)
02	directory writable by others, sticky bit set (a warning)
03	directory writable by others, sticky bit not set (a warning)

Key: 0 black, 1 red, 2 green, 3 brown, 4 blue, 5 magenta, 6 cyan, 7 light gray, x default (foreground or background); the first number is the foreground color, the second the background color.

Other than your prompt and regular files, `ls -G` will display other files according to its defaults, shown in Table 18-1 (and in the `ls` manual page).

Now comes the real fun. You can change the colors `ls -G` uses for different types of files by setting the LSCOLOR variable, which is by default:

```
LSCOLORS=4x5x2x3x1x464301060203
```

With this default directories will show up as blue on black (4x) and executables as red on black (1x). To get some lighter colors on the display, set `LSCOLORS` as follows:

```
$ LSCOLORS=2x5x0x4x6x464310160203
$ export LSCOLORS
```

which gives you green directories (2x), magenta symbolic links (5x), and cyan (6x) executables. Now we're getting somewhere. Try `ls -G /`. The / directory is a good one for testing because it contains the types of files you see most often—regular files, executables, directories, and symbolic links.

TIP

While you experiment with LSCOLORS, you can append its definition to a file in your home directory (say, `goodcolors`) for later use with:

```
$ echo $LSCOLORS >> ~/goodcolors
```

Return `LSCOLORS` to its default with:

```
$ LSCOLORS=
```

The next step in designing your own color scheme for the console is the `vidcontrol show` command, which displays the possible background colors (only those numbered 1 through 7) and the foreground colors you can choose (all 15). You get blue text on a white background, for example, with:

```
$ vidcontrol blue white
```

If you choose something non-functional like CIA/KGB colors (black on black) or Mafia colors (white on white), keep in mind `vidcontrol white black` for disaster recovery; you type it blind.

With `vidcontrol` providing blue text on a white background and `LSCOLORS` using defaults, directories will be blue on white (but so will regular files) and executables will be red on white, a nice patriotic color scheme for the United States, Russia, Norway, the United Kingdom, Liberia, and quite a few other countries. Your text editor will also display blue text on a white background, and so will man pages. (Notice that the `LSCOLOR` color codings are not the same as those for `vidcontrol`. Nobody said it would be easy, and nobody was right.)

Suppose, however, you want something a bit more subdued (also suitable for Swedish patriots):

```
$ vidcontrol blue brown
$ LSCOLORS=0x7x6x5x1x464301060203
```

That would make your prompt and regular files blue, most directories black, most executables red, and symbolic links light gray, all on a brownish-yellow background.

Changing the color assignments for the other types of files may be a waste of time because they are either uncommon, limited (usually) to `/dev`, or are meant as alerts, useful to have the same in all color schemes. In this scheme, though, character device files (43) are blue on brown, which is identical to your `vidcontrol` settings, and thus they are not distinguished from regular files (this is not the only overlap). Change 43 to x2 and do `ls -G /dev` (the x can be used as the first number as well as the second, where it stands for the foreground you set with `vidcontrol`). Ugly but informative.

Military Colors

This is the Army, Mr. Green
No fancy colors on the screen
You liked magenta with a blue foregound
Now it's black on a brown background.

For a more psychedelic look, try:

```
$ vidcontrol white magenta
$ LSCOLORS=2x3x0x4x6x464310160203
```

The problem with this Kool-Aid color scheme is that editing files and reading manual pages on a magenta background may be a bit more magenta than you want. Probably only black, white, and brown backgrounds are tolerable for more than a few minutes. Note also that if your color scheme has some identical (or close) background and foreground colors for a given file type, `ls -G` shows some blank lines or symbols without text (if you use the `-F` switch to `ls`, either at the command line or because it's set as an alias). The text is there, but you can't see it. That's why there's no 5x in the `LSCOLORS` definition suggested for a magenta background.

TIP

For each color scheme you like, you can create a file with three lines (the `vidcontrol` line, the `LSCOLORS` line, and the `export` line) in your home directory and use the `source` command (an internal shell command) to change the colors on your screen. Add a line reading `alias ls='ls -G'` to it as well if you like. With a few such color scheme files, you can switch color schemes at will.

Finally, a file containing the following (you could call it `nocolor`) will turn off all the color when you type `source nocolor`:

```
vidcontrol white black
LSCOLORS=
```

Booting from a Floppy

Sometimes you want to boot FreeBSD from the hard drive using a floppy rather than a boot manager. Maybe you have permission to install FreeBSD on someone else's computer on the condition that you don't install a boot manager or do anything that prevents an automatic boot into Windows (no boot manager).

You do this using a fixit floppy, creating it as described in Chapter 2 or from FreeBSD (if you have the `fixit.flp` image on your hard drive) as follows:

1. **Put a freshly formatted floppy in the floppy drive (don't mount it).**

2. **Type** `dd if=fixit.flp of=/dev/fd0` **to write the floppy image to the floppy disk.**

3. Reboot the computer with the floppy in the drive. This floppy is not capable of booting by itself, but it can boot from your hard drive. You see:

```
>> FreeBSD/i386 BOOT
   Default: 0:fd(0,a)/kernel
   boot:
```

4. Enter the correct incantation for booting from your hard drive, something like the following (the first number identifies the drive and the second the slice; for a SCSI disk use `da` instead of `ad`):

```
boot: 0:ad(2,a)/boot/loader
```

5. When you know exactly what needs to be typed in to boot from your hard drive, mount the floppy disk with:

```
# mount /dev/fd0 /mnt
```

6. Create a file with your text editor called `kernel.conf` and put this line in the file (changing the `0:ad(2,a)` part to the appropriate disk and slice for your computer, although slice 0 usually works if the disk is right):

```
boot: 0:ad(2,a)/boot/loader
```

7. Copy the file to the floppy by typing:

```
# cp kernel.conf /mnt
```

8. Dismount the floppy and test it to make sure it can boot right into FreeBSD on your computer and label the floppy as a hard-drive boot disk; it will no longer work as a `fixit` disk unless you delete the `kernel.conf` file or move that file to a different name.

Setting Up Your Mail System

Electronic mail is the Internet service used by more people than any other. A full mail system has the following components:

- **A mail transport agent**, or MTA. MTAs move mail around the Internet. FreeBSD comes with the most-used mail transport agent on the planet—`sendmail`—enabled on installation. If it's running, you see the following when you type `ps auxw | grep sendmail`:

```
root      158  0.0  0.3  1424 1212  ??  Ss
     10:10PM   0:00.01 sendmail: accepting
     connections on port 25 (sendmail)
```

  If it's not running, you enable it by putting this line in `/etc/rc.conf`:

```
sendmail_enable="YES"
```

  The other information `sendmail` needs to run is in the line that reads `sendmail_flags="-bd -q30m`, which is already included in `/etc/defaults/rc.conf` and does not need to be repeated in `/etc/rc.conf`. But if you want to start `sendmail` at the command line, you type:

```
# sendmail -bd -q30m
```

- **Mail user agents**, or MUAs. Another ugly UNIXism. These are the programs you're familiar with—programs for users to read and answer or compose mail, like `pine`, `elm`, `mutt`, and `xmh`. They are usually configurable in many ways (how to sort the mail for display, for example) but usually need only a few items of information to run, like your name, a "From:" address to use (possibly not that of the machine), or a Reply to: address, and a real name if different from the user's full name in the `/etc/password` file. MUAs also need to know how to send the mail—whether to use (by default) `sendmail` on the local machine, or some other MTA, like that of your ISP.

  You start `pine`'s configuration by typing `pine` and pressing `S` for Setup and then `C` for Configure. Extensive help is only a ? away at any time. You can leave many items blank and fill them in later when you have a better idea about how you want `pine` to behave—or you can look at and edit the file in your home directory called .pinerc, which is where the configuration settings are stored.

In the .pinerc file, you might want to add to the feature-list allow-changing-from, perhaps with additional features enabled. Note that each feature except the last ends with a comma.

- **A mail delivery agent**, /bin/mail on FreeBSD, that handles local delivery. (You can also use the mail program as a user agent.) You can usually ignore the MDA, even though it's necessary.

- **Programs for getting mail from a mail server** that receives a user's mail. Your mail probably arrives at your Internet service provider and is stored there waiting for you to download it. These programs can be part of a mail user agent, but on FreeBSD they're often separate. An example is fetchmail, installable as a port or a package. It comes with a graphical configuration tool called fetchmailconf.

- **Programs run by an ISP on a mail server to let users get the mail that arrives for them.** The cucipop application is an example. It lets the user upload the contents of /var/mail/<*username*>.

- **Programs for sorting your mail when it arrives**—especially convenient if you subscribe to mailing lists and get a lot of messages that aren't personally directed to you. You can get these messages sorted into mailboxes separate from personal mail. The procmail application is the standard.

Keeping Time and Serving Time

You update the system clock by typing:

```
# ntpdate <timeserver>
```

Table 18-2 lists a few timeservers; you can use more than one on the command line. This is a good command to put in a short script and call daily or more often (even every hour) from /etc/crontab. You can enable a check with a timeserver on boot by putting enable_ntpdate="YES" and ntpdate_flags="<timeservers>" in /etc/rc.conf, but if your network doesn't come up on boot it will slow down the boot process.

Table 18-2 Time Servers

Server	*Location*
swisstime.ethz.ch	Switzerland
bitsy.mit.edu	U.S. East Coast
otc1.psu.edu	U.S. East Coast
clepsydra.dec.com	U.S. West Coast
ncar.ucar.edu	U.S. Midwest

You can get an extensive worldwide list of public timeservers from the web site http://www.eecis.udel.edu/~mills/ntp/clock2.htm.

FreeBSD can also function as a timeserver with `ntpd` running. See the manual page for how to set it up. If `ntpd` is running, `ntpdate` won't work.

Tarring Up Your Driveway?

You don't want to tar up your driveway or repair your roof—you just want to extract the files from a tarball.

You place a `tar` archive so that it extracts where you want it. For example, `ports.tgz`, which is a compressed (the `z` shows that) tar archive, would be moved to `/usr` and extracted as follows:

```
# mv ports.tgz /usr
# cd /usr
# tar xzf ports.tgz
```

Because the first letter after `tar` is `x` (for extract), the filename, which comes after the `f`, is the name of the file to extract and decompress. A `v` added to the list of options (e.g., `tar xzvf`) makes `tar` verbose (sometimes known as noisy), listing on the screen each file it extracts and decompresses. The resulting hierarchy of files will have the same structure as the files used to make the tarball.

You can tar up a bunch of files in a directory (and all its subdirectories) with the command:

```
$ tar cf <filename to create> dirname
```

Because the first letter after `tar` is `c` (for create) instead of `x`, the filename you type following `f` is the name of the file to create. You don't have to be `root` to use `tar`, but you do need write privileges for the directories to which `tar` will be writing files. If you want to compress the files at the same time, add a `z`:

```
$ tar czf <filename to create> dirname
```

The filename to which the tar archive is written can be anything you like, but it's useful to give it a name, including an extension, that helps you remember what it is. If you're tarring up and compressing `spike`'s home directory, for example:

```
# cd /home
# tar czf spike.tgz spike
```

If you want to look at the table of contents of a tarball without extracting or decompressing, you use `t` as the first instruction to `tar` instead of `x` or `c`. This command would give you a listing of the directories and files in `spike.tgz`:

```
$ tar tzf spike.tgz
```

Tar has other options to ignore a file or files that match a particular pattern that can work whether you're creating a tar archive, extracting one, or just looking at the table of contents.

Using FreeBSD Security

When your computer is on the Internet, it's at risk. Unfortunately there are lots of kids out there who think it's fun to try to break into other people's computers.

Computer security comes in layers. No simple security precaution makes your computer entirely invulnerable, but everything you do to protect it helps a little. Although someone can break your car windows to get in and steal the stereo, locking the doors may discourage many a thief.

Chapter 12 describes basic firewall installation in the context of its use for allowing other computers on a local network to reach the Internet. Read `man ipfw` for information on adding rules to your firewall. You can also change the basic firewall rules by changing the type of firewall you run at boot in `/etc/rc.conf`. Read the file `/etc/rc.firewall` to see what rules will be invoked on boot for the different types of firewalls.

Tightening Up

You can easily increase security by editing `/etc/inetd.conf` to make it impossible for users to log in remotely using `rsh` or `rlogin`. To do so, you comment out these lines in `/etc/inetd.conf` by putting a # at the beginning of each of them:

```
shell stream tcp nowait root /usr/libexec/rshd rshd
login stream tcp nowait root /usr/libexec/rlogind rlogind
```

WARNING Allowing users to log in remotely using `rsh` and `rlogin` is very insecure.

After you make a change in `inetd.conf`, you type the following to cause `inetd` to reread the configuration file:

```
# killall -HUP inetd
```

You might also want to comment out `finger`, which provides information on users. Try the following, substituting your username for `spike`:

```
$ finger spike@localhost
```

Finally, as installed FreeBSD allows logins (with password authentication) via `telnet`. `Telnet`'s major problem is that passwords are sent over the local network in plain text—unencrypted. If you don't use `telnet`, you should comment `telnetd` out of `/etc/inetd.conf`. If you do use `telnet` to reach your FreeBSD computer, it would be a good idea to set up `ssh` and `sshd` (maintained by Kris Kennaway, who works on FreeBSD security matters) to use instead, as a replacement for `rsh`, `rlogin`, and `telnet`. They are explained in the next section.

Using ssh and sshd

I usually think of clients as people who maintain the lifestyles of lawyers and plumbers, but in the UNIX universe, clients are computer programs run by users. These clients send requests to servers. The servers are the computers (or the software running on them) that respond to these requests.

Thus `ssh` is the client you run on FreeBSD when you want to connect to another computer using `ssh`, which stands for secure shell. It's a substitute for `telnet`. As with `telnet`, you get a shell login.

If you want to connect to your FreeBSD computer over a network using `ssh` from another computer (your workstation at the time), FreeBSD is the server and runs `sshd`. The workstation can be any computer that has an ssh client program installed. A FreeBSD workstation or a workstation running some other variety of UNIX calls its client `ssh`. SecureCRT is a commercially available `ssh` (and `telnet`) client for Windows (www.vandyke.com). Putty is a free `ssh` and `telnet` client available for Windows and other platforms (http://www.chiark.greenend.org.uk/~sgtatham/putty/).

Setting up ssh and sshd

To enable `sshd,` you put this line in `/etc/rc.conf`:

```
sshd_enable="YES"
```

When the computer is rebooted, it will create key pairs of two kinds (RSA, for the ssh1 protocol, and DSA, for the ssh2 protocol) in /etc/ssh and start sshd.

If you have a version of FreeBSD older than 4.1.1, you may need to install rsaref as a port (/usr/ports/security/rsaref) to get the libraries you need. If you need to do this, an error message will alert you , or you can type ssh-keygen -R to find out if it's installed. If it's not:

```
# cd /usr/ports/security/rsaref
/usr/ports/security/rsaref # make install
```

The following shows what happens in older versions when you need to create keys yourself following an attempt to run sshd manually:

```
root@pninety /etc/ssh # sshd
error: Could not load host key: /etc/ssh/ssh_host_
     key: No such file or directory
Disabling protocol version 1
error: Could not load DSA host key: /etc/ssh
     /ssh_host_dsa_key
Disabling protocol version 2
sshd: no hostkeys available -- exiting.
sshd: no hostkeys available -- exiting.
```

I want to generate a pair (one public, one private) of RSA keys to go in /etc/ssh/ssh_host_key, so I use the -f parameter to ssh-keygen to tell it where to put the key:

```
/etc/ssh # ssh-keygen -f /etc/ssh/ssh_host_key
Generating RSA keys:  Key generation complete.
Enter passphrase (empty for no passphrase): [***]
Enter same passphrase again: [***]
Your identification has been saved in
     /etc/ssh/ssh_host_key.
Your public key has been saved in
     /etc/ssh/ssh_host_key.pub.
The key fingerprint is:
13:9c:6a:21:26:c9:c7:ba:16:83:b4:42:2a:dd:20:44
```

```
     root@pninety.stanford.edu
```

I also want DSA (ssh2) keys, so I repeat the process with the -d switch (this should all be on one line):

```
# ssh-keygen -d -f /etc/ssh/ssh_host_dsa_key
```

I also need pairs of RSA and DSA keys for myself as a user, so I exit from the root account. These keys you always have to create yourself. They go in the .ssh subdirectory of the user's home directory.

```
xanne@pninety ~ $ ssh-keygen
Generating RSA keys:  Key generation complete.
Enter file in which to save the key
     (/usr/home/xanne/.ssh/identity): Enter
Enter passphrase (empty for no passphrase):[***]
Enter same passphrase again: [***]
Your identification has been saved in
     /usr/home/xanne/.ssh/identity.
Your public key has been saved in
     /usr/home/xanne/.ssh/identity.pub.
The key fingerprint is:
7a:c5:79:c3:ae:d5:11:43:7b:b9:ea:8e:6c:e7:63:0f
     xanne@pninety.stanford.edu
```

I run ssh-keygen -d to get a DSA key pair:

```
xanne@pninety ~ $ ssh-keygen -d
Generating DSA parameter and key.
Enter file in which to save the key
     (/usr/home/xanne/.ssh/id_dsa): Enter
Enter passphrase (empty for no passphrase): [***]
Enter same passphrase again: [***]
Your identification has been saved in
     /usr/home/xanne/.ssh/id_dsa.
Your public key has been saved in
     /usr/home/xanne/.ssh/id_dsa.pub.
```

```
The key fingerprint is:
bf:eb:a2:be:a6:c9:33:ef:17:c0:73:01:ce:6c:d5:8c
    xanne@pninety.stanford.edu
```

Passphrases

Your passphrase prevents someone else from sitting down at your computer and using `ssh` to log in as you to another computer, because your passphrase will be required for you to use your keys unless you use password authentication.

Logging in to Your FreeBSD Computer with ssh

You should now be able to use an `ssh` client (SecureCRT or `putty` or an `ssh` client on Linux) to log in to your account on your FreeBSD computer. You will have to generate keys on the client computer in SecureCRT or whatever client you use. You use the conventions of the client program to tell it the name or `ip` address of your FreeBSD computer, your username on the FreeBSD computer, the fact that you want to use `ssh` (not `telnet`), and the method of authentication—at this time, password authentication. The client will probably let you enter and save a password. Now all your communication with your FreeBSD computer from the workstation you are using will be encrypted in both directions.

If you want to use RSA authentication, you copy the `identity.pub` file on the client to your FreeBSD computer, putting it in a file called `authorized_keys` in the `.ssh` subdirectory of your home directory. Be careful not to overwrite the `identity.pub` file that's already there; you can accomplish this by copying it to a new name, say `winbox.pub` if you're using some variety of Windows:

```
C:\putty> copy identity.pub winbox.pub
```

Move the file (by FTP or floppy) to the `.ssh` subdirectory of your home directory on your FreeBSD machine. Then append the file to the `authorized_keys` file (which will be created if it doesn't exist):

```
~/.ssh $ cat winbox.pub >> authorized_keys
```

The example shows the `winbox.pub` file being appended because you may have other identity.pub files from other computers (a laptop, perhaps) to add to authorized_keys.

Logging in to Another Computer from FreeBSD

With ssh keys in your home directory, you should also be able to log in to a computer (a server) on which you have an account using password authentication. If your username on the server is spike and you want to log in to comphost.example.com, you type:

```
$ ssh -l spike comphost.example.com
```

You will be asked for a password and logged in to your account.

To use RSA authentication, you create a subdirectory of your home directory on comphost.example.com called .ssh, and in that directory you create a file called authorized_keys. You put the identity.pub file from the FreeBSD machine on which you created your key in the authorized_keys file. First you copy it to another name (say, pninety.pub) so it doesn't overwrite any identity.pub file you may have on comphost.example.com. You get it there any way you can—on a floppy, by ftp, or whatever. Then you append it to the authorized_keys file by typing:

```
~/.ssh $ cat pninety.pub >> authorized_keys
```

Other Security Matters

The security manual page (man security) written by Matt Dillon, who has extensive experience with systems that have many users, gives some idea of the challenges that confront ISPs and others running large systems with many users.

The tripwire port keeps track of changes in files (you can select which ones) on your hard drive, generating a report on what has changed each time you run it. If you have a tripwire database in which you have confidence, you have an early warning system about intrusion. If a copy of the database is kept off-site (not just on the computer), you can determine which files were changed by an intruder and replace them. Otherwise the only recourse for a system that's been "rooted" is burning it to the ground—or to put it less dramatically, reinstalling.

`Tripwire` is only one of many security checking and monitoring programs available. Security ultimately depends on setting up a security regime, paying attention to the information it generates for you, and taking action. Mailing lists report on new security vulnerabilities in UNIX and other systems as they become known. Greater security almost always means less convenience.

Earlier chapters mentioned the `securelevel` at which you choose to run your computer because on installation you may have chosen a `securelevel` that makes it impossible to install a new kernel without first changing the `securelevel` and rebooting. The `init` manual page explains secure levels.

Chapter 19

Crisis Management

Getting into trouble is no fun, but getting out can be a great learning experience.

Half the battle is doing some advance preparation so that when the crisis arrives (and it is always, of course, unexpected) you have the tools you need handy.

The ultimate solution is reinstalling. It is possible to damage your system to the point where reinstalling is necessary. Once you reach the point where you are convinced you have to reinstall FreeBSD, you have the freedom to experiment.

The FAQ (frequently asked questions and answers) has a great deal of good information about specific problems. It is available on the FreeBSD web site, http://www.freebsd.org in case you can't get to the copy on your hard drive in `/usr/share/doc/faq`.

Information for Crises

Hard copy and a DOS floppy copy of the text files created with these commands are useful to have at hand when you run into trouble:

```
$ cat /var/run/dmesg.boot > dmesg.txt
$ cat /etc/rc.conf > rcconf.txt
$ df > df.txt
$ cat /etc/fstab > fstab.txt
```

You may also find useful copies of other configuration files you finally got working just right—maybe `/etc/ppp/ppp.conf` and others in the `/etc` directory like `pccard.conf` and `dhclient.conf`.

For each slice on each disk (`ad0s1`, for example) that shows up in `df` and has a FreeBSD file system on it, keep a reference copy of the disklabel:

```
# disklabel -r /dev/ad0s1 > ad0s1.txt
```

Reinstalling the Boot Manager

Computers with two or more operating systems installed usually have a boot manager that makes it possible to select the operating system to be run. Installing Windows usually rewrites the boot manager (or the portion of it that lives in the Master Boot Record).

If one way or another you are able to get back into FreeBSD (say, with a boot floppy), you run as `root` the following command to reinstall the boot manager on the first IDE drive (change `ad0` to suit your own situation):

```
# boot0cfg -B /dev/ad0
```

If you are unable to get into FreeBSD, you boot a DOS floppy with `bootinst.exe` and `boot.bin` on it, and type:

```
A:\>bootinst.exe boot.bin
```

To install the `osbsbeta` boot manager from your DOS boot floppy, assuming it has `osbsbeta.exe` on it, boot the floppy and type:

```
A:\>osbsbeta
```

Single-User Mode

Sometimes you go to single-user mode voluntarily, by pressing the spacebar when the boot sequence (the twirling baton) starts, telling the boot loader what kernel you want to load, and adding the `-s` switch:

```
boot: kernel -s
```

Sometimes you are summarily thrown into single-user mode because the system can't fully boot. You are asked to enter a shell or accept the default.

```
Enter the full path name of the shell or RETURN for
     /bin/sh:
```

Press Enter. If the default doesn't work, type /bin/csh.

First you want to re-mount the / partition read-write with the command:

```
# mount -u /
```

That gives you a writable / so you can fix a file like /etc/rc.conf, where you might have left out a closing " or done something else that confuses the boot process.

Until you mount your /usr partition, you have only the /bin/ed line editor available (see the section An Editor for Crises below—it's not so bad). Try to mount your other partitions in /etc/fstab with the command:

```
# mount -a
```

If that doesn't work (perhaps because the problem that prevented booting is a bad line in /etc/fstab), look at what's in /etc/fstab with

```
# /bin/cat /etc/fstab
```

and then mount the /var and /usr partitions (and any other partitions you might need) with commands like these, substituting the appropriate disk and slice:

```
# /sbin/mount /dev/ad0s1e /var
# /sbin/mount /dev/ad0s1f /usr
```

In single-user mode your default editor will be vi. With /usr mounted, you can change your default editor. Then vipw (which you type without arguments to edit /etc/master.passwd) will use your default editor, for example, ee:

```
# EDITOR=/usr/bin/ee
# export EDITOR
```

If you are using csh in single user mode, type:

```
% setenv EDITOR ee
```

When you've done whatever needs doing, to leave single user mode and continue booting simply type:

```
# exit
```

An Editor for Crises

When you end up in single-user mode because something went wrong, the only editor you have available is ed, an old line editor. That's because the editors are in /usr/bin or /usr/local/bin and you may not be able to get to anything in /usr until you fix whatever got broken.

Copying ee to /bin won't help, because ee depends on other files—those pesky libraries—that live in /usr/lib. Even compiling ee statically (so it doesn't depend on libraries) doesn't help, because ee and other full-screen editors (like vi and pico) need terminal capabilities that aren't available in /. Only a line editor will work when you are unable to access /usr.

The following sequence shows /etc/rc.conf being edited with ed. The commands are similar to vi commands but are not preceded by a colon. The first number ed puts on your screen is the number of characters in the file. Typing a number displays a line, and that's the line on which commands will operate unless ed is told differently. The s command is a substitution, and I use + as a separator instead of a slash (/) because I may want to change some lines that include slashes as part of the text. I press w to write the file, and it shows me how many characters are now in the file:

```
# ed rc.conf
1137
1
# This file now contains just the overrides from
    /etc/defaults/rc.conf
2
# please make all changes to this file.
s+changes+appropriate changes+
2
# please make all appropriate changes to this file.
w
1149
```

Continuing, I want to put a # at the beginning of a line to comment it out and add something to the end of another line. Line 3 in this file is a blank line:

```
3

4
# -- sysinstall generated deltas -- #
5
ifconfig_dc0="inet 10.10.10.20  netmask
    255.255.255.0"
s+^+#+
5
#ifconfig_dc0="inet 10.10.10.20  netmask
    255.255.255.0"
7
moused_port="/dev/psm0"
s+$+ # My mouse port+
7
moused_port="/dev/psm0" # My mouse port
8
moused_enable="YES"
```

I go back to line 7 because I want to insert a new line. I use the `i` command to start inserting and a **.** alone on a line to end insertion mode. The new line is just a comment, so it begins with a #:

```
7
moused_port="/dev/psm0" # My mouse port
i
# The next line is my mouse port
.
7
# The next line is my mouse port
8
moused_port="/dev/psm0" # My mouse port
```

I go back to line 7 because I want to delete it. After the deletion, line 7 is what used to be line 8:

```
7
# The next line is my mouse port
d
7
moused_port="/dev/psm0" # My mouse port
```

I want to delete the # I put at the beginning of the `ifconfig` line, so I find the line (it's line 5) and substitute nothing for # (thus, ++):

```
5
#ifconfig_dc0="inet 10.10.10.20  netmask
     255.255.255.0"
s+#++
5
ifconfig_dc0="inet 10.10.10.20  netmask
     255.255.255.0"
```

I save the file (`w`) and quit (`q`):

```
w
1165
```

```
q
#
```

Like vi, ed can deal with a range of lines at once and has other capabilities as well. But all you need are a few basic commands so that you can fix a few lines when you can't mount /usr to get to your favorite text editor. One somewhat complex command you might find useful, which puts a # at the beginning of every line in a file (lines 1 to the end, represented by $) and thus makes it inoperative, looks like this:

```
1,$s+^+#+
```

You might use that (followed by w and q on the next lines, to write and quit) if a file like rc.conf is giving you trouble but you can't easily figure out what's wrong.

Using the Fixit Floppy

The purpose of fixit.flp is to boot with a working FreeBSD kernel and some useful utilities so that you can get at a FreeBSD installation on your hard drive and fix it. The fixit.flp is not a boot disk (even though Chapter 18 tells you how to use a fixit.flp to boot from the hard drive). Nor does it have any special routines for repairing a disk; it has selected FreeBSD utilities.

To use fixit.flp, you boot as though you were installing (with the floppies kern.flp and then mfsroot.flp). You see the main menu of the installer. Select:

```
Fixit  Enter repair mode with CDROM/floppy or start
    shell
```

The next menu gives you three fixit options: the second "live" CD-ROM from the distribution, a fixit floppy, and an emergency holographic shell. The live CD-ROM is the easiest to use and should be your first choice if you have one (it's bootable).

Otherwise put the fixit.flp in the floppy drive when asked and press

Alt+F4 when requested. It will be mounted on `/mnt2`. Utilities will be in the `/mnt2/stand` directory:

```
Fixit# cd /mnt2/stand
```

You might do an `ls` here to see the utilities available to you. They are in the path of the running shell and you do not need a full path name to use them.

You should be able to mount your / partition, with adjustments for your own installation, as follows (in the example FreeBSD is installed on the second slice on the first IDE drive):

```
Fixit# mount /dev/ad0s2 /mnt
```

You can now change to the `/mnt` directory, which is the / partition on your hard drive, with `cd/mnt`. There you can edit files such as `rc.conf`, which will be in `/mnt/etc`. It's slow because `vi` (the available editor) is being loaded from the floppy, so don't give up too soon.

If you need to run `fsck` on filesystems, remember that your hard drive devices are in `/mnt/dev`:

```
Fixit# fsck /mnt/dev/ad0s2f
```

To see the other file systems on your hard drive, type:

```
Fixit# cat /mnt/etc/fstab
```

To mount `/usr`, if you need it, type:

```
Fixit# mount /mnt/dev/ad0s2f  /mnt2/mnt3
```

The `df` command then shows you the following, depending on your hard drive type and file systems:

```
Fixit# df
Filesystem                    Mounted on
/dev/md0c                     /
```

```
/dev/fd02                   /mnt2
/dev/ad0s2                  /mnt
/mnt/dev/ad0s2f             /mnt2/mnt3
```

The Second CD-ROM

Much better than the fixit floppy is the second CD-ROM, which has a live file system on it. Once you mount your file systems on the hard drive, you can then do things like replacing damaged or accidentally erased files or repairing damaged configuration files.

The Ultimate in Fixit

The most convenient fixit facility is another installation of FreeBSD on another hard drive in the same machine (or the same hard drive, if you have a boot manager that can boot either one). It can be a minimal installation, perhaps just the `bin`, `doc`, and `man` distributions and a few packages so you have the shell and editor you prefer. From there you can check file systems with `fsck`, mount them, and edit at will.

Awful Messages

Here are a number of problem messages you might see (not a complete list, by any means) and what to do about them.

File System Full

Running out of file space is serious, and you should do something about it right away. A file system is considered full when it's at about 92 percent of total space, since 8 percent of used space is added on to determine available space. Run `df` immediately to see which file system is over capacity.

Then try to figure out what's taking up the space. Is a process writing so many error messages to its log file that `/var` is filling up, or have you just done an upgrade from source and the combination of `/usr/src` and `/usr/obj` is overwhelming `/usr`?

If `/usr` is the problem, you can delete `/usr/obj` (`rm -rf /usr/obj`) after you build a new kernel and do `installworld` because `/usr/obj` is created by the `buildworld` process and deleted, if it exists, by buildworld when another buildworld is started.

Another `/usr` problem is `/usr/ports`, where a lot of space can be taken up by distfiles located in `/usr/ports/distfiles.` Work directories for the ports you've built also take space. Your own home directory may be the problem if you save a lot of mail messages. Perhaps you just installed Linux support, Netscape, `emacs`, `apsfilter`, The Gimp, and `wine`. (Go shopping! You need another hard drive.)

Many causes of a full file system are possible in `/var`. The `/var/tmp` directory may see a lot of action. If so you should consider moving `/var/tmp` to a place with more space, like `/usr/tmp`, and making a symbolic link from `/var/tmp` to `/usr/tmp`, as described in Chapter 7 for the `tmp` directory in `/`.

The `/var/log` directory may be getting bigger and bigger. Find out which log files are the problem and use `newsyslog` to compress them and eventually delete them on a regular basis (see Chapter 7).

Other `/var` problems can be `/var/mail/*` and `/var/spool/mqueue`, resulting from large mail messages (probably attachments). If you run `tripwire`, `/var/db/*` can be the cause of `/var`'s problems.

A problem in / can arise from too many kernels. You can always move (or delete) an old kernel you saved as a backup. This is a quick way to get 4MB or so. But a / problem can also be the result of downloading to / or inadvertently copying something there (you copy by mistake to `/myfile` instead of `~/myfile` or just `myfile`).

The command `ls -lrt` in any directory will show you the files in the order created, with the most recent ones last. This may help find a large new file. The following will sort the files in order of size and show you the largest ten:

```
$ ls -la | sort -k5 | tail -n 10
```

You can put that in a shell script and call it `worst` if you like. Here's a shell script that shows you the sizes of the subdirectories in a directory, but only the ones of megabyte magnitude (and unsorted). You call it `dirsize`, put it in your ~`/bin` directory, make it executable with `chmod 755 dirsize`, and run it with the name of the directory (that's the `$1`) for which you want subdirectory size information, for example, `dirsize /usr/ports`:

```
#!/bin/sh
for i in $1/* ; do
if [ -d $i ]; then
du -sh $i
fi
done | grep M
```

It's best done as `root` to avoid "permission denied" responses. You can also run the commands at the command line:

```
root@killer ~ # for i in /usr/ports/* ; do
for> if [ -d $i ] ; then
for then> du -sh $i
for then> fi
for> done | grep M
322K     /usr/ports/Mk
1.3M     /usr/ports/archivers
109M     /usr/ports/audio
1.1M     /usr/ports/databases
...
```

As you can see `/usr/ports/audio` must have something in it I built and is a place where I could recover some space.

Developers have experimented with utilities to resize slices on FreeBSD, but 4.x doesn't yet have one. So you're stuck with what you chose at installation. Although you can't change the size of /usr or /var, you can locate directories elsewhere and use symbolic links, and you can add a drive, partition and disklabel it, and mount `/home` or `/usr/local` (or both) on the file systems you create.

Timecounter Went Backwards

If you get a message that "microtime went backwards," change the kernel's timecounter method to `1`. To see what it is, type:

```
# sysctl -a | grep timecounter
kern.timecounter.method: 0
kern.timecounter.hardware: i8254
```

Change it to `1` with this command:

```
# sysctl -w kern.timecounter.method=1
```

Too Many Open Files

If you get a message about too many open files, you may need to recompile your kernel with a high number for `maxusers`. See Chapter 16. Meanwhile, close some files.

No aout Libraries

You sometimes get an error when installing Netscape that `X aout` libraries are missing.

If you have no libraries in `/usr/X11R6/lib/aout`, installing `/usr/ports/x11/XFree86-aoutlibs` will probably take care of it. If this port won't install, you may need to install the `compat22` distribution from CD-ROM or by FTP (start with `/stand/sysinstall` and choose `Configure->Distributions`). You may have `aout` libraries in `/usr/lib/aout` or `/usr/lib/compat/aout` or both; these are not the ones Netscape needs. See Chapter 7 for how to use `ldconfig` to check up on libraries.

Out of File Descriptors

It was a dark and stormy night, and the wind was whistling through the tree tops. The men sat around the fire trying to keep warm, and one of them said, "Sam, read us a story." And Sam grabbed a file and began to read: "It was a dark and stormy night . . .

And so on, until Sam ran out of files—or rather file descriptors, which are needed to open files.

In FreeBSD 4.1, `/etc/defaults/rc.conf`, like Sam and his story telling, is recursive. The `/etc/defaults/rc.conf` file is read on boot, and it has instructions in it to read `/etc/rc.conf`. So if you put it in `/etc/rc.conf`, `/etc/rc.conf` reads itself. And then reads itself again. But not forever—only until the system runs out of file descriptors.

FreeBSD then goes into single-user mode because it can't open any more files to boot the system. You recover by booting into single-user mode, typing `/sbin/mount -u /` to mount / read-write, and deleting `/etc/rc.conf` (or moving it to another name not beginning with `rc`, like `hold.rc.conf`). This problem does not exist in FreeBSD 4.2 and later versions.

Chapter 20

Other Resources

The amount of information "out there" is astounding. Probably every one of your questions has been answered somewhere, sometime; the problem is finding the gold.

This chapter looks at major resources on the Internet, recommends some books, and considers what you already have on your own hard drive.

The FreeBSD Web Page

The FreeBSD web page at http://www.freebsd.org is the mother lode—the place you're most likely to find a pertinent answer to any question about FreeBSD.

The left-hand side of the page has useful links in several categories including News, Software, Documentation (*The FreeBSD Handbook* and the FAQ on-line, and a link for new users), and Support. The Support links tell you about the mailing lists, user groups around the world, and other on-line resources.

Of special importance under Software is Release Information, where you can find out about any errors in release versions and how to correct them.

The Search link under This Site lets you search the mailing lists, one or more at a time.

At the bottom of the page is a link to The FreeBSD Mall, where you can buy everything from sets of FreeBSD CD-ROMs, books, and T-shirts, to stuffed toys.

The FAQ

The FAQ (Frequently Asked Questions) is a collection of answers to questions on common and uncommon problems including installation problems, how to get a special mouse to work or how to get the mouse to work on all screens, using a USB keyboard and mouse, what to do if you get a message that the file table is full, how to allow ordinary users (not just `root`) to mount the floppy and CD drives, and many other topics.

Unless you did a minimal installation, you will find the FAQ on your hard drive in `/usr/share/doc/faq`. You can read the html version in Netscape or with a text browser like `lynx` by changing to that directory and typing `lynx index.html`.

The FreeBSD Handbook

The FreeBSD Handbook is the basic reference for FreeBSD. It too should be on your hard drive, in `/usr/share/doc/handbook`.

Updating Your On-Disk Documents

TIP

Updating your system doesn't update your documents. The web page link to the FAQ or the Handbook has another link for getting the most recent version of the documents (and others as well) in whatever format you would like, or get them directly from `ftp.freebsd.org`.

For the *Handbook* in English, log in to `ftp ftp.freebsd.org,` enter `ftp` as your username and your email address as the password, and type:

```
cd /pub/FreeBSD/doc/en/books/handbook
```

and find the *Handbook* in the format you like—PDF, html, text, RTF—and compressed as you like. Download it (with `get` *<filename>*) and uncompress it. You can do the same for the FAQ.

WARNING

Both the FAQ and the *Handbook* have been written over a period of several years by many different people. Some of the entries apply to older versions of FreeBSD and may be wrong for more recent versions, so be alert for tip-offs like "in versions 2.1 of FreeBSD and later . . . ", which may or may not apply to versions 3.x or 4.x.

FreeBSD Mailing Lists

The FreeBSD mailing lists are the major source of support for FreeBSD.

You search the archives of the mailing lists using your browser and the link on the FreeBSD web page or http://www.freebsd.org/search/#mailinglists.

Searching the FreeBSD mailing lists is a wonderful way to find out about a specific topic, an error message you're getting, or special hardware like a laptop or motherboard. Table 20-1 lists some of the mailing lists and what they cover.

Table 20-1 The FreeBSD Mailing Lists

List	*Topic*
freebsd-questions	general questions; new users welcome
freebsd-stable	developments in the -stable branch
freebsd-current	developments in the -current branch
freebsd-hackers	technical discussions
freebsd-mobile	laptops and related hardware
freebsd-announce	important announcements; read only
freebsd-advocacy	promoting FreeBSD
freebsd-chat	conversation on various topics
freebsd-isp	Internet service provider issues
freebsd-jobs	employers and searchers
freebsd-newbies	chat for new users
freebsd-test	a place to send test messages

For a search on a general topic, `freebsd-questions` is most likely to produce results. To broaden your search, you might add `freebsd-stable` and `freebsd-hackers` (and `freebsd-current` if you decide to install it). Other lists are more specific. For laptop issues, search `freebsd-mobile`.

You subscribe to a mailing list by sending an email message to:

```
majordomo@freebsd.org
```

and putting in the body of the message something like:

```
subscribe freebsd-questions
```

The `freebsd-questions` mailing list is where questions from new users are most welcome. You ask a question by sending email to freebsd-questions@freebsd.org. (Don't send your subscription message there.) It helps to explain what you're trying to do, what you've tried, what version of FreeBSD you're running, and the relevant hardware.

TIP

Often you get an answer in a day or two or even a few hours, possibly from an expert. If you get a wrong answer, someone is likely to correct it in a follow-up message.

The mailing list archives are updated weekly, which isn't often enough to give you the latest information you need when you upgrade your system as described in Chapter 17. For that you need to subscribe, so you can check the lists in real time. Subscribe to `freebsd-stable` to follow the `-stable` branch, or `freebsd-current` for the bleeding edge.

Several of the mailing lists are high volume; `freebsd-questions` gets over 100 messages a day. Be prepared to store or delete a lot of mail (at least you don't have to answer it).

Books

The *FreeBSD Handbook* is available on your hard drive and, continually updated, on the web, but you can also buy a printed version.

- The FreeBSD Documentation Project (ed. Jim Mock), *The FreeBSD Hand-*

book. Walnut Creek, Calif.: BSDi, 1999. ISBN 1-57176-241-8.

Two other books specifically about FreeBSD are available. Greg Lehey's book is a standard, systematic reference to FreeBSD. It covers basics as well as topics like setting up a nameserver and installing a new disk. Ted Mittelstaedt's book is extremely useful for network administrators working with both FreeBSD and computers running Microsoft Windows.

- Greg Lehey, *The Complete FreeBSD*. 3rd ed. Walnut Creek, Calif.: Walnut Creek CDROM, 1999. ISBN 1-57176-246-9.

- Ted Mittelstaedt, *The FreeBSD Corporate Networker's Guide*. Boston, Mass.: Addison-Wesley, 2000. ISBN 0-201-70481-1.

The third edition (purple cover) of the *UNIX System Administration Handbook* is 890 pages of pure gold for a fair chunk of yours. It uses FreeBSD as one of its four example systems (the others are RedHat Linux, Solaris, and HPUX). This book will give you an overview of how the system works, from how it boots to how packets are sent over the Internet.

- Evi Nemeth, Garth Snyder, Scott Seebass, and Trent R. Hein, *UNIX System Administration Handbook*. 3rd ed. Upper Saddle River, N.J.: Prentice Hall PTR. ISBN 0-13-020601-6.

Unix for the Impatient is considered the best book on UNIX utilities by Professor Eugene W. Stark, who uses FreeBSD as the operating system in the undergraduate computer labs at the State University of New York at Stony Brook. It covers everything from `ls` to `emacs`. It's good to have one such virtually comprehensive reference on UNIX. If you want to find out how to delete that pesky file that has weird characters in it, this book will tell you. Not a handholder, though.

- Paul W. Abrahams and Bruce R. Larson. *UNIX for the Impatient*. 2nd ed. & CD. Reading, Mass.: Addison-Wesley, 1997. ISBN 0-201-41979-3.

Some gurus think knowing your shell and getting it to do what you want it to do is critical to being happy with UNIX. *Learning the bash Shell* is an excellent book on the `bash` shell for users. If you prefer `tcsh`, a book on it is also available.

- Cameron Newham and Bill Rosenblatt, *Learning the bash Shell*. 2nd ed. Sebastopol, Calif.: O'Reilly, 1998. ISBN 1-56592-347-2.

- Paul DuBois. *Using csh and tcsh.* Sebastopol, Calif.: O'Reilly, 1995. ISBN 1-56592-132-1.

The Samba suite is designed to allow computers running some variety of UNIX to communicate with computers running some variety of Microsoft Windows over a network using Microsoft's SMB (Server Message Block) protocol. The computers can then share files and printers.

Installing (and configuring) Samba makes it possible to see file systems on the UNIX (FreeBSD) machine from a Windows box just as other shared file-systems on other Windows computers can be seen. For viewing a Windows directory on a FreeBSD machine, you use `sharity-lite` or `smbfs`. They're in `/usr/ports/net` and can also be installed as packages.

Although some shortcut how-to's are available on the Internet, so is an entire book called *Using Samba*, available in PDF or html format at http://www.oreilly.com/catalog/samba; click the link to the on-line book. Because the Samba suite is complicated—after all, SMB is a complicated protocol—and somewhat different steps are involved in configuring different versions of Windows, if one of the how-to's doesn't work for you, go for the book, on line or in print.

- Robert Eckstein, David Collier-Brown, and Peter Kelly. *Using Samba.* Sebastopol, Calif.: O'Reilly, 2000. ISBN 1-56592-449-5.

Newsgroups

Newsgroups are like bulletin boards—you post messages everyone can read, and you can read everything other people post and reply to the newsgroup or by email to the author. Tens of thousands of newsgroups exist on topics from computer programming languages to "Saturday Night Live" (`alt.tv.snl`).

The primary newsgroup about the FreeBSD operating system is:

```
comp.unix.bsd.freebsd.misc
```

Announcements are posted on:

```
comp.unix.bsd.freebsd.announce
```

It's a good idea to read through a bunch of postings before jumping into the bitstream. Every few weeks the FAQ for the newsgroup will be posted. If you ask a question already answered in the FAQ, you risk getting *flamed*, or just ignored if you're lucky.

You read newsgroups with a news reader installed as a port or a package or with conventional browsers like Netscape and IE. The `tin` port is one of the easier ones to get running. You tell your news reader your NNTP server; mine is `nntp.stanford.edu`. The news server for Earthlink might be `nntp.earthlink.net`. Then you subscribe to the groups you want to read.

The messages are not actually downloaded to your computer. You just browse through the list and display the ones of interest, saving an occasional one to your hard drive or mailing it to yourself. Usually you can search for a string in the message titles to find ones of interest. You can of course post a message or respond to one. You may find your question has already been asked and answered.

Often you can configure a news reader to post a modified or fake "From" address, like `angel@nospam.heaven.org`. You avoid the risk of spam that way, but you give up getting answers to your postings by email.

Besides the FreeBSD groups, Table 20-2 includes a few others of interest.

The topics under discussion at any given time on a newsgroup vary a lot, and possibly no one who's expert or interested in your areas of concern may be around to answer. That could change in a few days or weeks. Some of the people providing answers know their stuff; others can give incomplete or incorrect answers or fail to understand your question.

Occasional threads go off into the wild blue yonder, and sometimes there are trolls or snappers around whose main interest is in making the case that your operating system is a good-for-nothing amateurish effort deficient in the right kinds of bells and whistles. Newsgroups are not really a battlefield on which to fight; they're just a place for relatively anonymous exchanges some of which may be useful to you.

Table 20-2 News Groups

Name	*Topic*
comp.unix.bsd.freebsd.misc	FreeBSD operating system
comp.unix.bsd.freebsd.announce	Announcements about FreeBSD
comp.unix.questions	UNIX neophytes group
comp.mail.pine	The PINE mail user agent
news.software.readers	Software used to read news
comp.unix.shell	Using and programming the Unix shell
comp.mail.sendmail	Configuring and using sendmail
comp.lang.awk	The AWK programming language
comp.lang.c	The C programming language
comp.unix.admin	Administering a UNIX system

Internet Relay Chat

Never venture onto IRC without your asbestos cape.

IRC can be useful, but if you haven't been through the Army's basic training, you may learn some new vocabulary. Parental guidance advised.

To access IRC, you install an IRC client as a port or package. You tell the client the name of the IRC server you want to access, often with the `/server` command. The servers are networked together, each being connected to others on the same IRC network, the four largest of which are EFnet, Undernet, IRCnet, and DALnet. You can find out the names of servers (and other information on using IRC) at http://www.irchelp.org.

Once you log on to a server, you provide a nickname for yourself with the `/nick` command. You then join a channel with the `/join` command. Most of the IRC networks have a #freebsd channel, so you type `/join #freebsd`. On EFnet the main help channel for FreeBSD is `#freebsdhelp`. The `#freebsd` channel is mainly miscellaneous chat.

The quality of help on IRC runs from the superb to the malicious. You may be told to run a command that will delete critical files on your hard drive. At the time you log on, no one may be present who understands your question or cares to answer—and no one has any obligation to answer at all. Other times you'll get just the hint you need.

Other Web Sites

Several web sites offer news and how-to's on FreeBSD. Most offer links to other sites.

http://www.daemonnews.org

The Daemon News, run by Chris Coleman and Gregory Sutter, site has many useful articles and how-to's. It indexes other BSD sites and lets you search the index. You can subscribe to the printed magazine at http://www.bsdmall.com.

http://www.mostgraveconcern.com/freebsd

This is a collection of what the author, Daniel O'Connor, calls FreeBSD Cheat Sheets. They're straightforward, precise, and very, very good.

http://www.freebsdzine.org

Started and run by Jim Mock, this site, The FreeBSD 'zine, provides information and help on FreeBSD.

http://www.freebsddiary.org and http://freshports.org

Practical examples of how the author (Dan Langille) accomplished specific tasks, the problems he ran into, and how he went about finding the information he needed. Plus the latest on new or modified FreeBSD ports. And more.

http://www.onlamp.com/pub/au/73

This site is part of www.oreillynet.org. This particular page lists articles on FreeBSD by Dru Lavigne, a networking instructor at a private technical college in Kingston, Ontario. Dru manages to explain the underlying principles while she outlines the steps for each task or objective. The site http://www.oreillynet.com/bsd has articles on FreeBSD by other authors.

http://www.defcon1.org

DefCon1 is a site maintained by some of the people involved in the EFnet IRC channel #freebsdhelp. Many informal how-to's and other links.

http://www.geek-girl.com/resources.html

No kidding. The Geek Girl maintains many useful links (not FreeBSD-specific), including information on UNIX basics called the UNIX Reference Desk.

http://www.ugu.com

This site, the UNIX Guru Universe, is for UNIX system administrators. There's a BSD link and specific FreeBSD links, most of which link back to www.freebsd.org.

http://www.freshmeat.net

Information on all the open-source software available for UNIX platforms. Announcements of the latest versions and where to get them if they haven't yet found their way into the FreeBSD ports collection.

http://people.freebsd.org/~will/almanac.htm

This site has over 160 well-organized links to web sites about FreeBSD. Maintained by Will Andrews, a young FreeBSD developer.

Other Sites

Hardware manufacturers provide information about hardware and how it's put together. You can get specs and downloadable manuals, even for old hardware, on these pages. If your motherboard is beeping on boot, the BIOS manufacturer's web page will tell you what the beep codes mean.

Visit www.slashdot.org to get news for nerds and stuff that matters (their terms).

And don't forget the standard search engines, like www.google.com.

On Your Hard Drive

Basic tools for finding files (`locate` and `find`) and for finding text within files (`grep`) are covered in earlier chapters, as are commands for finding relevant manual pages. The `glimpse` port is an addition to these tools that indexes your files and lets you search the index in various sophisticated ways.

TIP Take a look at `/usr/share`, especially the directories doc (already mentioned, of course), `misc`, and `examples`. You may be surprised by what's there. After you install ports or packages, `/usr/local/share` will also have files of interest.

You can find out quite a lot about what happens on boot by using `grep` in your `/etc` directory. For example, if you wonder what happens when you put `sshd_enable="YES"` in `/rc.conf`, this command will show you which files act on that instruction:

```
/etc # grep sshd_enable *
```

Which Port Installed the File?

Sometimes you want to know which package or port installed a particular file, or if a file is installed at all. One way to find out if `libtiff.so.*` is installed is (from `/var/db/pkg`):

```
$ pkg_info -av | grep libtiff.so
```

but that doesn't tell you where it is. You can create a little script to give you this information. In your home directory:

1. **Type** `cd bin`
2. **Use your favorite editor to create a file (you could called it** `ftf`**) and put only this in it:**

```
#!/bin/sh
grep -r $1 /var/db/pkg/*/
```

3. **Save the file.**
4. **Type** `chmod 755 ftf` **to make it executable.**

   It's now ready to run with its name plus any filename, or piece of a filename, you want to find out about. What you type after the name of the file you created is substituted for the `$1` in the script.

5. **To find** `libtiff.so` **and its brethren, type:**

```
$ ftf libtiff.so
```

   You see (depending on what's installed) lines like the following:

```
/var/db/pkg/tiff-3.5.5/+CONTENTS:lib/libtiff.so
/var/db/pkg/tiff-
     3.5.5/+CONTENTS:lib/libtiff.so.4
```

Which Port Has That *&! Library?

Searching all the `pkg-plist` files in ports to find out which port installs a particular file is the sort of thing computers do better than people.

If you need a particular library (or if you think you do—usually the ports mechanism handles dependencies without your intervention) here's a script you can run:

Use your favorite text editor to create a file in `~/bin` called `ff`:

```
#!/bin/sh
for i in /usr/ports/*/*/pkg-plist ; do
grep -isH $1 $i
done
```

Save the file; make it executable by typing:

```
~/bin $ chmod 755 ff
```

Now you can type:

```
$ ff libtiff
```

and see (after a while, since there's a `pkg-plist` for virtually every port):

```
/usr/ports/graphics/tiff/pkg-plist:lib/libtiff.a
/usr/ports/graphics/tiff/pkg-plist:lib/libtiff.so
/usr/ports/graphics/tiff/pkg-plist:lib/libtiff.so.4
/usr/ports/graphics/tiff/pkg-
     plist:share/doc/tiff/libtiff.html
```

The script searches all the `pkg-plist` files, one by one. The `-i` switch makes it case-insensitive, so searching for `xaw` will also find `Xaw`. The `-s` switch suppresses errors and the `-H` switch causes `grep` to print the full file names along with the lines of text that match your query. You might wish to direct the output to a file to read later and run it in the background, for example:

```
$ ff xaw >xaw.txt &
```

It's still a slow process, but it's still faster than doing it yourself.

Appendix A

Supported Hardware

FreeBSD supports, on installation and boot, a wide variety of hardware including ISA, VLB, EISA, Microchannel and PCI bus-based personal computers. Additional hardware is supported with loadable kernel modules (installed automatically when you install FreeBSD) or by compiling a custom kernel.

The lists of hardware supported on installation or kernel recompile are based on the `HARDWARE.TXT` file maintained by Mike Smith. It is available in the root directory of the installation CD-ROM. After you install FreeBSD the same file will be in gzipped format as `/stand/help/HARDWARE.TXT.gz` on your hard drive.

Hardware Supported on Installation

FreeBSD installer includes support for a wide variety of hardware. The same hardware supported during installation is supported after FreeBSD is installed, in the `GENERIC` kernel, called `kernel`. Table A-1 shows you the name of the device driver (what FreeBSD calls it) for the hardware, the port at which FreeBSD will look for it, the IRQ and DRQ FreeBSD will use for the hardware, and the starting memory address (IO). An `n/a` in a column means "not applicable."

If your hardware is set to use different resources, you either reconfigure your hardware to match what FreeBSD expects, or you configure FreeBSD before it boots to match your hardware—unless the resource is listed as "dyn." Then it's dynamically configured, and you don't have to worry about it. Changing the default settings FreeBSD uses for your hardware is explained in Chapter 16.

Three drivers in the GENERIC kernel are disabled by default but can be enabled—those for a second pccard controller and the third and fourth serial ports. Chapter 16 tells you how to enable them and also how to disable drivers on boot.

Hardware supported by FreeBSD but not included in the GENERIC kernel can be added later by compiling a kernel that includes support for it.

Table A-1 Hardware Supported in the GENERIC Kernel

Driver	*Port*	*IRQ*	*DRQ*	*IO*	*Description*
fdc0	3f0	6	2	n/a	Floppy disk controller
ata0	170	14	n/a	n/a	ATA/ATAPI controller
ata1	170	15	n/a	n/a	ATA/ATAPI controller
atadisk0	n/a	n/a	n/a	n/a	ATA disk drives
atapicd0	n/a	n/a	n/a	n/a	ATAPI CDROM drives
atapifd0	n/a	n/a	n/a	n/a	ATAPI floppy drives
atapist0	n/a	n/a	n/a	n/a	ATAPI tape drives
adv0	n/a	n/a	n/a	n/a	AdvanSys Narrow SCSI controllers
adw0	n/a	n/a	n/a	n/a	AdvanSys Wide SCSI controllers
amd0	n/a	n/a	n/a	n/a	AMD 53C974 (Tekram DC390(T))
ncr0	n/a	n/a	n/a	n/a	NCR PCI SCSI controller
bt0	330	dyn	dyn	dyn	Buslogic SCSI controller
aha0	330	dyn	5	dyn	Adaptec 154x/1535 SCSI controller
ahb0	dyn	dyn	dyn	dyn	Adaptec 174x SCSI controller
ahc0	dyn	dyn	dyn	dyn	Adaptec 274x/284x/294x SCSI controller
aic0	340	11	dyn	dyn	Adaptec 152x/AIC-6360 /AIC-6260 SCSI controller
isp0	dyn	dyn	dyn	dyn	QLogic 10X0, 1240 Ultra

					SCSI, 1080/1280 Ultra2 SCSI, 12160 Ultra3 SCSI, 2X00 Fibre Channel SCSI controller
ncv	dyn	dyn	n/a	n/a	NCR 53C500 based PC-Card SCSI
nsp	dyn	dyn	n/a	n/a	Workbit Ninja SCSI-3 based PC-Card SCSI
dpt0	dyn	dyn	n/a	n/a	DPT RAID SCSI controllers
amr0	dyn	dyn	n/a	n/a	AMI MegaRAID controllers
mlx0	dyn	dyn	n/a	dyn	Mylex DAC960 RAID controllers
twe0	dyn	dyn	n/a	n/a	3ware Escalade RAID controllers
asr0	dyn	dyn	dyn	dyn	DPT SmartRAID V, VI, and Adaptec SCSI RAID
myl0	dyn	dyn	dyn	dyn	Mylex AcceleRAID/ eXtremeRAID
aac	dyn	dyn	dyn	dyn	Adaptec FSA family PCI SCSI RAID
wt0	300	5	1	dyn	Wangtek and Archive QIC-02/QIC-36
psm0	60	12	n/a	n/a	PS/2 Mouse
mcd0	300	10	n/a	n/a	Mitsumi CD-ROM
matcd0	230	n/a	n/a	n/a	Matsushita/Panasonic CD-ROM
scd0	230	n/a	n/a	n/a	Sony CD-ROM
sio0	3f8	4	n/a	n/a	Serial Port 0 (COM1)
sio1	2f8	3	n/a	n/a	Serial Port 1 (COM2)
sio2	3e8	5	n/a	n/a	Serial Port 2 (COM3) (disabled)
sio3	2e8	9	n/a	n/a	Serial Port 3 (COM4) (disabled)
ppc0	dyn	7	n/a	n/a	Printer ports
pcic0	3e0	10	n/a	d4000	Pc-Card controller
pcic1 (disabled)	3e2	11	n/a	d4000	Pc-Card controller

dc0	n/a	n/a	n/a	n/a	DEC/Intel 21143 cards and workalikes
de0	n/a	n/a	n/a	n/a	DEC DC21x40 PCI based cards (including 21140 100bT cards)
ed0	280	10	dyn	d8000	WD & SMC 80xx; Novell NE1000 & NE2000; 3Com 3C503; HP PC Lan+
ep0	300	10	dyn	dyn	3Com 3C509
ex0	dyn	dyn	dyn	n/a	Intel EtherExpress Pro/10 cards
fe0	300	dyn	n/a	n/a	Allied-Telesyn AT1700, RE2000 and Fujitsu FMV-180 series cards
fxp0	dyn	dyn	n/a	dyn	Intel EtherExpress Pro/100B and Intel PRO/100+ Management Adapter
ie0	300	10	dyn	d0000	AT&T StarLAN 10 and EN100; 3Com 3C507; NI5210; Intel EtherExpress (8/16,16[TP]) cards
lnc0	280	10	n/a	dyn	Lance/PCnet cards (Isolan, Novell NE2100, NE32-VL, some PCnet-PCI cards)
pcn0	dyn	dyn	n/a	dyn	AMD PCnet/FAST, PCnet/FAST+, PCnet/FAST III, PCnet/PRO, PCnet /Home, and HomePNA cards
rl0	dyn	dyn	n/a	dyn	RealTek 8129/8139 fast ethernet
sf0	dyn	dyn	n/a	dyn	Adaptec AIC-6915 fast ethernet
sis0	dyn	dyn	n/a	dyn	SiS 900/SiS 7016 fast ethernet
sn0	0x300	10	n/a	n/a	SMC 91xx ethernet
ste0	dyn	dyn	n/a	dyn	Sundance ST201 Fast Ethernet
tl0	dyn	dyn	n/a	dyn	TI TNET100 'ThunderLAN' cards

tx0	dyn	dyn	n/a	dyn	SMC 9432 'Epic' Fast E Ethernet
wb0	dyn	dyn	n/a	dyn	Winbond W89C840F PCI based cards
vr0	dyn	dyn	n/a	dyn	VIA VT3043/VT86C100A PCI based cards
vx0	dyn	dyn	n/a	dyn	3Com 3c59x ((Fast) Etherlink III)
xe0	dyn	dyn	n/a	dyn	Xircom CreditCard adapters (16 bit)
xl0	dyn	dyn	n/a	dyn	3Com 3c900, 3c905, 3c905B, 3c905C, 3c980, 3cSOHO100 ((Fast) Etherlink XL)
cs0	0x300	dyn	n/a	n/a	Crystal Semiconductor CS89x0-based cards

All Supported Hardware

Here's a list of all hardware listed as working with FreeBSD 4.3. The installation CD-ROM always has a file called HARDWARE.TXT with the information for the version of FreeBSD on the CD. Note that it's not the manufacturer of the board that's critical, but the name of the chip the manufacturer uses on its board.

Disk Controllers

IDE disk controllers.

ATA disk controllers.

All supported SCSI controllers fully support SCSI-I & SCSI-II peripherals, including hard disks, optical disks, tape drives (including DAT and 8mm Exabyte), medium changers, process or target devices and CDROM drives.

WORM (write-once, read many) devices that support CD-ROM commands are supported for read-only access by the CD-ROM driver. WORM/CD-R/CD-RW writing support is provided by `cdrecord`, which is in the ports tree.

ATA disk controllers: Acerlabs Aladdin; AMD 756; CMD 646; Cypress 82C693; HighPoint HPT366; HighPoint HPT370; Intel PIIX; Intel PIIX3; Intel PIIX4; Intel ICH; Intel ICH2; Promise Fasttrak-33; Promise Fasttrak-66; Promise Fasttrak-100; Promise Ultra-33; Promise Ultra-66; Promise Ultra-100; SiS 5591; VIA 82C586; VIA 82C686a; VIA 82C686b.

Adaptec: 1535 ISA SCSI controllers; 154x series ISA SCSI controllers; 174x series EISA SCSI controller in standard and enhanced mode; 274X /284X/2920C/294x/2950/19160/29160/3940/3950/39160; Narrow/Wide /Twin series EISA/VLB/PCI SCSI controllers; AIC7850, AIC7860, AIC7880, AIC789x, on-board SCSI controllers; 1510 series ISA SCSI controllers (not for bootable devices); 152x series ISA SCSI controllers; AIC-6260 and AIC-6360 based boards, which includes the AHA-152x and SoundBlaster SCSI cards.

Adaptec 2100S, 2400A, 3200S, and 3400S SCSI RAID controllers.

Adaptec FSA family RAID controllers: AAC-2622; AAC-364; AAC-3642; Dell PERC 2/QC; Dell PERC 2/Si; Dell PERC 3/Di; Dell PERC 3/QC; Dell PERC 3/Si; HP NetRAID-4M.

AdvanSys SCSI controllers (all models).

BusLogic: MultiMaster "W" Series Host Adapters: BT-948, BT-958, BT-958D; MultiMaster "C" Series Host Adapters: BT-946C, BT-956C, BT-956CD, BT-445C, BT-747C, BT-757C, BT-757CD, BT-545C, BT-540CF; MultiMaster "S" Series Host Adapters: BT-445S, BT-747S, BT-747D, BT-757S, BT-757D, BT-545S, BT-542D, BT-742A, BT-542B; MultiMaster "A" Series Host Adapters: BT-742A, BT-542B. AMI FastDisk controllers that are true BusLogic MultiMaster clones are also supported. BusLogic/Mylex "Flashpoint" adapters are NOT yet supported.

DPT: DPT SmartCACHE Plus, SmartCACHE III, SmartRAID III, SmartCACHE IV and SmartRAID IV SCSI/RAID controllers are supported.

DPT SmartRAID V and VI SCSI RAID controllers: PM1554, PM2554, PM2654, PM2865, PM2754, PM3755, PM3757.

AMI: AMI MegaRAID Express and Enterprise family RAID controllers: MegaRAID Series 418; MegaRAID Enterprise 1200 (Series 428); MegaRAID Enterprise 1300 (Series 434); MegaRAID Enterprise 1400 (Series 438); MegaRAID Enterprise 1500 (Series 467); MegaRAID Enterprise 1600 (Series 471); MegaRAID Elite 1500 (Series 467); MegaRAID Elite 1600 (Series 493); MegaRAID Express 100 (Series 466WS); MegaRAID Express 200 (Series 466); MegaRAID Express 300 (Series 490); MegaRAID Express 500 (Series 475); Dell PERC; Dell PERC 2/SC; Dell PERC 2/DC; Dell PERC 3/DCL; HP NetRAID-1si; HP NetRAID-3si; HP Embedded NetRAID. Booting from these controllers is supported.

Mylex: Mylex DAC960 and DAC1100 RAID controllers with 2.x, 3.x, 4.x and 5.x ;firmware: DAC960P; DAC960PD; DAC960PDU; DAC960PL; DAC-960PJ; DAC960PG; AcceleRAID 150; AcceleRAID 250; eXtremeRAID 1100. This list includes controllers sold by Digital/Compaq in Alpha systems in the StorageWorks family, e.g., KZPSC, KZPAC. EISA adapters are not supported.

Mylex PCI to SCSI RAID controllers with 6.x firmware: AcceleRAID 160; AcceleRAID 170; AcceleRAID 352; eXtremeRAID 2000; eXtremeRAID 3000; Compatible Mylex controllers not listed should work, but have not been verified.

3ware: All members of the 5000, 6000, and 7000 series of 3ware Escalade ATA RAID controllers are supported.

Qlogic: Qlogic Controllers and variants: Qlogic 1020, 1040 SCSI and Ultra SCSI host adapters; Qlogic 1240 dual Ultra SCSI controllers; Qlogic 1080 Ultra2 LVD and 1280 Dual Ultra2 LVD controllers; Qlogic 12160 Ultra3 LVD controllers; Qlogic 2100 and Qlogic 2200 Fibre Channel SCSI controllers; Performance Technology SBS440 ISP1000 variants; Performance Technology SBS450 ISP1040 variants; Performance Technology SBS470 ISP2100 variants; Antares Microsystems P-0033 ISP2100 variants.

SymBios (formerly NCR): 53C810, 53C810a, 53C815, 53C820, 53C825a, 53C860, 53C875, 53C875e, 53C875j, 53C885, 53C895 and 53C896 PCI SCSI controllers: ASUS SC-200; Data Technology DTC3130 (all variants); DawiControl DC2976UW; Diamond FirePort (all); NCR cards (all); Symbios cards (all); Tekram DC390W, 390U and 390F; Tyan S1365.

NCR 53C500 based PC-Card SCSI host adapters: IO DATA PCSC-DV; KME KXLC002 (TAXAN ICD-400PN, etc.), KXLC004; Macnica Miracle SCSI-II mPS110; Media Intelligent MSC-110, MSC-200; NEC PC-9801N-J03R; New Media Corporation BASICS SCSI; Qlogic Fast SCSI; RATOC REX-9530, REX-5572 (as SCSI only).

TMC 18C30, 18C50 based ISA/PC-Card SCSI host adapters: Future Domain SCSI2GO; IBM SCSI PCMCIA Card; ICM PSC-2401 SCSI; Melco IFC-SC; RATOC REX-5536, REX-5536AM, REX-5536M, REX-9836A.

DTC 3290 EISA SCSI controller in 1542 emulation mode.

Tekram DC390 and DC390T controllers (maybe other cards based on the AMD 53c974 as well).

Workbit Ninja SCSI-3 based PC-Card SCSI host adapters: Alpha-Data AD-PCS201; IO DATA CBSC16.

CD-ROM Drives

Any SCSI CD-ROM drive should work, including the SoundBlaster SCSI. SCSI CD-ROMs use the `cd` device.

ATAPI CD-ROM devices are also supported and use `acd`. Support is also provided for the following proprietary CD-ROM drives: Matsushita/Panasonic (Creative SoundBlaster) proprietary interface (562/563 models) (`matcd`); Sony proprietary interface (all models) (`scd`); Mitsumi proprietary CD-ROM interface (all models, `mcd`) but this last one is unmaintained, and may or may not work for your hardware.

Writable CD-ROM devices are supported for reading. Software for writing CDs on a CD-Recorder is provided by `cdrecord`, installable as add-on software to FreeBSD as a port. It is known to work on the Philips CDD 521, COMPRO/Matsushita/Panasonice CW-7502, Philips CDD-2000, TEAC CD-R55S, and Yamaha CDR-400. It should also run on all SCSI-3/mmc complaint drives and all ATAPI/mmc compliant drives. It includes a CD-DA ripping program for making sound CDs.

Network Cards

Ethernet cards (and hubs) have been getting faster and cheaper at the same time, so it's getting reasonable to network your home computers. Many network cards work with FreeBSD.

Adaptec Duralink PCI fast ethernet adapters based on the Adaptec AIC-6915 fast ethernet controller chip, including the following: ANA-62011 64-bit single port 10/100baseTX adapter; ANA-62022 64-bit dual port 10/100baseTX adapter; ANA-62044 64-bit quad port 10/100baseTX adapter; ANA-69011 32-bit single port 10/100baseTX adapter; ANA-62020 64-bit single port 100baseFX adapter

Allied-Telesyn AT1700 and RE2000 cards.

Alteon Networks PCI gigabit ethernet NICs based on the Tigon 1 and Tigon 2 chipsets, including the following: Alteon AceNIC (Tigon 1 and 2); 3Com 3c985-SX (Tigon 1 and 2); Netgear GA620 (Tigon 2); Netgear GA620T (Tigon 2, 1000baseT) Silicon Graphics Gigabit Ethernet; DEC/Compaq EtherWORKS 1000; NEC Gigabit Ethernet; Farallon PN9000SX.

AMD PCnet/PCI (79c970 & 53c974 or 79c974); AMD PCnet/FAST, PCnet/FAST+, PCnet/FAST III, PCnet/PRO, HomePCI, and Home PNA.

SMC Elite 16 WD8013 ethernet interface, and most other WD8003E, WD8003EBT, WD8003W, WD8013W, WD8003S, WD8003SBT and WD8013EBT based clones. SMC Elite Ultra is also supported.

RealTek 8129/8139 fast ethernet NICs including the following: Allied Telesyn AT2550; Allied Telesyn AT2500TX; Genius GF100TXR (RTL8139); NDC Communications NE100TX-E; OvisLink LEF-8129TX; OvisLink LEF-8139TX; Netronix Inc. EA-1210 NetEther 10/100; KTX-9130TX 10/100 Fast Ethernet; Accton "Cheetah" EN1027D (MPX 5030/5038; RealTek 8139 clone); SMC EZ Card 10/100 PCI 1211-TX.

Lite-On 82c168/82c169 PNIC fast ethernet NICs including the following: LinkSys EtherFast LNE100TX; NetGear FA310-TX Rev. D1; Matrox FastNIC 10/100; Kingston KNE110TX.

Macronix 98713, 98713A, 98715, 98715A and 98725 fast ethernet NICs; Accton EN1217 (98715A); Adico AE310TX (98715A); Complex RL100-TX; CNet Pro120A (98713 or 98713A); CNet Pro120B (98715); NDC Communications SFA100A (98713A); SVEC PN102TX (98713).

Macronix/Lite-On PNIC II LC82C115 fast ethernet NICs including the following: LinkSys EtherFast LNE100TX Version 2.

Winbond W89C840F fast ethernet NICs including the following: Trendware TE100-PCIE.

VIA Technologies VT3043 "Rhine I" and VT86C100A "Rhine II" Fast Ethernet NICs including the following: Hawking Technologies PN102TX; D-Link DFE-530TX; AOpen/Acer ALN-320.

Silicon Integrated Systems SiS 900 and SiS 7016 PCI fast ethernet NICs.

Sundance Technologies ST201 PCI fast ethernet NICs including the following: D-Link DFE-550TX.

SysKonnect SK-984x PCI Gigabit Ethernet cards including the following: SK-9841 1000baseLX single mode fiber, single port; SK-9842 1000baseSX multimode fiber, single port; SK-9843 1000baseLX single mode fiber, dual port; SK-9844 1000baseSX multimode fiber, dual port.

Texas Instruments ThunderLAN PCI NICs, including the following: Compaq Netelligent 10, 10/100, 10/100 Proliant, 10/100 Dual-Port; Compaq Netelligent 10/100 TX Embedded UTP, 10 T PCI UTP/Coax, 10/100 TX UTP; Compaq NetFlex 3P, 3P Integrated, 3P w/ BNC; Olicom OC-2135/2138, OC-2325, OC-2326 10/100 TX UTP; Racore 8165 10/100baseTX; Racore 8148 10baseT/100baseTX/100baseFX multi-personality.

ADMtek AL981-based PCI fast ethernet NICs; ADMtek AN985-based PCI fast ethernet NICs; ADMtek Inc. AN986-based USB ethernet NICs including the following: LinkSys USB100TX; Billionton USB100; Melco Inc. LU-ATX; D-Link DSB-650TX; SMC 2202USB.

CATC USB-EL1210A-based USB ethernet NICs including the following: CATC Netmate; CATC Netmate II; Belkin F5U111.

Kawasaki LSI KU5KUSB101B-based USB ethernet NICs including the following: LinkSys USB10T; Entrega NET-USB-E45; Peracom USB Ethernet Adapter; 3Com 3c19250; ADS Technologies USB-10BT; ATen UC10T; Netgear EA101; D-Link DSB-650; SMC 2102USB; SMC 2104USB; Corega USB-T.

ASIX Electronics AX88140A PCI NICs, including the following: Alfa Inc. GFC2204; CNet Pro110B.

DEC EtherWORKS III NICs (DE203, DE204, and DE205); DEC EtherWORKS II NICs (DE200, DE201, DE202, and DE422); DEC DC21040, DC21041, or DC21140 based NICs (SMC Etherpower 8432T, DE245, etc.); DEC FDDI (DEFPA/DEFEA) NICs.

Davicom DM9100 and DM9102 PCI fast ethernet NICs, including the following: Jaton Corporation XPressNet.

Efficient ENI-155p ATM PCI.

FORE PCA-200E ATM PCI.

Fujitsu MB86960A/MB86965A., including the following: CONTEC C-NET(PC)C Ethernet; Eiger Labs EPX-10BT; Fujitsu FMV-J182, FMV-J182A, MBH10302, MBH10303 Ethernet PCMCIA; Fujitsu Towa LA501 Ethernet; HITACHI HT-4840-11;NextCom J Link NC5310; RATOC REX-5588, REX-9822, REX-4886, REX-R280; TDK LAK-CD021, LAK-CD021A, LAK-CD021BX.

HP PC Lan+ cards (model numbers: 27247B and 27252A).

Intel EtherExpress (not recommended due to driver instability).

Intel EtherExpress Pro/10; Intel EtherExpress Pro/100B PCI Fast Ethernet; Intel PRO/100+ Management Adapter; Intel Gigabit Ethernet (PRO/1000).

Isolan AT 4141-0 (16 bit); Isolink 4110 (8 bit).

Novell NE1000, NE2000, and NE2100 Ethernet interface; PCI network cards emulating the NE2000: RealTek 8029, NetVin 5000, Winbond W89C940, Surecom NE-34, VIA VT86C926, etc.

3Com 3C501 cards; 3Com 3C503 Etherlink II; 3Com 3C507 Etherlink 16/TP; 3Com 3C509, 3C579, 3C589/589B/589C/589D/589E/XE589ET/574TX /574B (PC-card/PCMCIA), 3C590/592/595/900/905/905B/905C PCI, 3C556/556B MiniPCI, and EISA (Fast) Etherlink III / (Fast) Etherlink XL; 3Com 3c980/3c980B Fast Etherlink XL server adapter; 3Com 3cSOHO100-TX OfficeConnect adapter.

Toshiba ethernet cards.

NE2000 compatible PC-Card (PCMCIA) Ethernet/FastEthernet cards, including the following: AR-P500 Ethernet card; Accton EN2212/EN2216/UE2216(OEM); Allied Telesis CentreCOM LA100-PCM_V2; AmbiCom 10BaseT card; BayNetworks NETGEAR FA410TXC Fast Ethernet; CNet BC40 adapter; COREGA Ether PCC-T/EtherII PCC-T/FEther PCC-TFX/PCC-TXD; Compex Net-A adapter; CyQ've ELA-010; D-Link DE-650/660; Danpex EN-6200P2; ELECOM Laneed LD-CDL/TX; IO DATA PCLA/TE, PCET/TX, PCET/TX-R; IBM Creditcard Ethernet I/II; IC-CARD Ethernet/IC-CARD+ Ethernet; Linksys EC2T/PCMPC100, EtherFast 10/100 PC Card (PCMPC100, V2, V3; Melco LPC-T/LP2-T/LPC2-TX/LPC3-TX/LPC3-CLX; NDC Ethernet Instant-Link; National Semiconductor InfoMover NE4100; Network Everywhere Ethernet 10BaseT PC Card; Planex FNW-3600-T; Socket LP-E; Surecom EtherPerfect EP-427; TDK LAK-CD031, Grey Cell GCS2000 Ethernet Card; Telecom Device SuperSocket RE450T.

Megahertz X-Jack Ethernet PC-Card CC-10BT.

Xircom CreditCard adapters(16bit) and workalikes: Accton EN2226/Fast EtherCard (16-bit verison); Compaq Netelligent 10/100 PC Card; Intel EtherExpress PRO/100 Mobile Adapter (16-bit verison); Xircom 10/100 Network PC Card adapter; Xircom Realport card + modem(Ethernet part); Xircom CreditCard Ethernet 10/100; Xircom CreditCard 10Base-T "CreditCard Ethernet Adaptor IIps" (PS-CE2-10); Xircom CreditCard Ethernet 10/100 + modem (Ethernet part).

National Semiconductor DP8393X (SONIC) Ethernet cards: NEC PC-9801-83, -84, -103, and -104; NEC PC-9801N-25 and -J02R.

USB Devices

Many USB peripherals are supported. With some exceptions any device of a given class will be supported even if not explicitly listed here:

USB keyboards, mice, printers and parallel printer conversion cables, hubs, ethernet controllers.

USB host controllers: ALi Aladdin-V; AMD-756; CMD Tech 670 & 673; Intel

82371SB (PIIX3); Intel 82371AB and EB chipsets (PIIX4); NEC uPD 9210; OPTi 82C861 (FireLink); SiS 5571; VIA 83C572 USB; and any other UHCI or OHCI compliant motherboard chipset (no exceptions known).

PCI plug-in USB host controllers: ADS Electronics PCI plug-in card (2 ports); Entrega PCI plug-in card (4 ports).

Specific devices reported to be working (see the list of network cards for specific USB ethernet device names): ActiveWire I/O Board; Agiler Mouse 29UO; Andromeda hub; Apple iMac mouse; Apple iMac keyboard; ATen parallel printer adapter; Belkin F5U002 parallel printer adapter; Belkin Mouse; BTC BTC7935 keyboard with PS/2 mouse port; Cherry G81-3504 keyboard; Chic mouse; Cypress mouse; Entrega USB-to-parallel printer adapter; Genius Niche mouse; HP ScanJet 4100C, 5200C, 6300C; Iomega USB Zip 100Mb (primitive support still); Kensington Mouse-in-a-Box; Logitech M2452 keyboard; Logitech wheel mouse (3 buttons); Logitech PS/2 / USB mouse (3 buttons); MacAlly mouse (3 buttons); MacAlly self powered hub (4 ports); MacAlly iKey keyboard; Matshita CF-VFDU03 floppy drive; Microsoft IntelliMouse (3 buttons); Microsoft keyboard; Microtec USB-SCSI-HD 50 USB to SCSI cable; NEC hub; Panasonic floppy drive; Perfection 636U scanner; 3Com 5605 modem; Trust Ami Mouse (3 buttons); Y-E Data floppy drive (720/1.44/2.88MB).

ISDN (European DSS1 Protocol)

The DSS1 protocol is also known as Q.921/Q931.

The devices supported are: Asuscom ISDNlink 128K PnP; AVM A1; AVM Fritz!Card classic; AVM Fritz!Card PCI; Creatix ISDN-S0/8; Creatix ISDN-S0/16; Creatix ISDN-S0 PnP; Dr.Neuhaus Niccy 1008; Dr.Neuhaus Niccy 1016; Dr.Neuhaus Niccy GO@ (ISA PnP); ELSA QuickStep 1000pro ISA; ELSA MicroLink ISDN/PCI (same as ELSA QuickStep 1000pro PCI); ELSA PCC-16; Sagem Cybermod (ISA PnP); Sedlbauer Win Speed; Siemens I-Surf 2.0; Teles S0/8; Teles S0/16; Teles S0/16.3 (the "c" Versions - like 16.3c - are NOT supported); Teles S0/16.3 PnP.

Miscellaneous

Bus mice

PS/2 mice

Standard PC Joystick

Other supported devices include:

AST 4 port serial card using shared IRQ.; ARNET 8 port serial card using shared IRQ.; ARNET (now Digiboard) Sync 570/i high-speed serial.; Boca BB1004 4-Port serial card (modems NOT supported); Boca IOAT66 6-Port serial card (modems supported); Boca BB1008 8-Port serial card (modems NOT supported); Boca BB2016 16-Port serial card (modems supported); Comtrol Rocketport card; Cyclades Cyclom-y Serial Board.; STB 4 port card using shared IRQ; SDL Communications Riscom/8 Serial Board; SDL Communications RISCom/N2 and N2pci high-speed sync serial boards; Specialix SI/XIO/SX multiport serial cards, with both the older SIHOST2.x and the new "enhanced" (transputer based, aka JET) host cards (ISA, EISA and PCI are supported); Stallion multiport serial boards: EasyIO, EasyConnection 8/32 & 8/64, ONboard 4/16 and Brumby; HP4020, HP6020, Philips CDD2000/CDD2660 and Plasmon CD-R drives; X-10 power controllers; GPIB and Transputer drivers; Genius and Mustek hand scanners.

Lucent Technologies WaveLAN/IEEE 802.11 PCMCIA and ISA standard speed (2Mbps) and turbo speed (6Mbps) wireless network adapters and workalikes; 3COM 3crwe737A AirConnect Wireless LAN PC Card; Cabletron RoamAbout 802.11 DS; Compaq WL100; Corega KK Wireless LAN PCC-11, PCCA-11; Laneed Wireless card; ELECOM Air@Hawk/LD-WL11/PCC; Farallon Skyline 11Mbps Wireless; ICOM SL-1100; Intel PRO/Wireless 2011 LAN PC Card; IO Data WN-B11/PCM; Melco Airconnect WLI-PCM-L11; NCR WaveLAN/IEEE 802.11; NEC Wireless Card CMZ-RT-WP, PC-WL/11C, PK-WL001; PLANEX GeoWave/GW-NS110; TDK LAK-CD011WL. Note: the ISA versions of these adapters are actually PCMCIA cards combined with an ISA to PCMCIA bridge card, so both kinds of devices work with the same driver.

Aironet 4500/4800 series 802.11 wireless adapters. The PCMCIA, PCI and ISA adapters are all supported.

Cisco Systems Aironet 340 Series (includes 340, 341, and 342 models) 11Mbps 802.11 wireless NIC.

Webgear Aviator 2.4GHz wireless adapters.

Toshiba Mobile HDD MEHDD20A (Type II).

Panasonic Flash ATA BN-040ABP3.

Hewlett Packard M820e (CD-writer).

Microchannel

Experimental support for Microchannel systems became available with FreeBSD 4.0.

Drivers with support for Microchannel peripherals are: aha (Adaptec AHA-1640 SCSI controller); bt (Buslogic BT-640A and Storage Dimensions SDC3211 SCSI controllers); ep (3Com 3C529 network adapter).

Sound Cards and Multimedia

Sound cards supported by the Voxware drivers: Adlib, SoundBlaster, SoundBlaster Pro, ProAudioSpectrum, Gravis UltraSound and Roland MPU-401 sound cards.

Sound cards supported by the newpcm (pcm) driver: Advance Asound 100, 110 and Logic ALS120; C-Media CMI-8x38; Crystal Semiconductor CS461x /462x/428x; Crystal Semiconductor CS4281; ENSONIQ AudioPCI ES1370 /1371; ESS ES1868, ES1869, ES1879 and ES1888; ESS Maestro-1, Maestro-2, and Maestro-2E; ESS Maestro-3/Allegro; ForteMedia fm801; Gravis UltraSound MAX/PnP; MSS/WSS Compatible DSPs; NeoMagic 256AV/ZX; OPTi 931/82C931; SoundBlaster, Soundblaster Pro, Soundblaster AWE-32, Soundblaster AWE-64; Trident 4DWave DX/NX; VIA Technologies VT82C686A; Yamaha DS1 and DS1e.

Other supported multimedia hardware: Matrox Meteor Video frame grabber; Creative Labs Video Spigot frame grabber; Cortex1 frame grabber; various Frame grabbers based on Brooktree Bt848 and Bt878 chip.

Modems

Modems come in two varieties: hardware modems and software modems. The software modems are cheaper because they use your system's hardware instead of their own. They're usually called WinModems and come in many varieties. FreeBSD doesn't support them. Unfortunately many laptops have built-in WinModems.

Modems, whether they're internal modems that come on a card you install in your computer or external modems that you plug into the back of your computer, use a serial port. An internal modem sometimes requires a cold reboot (shutting down the operating system and turning off the computer for a few seconds) to be reset if you've sent it commands that confuse it. Most people think the extra cost of an external modem is worthwhile. Besides, they have blinking lights.

Most modems use standard Hayes modem commands, but some of them understand more commands than others. The modem's manual is worth keeping around so you know how to talk to it for its initial set-up.

Laptops

FreeBSD runs on many laptops—IBM ThinkPads, Sony VAIOs, various Toshibas, and many others. Laptops are always a compromise between features and luggability. Installation is tricker than on a desktop computer. Not all laptops have CD-ROM drives recognized by FreeBSD. If the laptop has a pcmcia ethernet card supported by FreeBSD, connecting to a network and installing by FTP is one option; installing from DOS is another.

FreeBSD has support for many, but not all, pcmcia cards. These cards provide you with devices for your laptop like a modem, an ethernet card, a scsi adapter, and so forth. Support is built in to the GENERIC kernel (and available on installation) for basic card-reading services, but drivers are also needed for the specific device on the card.

After installation, you can read `/etc/defaults/pccard.conf` for the cards supported by FreeBSD, although others may work as well.

Video Cards

Just about any video card works with FreeBSD in text mode. What works for graphics depends on X, the graphical user interface. FreeBSD 4.3 comes with version 3.3.6 of X (also known as XFree86). Version 4 of X was released in June 2000 and is available in the FreeBSD ports collection, but at least initially it didn't support as many video cards as X-3.3.6. You can check the X web page at http://www.XFree86.org for the latest information about what cards are supported. The cards of all the major manufacturers are supported, but the very latest card, or some of its features, may be unsupported. Information on video cards can also be found in the file `/usr/X11R6/lib/X11/Cards` on your hard drive after installation.

Scanners

Software that handles many scanners is in the FreeBSD ports collection, in `/usr/ports/graphics/sane`. If you already have a scanner, try it. If you're thinking of buying one and want it to work with FreeBSD, install `sane` and look at the documentation. The scanners supported best are SCSI scanners—yep, the most expensive ones.

Appendix B

The FreeBSD CD-ROM

The CD-ROM in this book is virtually identical to the first CD-ROM in the set of four sold by Wind River Systems (http://www.freebsdmall.com) and available as an ISO-image by FTP. It can be used to install the version of FreeBSD on the CD-ROM. FreeBSD 4.3-RELEASE is the version originally distributed with this book. It includes the complete FreeBSD operating system and source code, the X Window System (graphical user interface), and many third-party software programs ready to install.

Chapters 2 through 4 of the text explain how to install the FreeBSD operating system on a personal computer that also runs some version of Microsoft Windows (or perhaps Linux). To install FreeBSD you need:

- A computer with a 486 or better (a Pentium is better!) CPU, although an 386SX might work. AMD and Cyrix CPUs are also supported.

- At least 8MB RAM—16 is better.

- An IDE or SCSI hard drive with at least 110MB available. For the total experience, a gigabyte or even two.

- A CD-ROM drive and, if it's not a bootable CD-ROM drive, a floppy drive.

- A floppy drive and a good Internet connection if you don't have a CD-ROM drive and want to install from the Internet.

- Keyboard, monitor, and video card.

- Optional: mouse (but required for X, the graphical user interface), sound card, modem, ethernet card, and printer.

Most of the information in this book is also valid for versions 4.0, 4.1, and 4.2

of FreeBSD, although some differences in the installation dialogs and some differences in utilities exist among versions. Version 4.4 of FreeBSD is expected to be available on CD-ROM in September 2001 and to differ in only minor ways from version 4.3.

Index